CRISIS INTERVENTION HANDBOOK

OTHER WADSWORTH TITLES OF RELATED INTEREST IN SOCIAL WELFARE

Marion L. Beaver, Don Miller **Clinical Social Work**

Ira Colby **Social Welfare Policy: Perspectives, Patterns and Insights**

Danya Glaser, Stephen Frosh **Child Sexual Abuse**

Dean H. Hepworth, Jo Ann Larsen **Direct Social Work Practice: Theory and Skills, Second Edition**

Bruce S. Jansson **The Reluctant Welfare State**

Bruce S. Jansson **Social Welfare Policy: From Theory to Practice**

Betty Piccard **Introduction to Social Work: A Primer, Fourth Edition**

Albert R. Roberts **Juvenile Justice: Policies, Programs and Services**

Allen Rubin, Earl Babbie **Research Methods for Social Work**

Myron E. Weiner **Human Services Management, Second Edition**

Charles Zastrow **Introduction to Social Welfare: Social Problems, Services, and Current Issues, Fourth Edition**

Charles Zastrow **The Practice of Social Work, Third Edition**

CRISIS INTERVENTION HANDBOOK

Assessment, Treatment and Research

Edited by

Albert R. Roberts, D.S.W.

Rutgers—The State University of New Jersey

Wadsworth Publishing Company

Belmont, California

A Division of Wadsworth, Inc.

Social Welfare Editor **Peggy Adams**

Editorial Assistant **Karen Moore**

Production Editor **Donna Linden**

Managing Designer **Carolyn Deacy**

Print Buyer **Barbara Britton**

Designer **Christy Butterfield**

Cover **Vargas/Williams Design**

Copy Editor **Dave Cole**

Compositor **Omegatype, Champaign, Illinois**

Printed in the United States of America   50

1 2 3 4 5 6 7 8 9 10—94 93 92 91 90

Library of Congress Cataloging-in-Publication Data

Crisis intervention handbook: assessment, treatment and research /
    edited by Albert R. Roberts.
        p.   cm.
        Includes bibliographical references.
        ISBN 0-534-12510-7
        1. Crisis intervention (Psychiatry)
        I. Roberts, Albert R.
        [DNLM: 1. Crisis Intervention—
        handbooks.   WM 34 C932]
    RC480.6C744   1990
    616.89'025—dc20
    DNLM/DLC
    for Library of Congress   89-2274
                                                CIP

Brief Contents

Detailed Contents

Chapter 2

Chapter 3

Chapter 4

Chapter 7

Assessment and Crisis Intervention with Rape and Incest Victims: Strategies, Techniques, and Case Illustrations   124

PATRICIA PETRETIC-JACKSON, PH.D., AND TOM JACKSON, PH.D.

Chapter 8

Crisis Intervention with Abusing Families: Short-Term Cognitive Coercive Group Therapy Using Goal Attainment Scaling   153

RITA JUSTICE, PH.D., AND BLAIR JUSTICE, PH.D.

Chapter 12

Time-Limited Cognitive Therapy with Women in Crisis of Reproductive Failure   237

DIANE B. BRASHEAR, PH.D., A.C.S.W.

Chapter 13

Male Erectile Difficulty: Crisis Intervention and Short-Term Treatment   255

BARRY COURNOYER, D.S.W., A.C.S.W.

Chapter 14

Post-Disaster Mobilization and Crisis Counseling: Guidelines and Techniques for Developing Crisis-Oriented Services for Disaster Victims   279

RAQUEL E. COHEN, M.D., M.P.H.

Part V

RESEARCH   301

Chapter 15

Designs and Procedures for Evaluating Crisis Intervention   303

GERALD T. POWERS, PH.D.

Foreword

C risis intervention approaches have become the treatment of choice in a large number of human service settings. There are many reasons for this. In an increasingly complex society in the midst of rapid social and technological change individuals and families face many more stressors than in the past. Their need for help is not only greater and more apparent but also more acceptable. Further, during a crisis the individual or family is at a point when change is most possible. Old behavior patterns no longer work or work well and therefore new adaptations are demanded. The individual or family is more open to change than at other periods in their life history. This may be one reason why short-term therapy has been found to be as successful as longer term treatment approaches. Crisis intervention methods are short term. And with the shortage of professionally trained therapists who have too many clients and patients to serve—who often need help immediately—the movement to crisis intervention approaches seems almost inevitable.

We have come a long way since the first studies of the phenomenon of crisis. The very first by Waller (1930) on divorce demonstrated the difficulties faced by those in the midst of a crisis, and laid the groundwork for much of what was to follow. He delineated four major stages in the process: (1) breaking old habits, (2) beginning to reconstruct life, (3) seeking new love objects, and (4) completed readjustment. Next there were a series of studies of family adjustment to the Depression by Angell (1936), Cavan and Ranck (1938), Komarovsky (1940), and Bakke (1940). Koos went on to study families' reactions to trouble and illness (1946), and then Hill (1949) tested all of the previous findings by independently analyzing quantitative questionnaire data and qualitative case study material in his study of the stress of wartime separation and reunion caused by the husband's entry into the armed forces during World War II. The famous study by Lindemann (1944) of the reactions of loved ones to the deaths of those in the Coconut Grove night club fire in Boston, Massachusetts, and the work of Gerald Caplan and his colleagues (1961) have brought us to the modern era.

Since then this approach has been applied to a great many different problems and in a great many different settings. Still under development are differential treatment profiles that can be used with persons who experience specific stressor events, all within the framework of the crisis intervention method. The research that evaluates the outcomes of specific intervention techniques also is just beginning. But nowhere is this important material brought together in a systematic way.

This is the major advantage of this comprehensive handbook. For the first time we have the experts in this field summarizing what is known about crisis situations and how to effectively intervene in each of them. The book will be particularly helpful to students and practitioners in the helping professions because each chapter is organized in a similar way. While the focus is on the nature and ramifications of the particular problem being discussed and the most effective change techniques currently available, each chapter provides case illustrations that bring the material to life, and then summarizes the accumulated research. The final chapter looks to the future, suggesting ways each of us can evaluate our own practice as well as contribute to the knowledge of others who work with similar clients.

The crisis intervention approach is distinctively different from many of the other methods previously utilized in psychology, psychiatry, and social work. It makes the assumption that most persons have performed normally prior to the introduction of the stressor event. While their observed behavior may seem dysfunctional, it is a product of the difficult and often unexpected situation in which they find themselves. Therapeutic goals are focused on resumption of typical constructive activities. In most cases psychopathology is not an issue. Rather, the client's or patient's strengths are given primary attention. It is his or her reactions to the situation and methods to deal with it that are of greatest significance in the therapeutic process. It assumes that all of us, at one time or another, have stressors placed upon us with which we find it difficult to deal, and that all of us seek and need help under these circumstances. Thus, in my opinion, the crisis intervention approach maximizes respect for human beings and their social and psychological potential.

Why do bad things happen to good people? This is a question that the philosophers have been trying to answer since the beginning of time, and I will not attempt an answer here. But we do know that bad things happen to too many of us, and in our modern society, too often. No adult or child wants to be sexually abused or beaten, or lose a loved one, or have their home and possessions destroyed through no fault of their own. But it happens every day. When it does we have reason to be upset, to feel that our lives are out of balance, to not know what to do next. It is the people in these situations that the crisis intervention approach addresses. Increasingly, it is these people who come to our clinics and hospitals for help. And it is the crisis intervention approach that seems to be the most helpful. This handbook will be a major aid to those who work with such people every day, and for those who are preparing to do such work. It is a volume that has been needed by human services professionals for some time.

Paul H. Glasser, Ph.D.
Dean, School of Social Work
Rutgers—The State University of New Jersey

References

Angell, R. C. (1936). *The Family Encounters the Depression*. New York: Charles Scribner's Sons.

Bakke, E. (1940). *Citizens Without Work*. New Haven: Yale University Press.

Caplan, G. (1961). *An Approach to Community Mental Health*. New York: Grune and Stratton.

Cavan, R. & Ranck, K. (1938). *The Family and the Depression*. Chicago: University of Chicago Press.

Hill, R. (1949). *Families Under Stress*. New York: Harper & Row.

Komarovsky, M. (1940). *The Unemployed Man and His Family*. New York: Dryden Press.

Koos, E. L. (1946). *Families in Trouble*. New York: King's Crown Press.

Lindemann, E. (1944). "Symptomatology and Management of Acute Grief." *American Journal of Psychiatry, 101,* 141–148.

Waller, W. (1930). *The Old Love and the New: Divorce and Readjustment*. Philadelphia: Horace Liveright, Inc.

Preface

S ince the publication of the now-classic *Crisis Intervention* (1965), edited by Howard J. Parad, the practice of crisis intervention has changed dramatically. Professional and public interest in crisis intervention has grown tremendously in the past two decades, partially due, no doubt, to the prevalence of crisis events in almost everyone's life. Hundreds of thousands of persons in distress call or come to health or mental health facilities throughout the United States each day, most in some form of crisis. Crisis situations can often be critical turning points in a person's life. Persons in crisis provide clinicians with a focus and method of providing immediate and efficacious intervention. In addition, given the current limitations of clinical resources in child and family, health, and mental health settings, the use of time-limited crisis intervention has become both economically feasible and the treatment of choice for many clients.

Rapid assessment and crisis intervention require specialized knowledge and intervention skills. With increasing frequency, clinicians and graduate students in field placements are called upon to intervene in acute crisis situations (e.g., adolescent suicide attempts, severe battering episodes, drug overdoses). It is therefore essential that students and clinicians be provided with the applicable information, knowledge base, and intervention strategies. This handbook is intended as a key resource for those called upon to intervene.

This handbook was written for clinicians and graduate students who work with people in crisis and who need to know the latest steps and methods for intervening. Crisis theory and practice principles cut across several professional affiliations and professions, including social work, psychology, and psychiatry. Therefore, an interdisciplinary approach has been used in compiling this handbook of all specially written chapters.

This handbook will also be useful as the primary text in graduate-level courses in crisis intervention and brief treatment, crisis counseling, social work practice, and community mental health, and as the supplementary text in health social work, mental health practice, and psychological assessment and treatment.

Professors, clinicians, and graduate students have been searching for a book that provides the latest applications of crisis theory, principles, and techniques to persons in crisis. This handbook is designed to meet that need. It offers challenging methods, techniques, and case illustrations for those who are concerned with helping persons in crisis.

This handbook is a collaborative work with original chapters written by prominent clinical social workers, health social workers, counseling psychologists, clinical psychologists, and child psychiatrists. My wholehearted appreciation is extended to all members of my author team for following my guidelines. Each practice chapter generally begins with one or two case vignettes, then provides a brief review of the research literature on the appropriateness of crisis intervention with a particular group. The major part of each chapter includes a framework for the practice of crisis intervention with a specific target group. Several detailed cases are included in each chapter to demonstrate the steps in the operation of the crisis intervention model. Also highlighted in each practice chapter are clinical issues, roles, and skills. Many of the chapters conclude by summarizing outcome research and methods of determining the effectiveness of crisis intervention with a particular target group such as college students in crisis, abusive parents, or rape victims.

The chapter authors have extensive expertise gained over many years of studying and practicing crisis intervention with vulnerable populations. All of the chapters share a common theme: that effective crisis intervention is based on the application of the basic principles of crisis theory. The focus is on quickly assessing the situation, providing support, exploring possible solutions, assisting the person in crisis in taking concrete steps to reestablish coping, and ultimately facilitating the client's growth and crisis resolution.

In crisis intervention, the clinician's primary focus is on helping the person in crisis handle and lessen the impact of the crisis event on each segment of his or her life. Crisis resolution depends on the severity of the precipitating event; the mobilization of the individual's personal and social resources, such as ego strengths; the person's experience resolving previous crises; and assistance from family members.

This handbook originated, in part, because of my interest in and study of suicide prevention, which began more than 20 years ago with my master's thesis entitled *The Organizational Structure and Function of Suicide Prevention Agencies in the United States* (1967). By 1978, my interest in crisis intervention had been expanded to adolescent runaways. My 1978 doctoral dissertation was a qualitative study of adolescent runaways in crisis. A slightly condensed version of the dissertation, entitled *Runaways and Nonrunaways in an American Suburb,* was published in 1981 by the John Jay College Press of the City University of New York; it was reprinted in 1987 by the Dorsey Press of Chicago. From the late 1970s until the present, I have concentrated on the study of victims of family violence and of other violent crimes, and on the development of crisis intervention services for crime victims. Several of my publications have reported on the findings of my research on victimization and crisis intervention. These include *Sheltering Battered Women: A National Study and Service Guide* (1981); *Battered Women and*

Their Families: Intervention Strategies and Treatment Programs (1984); and *National Survey of 184 Victim Service and Witness Assistance Programs: Final Report* (July, 1987). I mention these prior contributions to the literature because this handbook represents an outgrowth of my earlier work.

The primary thrust of this handbook is to examine the application of crisis theory and the crisis model in child and family, emergency health, mental health, and private practice settings. The book is divided into five parts. Part I summarizes the literature on crisis theory and crisis intervention programs and presents the foundation assumptions and the seven steps in the crisis intervention model. Part II examines four crisis intervention models designed to aid children, adolescents, and college students. In Part III recent rapid assessment and crisis intervention programs for survivors of victimization and their abusers are described and analyzed.

During the past decade, health and mental health professionals have taken a more active role in providing crisis intervention services to cocaine addicts in crisis, violent crime victims, pregnant teens, persons experiencing a medical crisis, and disaster victims. Part IV brings together six chapters that provide detailed descriptions of crisis intervention units, programs, and practices in health, mental health, and private practice settings.

Part V includes a comprehensive explanation of the methods applicable for conducting research and evaluating the effectiveness of crisis intervention programs. It discusses a range of quantitative and qualitative methods.

Albert R. Roberts, D.S.W.

Acknowledgments

I would like to express my sincere appreciation to Lilian Schein, Director of Macmillan's Behavioral Science Book Club for encouraging me to develop this handbook. I deeply appreciate the contributions made by my author team, and their patience with the inevitable delays. Their willingness to make editorial changes made my tasks as volume editor much more manageable.

I gratefully acknowledge the painstaking and insightful comments of the reviewers of this manuscript. They include Professors Gilbert Greene, Michigan State University; Anne L. Horton, Brigham Young University; David Royse, University of Kentucky; Charles L. Schwartz, University of South Dakota; and Michael Smith, Hunter College, City University of New York. Special thanks go to Peggy Adams, Senior Editor at Wadsworth, who has skillfully helped me produce a volume of which we can all be proud, and to Donna Linden who did a very thorough and professional job with the final production stages of this handbook.

My wife, Beverly, came through again and provided the important finishing touches to the book. She worked with me in completing those final tasks that no one ever wants to do—proofreading the page proofs and preparing the index. Finally, my thanks go to my former colleague, Dr. Robert S. Nevin who, with very little lead time, juggled his schedule in order to prepare the detailed Glossary.

About the Contributors

DIANE B. BRASHEAR, PH.D., A.C.S.W. Assistant Professor, Department of Obstetrics and Gynecology, Indiana University School of Medicine, Indianapolis, Indiana; and President, Community Council of Central Indiana

JAMES A. COCORES, M.D. Medical Director, Outpatient Recovery Centers, Fair Oaks Hospital, Summit, New Jersey; and Research Psychiatrist, Research Facilities, Fair Oaks Hospital

RAQUEL E. COHEN, M.D., M.P.H. Professor of Child Psychiatry, University of Miami Medical School and Jackson Memorial Hospital, Miami, Florida

ELAINE P. CONGRESS, D.S.W., A.C.S.W. Assistant Professor, Graduate School of Social Services, Fordham University at Lincoln Center, New York, New York; and former Director of Social Work, Sunset Park Mental Health Center of Lutheran Medical Center, Brooklyn, New York

BARRY COURNOYER, D.S.W., A.C.S.W. Associate Professor, Indiana University School of Social Work, Indianapolis, Indiana; and Clinical Social Worker in independent practice

LYNN FISHER-MCCANNE, PH.D. Associate Director, Counseling and Student Development Center, Northern Illinois University, DeKalb, Illinois

MARK S. GOLD, M.D. Director of Research, Research Facilities, Fair Oaks Hospital, Summit, New Jersey, and Delray Beach, Florida; and Founder, 800-Cocaine, The National Cocaine Helpline at Fair Oaks Hospital

HOWARD J. HESS, D.S.W. Associate Professor and Assistant Dean for Student Services, Indiana University School of Social Work, Indianapolis, Indiana

TOM JACKSON, PH.D. Associate Professor and Director of Clinical Training, Department of Psychology, University of Arkansas, Fayetteville, Arkansas

BLAIR JUSTICE, PH.D. Professor of Psychology, Health Sciences Center, School of Public Health, The University of Texas, Houston, Texas

RITA JUSTICE, PH.D. Clinical Psychologist in private practice, Houston, Texas

ROBIN LEWIS, PH.D. Lecturer, Department of Counseling, University of Southern California, Los Angeles, California

BRIAN J. MCCONVILLE, M.D. Professor of Child Psychiatry and Pediatrics and Director, Division of Child and Adolescent Psychiatry, University of Cincinnati College of Medicine, Cincinnati, Ohio

MARILYN MEHR, PH.D. Associate Clinical Professor, Department of Family Medicine, Loma Linda University Medical School, Loma Linda, California, and School of Medicine, University of Southern California, Los Angeles, California

ALLEN J. OTTENS, PH.D. Coordinator of Student Development Programming and Staff Psychologist, Counseling and Student Development Center, Northern Illinois University, DeKalb, Illinois

PATRICIA PETRETIC-JACKSON, PH.D. Associate Professor, Department of Psychology, University of South Dakota, Vermillion, South Dakota

GERALD T. POWERS, PH.D. Professor, Indiana University School of Social Work, Indianapolis, Indiana

ALBERT R. ROBERTS, D.S.W. Associate Professor, School of Social Work, Rutgers—The State University of New Jersey, New Brunswick, New Jersey

PAMELA L. RUSTER, M.S.S.W. Manager, Social Services, Bartholomew County Hospital, Columbus, Indiana

BEVERLY SCHENKMAN ROBERTS, M.ED. Consultant, Community Service Council of Central Indiana, Indianapolis, Indiana

NORMAN M. SHULMAN, ED.D. Emergency Services Program Coordinator, Central New Hampshire Community Mental Health Services, Inc., Concord, New Hampshire

BETTY A. WALKER, PH.D. Associate Professor, Department of Counseling, University of Southern California, Los Angeles, California

Part I

OVERVIEW

Chapter 1

An Overview of Crisis Theory and Crisis Intervention

Albert R. Roberts, D.S.W.

Mary R. was a 22-year-old college senior when she was raped. It was 11 P.M. and Mary had just left the health sciences library at the university and was walking the three long blocks to the parking lot where her car was parked. She recalls her reactions a week later:

> I was sort of in shock and numb. It was a terrifying, painful, and degrading experience. It was something you don't expect to happen. But it could have been much worse. He held a knife to my throat while raping me. I thought he was going to kill me afterwards. I'm glad to be alive.

John A., a 24-year-old blind white male, was a victim of robbery. John was returning to his apartment following an afternoon appointment with his physician when he was robbed. John recalled what took place:

> A guy came up to me and pressed the cold barrel of his gun on my neck. He said if I don't give him what I got he would shoot me and the dog. I gave him the twenty-one dollars I had. Nobody helped me. Everybody's afraid to intervene. They're afraid because they know the guy will get off or be put on probation and may come after them.

> About a week after the robbery, I woke up sweating and had a serious asthma attack. I was hospitalized for a week. Now I try not to visit friends or my cousin in Manhattan. I go out a lot less. I stay home and listen to the radio or TV most of the time.

Judy B., a 27-year-old surgical nurse, was a survivor of wife battering. She had two children with Ray and they had been married for six years. As his drinking increased, so did his beatings. The final straw was a violent attack when he punched her many times in her face. The day after this last assault, after Judy looked at her swollen face in the mirror, she went to a gun store and purchased a Smith and Wesson handgun. As she drove home looking at the gun by her side she finally decided to seek help. She called the battered women's shelter hotline and said, "I'm afraid that I'm going to kill my husband."

Persons in acute crisis have had similar reactions to traumatic events, from initial feelings of disruption and disorganization to the eventual readjustment of the self. During the impact phase, survivors of victimization and other crisis events often feel numb, disoriented, shattered, fearful, vulnerable, helpless, and lonely. The survivors may seek help, consolation, and advice from friends or professionals within several hours or days after the crisis event.

Helping a person in crisis—whether it be in the aftermath of a violent crime, a suicide attempt, a drug overdose, a natural disaster, a divorce, a broken romance, sexual impotence, or an automobile crash—requires exceptional sensitivity and active listening skills on the part of the crisis intervenor. If a hotline worker, crisis counselor, social worker, or psychologist is able to establish rapport with the person in crisis soon after the crisis event, many hours of later therapy may be saved.

Where can persons in crisis turn for help? How do they find the phone number of the crisis intervention service in their area? Police officers and hospital emergency room staff are available 24 hours a day, 7 days a week. In fact, on weekends and at night they are often the only help available. The police or an information operator can give a person in crisis the name of a local hotline, a community crisis center, the crisis intervention unit at the local community mental health center, a rape crisis center, a battered women's shelter, or a family crisis intervention program which provides home-based crisis services. In addition, many large cities have information and referral networks funded by the United Way, the Community Service Society, or the American Red Cross. These information and referral (I and R) services give crisis callers the phone numbers of community agencies in their localities. Unfortunately, because of limited resources, some of these information and crisis lines are only available from 8:30 A.M. to 5 P.M.

The information and referral services throughout the United States, which number in excess of 4,900, are operated under different organizational auspices, including traditional social services agencies, community mental health centers, public libraries, police departments, shopping malls, domestic violence shelters, women's centers, travelers' aid centers, youth crisis centers, and area agencies on aging. The goal of information and referral networks is to facilitate access to services and to overcome the many barriers that obstruct entry to needed resources (Levinson, 1988, p. 7). According-ing to the United Way of America (1980), "I and R is a service which informs, guides, directs and links people in need to the appropriate human service which alleviates or eliminates the need."

Some information and referral networks are generic and provide information to the public on all community services, including crisis centers, while others are more specialized and focus on meeting the needs of callers such as those who are depressed and have suicide ideation, children and youths in crisis, women in crisis, survivors of violent crimes, runaways and homeless youths, or the elderly.

Crisis Centers and Specialized Hotlines and Services

D uring the past two decades thousands of crisis intervention programs have been established throughout the United States and Canada. There are over 1,400 grass-roots crisis centers and crisis units affiliated with the American Association of Suicidology or a local community mental health center. There are also over 900 victim assistance, rape crisis, and child sexual abuse intervention programs, as well as 1,250 battered women's shelters and hotlines. In addition, crisis services are provided at thousands of local hospital emergency rooms, hospital-based trauma centers and emergency psychiatric services, suicide prevention centers, and pastoral counseling services.

24-Hour Hotlines

Crisis centers and hotlines provide information, crisis assessments, crisis counseling, and referrals for callers with such problems as depression, suicide ideation, alcoholism, chemical dependency, impotence, infertility, child battering, woman battering, and crime victimization. Because of their 24-hour availability, they can provide immediate, though temporary, intervention. Some crisis victims do not have a caring friend or relative to whom they can turn; they often benefit from an empathetic, active listener. Even when significant others are available to aid the person in crisis, hotlines provide a valuable service by linking the caller to appropriate community resources.

With the development of crisis centers nationwide, there has been a considerable increase in the use of the telephone as a method of rapid crisis assessment and management. The 24-hour telephone crisis service maximizes the immediacy and availability of crisis intervention. It also provides anonymity to the caller while assessing the risk of suicide and imminent danger. The telephone crisis intervenor is trained to establish rapport with the caller, conduct a brief assessment, provide a sympathetic ear, help develop a crisis management plan, and/or refer the caller to an appropriate treatment program or service. In most cases effective crisis resolution can be facilitated by suicide prevention hotlines as long as they provide referral and follow-up services.

Suicide Prevention and Crisis Centers

Suicide prevention services began in London, England, in 1906 when the Salvation Army opened an antisuicide bureau aimed at helping persons who attempted suicide. At about the same time, Reverend Harry M. Warren opened the National Save-a-Life League in New York City. Over the years the league's 24-hour hotline has been answered by full-time staff, trained volunteers, and in a few instances by consulting psychiatrists who have served on the agency's board of directors.

In the 1960s and early 1970s federal funding was made available as a result of the Community Mental Health Center Act of 1963 and by the National Institute of Mental Health (NIMH). Between 1968 and 1972 almost 200 suicide prevention centers were established (Roberts, 1979, p. 398). In the United States and Canada that number now has increased more than sevenfold. See Chapters 2, 3, and 7 for detailed examinations of crisis intervention and follow-up treatment of depressed persons and those with suicide ideation who have been referred to college counseling centers.

National Hotline: 800–COCAINE

On May 6, 1983, New Jersey's Fair Oaks Hospital in Summit created the first nationwide hotline for cocaine users and their families. The need for such a hotline had arisen because of a threefold increase in cocaine-related emergency room visits and a fourfold increase in cocaine-related deaths. The purpose of the toll-free 800–COCAINE hotline is to provide callers with immediate assessment, crisis intervention, and referral.

In its first year of operation, the helpline provided information, crisis intervention, and referral to over 400,000 callers. As of 1988, this program was receiving an average of 1,200 calls a day, or over 430,000 calls annually. The hotline has a professional staff of 40 specialists who have received one or more years of training in crisis intervention with substance abusers. Callers are referred to self-help groups and treatment programs in all parts of the United States.

In many cases, the cocaine user denies the severity of the problem. Many of the callers who enter time-limited treatment programs do so as a result of a crisis event such as the threat of job loss, family violence, marital discord or separation, a natural disaster, bankruptcy, serious physical illness, and/or legal problems. A thorough examination of crisis intervention with cocaine (including crack) users at Fair Oaks Hospital is presented by Doctors James Cocores and Mark Gold (founder of the 800–COCAINE hotline) in Chapter 9.

Child Abuse Hotlines and Referral Networks

A number of states, cities, and counties have developed child abuse hotlines for reporting suspected cases of child abuse and neglect. Early case finding and rapid investigation and intervention can lead to resolving crisis situations and preventing further child maltreatment. Many communities have also developed parental stress hotline services, which provide immediate intervention for potentially abusive parents who are at risk of injuring their child. These crisis intervention hotlines offer supportive reassurance, advice, and nonjudgmental listening from trained volunteers. They also provide a stressed-out parent with information and referral to individual and group parenting treatment. The hotlines are usually available on a toll-free basis, 24 hours a day, 7 days a week.

Respite centers or crisis nurseries are available in most large cities to provide parents in crisis with temporary relief from child care. For example, New York City's Foundling Hospital has a crisis nursery where parents can take their children and leave them overnight when they fear they may lose control and inflict injury. The average stay is three days (Kadushin and Martin, 1988, p. 251). These nurseries are usually operated on a 24-hour basis and generally provide shelter care for children under 6 years of age. The crisis nursery staff encourages abusing parents to seek professional treatment. In Chapter 8, Doctors Rita and Blair Justice describe the crisis intervention group therapy model (also known as short-term cognitive coercive group therapy) they use with abusing families in Texas.

Rape Crisis Programs

Programs for rape crisis have been developed by medical centers, community mental health centers, women's counseling centers, crisis clinics, and police departments. Social workers at rape crisis organizations provide crisis intervention, advocacy, support, education, and referral to community resources. Crisis intervention generally involves an initial visit from a social worker, crisis counselor, or nurse while the victim is being examined in the hospital emergency room. Although follow-up is often handled through telephone counseling, in-person counseling sessions may take place when the victim is in distress. In several parts of the country, rape crisis programs have begun support groups for sexual assault victims. See Chapter 7 for a comprehensive review of assessment and crisis intervention strategies for rape and incest survivors.

Battered Women's Shelters and Hotlines

A number of state legislatures have enacted special legislation that provides funding for hotlines and shelters for victims of domestic violence. There are crisis intervention services for battered women and their children in every state and major metropolitan area in the country. The primary focus of these services is to ensure the women's safety, but many shelters have evolved into much more than just a place for safe lodging. Crisis intervention for battered women generally entails a 24-hour telephone hotline, safe and secure emergency shelter (the average length of stay being three to four weeks), an underground network of volunteer homes and shelters, and welfare and court advocacy by student interns and other volunteers (Roberts, 1984). Shelters also provide peer counseling, support groups, information on women's legal rights, and referral to social service agencies.

In some communities, emergency services for battered women have been expanded to include parenting education workshops, assistance in finding housing, employment counseling and job placement for the women, and group counseling for batterers. In the all-too-often neglected area of assessment and treatment for the children of battered women, a small but growing number of shelters provides either group counseling or referral to mental health centers, as needed. For a more complete discussion of crisis intervention model building for battered women and their children, see Chapter 6.

Crisis Intervention and Groups to Aid Impotent Men

"Researchers estimate that 10 million American men suffer from . . . impotence. Help is available, but men are often too embarrassed—or feel too hopeless to seek it. . . . Impotence is defined as the inability to maintain an erection firm enough for intercourse" (Blaun, 1987, p. 50). An international organization with over 100 chapters, called Impotence Anonymous, began in 1982. The Manhattan chapter of Impotence Anonymous meets at Beth Israel Medical Center on the third Tuesday of each month. Every regular meeting features a group discussion with a consulting physician and a lay volunteer coordinator—a man who is now potent. Women who are partners of current or formerly impotent men frequently attend and answer questions as well. Crisis intervention and time-limited brief treatment has been very effective with impotence cases caused by psychological problems. See Chapter 13 for a description of successful crisis resolution with men who have had erectile difficulties.

Defining a Crisis and Crisis Concepts

C risis may be viewed in various ways, but most definitions emphasize that a crisis can be a turning point in a person's life. According to Bard and Ellison (1974, p. 68), crisis is "a subjective reaction to a stressful life experience, one so affecting the stability of the individual that the ability to cope or function may be seriously compromised."

It has been established that a crisis can develop when an event, or a series of events, takes place in a person's life and the result is a hazardous situation. However, it is important to note that the crisis is not the situation itself (e.g., being victimized); rather, it is the person's *perception of and response to* the situation (Parad, 1971, p. 197).

The most important precipitant of a crisis is a stressful or hazardous event. But two other conditions are also necessary to have a crisis state: (a) the individual's perception that the stressful event will lead to considerable upset and/or disruption;

and (b) the individual's inability to resolve the disruption by previously used coping methods.

Crisis intervention refers to a therapist entering into the life situation of an individual or family to alleviate the impact of a crisis in order to help mobilize the resources of those directly affected (Parad, 1965).

In conceptualizing crisis theory, Parad and Caplan (1960) examine the fact that "crises have a peak or sudden turning point" and as the individual reaches this peak, tension increases and stimulates the mobilization of previously hidden strengths and capacities. They urge timely intervention to help individuals cope successfully with a crisis situation. Caplan (1961, p. 293) states that "a relatively minor force, acting for a relatively short time, can switch the balance to one side or another, to the side of mental health or the side of mental ill health."

There is a general consensus among clinical social workers and psychologists that the following are characteristic of a person in crisis:

1. Perceiving a precipitating event as being meaningful and threatening
2. Appearing unable to modify or lessen the impact of stressful events with traditional coping methods
3. Experiencing increased fear, tension, and/or confusion
4. Exhibiting a high level of subjective discomfort
5. Proceeding rapidly to an active state of crisis—a state of disequilibrium

The term *crisis* as it has been described here is applicable to most of the clients of the social workers, psychologists, and child psychiatrists who prepared chapters for this handbook. The definition of a crisis stated previously is particularly applicable to persons in acute crisis because these individuals usually seek help only after they have experienced a hazardous event and are in a vulnerable state, have failed to cope and lessen the crisis through customary coping methods, and want outside help.

Foundation Assumptions and the Crisis Theory Framework

T he conceptual framework for crisis intervention practice presented in this handbook incorporates the basic principles of crisis theory. The crisis intervention specialization is built on a basic knowledge of crisis theory and practice. Crisis theory includes a cluster of principles upon which crisis clinicians and researchers usually agree. In this handbook the prominent authorities on crisis intervention demonstrate the application of the crisis intervention process and practices to special groups at high risk of crisis. But first it will be helpful to summarize the foundation principles of crisis theory and place them into a step-by-step crisis management framework.

Basic Tenets of Crisis Theory

As mentioned earlier, a crisis state is a temporary upset, accompanied by some confusion and disorganization and characterized by a person's inability to cope with a specific situation through the use of traditional problem-solving methods.

According to Naomi Golan (1978), the heart of crisis theory and practice rests in a series of basic statements:

Crisis situations can occur episodically during "the normal life span of individuals, families, groups, communities and nation." They are often initiated by a hazardous event. This may be a catastrophic event or a series of successive stressful blows which rapidly build up a cumulative effect (p. 8).

"The impact of the hazardous event disturbs the individual's homeostatic balance and puts him in a vulnerable state" (p. 8).

"If the problem continues and cannot be resolved, avoided, or redefined, tension rises to a peak, and a precipitating factor can bring about a turning point, during which self-righting devices no longer operate and the individual enters a state of disequilibrium . . . [an] active crisis" (p. 8).

During the development of the crisis situation, the person "may perceive the initial and subsequent stressful events primarily as a threat, either to his instinctual needs or to his sense of autonomy and well-being; as a *loss* of a person, an ability, or a capacity; or as a *challenge* to survival, growth or mastery" (p. 8).

A crisis state "is neither an illness nor a pathological experience; it reflects instead a realistic struggle in the individual's current life situation" (p. 8).

The time span between the initial hazardous event and the final crisis resolution may vary. "Depending upon the specific nature of the situation, the cognitive, affective, and behavioral tasks that have to be accomplished and the situational supports and resources available, the actual state of active disequilibrium is time-limited, usually lasting up to four to six weeks" (p. 9).

The phase known as crisis resolution is the period when the person seems to be especially amenable to help. Traditional defense mechanisms have broken down, traditional coping patterns have been found to be ineffective, "and the ego has become more open to outside influence and change. . . . A small amount of help, appropriately focused, can prove more effective than more extensive help at a period of less emotional accessibility" (p. 9).

During the phase known as reintegration, ego strengths may surface along with new patterns of adaptation in order to enable the individual to cope with similar hazardous events in the future. "However, if help is not available during this critical period . . . maladaptive patterns may be adopted which can result in weakened ability to function adequately in the period ahead" (p. 9).

Central to the crisis state is severe emotional upset or disequilibrium (Rapoport, 1965; Halpern, 1973), vulnerability and reduced defensiveness (Tyhurst, 1958; Halpern, 1973), and failed attempts at coping.

Duration of the Crisis

Persons in a crisis state cannot remain indefinitely in a state of psychological turmoil and survive. Caplan (1964) noted, and other clinical supervisors have concurred, that in a typical crisis state equilibrium will be restored in four to six weeks. However, the magical figure of four to six weeks has been confusing. Several authors note that crisis resolution can take from several weeks to several months. In order to clarify the confusion concerning this period, it is useful to explain the difference between restoring equilibrium and crisis resolution.

Disequilibrium, which is characterized by confusing emotions, somatic complaints, and erratic behavior, is reduced considerably within the first six weeks of crisis intervention. The severe emotional discomfort experienced by the person in crisis propels him or her toward action that will result in reducing the subjective discomfort. Thus, *equilibrium is restored* and the disorganization is time limited.

Viney (1976) aptly describes *crisis resolution* as restoration of equilibrium as well as cognitive mastery of the situation and the development of new coping methods. Fairchild (1986) refers to crisis resolution as an adaptive consequence of a crisis in which the person grows from the crisis experience through the discovery of new coping skills and resources to employ in the future. In this handbook, *crisis intervention* is viewed as the process of working through the crisis event so that the person is assisted in exploring the traumatic experience and his or her reaction to it. Emphasis is also placed on helping the individual:

Make behavioral changes and interpersonal adjustments

Mobilize internal and external resources and supports

Reduce unpleasant or disturbing affects related to the crisis

Integrate the event and its aftermath into the individual's other life experiences and markers

The goal of effective crisis resolution is to remove vulnerabilities from the individual's past and bolster the individual with an increased repertoire of new coping skills to serve as a buffer from similar stressful situations in the future.

Crisis Intervention Models and Strategies

Several systematic practice models and techniques have been developed for crisis intervention work. The crisis intervention model applied in this handbook synthesizes the models developed by Aguilera and Messick (1982), Beck (1976), Burns (1980),

Caplan (1964), Golan (1978), Parad (1965), and Puryear (1979). All of these practice models and techniques are focused on resolving immediate problems and emotional conflicts through a minimum number of contacts. Crisis-oriented treatment is time limited and goal directed, in contrast to long-term psychotherapy, which could take several years to complete.

Crisis intervenors should "adopt a role which is active and directive without taking problem ownership" away from the individual in crisis too prematurely (Fairchild, 1986). The skilled crisis intervenor should display acceptance and hopefulness in order to communicate to persons in crisis that their intense emotional turmoil and threatening situations are not hopeless, and that in fact they (like others in similar situations before them) will survive the crisis successfully and become better prepared for potentially hazardous life events in the future.

In order to become an effective crisis intervenor, it is important to gauge the stages and completeness of the intervention. Keep in mind that the following paradigm and steps should be viewed as a guide, not as a rigid process, since with some clients the steps may overlap.

The procedural steps, or crisis counseling strategies, for helping persons in crisis are as follows:

1. Make psychological contact and rapidly establish the relationship.
2. Examine the dimensions of the problem in order to define it.
3. Encourage an exploration of feelings and emotions.
4. Explore and assess past coping attempts.
5. Generate and explore alternatives and specific solutions.
6. Restore cognitive functioning through implementation of action plan.
7. Follow-up.

1. Make psychological contact and rapidly establish the relationship. This first step involves the initial contact between the crisis intervenor and the potential client. The major task for the clinician at this point is to establish rapport by conveying genuine respect for and acceptance of the client. The client also often needs reassurance and reinforcement that he or she can be helped and that this is the appropriate place to receive such help.

2. Examine the dimensions of the problem in order to define it. It is useful to try to identify the following: (a) the "last straw" or precipitating event that led the client to seek help; (b) previous coping methods; and (c) dangerousness or lethality. Crisis counselors should explore these dimensions of the problem through specific open-ended questions. The focus must be on *now and how* rather than *then and why.* For example, key questions would be:

"What situation or event led you to seek help?"

"When did this event take place?"

3. Encourage an exploration of feelings and emotions. Step three is closely related to examining and defining the dimensions of the problem, particularly the precipitating event. It is presented here as a separate step because some therapists overlook it in their attempt to make rapid assessment and find the precipitating event. It is extremely therapeutic for a client to ventilate and express feelings and emotions in an accepting, supportive, private, and nonjudgmental setting.

The primary technique for identifying a client's feelings and emotions is through *active listening*. This involves the crisis intervenor listening in an empathic and supportive way to both the client's reflection of what happened and how the client feels about the crisis event.

4. Explore and assess past coping attempts. Most youths and adults have developed several coping mechanisms, some adaptive, some less adaptive, and some inadequate as responses to the crisis event. Basically, an emotionally hazardous event becomes an emotional crisis when the "usual homeostatic, direct problem-solving mechanisms do not work" (Caplan, 1964, p. 39). Thus, attempts to cope fail. One of the major foci of crisis intervention involves identifying and modifying the client's coping behaviors at both the preconscious and conscious levels. It is important for the crisis intervenor to attempt to bring to the conscious level the client's coping responses that now operate just below the surface at the preconscious level, and then to educate the client in modifying maladaptive coping behaviors.

Specifically, it is useful to ask the client how certain situations are handled, such as feelings of intense anger, loss of a loved one (a child or spouse), disappointment, or failure.

5. Generate and explore alternatives and specific solutions. If possible, this involves the collaborative effort between the client and crisis intervenor to generate alternatives. It is also important at this stage to explore the consequences and feelings about each alternative.

Most clients have some notion of what should be done to cope with the crisis situation, but they may well need assistance from the crisis clinician in order to define and conceptualize more adaptive coping responses to the crisis. In cases where the client has little or no introspection or personal insights, the clinician needs to take the initiative and suggest more adaptive coping methods. Defining and conceptualizing more adaptive coping behaviors for the client can be a highly productive component in helping the client resolve the crisis situation.

6. Restore cognitive functioning through implementation of action plan. The basic premise underlying a cognitive approach to crisis resolution is that the ways in which external events and a person's cognitions of the events turn into personal crisis are based on cognitive factors. The crisis clinician using a cognitive approach helps the client focus on why a specific event leads to a crisis state (e.g., it violates a person's expectancies) and, simultaneously, what the client can do to effectively master the experience and be able to cope with similar events should they occur in the future.

Cognitive mastery involves three phases. First, the client needs to obtain a realistic understanding of what happened and what led to the crisis. In order to move through and past the crisis and get on with life, it is important that the client have an understanding of what happened, why it happened, who was involved, and the final outcome (e.g., a suicide attempt, a divorce, a child being battered).

Second, it is useful for the client to understand the specific meaning the event has for him or her, how it conflicts with his or her expectations, life goals, and belief system. The client's thoughts and belief statements usually flow out freely when a client in crisis talks. The crisis intervenor should listen carefully and note any cognitive errors or distortions (overgeneralizing, catastrophizing) or irrational beliefs. The clinician should avoid prematurely stating the rational beliefs or reality-based cognitions for the client. Instead, the clinician should help the client discover distortions and irrational beliefs. This can be facilitated through carefully worded questions such as "Do you still want to move out of state now that you know that the person who raped you and brutally killed his previous two victims will be electrocuted today in the electric chair?" or, "Have you ever asked your doctor whether he thinks you are a workaholic and will die from a heart attack at a young age, or what your actual risk of cardiac failure is if you do not lessen your seventy-hour work weeks?"

The third and final part of cognitive mastery involves restructuring, rebuilding, or replacing irrational beliefs and erroneous cognitions with rational beliefs and new cognitions. This may involve providing new information through cognitive restructuring, homework assignments, or referral to others who have lived through and mastered a similar crisis (e.g., a support group for widows, for impotent men, for rape victims, or for infertile couples).

7. Follow-up. At the final session the client should be told that if at any time in the future he or she needs to come back for another session, the door is open and the clinician is available. Sometimes clients cancel their second, third, or fourth appointment prior to resolving the crisis. For example, the client who was raped at knifepoint is up half the night prior to her appointment with her clinician. She mistakenly thinks her nightmares and insomnia are caused by the clinician. In actuality, she has not come to grips with her vulnerabilities and fears that the rapist will return. The clinician, knowing that victims of violent crimes often go into crisis at the anniversary of the crime—exactly one month or one year after the victimization—informs the client that she would like to see her again and that as soon as she calls she will be given an emergency appointment the same day.

Summary

I t is clear, in reviewing the current progress in applying time-limited crisis intervention approaches to persons in acute crisis, that we have come a long way in the past decade. Crisis intervention is provided by all of the 600-plus voluntary crisis centers and crisis lines; by most of the 760 community mental health centers and their satellite programs; and by the majority of the 900 victim assistance programs and 1,250 battered women's programs available throughout the country. In addition, crisis services are provided at thousands of local hospital emergency rooms, hospital-based emergency psychiatric services, suicide prevention centers, child abuse hotlines and crisis nurseries, local United Way–funded info lines, and pastoral counseling services. The rapid proliferation of crisis services developed across the country in recent years is often directed toward particular groups of persons in crisis, such as rape victims, battered women, adolescent suicide attemptors, cocaine abusers, infertile couples, abusive parents, and victims of disasters. The increased development of crisis services and units reflects a growing awareness among public health and mental health administrators of the critical need for community crisis services.

This handbook provides an up-to-date and comprehensive examination of the crisis model and its application to persons suffering from an acute type of crisis. There is consensus among most social workers, clinical psychologists, and psychiatrists that crisis theory and the crisis intervention approach provide an extremely useful focus for handling all types of acute crisis. Almost every distressed person who calls or visits a community mental health center, victim assistance program, rape crisis unit or program, battered women's shelter, substance abuse treatment program, or suicide prevention program can be viewed as being in some form of crisis. By providing rapid assessment and timely responses, clinicians can formulate effective and economically feasible plans for time-limited crisis intervention.

References

Aguilera, D. C., & Messick, J. M. (1982). *Crisis Intervention: Theory and Methodology.* St. Louis, MO: C.V. Mosby.

Bard, M., & Ellison, K. (1974, May). "Crisis Intervention and Investigation of Forcible Rape," *The Police Chief, 41,* 68–73.

Beck, A. T. (1976). *Cognitive Therapy and the Emotional Disorders.* New York: The New American Library.

Bellak, L., & Siegel, H. (1983). *Handbook of Intensive Brief and Emergency Psychotherapy.* Larchmont, NY: C.P.S.

Blaun, R. (1987, March 30). "Dealing With Impotence." *New York,* pp. 50–58.

Burns, D. D. (1980). *Feeling Good.* New York: The New American Library.

Caplan, G. (1961). *An Approach to Community Mental Health.* New York: Grune and Stratton.

Caplan, G. (1964). *Principles of Preventive Psychiatry.* New York: Basic Books.

Fairchild, T. N. (1986). *Crisis Intervention Strategies for School-Based Helpers.* Springfield, IL: Charles C. Thomas.

Golan, N. (1978). *Treatment in Crisis Situations.* New York: Free Press.

Halpern, H. A. (1973). "Crisis Theory: A Definitional Study." *Community Mental Health Journal, 9,* 342–349.

Kadushin, A., & Martin, J. A. (1988). *Child Welfare Services* (4th ed.). New York: Macmillan.

Levinson, R. W. (1988). *Information and Referral Networks.* New York: Springer.

Lindemann, E. (1944). "Symptomatology and Management of Acute Grief." *American Journal of Psychiatry, 101,* 141–148.

Meichenbaum, D., & Jaremko, M. E. (1983). *Stress Reduction and Prevention*. New York: Plenum.

Parad, H. J. (1965). *Crisis Intervention: Selected Readings*. New York: Family Service Association of America.

Parad, H. J. (1971). "Crisis Intervention." In Robert Morris (Ed.), *Encyclopedia of Social Work* (Vol. 1, pp. 196–202). New York: National Association of Social Workers.

Parad, H. J. & Caplan, G. (1960). "A Framework for Studying Families in Crisis." *Social Work, 5* (3), 3–15.

Puryear, D. A. (1979). *Helping People in Crisis*. San Francisco: Jossey-Bass.

Rapoport, L. (1965). "The State of Crisis: Some Theoretical Considerations." In H. J. Parad (Ed.), *Crisis Intervention: Selected Readings*. New York: Family Service Association of America.

Ripple, L., Alexander, Ernestina, & Polemis, Bernice. (1964). *Motivation, Capacity, and Opportunity*. Chicago: University of Chicago Press.

Roberts, A. R. (1979). "Organization of Suicide Prevention Agencies." In Leon D. Hankoff & Bernice Einsidler (Eds.), *Suicide: Theory and Clinical Aspects* (pp. 391–399). Littleton, MA: PSG Publishing.

Roberts, A. R. (1984). *Battered Women and Their Families*. New York: Springer.

Slaby, A. E. (1985). "Crisis-Oriented Therapy." In Frank R. Lipton & Stephen M. Goldfinger (Eds.), *Emergency Psychiatry at the Crossroads* (pp. 21–34). San Francisco: Jossey-Bass.

Stotland, E. (1969). *The Psychology of Hope*. San Francisco: Jossey-Bass.

Tyhurst, J. S. (1957). "The Role of Transition States—Including Disasters—in Mental Illness." In *Symposium on Preventive and Social Psychiatry* (pp. 1–23). Washington, DC: Walter Reed Army Institute of Research.

Viney, L. L. (1976). "The Concept of Crisis: A Tool for Clinical Psychologists." *Bulletin of the British Psychological Society, 29,* 387–395.

United Way of America. (1980). *Information and Referral: Programmed Resource and Training Course*. Alexandria, VA: Author.

Part II

CRISIS ASSESSMENT AND INTERVENTION MODELS WITH CHILDREN AND YOUTH

DEVELOPING crisis intervention programs specifically for children, youth, and college students is a crucial step toward meeting their psychosocial needs. Children and youths have a somewhat limited experiential background with which to deal with acute crisis events. Depending on their age, they may have limited cognitive abilities, limited education, and an immature emotional level of development with which to handle a crisis. Thus it is vital for the crisis intervenor to be warm, reassuring, and patient, as well as open and directive, so the young person can learn and grow from the experience.

Some hazardous events—such as divorce of parents, sexual abuse, or an unwanted pregnancy—can quickly develop into a personal crisis for the individual(s) directly involved. Other events are devastating to an entire class, school, or college community, such as a student's suicide or a gunman entering the school and injuring or killing one or more persons.

Children and adolescents who lose a loved one often have strong responses, the nature of which has until recently not been clear. In Chapter 2 there is a discussion of the research literature and the provision of crisis intervention and time-limited cognitive therapy with children who have experienced their parents' divorce, a long-term physical or emotional illness of a parent, or the death of a loved one through illness, disaster, or extreme events such as homicide or suicide. The chapter discusses children's reactions of grief versus depression and points out that time-limited cognitive strategies place emphasis on the treatment of cognitive distortions and also on cognitive restructuring. A number of case illustrations are provided, and the chapter stresses that although crisis intervention is important, the family interaction approach may also be useful. Finally, it is important that given the broad array of possible disorders and intervention, careful diagnosis and therapeutic planning be done. Of utmost importance for the grieving child during the period immediately following the loss of a loved one is a basic supportive structure and nurturance. At a later time, the clinician initiates behavioral and cognitive restructuring and exploration of the child's inner thoughts leading to planning for the future.

Dramatically increasing adolescent suicide rates have brought widespread attention and concern to the issue of teen suicide. Chapter 3 presents a crisis model for adolescent suicidal clients and their families. It integrates traditional crisis intervention with an expanded orientation which not only focuses intervention on the suicidal teen and his or her attendant developmental issues, but includes the familial and societal context as factors which require attention and focus in the therapeutic setting. This chapter emphasizes the importance of including the family in crisis intervention with the suicidal teen. Guidelines, including case materials, are presented to assist the mental health professional in both crisis resolution as well as in laying the groundwork for continuing improvement in adolescent and family healing, stability, and growth.

Schools and colleges provide a unique opportunity for individual and group crisis intervention. Children and youths often spend as much time in educational settings as they do at home. The result is that school personnel (including teachers, guidance counselors, school social workers, and coaches) may spend as much or more time with youths as their parents do. Therefore, school and college faculty and staff have many opportunities to observe changes in students' appearance, behavior, and attitude toward school which may indicate a crisis situation. They also have special opportunities to provide crisis intervention services.

There is a major similarity between the goals of schools and colleges and those of crisis intervention programs: Both focus on growth and development as a result of learning. In fact, crisis theory purports that each crisis experienced by a youth represents a unique opportunity that may never occur again.

Traumatic events which have emotional consequences for an entire school population seem to be increasing in frequency across the United States. Chapter 4 provides a special opportunity to learn how to provide crisis consultation and crisis intervention in times of tragedy. The author describes two detailed crisis management plans he developed at Concord (New Hampshire) High School following two tragedies: the fatal police shooting of a 16-year-old former student at the high school and the freeing of his two hostages; and the tragic death of a popular teacher at the school, the nationally acclaimed Christa McAuliffe, the first teacher chosen to participate in a space mission, who was killed with six astronauts aboard the space shuttle on January 28, 1986. This chapter explicates practice guidelines and two detailed crisis management plans implemented to cope with the students' need for crisis intervention in the aftermath of these events. The chapter concludes with a description of concrete preintervention, intervention, and postvention guidelines which can be used by other school settings to limit the potential negative impact that traumatic events such as these can have on students and teachers.

Chapter 5 examines the delivery of crisis intervention services by college and university counseling centers. The chapter begins with documentation of the appropriateness of crisis intervention for college students at Stanford University, the University of Massachusetts, and other higher education centers. Then the chapter presents a practice framework for crisis intervention with college students, staff, and faculty. Crisis precipitants common among college students include physical assault/date rape, unwanted pregnancy, abortion, death of a parent, hospitalization of a parent, a broken romance, and impending academic failure. The chapter then contains a crisis intervention model and case illustrations of the model in operation.

Chapter 2

Assessment, Crisis Intervention, and Time-Limited Cognitive Therapy with Children and Adolescents Grieving the Loss of a Loved One

BRIAN J. MCCONVILLE, M.D.

Introduction

C hildren and adolescents frequently lose a loved one or loved ones through sickness or accident, and particularly through divorce. These situations may occur by acute crises or by a sudden worsening of long-term concerns.

Practice Frameworks: An Overview

D avid is a bright appealing 7-year-old boy whose parents have been talking about separating for six months but still live in the same house. Each parent insists on the right to stay and will not make a move toward full divorce or separation. Each parent also uses David as a confidant and attempts to have him take sides.

David is sad and tearful and shows little zest for living, with decreased appetite and difficulty in sleeping. At night he dreams of frightening monsters with indistinct faces who try to pull him in different directions. He has begun to lose weight and talks wistfully about his hope that his parents will stay together. He is particularly anxious about being asked to choose between the parents and fears he may do "something bad" which might precipitate a divorce.

In David's viewpoint there is no solution to his problem, and the clinician first goes over the difficulty of his situation with him, encouraging him to talk about his feelings about the separation. David is very angry at both parents but is afraid to express his anger. This is most marked with his father, because David feels the father is more likely than the mother to leave. The clinician tells him that he has the right to have his opinions and that many children in similar situations share his feelings. However, the clinician says, David is not responsible for what his parents may or may not do. The clinician later talks with both parents about how David needs to have them come to a reasonable solution despite their individual differences, since they are still David's parents, and they both love him.

After some hesitation and mutual blaming, the parents agree with this, and the separation occurs reasonably amicably. David spends most of his time with his mother, shows less depressive symptoms, and begins to learn again at school. He can also let go of his prior pattern of being more mature than his years, and he no longer needs to act as confidant and parent to his own parents. The time in therapy has been eight weeks, and at follow-up after three months David continues to do well.

This example indicates how short-term crisis intervention may work with children, and it exemplifies the usefulness of direct work with both David and his parents.

The therapy has included an early assessment of the degree of the child's depression, especially in terms of any possible suicidal tendencies. The dimensions of the problem and David's feelings and emotions are explored, and some coping responses are suggested. David's willingness and capacity to talk freely to adults are used, but his tendency to act as parent to his parents is agreed to be not useful. Alternative solutions are explored, which include a realistic appraisal of the child's limitations in ensuring change. An alternate approach is selected and followed through, and the parents are actively interested in a transcendent role of being parents to David, rather than warring parties. The restructuring intervention is successful and David is encouraged to talk to other children at school with similar problems. At follow-up he continues to do well, although the situation continues to need careful monitoring.

This case, which is common in child psychotherapy, indicates the importance of crisis intervention with children. Other residual issues still exist, but at this time David continues to grow, learn, and be able to express cheerful emotions with others despite the need for intermittent but masterable grieving.

A child's or adolescent's loss of a loved one may give rise to devastating consequences, the nature of which is only now beginning to be fully understood. Sometimes loss of a significant person will result in a series of short-lived affectual and cognitive responses, and crisis intervention techniques will help to fully resolve the issues. For example, the latest revision of the *Diagnostic and Statistical Manual of Mental Disorders (DSM-III-R)* of the American Psychiatric Association (APA; 1987) describes a category of uncomplicated bereavement. In this, a depressive syndrome is frequently a normal reaction, with feelings of depression and such associated symptoms as poor appetite, weight loss, and insomnia. However, morbid preoccupation with worthlessness, prolonged and marked functional impairment, and marked psychoretardation are uncommon, unless the bereavement is complicated by the concurrent development of a major depressive episode.

In uncomplicated bereavement, guilt, if present, is largely about things done or not done by the survivor at the time of the death. Thoughts of death are usually limited to the person's thinking that he or she would be better off dead, or that he or she should have died with the deceased person. Ordinarily the person with uncomplicated bereavement regards feelings of depressed mood as "normal," although professional help may be sought for associated symptoms such as insomnia or anorexia. The reaction to the loss may not be immediate but rarely occurs after the first two to three months. The duration of normal bereavement is said to vary considerably among different cultural groups. The *DSM-III-R* definitions make it clear that there is a continuum associated with the response to loss between "uncomplicated" bereavement and the development of dysthymic disorders, major depressive episodes, and even full melancholia. Extreme cases could require psychotherapeutic intervention, possible pharmacotherapeutic intervention, and even hospitalization.

The obvious question is how to identify children most at risk for the more serious grief responses. In brief, those with previously unmastered losses, with parents who have themselves been depressed, with a history of serious illnesses requiring hospitalization, and with a genetic inheritance pattern for affective disorders are most at risk. There is also a spectrum of responses to bereavement which are not only affective but may also include behavior disorders (Furman, 1983; Marriage, Fine, Moretti, & Haley, 1986) as well as the possibility of somatization reactions (Maloney, 1980; Klykylo, McConville, & Maloney, in press). There may also be long-term effects on family interaction patterns (LaRoche, 1986).

What represents the loss of a loved one? In this chapter we will hold that grieving for loss (a) follows the death of a loved one due to an acute or chronic illness, a homicide or other violent interpersonal act, or a natural disaster; (b) follows divorce and separation; or (c) relates to the nonavailability of particular caring persons for long periods of time either from physical illness or emotional illness such as depression. It is probable that grieving will vary with age and developmental stage (McConville, Boag, & Purohit, 1972; Kazdin, 1981).

Brief Review of the Research Literature About Loss in Children and Adolescents

Grief Responses Versus Depression Following Loss

A number of writers, such as Bowlby (1980), have drawn parallels between grief and depression. Bowlby in particular has argued that mourning has a central role in the genesis of depression, so that it is important to inquire whether there are developmental changes in children's responses to bereavement. Rutter (1986) has discussed this in terms of the general developmental psychopathology of depression and notes that no one study yet provides adequate and comparable general population data on the severity and persistence of grief reactions at different ages. Such data as are available (Bowlby, 1980; Rutter, 1966; Kleiman, 1968; Van Eerdewegh, Bieri, Parilla, & Clayton, 1982) have suggested that immediate grief reactions are both milder and of shorter duration in young children than in adolescents or adults. McConville et al. (1972) also suggested this in a study of children of various ages who experienced a common bereavement.

It is ordinarily suggested that age differences in bereavement relate to the child's ability to conceptualize both the past and the meaning of death. Furman (1970) described the reaction of children of various ages to loss, including the child's early animistic concepts about death, and noted that children tended to equate the functions of the dead person with their own developmental stages. Regression from recently mastered skills often occurred, and sometimes this loss of skills was associated with a feeling of uselessness or futility about, for example, taking papers home from school which had always been seen by the dead mother. This in turn leads to the child's age-related concepts of death as described by Dunton (1970), following the work of Piaget (1951). The child has no understanding of the meaning of death until the age of 5 or 6. By age 8 or 9 causalogical thinking is used to some degree by every child, and by age 11 children use logical thinking. Before the age of 7, separation anxiety predominates over anxiety related to aggression, and after 7 the reverse is true. As Rutter (1986) pointed out, this does not mean that children are less affected by bereavement, but rather that they may not show depression in a manner typical of adults and may suffer instead in other ways.

The immediate reactions to loss may therefore be short-lived in younger children, but the delayed consequences may be considerable. Concerns about long-term effects of death such as breakup of home, changes of caretaker, financial disadvantage, and the effects of bereavement on the surviving parent with the arrival of a stepparent (Furman, 1974) may give rise to considerable uncertainty. In a study of bereavement reactions in kibbutz children who had lost their fathers, Elizur and Kaffman (1982) noted that "the common assumption that time will heal and problems will disappear seems misleading and may prevent indispensable help in intervention in critical stages in the first years of bereavement." In the same vein, Kalter, Riemer, Brickman, and Chen (1985), reporting on the implications of parental divorce for female development, reported what Wallerstein (1985) described as a "time bomb–like" reaction during adolescence in terms of precocious sexual activity, substance abuse, and running away from home in teenage girls. This leads to consideration of the importance of early intervention during divorce.

Responses to the Loss of a Loved One Through Illness

There has been considerable interest in the literature about terminally ill children and their families. Most of the studies have dealt with responses in families (Spinetta, Swarner, & Sheposh, 1981; Jurk, Ekert, & Jones, 1981; Wiener, 1970). These include continued grieving, guilt, and a tendency toward blaming behavior and family dissension, with possible marital breakup. Parents who adjusted best had a consistent philosophy of life during the course of the illness and gave their child information and emotional support. Few of these studies have dealt particularly with children's adjustment, and most have been limited to individual case studies with some reports in psychoanalytic publications (Cairns, Clark, Smith & Lansky, 1979; Berman, 1978; Pettle, Michael, & Lansdown, 1986). Responses reported include disturbed ego functioning, poor self-concept, guilt-laden reactions, death phobias, and character distortions.

Children in families with chronically or terminally ill siblings perceive themselves as more socially isolated (Cairns et al., 1979), and may present management difficulties for their parents, being more prone to adjustment problems, irritability, and withdrawal. Simeonsson and McHale (1981) found in surviving children identity problems, increased physical demands, and attempts to compensate the parents for the limitations of the sick sibling. Spinetta et al. (1981) report on general malaise, an inability to return to normal functioning, continued apathy and feelings of sadness, and inability to confront reminders of the dead child and to plan for the future.

The family structure seems to be the most powerful orienting force toward adjustment. Pettle et al. (1986) studied 28 children from 14 families in which a brother or sister died from cancer between an 18- and 30-month period, using behavior checklists completed by parents and teachers and a self-concept scale. Ten children experienced emotional or behavioral difficulties or both, and 26 of the children obtained negative self-esteem scores. Interestingly, parental and child adjustments were not found related inter se, nor did they relate to the child's self-esteem. This difference between children's subjective distress and parents' tendency to notice disturbing rather than disturbed internalizing behavior has also been shown in studies of children with depression (Fine, Moretti, Haley, & Marriage, 1985). Accordingly, for many children loss of a sibling can cause long-term distress, and children perceived themselves unfavorably with their dead sibling. There is some suggestion that the shorter the duration of illness, the greater the impact on the surviving sibling's negative view of himself or herself, suggesting that during long-term illness optimal preparatory mourning and grieving can take place.

Few studies deal with the issue of children's responses after sudden death, and those which exist are largely anecdotal. Peretz (1970) describes varieties of grief in these situations including normal, anticipatory, delayed, and chronic, along with depression, hypochondriasis, and acting out.

Responses to the Loss of a Loved One Through Disaster

A related area of concern has to do with children's response to loss of people during disaster. Following a tornado which struck a town in Mississippi in 1953, causing a number of deaths, Anthony (1986) found in children a tendency to cling to parents, an inability to sleep alone, hypersensitivity to noise, and a striking tendency to avoid situations associated with the tornado, which clearly resemble the stress disorders. Similar findings were found after the Buffalo Creek flood in which many people died (Newman, 1976), with the symptoms described by Anthony plus withdrawal, depression and hypochondriasis, and with evidence of personality changes from 7 years on.

In the Chowchilla disaster in 1976, Terr (1979) reviewed reactions of children 5 to 13 months afterward and then four years after that. Terr found recurrent dreams of the child's own death with pessimism about his or her future, fear of further trauma, repetitive monotonous compulsive activity to maintain the level of chronic anxiety, and personality changes.

Similar results were found by Galante and Foa (1986) following a severe earthquake in Italy. One striking finding was that not only did the frequency of expressed fears drop after treatment that allowed an opportunity to ventilate and talk about the situation, but also the children fought to be the first to enter treatment, had to be evicted at the end, and even bombarded the prefab treatment room with stones to storm their way back in after their turns were over!

Kinzie, Sack, Angell, and Manson (1986) described the psychiatric effects of massive trauma on Cambodian children using standardized interviews on 40 high school students who had suffered massive trauma from 1975 to 1979 with separation from family, forced labor, starvation, and the witnessing of many deaths. After two years of living in refugee camps the children immigrated to the United States between ages 4 and 14. Four years after leaving Cambodia 50 percent had developed post-traumatic stress disorder and mild but prolonged depressive symptoms which were more common and severe when the students did not reside with a family member. Those students receiving a psychiatric diagnosis also were more likely to be rated by their classroom teachers as withdrawn or daydreaming rather than disruptive; here the effect of possible contact with an alternate culture should be taken into effect.

On the other hand, Garmezy (1986) described stress-resistant children whose resilience stemmed from inherent biologic dispositions, satisfactory early development within a reasonably good environment, and supportive relationship with parents, families, and other supportive figures. Some children came through stress well, even with enhanced capacities.

Anthony (1986) remarked that instruments are needed to gain accessibility to the child's underlying feelings rather than those which follow direct observation, questionnaires, or other paper and pencil techniques.

Responses to the Loss of a Loved One Through Parental Homicide

An extreme form of personal stress relates to children who have witnessed the killing of one or both of their parents in homicidal violence. Pynoos and Eth (1986) described a semi-standardized interview for children with such unfortunate histories which proceeds in a three-stage approach, from projective drawing and story testing to discussing the actual traumatic situation and the perceptual impact, and then to the aftermath and its consequences for the child. Such an approach begins systematically with establishing rapport and moves to reenactment and understanding of both the cognitive and affectual components of the unmastered experience. It then includes active attempts to have the child work on mastery mechanisms, again both at a cognitive and affectual level. Often denial in fantasy allows the child to mitigate painful reality by imaginatively reversing the violent outcome. However, some leading comments from the interviewer suggesting a wish from the child to reverse the event will often cause a high degree of emotional release. Pynoos and Eth noted ⸱' ₊t the child "must attain a state where he does not feel too threatened by emotional responses and where he has at least the hope of being able to cope with them." This approach clearly suggests both cognitive and affective restructuring toward acceptance of death following traumatic events and is a good general model for therapy. Issues of human accountability and inner plans for action, punishment, or retaliation are then commented on and the child's impulse control, traumatic dreams, and future orientation and current stressors are asked about.

In the final stage of closure there is a recapitulation, with spelling out of realistic fears, of the expectable cause of the disorder, and comments about the child's courage. This approach is similar to that used by military psychiatrists with treatment of soldiers who had viewed a buddy either killed or maimed in combat; considerable success has been described for this approach. It also follows that used for adults by Horowitz, Wilner, Kaltneider, and Alvarez (1980) following severe trauma. Malmquist (1986) also addressed the issue of children who witness parental murder and found that those children who were comfortable about their support from others dealt better than those who could not affirm their own value and worth. The latter had episodes of anxiety and depression remaining long after the event.

Mourning Responses in Children Following Divorce

The population available for study of divorce mourning is enormous, given the rate of divorce in the United States, despite recent suggestions that figures showing that half of marriages fail are untrue because of errors in estimating incidence versus prevalence.

A number of the long-term effects of divorce and remarriage in the adjustment of children have now been studied. Hetherington, Cox, and Cox (1985), in a six-year follow-up of the effects of divorce on parents and children, found that divorce showed more adverse effects for boys, while remarriage was more disruptive for girls. The long-term effects in adjustment were externalized in boys and more internalized in girls. Children of divorced families encountered more negative life changes than those of nondivorced families, with behavior problems up to six years after divorce. Guidubaldi and Perry (1985) in a longitudinal study showed that children from divorced families performed more poorly than those in intact families. Kalter et al. (1985) found long-term negative effects of divorce on daughters, particularly when taking into account adolescent and adult subjects and looking beyond short-term effects into dimensions related to self-esteem and ultimate heterosexual adjustment.

Wallerstein (1985), in a 10-year longitudinal study, found that 40 young adults at the 10-year mark still regarded their parents' divorces as a continued major influence in their lives. A significant number had vivid memories of the marital rupture, with feelings of sadness, continuing resentment of the parents, and a sense of deprivation. They tended to have ideals of a lasting marriage and a conservative morality but were apprehensive about repeating their parents' unhappy marriage for the sake of their children.

A separate but related issue has to do with children in divorce going through custody concerns and court (Steinman, Zemmelman, & Knoblauch, 1985). Children involved in parental disputes making transitions from one parent's home to the other showed different patterns of coping and defensive response, often being different with either parent (Johnston, Campbell, & Mayes, 1985). It would therefore seem that the long-term sequelae of divorce are very considerable and efforts at early intervention are particularly important.

Responses to the Loss of Parents with Physical or Emotional Illness

Children who have been exposed to long-term physical illness with parents or to parents with depression are an important group of children experiencing loss. Many responses of children to their parents who are in the hospital over long periods of time are similar to those described earlier for children whose siblings are ill.

However, there is a considerable concern about the availability of the other parent. This availability may be highlighted in parents with psychiatric illness, and especially in children with depressed mothers who for various reasons are not available to their children. In this regard, LaRoche (1986) discussed prevention maneuvers in high-risk children of depressed parents, and discussed difficulties for the child with unexpected changes in the parent's mood, energy, or self-esteem in reality testing. Beardslee, Bemporad, Keller, and Klerman (1985) suggested from a review of studies that children of parents at risk for affective disorder were likely to develop depression and other kinds of psychopathology. In contrast, LaRoche (1986) found a relatively low incidence of affective problems and suggested that administration of lithium and other therapies on an outpatient basis may be a protective factor. They suggested that the presence of psychopathology in the child may lie in the failure of a supportive father to stabilize the emotional climate of the family when the mother is ill. This is particularly important in view of the finding by Weissman (1979) of a high degree of parental dysfunction in depressed mothers who had difficulty communicating with their children or who expressed loss of affection and anger toward their children. The making and keeping of affectional bonds is particularly important in young children;

in older children withdrawal of these bonds produces an absence of guidance and boundaries, which may give rise to antisocial behavior.

Research Approaches to Assessment, Crisis Intervention, and Time-Limited Cognitive Therapy

The assessment of children following loss has been described earlier in this chapter and particularly relates to the phenomena of grieving, possible associated depressive reactions, and some elements of post-traumatic stress disorder. There is also often an association with somatizing disorders, anxiety, and conduct disorders. This is particularly true for those children who are for special reasons vulnerable to stress (Garmezy, 1986). For them, the risk related to cumulative trauma is of considerable importance. A number of authors have focused on treating the parents and child by studying their interactions (Fraiberg, 1983), and similar studies have been done in the development of interpersonal psychotherapies. Minde, Shosenberg, Marton, and Ridley (1980) and Nurcombe et al. (1984) have described direct intervention programs for self-help skills in mothers of low-birth-weight infants, designed particularly to increase their feelings of competence. Similarly, LaRoche (1986) and Forest, Standish, and Baum (1982) have studied the effects of support and counseling after parental bereavement. This is an effective way to express feelings and learn new coping areas. LaRoche also commented that the common practice of encouraging a bereaved mother to become pregnant again to "forget the loss" is not a good strategy. Parents and children should probably be given the opportunity to hold or see the dead infant.

Cognitive strategies have been particularly useful in dealing with children with mourning and depression. The work of Beck (1967) and Kovacs and Beck (1977) has been of seminal importance. This in turn has caused an emphasis on studying cognitive distortions in depressed children, from concepts of locus of control (Rotter, 1966) to Beck's (1976) theory of cognitive error and distortion, and notions of attributional style (Abramson, Seligman, & Teasdale, 1978). Moyal (1977) found that self-esteem and depressive symptoms in school children correlated with an external locus of control and helpless self-blaming responses. Depressed children (Leon, Kendall, & Garber, 1980) attribute positive events to more external causes and negative events to more internal causes. Depression is long lasting if uncontrollable negative events are seen as due to stable, as distinct from transient, factors. Finally, the depression becomes pervasive when a person sees negative events as present in all situations (global) as opposed to some situations. This suggests a stage sequence in children thinking more negatively about themselves, and Seligman and Peterson (1986) found that internal stable and global attributions endured as depressive symptoms in children six months after the precipitating event. This finding was also indicated by some early work of McConville, Boag, and Purohit (1973) describing a negative self-esteem subtype in children's depression. Common errors by depressed subjects relating to overgeneralization, selective abstraction, personalizing, and catastrophizing can be reliably measured in schoolchildren through the Children's Negative Cognitive Error Questionnaire (Leitenberg, Yost, & Carroll-Wilson, 1986). Therapeutic maneuvers to offset these cognitive distortions are important.

As noted, parental depression may have a very significant effect on children not only because the parents are unresponsive, but also because the child of a depressed mother may mirror his or her mother's depressed behavior (Field, 1984). Hence the mother and child may maintain each other's depression, especially when both of them have an attributional style which makes them vulnerable to depression, so that dealing with both mother and child about more effective mastery is important.

The original work of Beck (Burns & Beck, 1978) stressed cognitive mediation of mood disorders by correcting cognitive distortions and decatastrophizing. Later work related to altering overgeneralization, minimization of positives, and selective abstraction. Sometimes written material in the form of diaries is useful for children to note their depression. Emery, Bedrosian, and Garber (1983) have discussed current concepts in cognitive therapy with depressed children and adolescents at some length. Whereas the targets of adult cognitive therapies can be classified as being cognitive errors, the focus of treatment in children should be on cognitive deficits in role-taking ability, empathy, interpersonal problem solving, and interpersonal understanding.

The literature on evaluation of crisis intervention and time-limited cognitive therapy is far from complete. Various reviews of child psychotherapy such as those of Shaffer (1984) and Dulcan (1984) have outlined the difficulties associated with doing adequate psychotherapy research. Urbain and Kendall (1980) found in their review of cognitive therapy with children that while most studies demonstrate that therapy improves problem solving, there is little evidence to show that this necessarily results in a reduction of behavior problems. Rather similar findings were made by Hobbs, Manguin, Tyroler, and Lahey (1980). Shaffer points out that changes in therapy should be assessed both particularly and generally. One not only should look at changes in thinking style or behavior patterns, but must also take global measures of pathology and more operational indices such as school attendance figures, recidivism rates, need for medication, and general adjustment in the community. One should also be clear that the changes seen are long lasting, or that there are not late-occurring effects. Proskauer (1971) discussed the effect of crisis-oriented and time-limited psychotherapy for children following loss and finds that this is useful as long as the current living situation is reasonably stable and nurturing. Obviously, more studies are needed.

There has been much discussion about the need for specifying psychotherapy in therapy manuals. But this essentially requires the conduct of therapy to continue relentlessly in the prescribed fashion regardless of the emerging material and is often not clinically useful. What seems to be more useful is that the therapist should behave consistently. The therapist should be flexible enough to explore a particular problem, use a consistent approach long enough to get changes set in place, and then be prepared to take up other material at a later time when it is more appropriate to do so. Crisis intervention cognitive strategies seem to be particularly useful in such planning for children undergoing grief and mourning, but well-planned studies are needed to further investigate this impression.

Critical Concepts in Crisis Intervention and Time-Limited Cognitive Therapy for Children and Adolescents Undergoing Loss

Crisis Intervention Versus Time-Limited Cognitive Therapy

Implicit in the concept of crisis is the sudden occurrence of some unmastered stress. At times this may be due to a disaster which affects a large number of people, as in children's responses to an earthquake or flood. At other times the crisis occurs as a personal tragedy which has particular meaning only for the child and family, as in an automobile accident. Responses of the child or adolescent are best expressed within the framework of acute post-traumatic stress reactions or stress disorder. However, as has been noted earlier, the exact impact on the child or adolescent relates to his or her expectations, goals, and belief systems, as well as his or her ordinary reaction to stress, relative invulnerability, or other constitutional factors.

If the child or adolescent experiencing an acute crisis has previously shown no evidence of emotional problems, has coped well and flexibly, and belongs to a caring family, then crisis therapy which focuses on modifying perception and coping responses to stress may well be effective. This would include changing personal and interpersonal factors and directing the child or adolescent in ways of integrating this experience into other life events. In cases where the crisis is more a precipitating event which pushes the child from a previous subclinical state into a full clinical disorder, the child may not have a sufficient number of satisfactory experiences or coping mechanisms to be able to reintegrate himself or herself to a previous good pattern of functioning. Here a more extensive cognitive and effectual restructuring may be needed. In practice— and especially in crisis-oriented programs—such interventions are necessarily time limited. The goal is to establish a pattern of satisfactory functioning.

At times, more extensive intervention may include psychopharmacologic and hospital treatment in the acute phases, as well as crisis and time-limited and cognitive therapy. Subsequently, more extensive therapy, including more historical exploration of restructuring, may be necessary in some children. The goal of therapy therefore is to intervene as promptly and precisely as possible, with clear goals of treatment and within a clearly understood relationship with the client. Such intervention may often indicate other areas in the child's life to be explored, but this does not mean it is mandatory to proceed with these areas. In what may be described as *stage-oriented therapy,* each child may be given an option to continue on to other aspects if he or she feels this is necessary. Such further exploration may be deferred to a later time. The important aspect in crisis intervention programs is to complete the task of therapy originally set up during the crisis.

All important concepts in both crisis intervention and time-limited cognitive therapy have to do with recognizing that children during periods of loss are undergoing extreme stress; this finding is often overlooked because of the actual bereavement and its direct effects on adults. Children also require specific interventions aimed at their age and developmental stage. The basic principles involve the early identification and treatment of problems associated with the mourning process, and the key is to have a skilled clinician or treatment team which automatically considers the responses of the various family members, especially the children.

Knowledge of the stress of a crisis on children and adolescents will help the clinician focus automatically on the necessity for intervention and avoid being unduly caught up with the more instrumental aspects of the loss, such as initial settlements or funeral arrangements, or with those adults who show more overt symptomatology. As noted earlier, Rutter (1986) has found that children's grief responses are truncated in observable phenomena but there is a later possibility of emergence in other symptoms, such as anxiety, post-traumatic stress disorders, conduct disorders, and somatizations. Prompt intervention with children at the time of the event will be useful in offsetting future problems, although there is not yet hard evidence of this. One overall model that might be used is that of Pynoos and Eth (1986), where the general model is rather similar to that used for intervention in other traumatic situations. This is equally true if the bereavement has been unexpected or sudden, so that both mourning and post-traumatic aspects will occur.

Hence the combination of gathering factual information, conducting associated cognitive and affectual restructuring, and doing some modeling of alternate ways in which the child may have wished the event to occur is useful as an initial model. Then it will be possible to take up issues of guilt, anger at the dead person, possible retribution fantasies toward those involved in the separation or bereavement, and then to plan realistic hopes for the future. An important feature in this model is a series of sessions during or soon after the bereavement or loss.

Another general concept is that some preparatory mourning should be allowed for if the separation or loss responses are predictable, with the therapist available to the child or family. In relatively common clinical groups such as children of divorced parents, group therapy may be possible to utilize peer guidance and support while talking through a shared concern. At other times, as with children who have a very ill sibling in the hospital, preparatory intervention will aid in the coping responses of the child and family. One of the more common models for intervention in this way has been described by Hoffman, O'Grady, McConville, and Harris (1986), who reported relaxation by hypnosis and problem- versus emotion-focused coping styles in parents and children during the child's severe illness. *Problem-focused coping* consists of direct actions (behavioral or cognitive) to remove or alter threatening circumstances. *Emotion-focused coping* includes actions or thoughts to control undesirable feelings resulting from stressful circumstances (Lazarus & Folkman, 1984).

Identification of Key Diagnoses

Most disorders are those associated with grief, mourning, and depression, as well as conduct, anxiety, or stress disorders. The clinical symptoms associated with these disorders are listed in the American Psychiatric Association's (APA; 1987) *DSM-III-R*. In addition, there are a number of interactions between siblings involving anger and guilt toward the ill sibling or involving the healthy sibling comparing himself or herself unfavorably. Children within a family context may assume particular roles such as being the "good" child, or the parental child, or at times may even be a scapegoat for various occurrences. These interactional problems may be addressed during the general context of family therapy.

Identification of Target Symptoms

The assignment of diagnoses per se does not necessarily indicate treatment, since the key component symptoms to make a particular diagnosis may be treated in different fashions. For example, clear vegetative signs of depression such as appetite problems, sleep disturbance, and alterations in motility may well respond to the antidepressant medication, whereas other symptoms such as negative self-esteem or guilt related to one's actions may not respond as easily and may therefore require cognitive or affectual reeducative therapy.

It may also prove simpler to look after the more obviously treatable components first. For example, many children in grief reactions following disaster or divorce may be particularly susceptible to basic nurturance anxiety, not knowing where they will be living or with whom they will be living. Resolution of these basic facets of survival will be necessary before any more substantive work can be done. It is therefore necessary for the clinician to have a broad variety of skills. These would certainly include such skills in cognitive therapy as inducing self-monitoring of mood, activities, pleasant events, and mastery experiences (Fixsen, Phillips, & Wolf, 1972). Behavioral techniques may include activity scheduling to help the children become more actively involved during the day and to decrease passivity and time spent ruminating over depressive symptoms.

Contingent reinforcement using manipulation of social contingencies, punishment, positive reinforcement, systematic desensitization, and modeling procedures can also be used to modify children's behavior (Petti, 1983). One problem, as Emery et al. (1983) pointed out, is that depressed or anhedonic children may not be rewarded by such ordinary modifiers as candy, toys, or games. Such children might be asked what would be fun for them if they did not feel so bad. Self-monitoring or recording thoughts, with alternate ways in which these may be described to oneself out loud or internally, can be of use. Children who cannot seek out pleasurable activities by themselves may need to have pleasurable activities scheduled. The use of graded task assignments can also be useful, since depressed children will often show decreased performance as a result of feeling overwhelmed.

Obviously the clinician has to be able to function broadly from a number of theoretical bases but should also be able to put these plans together into a meaningful framework. Some of these techniques will be described in the following section.

Case Examples

Four examples are given in this chapter. The first example—in the introduction—is of a clear crisis intervention for a child during separation of his parents. The next three case examples to be given illustrate the following:

1. Initial crisis intervention and then time-limited cognitive therapy in a child with separation anxiety
2. Crisis intervention and support of cognitive and affectual therapy for a dying child
3. Crisis hospitalization and supportive cognitive and affectual treatment for a sexually traumatized child with subsequent loss (through jail sentence) of parents, where initial crisis intervention has been unsuccessful

These cases have been selected to indicate a spectrum of increasing clinical complexity where the principles described for crisis intervention and cognitive treatment may be employed.

Case 1: A Child with Acute Separation Anxiety

Sally was a 7-year-old child with a three-month history of extreme anxiety while at school about her mother's well-being as well as fear of her teacher's anger. She earlier had a history of difficulty in separating from the mother during kindergarten, which was reinforced by the mother's difficulty in separating from the child. The mother took the child out from school more for her own reasons (as she said) than for the child. The present episode of school-based anxiety had been brought about by the death of a grandmother some three months earlier. Following this, the girl experienced a great deal of grief and mourning about the grandmother and felt that the grandmother's spirit had to stay with the body in the grave until the body was completely dissolved before it would be free to go up to heaven.

The child was also troubled by feelings that some person might break into her room at nighttime, and on questioning it emerged that this had to do with some frightening animistic concepts of the dead person. A diagnosis of separation anxiety disorder and a secondary diagnosis of adjustment disorder with depressed features were made and the child was taken into therapy. During the initial interview this verbal child not only vividly described her problems, but also had advanced some attempts at mastery. For example, she mentioned that she had been scared to visit the home of her dead grandmother, but that she was now able to do this by getting closer to her grandmother's house on repeated visits. She also asked to go to her other grandmother's funeral in due time!

She had difficulty flying to a nearby state to spend time with a relative, and described fear that the aircraft might crash because of the bumpiness of the ride. However, on the return visit she felt that the pilot now "knew what he was doing" and had relaxed and was able to master the trip. She was also pleased that she had been able to leave the mother and check with her by phone a number of times while she was away.

It therefore seemed that this girl already had put in place a number of cognitive structures leading to mastery attempts, so that she could be considered a good candidate for crisis intervention therapy.

In the initial sessions, however, which focused largely on her fears of the schoolteacher getting angry at her, she described how she might withdraw from the teacher's anger and might also feel that any anger the teacher directed at anybody else in the class was really directed at her. She would then fantasize being sent from the class and to the principal's office, where she would spend the day looking sadly out the window at the wind in the trees and would eventually be sent home, where she would be sent to bed but would at least feel safe.

Alternatively, when in role-playing enactment it was suggested to her that she might be the teacher, she responded with considerable severity by berating the clinician (who played the role of the child) for inadequate work done and saying that this would have to be done repetitively until the work was perfect. When in role reversal she was again in the position of the pupil, she would again become fearful. It therefore seemed clear that she had no intermediate position for being adequately assertive and that when she was faced with anger from a teacher or potential anger from her mother she became extremely depressed and sad.

A series of homework assignments was given to her in which she would try to write down things that had happened at school, with notes as to her response and with possible alternate solutions, and in continuation therapy these solutions were tried out in enactment. As part of this, the mother, who was excessively involved with the child, was in the room as an observer and later interacted with the child in role playing. The mother would allow the child to be more assertive, but not so much as to take over the role of a parentified child. Both the mother and child were very aware of their tendency to act as co-siblings in the family, and also of a family constellation in which the mother looked after her own mother excessively, and vice versa. The mother saw that she was setting up the same type of relationship with the child, making it difficult for this child to individuate satisfactorily. In this case the loss of the grandmother touched off the basic separation–individuation anxiety. Under extreme stress, as when she actually faced a teacher's anger or initially coped with the loss of the grandmother, the child would say she would not "give a care" and would just carry on either working or playing. This denial mechanism was useful as a first response but was not useful in a long-term adaptive sense. After five sessions, both her fear of her teacher and her separation anxiety had decreased.

In subsequent time-limited cognitive therapy, the girl showed an interesting series of coping responses and defenses of increasing complexity. There were a number of coping areas where she had already run through various solutions in her mind. These maneuvers came under the heading of *cognitive problem solving* as described by Lazarus and Folkman (1984) as part of a problem-focused approach. The behaviors were not well articulated but were nonetheless present in nascent form. Her major difficulties had more to do with emotion-focused coping when she had to assert herself, since she either went into withdrawal maneuvers—which left her withdrawn and lonely but secure within the original mother–child relationship—or turned to angry assertiveness with the teacher or parent when she feared she would be deserted or extruded.

Sessions therefore dealt with reinforcing her coping skills and running through in imagination and then in enactment sessions with the mother and child how it would be possible to foster the child's emotional independence without bringing about the feared rejection and loss.

As she worked on these mechanisms, her use of denial or counterphobic assertions of bravery diminished and she was able to interact more easily with others in her family. Concurrently, the mother was able to increase her separation from the girl and to encourage the girl's overall independence.

Case 2: Cognitive Affectual Therapy for a Dying Child and His Family

This case is of a 14-year-old boy in the bone marrow transplant unit in a large pediatric hospital. Here the boy and his parents had originally maintained with great hope that he was going to survive; this hope was seen as an important and almost self-fulfilling factor. As he became more ill, his protestations that he would be well increased, as did those of the family. The increased probability of death was a crisis event and the clinician became more active. In the final stages before death, the mother was able with assistance to use her emotion-focused coping by crying to a great extent, and to utilize such directed responses as hypnosis-promoted relaxation. On the other hand, the father tended to use more behavioral emotion-focused coping by increased drinking at times, by social withdrawal, and by becoming involved with practical business matters. His denial responses were supported.

As greater stress impinged on the family during the period of the child's dying, the mother became more involved in looking after the child's needs and was able to consider the possibility of the child's death. The father originally insisted that the child was going to survive and inquired about (nonuseful) lung transplants. This possibility was gently discouraged by the clinician and the hematologist. Among the two siblings, one younger child was able to grieve for the impending loss of her brother, whereas an older sister became excessively involved in sports and other activities that allowed her to avoid feeling states. Hence all family members had rather different coping mechanisms.

The patient's optimism was supported as long as possible, but eventually the boy stated his wish to die and at one time said, "Hurry, it's time." The family by now was able to unite in grieving responses as a family unit and went through the subsequent funeral well. However, one year after the death, in follow-up after brief therapy, the mother still said it helped her to cry every day. The father had become excessively immersed at work, and the younger girl still questioned why her brother had to die. The older girl was still involved in sports but developed some difficulties at school and some somatic pains of unknown etiology. Clearly the habitual responses shown by the family members had continued, and despite previous efforts there was a need for continued therapy for the family. This has now been arranged and is proceeding well.

Case 3: A Child Needing Crisis Hospitalization and Long-Term Therapy

This case is of a child whose parents had physically neglected and sexually abused him and the other children in the family; as a result both parents had been jailed for an indefinite period. He was placed in a foster home, and when he felt that the foster mother did not care sufficiently for him he became physically aggressive toward her and required hospitalization. In a prolonged period of hospitalization he displayed coping responses which indicated his extremely deprived life experiences when he recounted and enacted his skills in looking after himself, including living in the wooded area near his house. He also enacted his toughness through dressing in army clothing and by having a series of pictures connected with tigers, describing himself as being a tiger who could fight and survive. Sadly, the tiger was one of the few toys his mother had given him.

In cognitive-affectual therapy he could at times discuss the sexual abuse he had suffered and his guilt at being a key witness in the parents' trial. Often he could not tolerate such strong feelings.

In interactions with particular staff members with whom he eventually formed close attachments, he was able to work out better ways of being independent and strong while at the same time accepting that other people liked and could like him. This latter goal required a great deal of inpatient therapy over ward events, spelling out his mistrusting cognitive distortions. Finally as he began to trust he took his therapist to the areas where he had lived in the woods when things became too bad at home, and he shared more of his feelings. A teacher was able to take him initially to the zoo to look at tigers and later to her home for increasing periods of time, as he began to trust her more. Despite this, his guilt about having sent his parents to prison and his negative self-esteem required a great deal of excessive psychotherapy, with use of tricyclic medication for depression in the initial phases. In this case a combination of medication, an initial concrete behavior modification program, later alteration of negative cognitive distortions, enactment of mastery skills, and eventual grieving were necessary. But despite this, he remains in foster care, where he has occasional outbursts. It could be argued that more prompt handling of this child's initial anguish may have helped him integrate better, but the extreme and prolonged nature of his stress makes this unlikely.

Summary

I t will be seen that the crisis-oriented and time-limited cognitive therapies described form an essential but not exclusive part of the clinician's repertoire. The assessment of the child and family has to be done in the usual fashion, coming to a clear diagnosis and utilizing information from the child, family, and other sources. Consideration of externalizing behaviors involving familial, social, interactional, and behavioral concepts, and concurrent assessment of internalizing affectual, intrapsychic, and organic cognitive problems is needed. A range of immediate adaptations, coping styles, and problem- and emotion-focused coping mechanisms may be utilized. Consideration should also be given to the more classical mechanisms of defense, such as denial, rejection, and reaction formation. Characteristic patterns of family interaction should be assessed, as in the enmeshment patterns and difficulty in role definitions seen in

Case 1. Because of cognitive deficits, the child may not know how to behave in certain areas, but more emotionally based defense mechanisms and full resistance under the effects of anxiety can also occur in time. In other words, the crisis intervention and initial cognitive and affective restructuring strategies suggested in this chapter should not necessarily form the only approach to a child if opportunities exist for expressive and uncovering therapy, for structured family therapy, or even for psychopharmacologic intervention if necessary, for particular target groups of symptoms at certain times. Often behavioral approaches stressing a more Adlerian model will move a child or adolescent from fixed states of hopelessness and inability to function into areas of choice where he or she can negotiate with the parents about logical consequences and choices. This in turn may lead to contract formation which decreases the child's or adolescent's sense of helplessness and which sets external rules in the family.

More traditional psychodynamic approaches may also be extremely useful in understanding the richness and complexity of children's problems.

In dealing with children and adolescents, age and stage concepts are fundamental. Younger children often require information about the formality and irreversibility of death, since this fits in with their limited cognitive capacity, in a Piagetian sense. McConville et al. (1972) found that in responses of children to a common loss, younger children showed more denial and restitution and animistic fantasies about the dead people, whereas older children used more intellectual defenses, felt more guilty, and could think about longer term means of improving the situation. Children may also respond to strategic maneuvers such as role-playing techniques to enable a trial enactment of coping strategies after death or loss. Here the child can select, along with the clinician, strategies that work best for him or her at a particular age and stage.

It should also be noted that adolescents with underlying mourning responses and low self-esteem may often initially react with aggressive antisocial responses or alternatively with self-injurious behavior. The former pattern is more common in males and the latter in females. Setting clear limits and goals in a more behavioral pattern— especially within the family—may contain the adolescent and therefore allow for the later expression of grief. When grief does occur the adolescent is able to consider more abstract cognitive strategies that might be rehearsed verbally and later internally to alter perceptual/cognitive styles. Boredom and apathy in withdrawn teenagers may often occur, with concomitant depression and low self-esteem. A negative identity is often associated with the teenager's capacity to see himself or herself in terms of black and white options, and it is often necessary to suggest intermediate stages of functioning so that the adolescent is better able to express shades or degrees of mourning or grief.

Finally, many teenagers are exquisitely sensitive to rejection and loss, and empathic understanding by the clinician is an important first step. Dramatized enactments of how the teenager may be feeling by using role reversal situations may also allow for the degree of detachment the teenager needs to deal with loss, and in turn leads to the painful work of letting go of the loved person (Emery et al., 1983).

The steps in the crisis intervention and time-limited cognitive therapy model relate to a careful assessment of the clinical situation, with an initial selection of who is to be treated—the child alone, the child and parents, or the entire family. The various components of the problem should be carefully assessed in terms of key target groupings relating to externalizing social/interactional/familial and internalizing affectual/intrapsychic problems, as well as taking account of organic and cognitive factors which may modify the clinical picture.

It is useful at this point to be able to formulate a full *DMS-III-R* diagnosis in terms of the five axes. This will suggest target symptom groupings which may be treated in a variety of fashions. Some may require crisis stabilization of the situation, and others may require associated pharmacologic intervention and possible environmental manipulation. Once the initial crisis is stabilized so that the child or adolescent knows about basic structures and nurturance, work can progress toward dealing with the grieving and mourning processes.

Obviously the input of the therapist is best if he or she is involved early. In times of sudden death or loss—and particularly in disaster—this is very important; at other times early working with the family in cases of possible bereavement is a useful model. Case 2 given earlier relates to this, and Case 3 indicates the difficulties which may occur when such preventive intervention is either not thought of or is not possible.

Obviously, crisis intervention and brief cognitive therapy should not be thought of as the only intervention to be used in all cases. In addition to being a skilled diagnostician, a clinician should be able to recognize the necessary types of therapy required for various phases of the therapeutic process and should be willing to change frameworks as the clinical material alters, or as the phases of therapy alter from initial concerns about damage control and crisis containment toward longer term cognitive and affectual restructuring maneuvers.

This chapter has given an overview of the broad array of therapeutic interventions possible for children and adolescents grieving the loss of a loved one. The usefulness of the crisis intervention and cognitive therapy approaches has been stressed, and the breadth of the maneuvers involved requires the clinician to be skilled in a variety of therapeutic modalities and to be clear about the indications for particular therapeutic intervention.

Such therapeutic planning should follow a careful diagnosis, with selection of the optimal modes of therapeutic intervention for various target symptom groupings for a particular phase of therapy. Earlier moves should be directed toward establishing a supportive structure and nurturing the grieving child or adolescent so that he or she is taken care of in the initial stages of grief using the principles of crisis intervention. Later behavioral, cognitive, and affectual restructuring can then proceed, with exploration of the child's inner thoughts and planning for future directions.

Given this approach, many children and adolescents experiencing the loss of a loved one may be greatly helped by skilled and sensitive clinicians. Clearly the scope of early interventional psychotherapy for those with these devastating but common problems is advancing at a very rapid rate, and this provides great hope for the future.

References

Abramson, L. Y., Seligman, M., & Teasdale, J. (1978). "Learned Helplessness in Humans: Critique and Reformulation." *Journal of Abnormal Psychology, 78,* 49–74.

American Psychiatric Association. (1987). *Diagnostic and Statistical Manual of Mental Disorders (DMS-III-R).* Washington, DC: Author.

Anthony, E. J. (1986). "Children's Reactions to Severe Stress." *Journal of the American Academy of Child Psychiatry, 25,* 299–305.

Beardslee, W., Bemporad, J., Keller, M., & Klerman, G. (1985). "Children of Parents With Affective Disorders: A Review. *American Journal of Psychiatry, 140,* 825–832.

Beck, A. T. (1967). *Depression: Clinical, Environmental and Therapeutical Aspects.* Philadelphia: University of Pennsylvania Press.

Beck, A. T. (1976). *Cognitive Therapy and the Emotional Disorders.* New York: International Universities Press.

Berman, L. E. (1978). "Sibling Loss as an Organizer of Unconscious Guilt: A Case Study." *Psychoanalytic Quarterly, 47,* 565–587.

Bowlby, J. (1980). *Attachment and Loss. Loss, Sadness and Depression.* New York: Basic Books.

Burns, D., & Beck, A. T. (1978). Cognitive Behavior Modification of Mood Disorders. In A. Beck (Ed.), *Cognitive Behavior Therapy: Research and Application* (pp. 109–134). New York: Plenum Press.

Cairns, N., Clark, G., Smith, S., & Lansky, S. (1979). "Adaptation of Siblings to Childhood Malignancy." *Journal of Pediatrics, 95,* 484–487.

Dulcan, M. (1984). "Brief Psychotherapy With Children and Their Families: The State of the Art." *Journal of the American Academy of Child Psychiatry, 23,* 544–551.

Dunton, H. (1970). The Child's Concept of Grief. In B. Schoenberg, H. Carr, D. Peretz, & A. Kutscher (Eds.), *Loss and Grief.* New York: Columbia University Press.

Elizur, E., & Kaffman, M. (1982). "Children's Bereavement Reactions Following Death of the Father." *Journal of the American Academy of Child Psychiatry, 21,* 474–480.

Emery, G., Bedrosian, R., & Garber, J. (1983). Cognitive Therapy With Depressed Children and Adolescents. In D. Cantwell & G. Carlson (Eds.), *Affective Disorders in Childhood and Adolescents: An Update.* New York: Spectrum.

Field, T. M. (1984). Perinatal Risk Factors for Infant Depression. In J. Call, E. Galenson, & R. Tyron (Eds.), *Frontiers in Infant Psychiatry.* New York: Basic Books.

Fine, S., Moretti, M., Haley, G., & Marriage, K. (1985). "Affective Disorders in Children and Adolescents: The Dysthymic Disorder Dilemma." *Canadian Journal of Psychiatry, 30,* 173–177.

Fixsen, D., Phillips, E., & Wolf, M. (1972). "Achievement Place: The Reliability of Self-reporting and Peer-reporting and Their Effects on Behavior." *Journal of Applied Behavior Analysis, 5,* 19–30.

Forest, C., Standish, E., Baum, J. (1982). "Support After Perinatal Death: A Study of Support and Counselling After Perinatal Bereavement." *British Medical Journal, 285,* 1475–1479.

Fraiberg, S. (1983). "The Invisible Children." In E. J. Anthony, C. Koupernick, & C. Chiland (Eds.), *The Child in His Family.* Vol. 4, *Vulnerable Children.* New York: Wiley.

Furman, E. (1970). "The Child's Reaction to Death in the Family." In B. Schoenberg (Ed.), *Loss and Grief* (pp. 70–86). New York: Columbia University Press.

Furman, E. (1974). *A Child's Parent Dies. Studies in Childhood Bereavement.* New Haven: Yale University Press.

Furman, E. (1983). "Studies in Childhood Bereavement." *Canadian Journal of Psychiatry, 28,* 241–247.

Galante, R., & Foa, D. (1986). "An Epidemiologic Study of Psychic Trauma and Treatment Effectiveness for Children After a National Disaster." *Journal of the American Academy of Child Psychiatry, 25,* 357–363.

Garmezy, N. (1986). "Children Under Severe Stress: Critique and Commentary." *Journal of the American Academy of Child Psychiatry, 25,* 384–392.

Guidubaldi, J., & Perry, J. D. (1985). "Divorce and Mental Health Sequelae for Children: A Two-Year Follow-up of a Nationwide Sample." *Journal of the American Academy of Child Psychiatry, 25,* 531–537.

Hetherington, E. M., Cox, M., & Cox, R. (1985). "Long-Term Effects of Divorce and Remarriage on the Adjustment of Children." *Journal of the American Academy of Child Psychiatry, 24,* 518–531.

Hobbs, S. A., Manguin, L., Tyroler, M., & Lahey, S. (1980). "Cognitive Behavior Therapy With Children: Has Clinical Utility Been Demonstrated?" *Psychological Bulletin, 87,* 147–165.

Hoffman, C., O'Grady, D., McConville, B., & Harris, R. (1986). "Hypnosis With Parents and Children for Coping During Bone Marrow Transplantation." Paper presented to Society for Clinical and Experimental Hypnosis, Chicago, IL.

Horowitz, M., Wilner, N., Kaltneider, N., & Alvarez, W. (1980). "Signs and Symptoms of Post Traumatic Stress Disorder." *Archives of General Psychiatry, 37,* 85–92.

Johnston, J. R., Campbell, L., & Mayes, S. (1985). "Latency Children in Post Separation and Divorce Disputes." *Journal of the American Academy of Child Psychiatry, 24,* 563–574.

Jurk, I., Ekert, H., & Jones, H. (1981). "Family Responses and Mechanisms of Adjustment Following Death of Children With Cancer." *Australian Pediatric Journal, 17* (2), 85–88.

Kalter, N., Riemer, B., Brickman, A., & Chen, J. W. (1985). "Implications of Parental Divorce for Female Development." *Journal of the American Academy of Child Psychiatry, 24,* 538–544.

Kazdin, A., French, N., Unis, A., & Esveldt-Dawson, K. (1983). "Hopelessness, Depression and Suicidal Intent Among Psychologically Disturbed Inpatient Children." *Journal of Consulting and Clinical Psychology, 54,* 504–510.

Kazdin, E. (1981). "Assessment Techniques for Child Depression." *Journal of the American Academy of Child Psychiatry, 20,* 358–375.

Kinzie, J. D., Sack, W. H., Angell, R. H., & Manson, S. (1986). "The Psychiatric Effects of Massive Trauma on Cambodian Children (I, II)." *Journal of the American Academy of Child Psychiatry, 25,* 370–392.

Kleiman, G. W. (1968). *Psychological Emergencies of Children.* New York: Grune & Stratton.

Klykylo, W., McConville, B., & Maloney, M. (in press). "Somatoform and Eating Disorders." In *Handbook of Studies in Child Psychiatry.* New York: Elsevier.

Kovacs, M., & Beck, A. T. (1977). "An Empirical-Clinical Approach Towards a Definition of Childhood Depression." In I. Schulderbrandt & A. Raskin (Eds.), *Depression in Childhood: Diagnosis, Treatment, and Conceptual Models.* New York: Raven Press.

LaRoche, C. (1986). "Prevention in High Risk Children of Depressed Parents." *Canadian Journal of Psychiatry, 31,* 161–165.

Lazarus, R., & Folkman, S. (1984). *Stress, Appraisal and Coping.* New York: Springer.

Leitenberg, H., Yost, L., & Carroll-Wilson, M. (1986). "Negative Cognitive Errors in Children: Questionnaire Development, Normative Data, and Comparisons Between Children With and Without Self-reported Symptoms of Depression, Low Self-esteem and Evaluation Anxiety. *Journal of Consulting and Clinical Psychology, 54,* 528–536.

Leon, G. R., Kendall, P., & Garber, J. (1980). "Depression in Children: Parent, Teacher and Child Perspectives." *Journal of Abnormal Child Psychology, 8,* 221–235.

Malmquist, C. P. (1986). "Children Who Witness Parental Murder: Post Traumatic Aspects." *Journal of the American Academy of Child Psychiatry, 25,* 320–326.

Maloney, M. (1980). "Diagnosing Hysterical Conversion Reactions in Children." *Journal of Pediatrics, 96,* 1016–1020.

Marriage, K., Fine, S., Moretti, M., & Haley, G. (1986). "Relationship Between Depression and Conduct Disorders in Children and Adolescents." *Journal of the American Academy of Child Psychiatry, 25,* 687–691.

McConville, B., Boag, L., & Purohit, A. (1972). "Mourning Depressive Responses of Children in Residence Following Sudden Death of Parent Figures." *Journal of the American Academy of Child Psychiatry, 11,* 361–364.

McConville, B., Boag, L., & Purohit, A. (1973). "Three Types of Childhood Depression." *Canadian Journal of Psychiatry, 18,* 133–138.

McConville, B., & Bruce, R. T. (1985). "Depressive Illnesses in Children and Adolescents: A Review of Current Concepts." *Canadian Journal of Psychiatry, 30,* 119–129.

Minde, K., Shosenberg, N., Marton, J., & Ridley, J. (1980). "Self Help Groups in a Premature Nursery: A Controlled Evaluation." *Journal of Pediatrics, 96,* 933–939.

Moyal, B. R. (1977). "Locus of Control, Self-esteem, Stimulus Appraisal and Depressive Symptoms in Children." *Journal of Consulting and Clinical Psychology, 45,* 951–952.

Newman, C. J. (1976). "Children of Disaster: Clinical Observation at Buffalo Creek." *American Journal of Psychiatry, 133,* 306–312.

Nurcombe, B., Howell, D., Rauh, V., Teti, D., Ruoff, D., & Brennan, J. (1984). "An Intervention Program for Mothers of Low Birthweight Infants, Preliminary Results." *Journal of the American Academy of Child Psychiatry, 23,* 319–325.

Peretz, D. (1970). "Reaction to Loss." In G. Schoenberg, A. Carr, D. Peretz, & A. Kutscher (Eds.), *Loss and Grief.* New York: Columbia University Press.

Petti, T. (1983)."Behavioral Approaches in the Treatment of Depressed Children." In D. Cantwell & E. Carlson (Eds.), *Affective Disorders in Childhood and Adolescence—An Update.* New York: Spectrum.

Pettle, M. S., Michael, & Lansdown, R. (1986). "Adjustment to the Death of a Sibling." *Archives of Diseases in Childhood, 61,* 278–283.

Piaget, J. (1951). *The Child's Conception of the World.* New York: Humanities Press.

Proskauer, S. (1971). "Focused Time-Limited Psychotherapy With Children." *Journal of the American Academy of Child Psychiatry, 10,* 619–639.

Pynoos, R. S., & Eth, S. (1986). "Witness to Violence: The Child Interview." *Journal of the American Academy of Child Psychiatry, 25,* 306–319.

Rotter, J. B. (1966). "Generalized Expectancies for Internal Versus External Control of Reinforcement." *Psychological Monographs, 80,* 1–28.

Rutter, M. (1966). *Children of Sick Parents: An Environmental and Psychiatric Study.* (Maudsley Monograph No. 16). London: Oxford University Press.

Rutter, M. (1986). "The Developmental Psychopathology of Depression." In M. Rutter, C. Izard, & P. Reed (Eds.), *Depression in Young People: Developmental and Clinical Perspectives.* New York: Guilford Press.

Seligman, M. E., & Peterson, C. (1986). "A Learned Helplessness Perspective on Childhood Depression: Theory and Research." In M. Rutter, C. Izard, & P. Reed (Eds.), *Depression in Young People: Developmental and Clinical Perspectives.* New York: Guilford Press.

Shaffer, D. (1984). "Notes on Psychotherapy Research Among Children and Adolescents." *Journal of the American Academy of Child Psychiatry, 23,* 552–561.

Simeonsson, R., & McHale, S. (1981). "Review: Research on Handicapped Children: Sibling Relationships." *Child: Care, Health, and Development, 7,* 153–171.

Spinetta, J., Swarner, J., & Sheposh, J. (1981). "Effective Parental Coping Following the Death of a Child From Cancer." *Journal of Pediatric Psychology, 6,* 251–263.

Steinman, S. B., Zemmelman, S. E., & Knoblauch, T. M. (1985). "A Study of Parents Who Sought Joint Custody Following Divorce: Who Reaches Agreement and Sustains Joint Custody and Who Returns to Court." *Journal of the American Academy of Child Psychiatry, 24,* 554–562.

Terr, L. (1979). "Children of Chowchilla." *The Psychoanalytic Study of the Child, 34,* 552–623.

Urbain, E. S., & Kendall, D. C. (1980). "Review of Social-Cognitive Problem-Solving Interventions With Children." *Psychological Bulletin, 88,* 109–143.

Van Eerdewegh, M. M., Bieri, M. D., Parilla, R. H., & Clayton, P. (1982). "The Bereaved Child." *British Journal of Psychiatry, 139,* 213–220.

Wallerstein, J. (1985). "Children of Divorce: Preliminary Report of a Ten-Year Follow-up of Older Children and Adolescents." *Journal of the American Academy of Child Psychiatry, 24,* 545–553.

Wallerstein, J. (1985). "Children of Divorce: Recent Research." *Journal of the American Academy of Child Psychiatry, 24,* 515–517.

Weissman, M. (1979). "Depressed Parents and Their Children: Implications for Prevention." In I. Berlin & I. Stone (Eds.), *Basic Handbook of Child Psychology* (Vol. 4). New York: Basic Books.

Wiener, J. (1970). "Reactions of the Family to the Fatal Illness of the Child." In B. Schoenberg (Ed.), *Loss and Grief.* New York: Columbia University Press.

Chapter 3

Counseling with Adolescent Suicidal Clients and Their Families

Robin Lewis, Ph.D.,
Betty A. Walker, Ph.D.,
and Marilyn Mehr, Ph.D.

K aren sat cross-legged on the edge of her bed. Surrounding her on top of the quilt her grandmother had given her were an assortment of record jackets, ticket stubs to the last concert of the group Devil May Care, two marijuana cigarettes twisted tightly at opposite ends, and her last report card.

Over the insistent beat of "Soul-Mates," her mother knocked on her door. "Karen, can you hear me, honey? Daddy and I are going to the Petersons' for a barbecue. Be back around ten-thirty."

Karen picked up one of the cigarettes and lit it with the lighter her boyfriend, Steven, had given her last week. "Sure, Mom, have fun."

"We will, dear, and don't worry about Steven. He'll call."

"Sure, Mom."

There would be enough time, Karen thought. Most likely ten-thirty meant one-thirty, since her parents would tend to lose track of time after the first few rounds of drinks. No one would call to interrupt her. She was certain of that.

The smoke from the cigarette filled her lungs as she sucked in her breath. She held the cigarette lighter next to her cheek, wishing Steven were here with her. Why, of all people, did he leave me for my best friend? she thought, and she sunk her head into the patchwork quilt and began to cry.

As she reached for a tissue she picked up a corner of the crumpled report card. Opening it carefully, she hoped that the grades had somehow transformed themselves. Driver's ed, C; history, D; physical ed, D; and three F's—algebra, art, and English lit. She had loved English classes once and had wanted to be a writer. But she just hadn't been able to keep up.

Her parents would be furious. Everyone would know, since she would be unable to graduate. But there was a way. She got up, went to the medicine chest in her parents' bathroom, and found the small bottle with the pills her mother used for sleeping. She counted out 12 of them, poured herself some water from the tap, and swallowed each one separately.

Karen walked slowly back to her room, sat down at her desk, and wrote a short note. "Dear Mom and Dad, I am sorry. I let you down. Tell Grandma good-bye. And Steve. Love, Karen."

She lay across the stack of record jackets, curlers, and cigarette wrappers, closed her eyes, and waited.

Introduction

The importance of crisis intervention in response to adolescent suicide attempts cannot be overemphasized. Crisis intervention offers what has been recognized as the greatest potential for change within a short period of time (Pittman, De Young, Flomenhaft, Kaplan, & Lansley, 1966). If it is to be effective, crisis intervention must include the whole family.

Family therapy offers an opportunity for growth in the health of the entire family unit. The guidance, support, and knowledgeable intervention of a counselor, along with the active involvement of the family, can convert a potentially lethal action into an opportunity for positive change for all participants (Walker & Mehr, 1983). Treatment of the entire family recognizes the suicidal actions of the adolescent as a product of interpersonal, developmental, and societal issues, and most importantly as a function of family distress.

The multidimensional nature of adolescent suicide must be incorporated into effective crisis resolution. A family intervention approach seeks to draw on the mutual need and recognition for the family members to cooperate and support each other. This approach addresses the immediate crisis and builds a foundation for continued improved familial communication, growth, and stability.

Review of the Literature

There can be no doubt that adolescent suicide rates have skyrocketed. While estimates vary, research suggests that suicide rates have risen as much as 237 percent between 1960 and 1980 (Maris, 1985). Current estimates suggest that as many as 400,000 teenagers attempt suicide annually (Brody, 1986) and approximately 5,200 of these attempts are fatal (Cantor, 1987). The greatest increases have occurred among middle to late adolescents from 15 to 24 years old (Rosenkrantz, 1978).

As a leading cause of death, suicides are second only to accidents (Maris, 1985). The figures may be higher given research questioning "accidental" deaths which may, in fact, represent teen suicides.

In the past 25 years, in addition to soaring teenage suicide rates, we have also witnessed a substantial breakdown of the nuclear family and a dramatic surge in alcohol and drug abuse. Today's societal pressures, including the threat of nuclear holocaust, excessive competition, and emphasis on achievement and material success, have been identified as major stressors for both today's youth and adults (Valente, 1984). Add to these factors the developmental pressures of adolescence, when internal stress may be at its peak (Peck, 1968), and we see a portrait of struggling youth.

Adolescent suicide cuts across many personality profiles, family compositions, and demographic variables. Research suggests a variety of intentions in youth suicide, including escape, revenge, altruism, psychosis, imitation, and risk-taking (Maris, 1985). Although females outnumber males in terms of attempts by nearly three to one or more, males more frequently complete suicide. Additionally, a new profile of the "good" boy and girl attemptor from an upwardly mobile family with minimal family disturbance is emerging (Peck, 1984).

While the suicidal presentation may vary in the adolescent, family-related factors have consistently emerged as pertinent. Seiden (1969) characterized the home life of suicidal youths as chaotic. In a psychological autopsy study by Schafii, Carrigan, Whittinghill, and Derrick (1985) 55 percent of the sample of 20 completed adolescent suicides evidenced parental absence or abuse and 60 percent reflected parental emotional problems. Other work has identified highly significant family issues related to a lack of communication with parents (Corder, Page, & Corder, 1974); feeling misunderstood by parents, which was reported by 90 percent of one research sample (Mehr, Zeltzer, & Robinson, 1981); lack of stability of family structure and support (Schafii, et al., 1985); and the assessment by the suicidal youth of conflict with the family (Peck, 1968). The importance of family factors may in fact be underestimated. In a study by Mehr et al. (1981), heightened self-blame emerged as a significant characteristic of the adolescent suicidal population. Such internalization reduces the possibility of the adolescent identifying external contributing factors such as the family.

A family therapy approach to crisis intervention with the suicidal adolescent addresses the family context as one of the main features in teenage suicidal behavior (Kerfoot, 1980). Yet adolescent suicide may be seen as a family crisis which can provide an opportunity for maximizing position changes and efforts required in establishing healthy relationships among family members (Minuchin & Barcai, 1972).

Practice Frameworks

Crisis intervention aims at restoring the adolescent to the level of his or her functioning before the crisis (Aguilera & Messick, 1984). It is essential that crisis intervention make the entire family aware of the family dynamics which contributed to the adolescent's belief that suicide would accomplish something such as finally being heard, escaping, or taking revenge. Finding new ways of acknowledging and meeting the needs of the family members is essential. The suicide attempt forces the family to pay attention *now* to the adolescent and his or her needs as well as those of the entire family.

There is considerable clinical evidence (Doyle & Dorlac, 1978) that the family unit is most responsive to change during the crisis period. Restructuring previously maladaptive coping patterns is now possible. At this time, defenses are down and core issues are revealed. The desire to change and heal is at its peak. The therapist can attend to both the dangerous and opportune aspects of crisis in the individual and family by setting clear limits and encouraging communication.

Crisis intervention models emphasize brief, time-limited, focused treatment which is action oriented. It is not enough to merely make the family aware; active intervention must offer the opportunity to explore new resources for working through family struggles. Thus, the therapist must be able to provide strength, direction, support, reassurance, and hope.

MOTHER   I don't know what to do. I thought we were good parents. We sent her to camp, gave her music lessons. She was a great tennis player. . . .

CLINICIAN   When was that?

FATHER   It must have been, well, about the seventh grade.

CLINICIAN   And then what happened?

MOTHER   She just changed. Got more withdrawn, came home late from school. Some of her friends from grammar school would call and she wouldn't want to talk to them. She had new friends and always seemed to meet them.

CLINICIAN   Did you talk to her about these changes?

FATHER   Well, we tried, but she just got angry and went to her room and slammed the door.

CLINICIAN   I see. And you let her.

MOTHER   She had always been such a good child. We had never had to discipline her. Not like her sister, Susan, who was always in trouble.

CLINICIAN   So Karen was the 'good' child. Quite a responsibility, was it, Karen?

KAREN   (She begins to cry.) I just couldn't live up to it, to what they wanted.

CLINICIAN   And you thought you couldn't tell them when you started to get into trouble?

KAREN   Yeah. They wouldn't understand.

CLINICIAN   Well, Karen, they're here now, to understand, as you are. You can tell them now just what happened.

KAREN   But it will kill them!

CLINICIAN   You almost killed yourself and that would have 'killed' them. What you say and what they say will hurt, but it will be real. In time, it will allow you to heal and to move on. Let's begin.

The application of crisis intervention theory and technique has been most commonly applied to individuals rather than entire families. The application to whole families was not undertaken until the establishment of the Family Treatment Unit at Colorado Psychiatric Hospital in 1964 (Langsley & Kaplan, 1968). This program was based on the theory that hospitalizing someone allows him or her to be scapegoated by the family. All of the family dysfunction becomes projected onto the identified patient. With this belief in mind, the program directors formulated an outpatient treatment program in which the family received intensive therapy together.

Identification of Key Problems to the Individual and Agency

F requently, parents become so involved in coping with their own issues that the needs of the child are overlooked. This pattern may also emerge with agency clinicians who become absorbed with administrative demands. It is therefore important that an agency formulate a program that meets the needs of the adolescent suicide attemptor, the family, and the clinician. Key components of this program are as follows:

1. Education. The professionals and nonprofessionals in the program should be well trained and educated in issues of adolescent development, family dynamics, and crisis intervention following a suicide attempt. They must have adequate training in understanding adolescent developmental needs and family dynamics. Clinicians must be willing to explore their own adolescence—their own family issues, unfinished strivings, and conflicts, as well as their hopes and ideals. In addition, they must be able to appreciate and tolerate the intensity of the adolescent helplessness, rage, and despair which sought relief in a suicide attempt. If the caregivers deny or minimize the seriousness of the adolescent reaction, they will be unable to respond with the necessary involvement needed to resolve the crisis.

2. Availability. The agency or clinician must have the capacity for a quick and timely response. Unless response to an adolescent suicide is immediate, both the family and the adolescent will reconstruct defenses (necessarily, if help is not available), thus minimizing the crisis and returning to the former, potentially lethal method of coping. The agency must therefore have someone on call not only during working hours but around the clock. At the least there should be referral to a hotline or crisis intervention service capable of responding to emergencies outside normal working hours.

3. External resources. The agency or individual must have a network of intra-agency resources. Clearly, no single agency can provide 24-hour crisis intervention services adequate to respond to the needs of an adolescent population. It is therefore vital that agencies serving adolescents have a network of support services complementing their own resources. For example, the Samaritans in England maintain a well-trained network of paraprofessional volunteers who will befriend the suicide attemptor and lend companionship, comfort, and supervision to the attemptor throughout the crisis and afterward. The Samaritans are community volunteers who meet with the suicide attemptor and spend considerable time with him or her in the days, weeks, and months after the suicide attempt. In order to stabilize, the family and the adolescent often need the presence of an outside person—clinician, paraprofessional, or both—in the tenuous period after the suicide attempt. An agency must also have access to hospitalization; medical personnel for medication evaluation; and resource lists of support groups, community agencies, and social services which can provide economic, psychological, social, religious, or educational support in whatever ways are needed by the adolescent and family.

4. **Internal resources/self-care.** The effect of the crisis-helping process on the caregiver and the agency is often overlooked. Crisis intervention work makes uneven demands on the agency. Agency workers often experience a cycle characterized by a very energetic and active crisis response episode followed by periods of relative calm. Agencies can attend to breaking this cycle by arranging work projects for employees to avoid a "postsuicidal depression" and maintain an even flow of work and activities. Specifically, attention must be given to the personal responses and concerns of the caregivers (Hatton & Valente, 1984). Hatton and Valente have identified several areas of concern for the health professional which may require attention, including feelings of professional inadequacy, fear of responsibility for decisions, suicidal feelings in the caregiver, resentment of the client, listening difficulties, sociocultural stereotyping, and struggles with building rapport. The clinician practicing crisis work alone or as a part of an agency must have the opportunity to address such concerns. Agencies must place a premium on the well-being of their workers and evidence this care and attention in the form of group discussions of concerns, validation of the inherent stress of crisis work, and actions to build intra-agency support and care.

Target Systems

I n responding to the needs of a teenager and his or her family, the counselor must consider the overlapping relationships of the adolescent to the family, peers, the school, and the community.

Prevention is the most effective deterrent to adolescent suicide and must take place on three levels: primary, secondary and tertiary. Before a suicide occurs, these levels of intervention can be designed, organized, and implemented to prepare for a possible suicide crisis.

Primary Prevention

Primary prevention programs focus on education as a deterrent to a suicidal crisis and the need for crisis intervention. Peer counseling and other prevention programs have been developed across the country in response to rising concerns of adolescent suicide risk (Honig, 1986; Morris, 1982). California public schools report 203 schools (approximately 25 percent) have established peer counseling programs which in 1985–86 utilized 4,615 student peer counselors. At the present time, 93 percent of the schools provide training, including 68 percent which have a written course of study. To date, more than 9,000 students have completed peer counselor training, including more than 50 areas of skill and knowledge. Since the main concern of this chapter is the adolescent and the family, the target systems for education must be those which impact both. Teaching about the prevention and identification of possible suicide attemptors may occur in the schools, churches, or recreational and social organizations within the community. Before a curriculum is developed, a consensus should develop, through meetings with community and family representatives, that there is a need for education.

The curriculum itself must include not only information about suicide, but must explore the components of a physically and emotionally satisfying lifestyle. There should be time allotted to the discussion of self-esteem and value, developmental issues of separation and individuation, and the function of the family in supporting and protecting the adolescent's quest for identity. Further, the curriculum should examine the role of the peer group and the adolescent's need to balance family and peer influences in maintaining a steady sense of identity. Finally, the uses and abuses of sex and drugs must be evaluated by parents and adolescents in an open forum in which everyone can be heard.

Secondary Prevention

Secondary prevention involves the identification of the at-risk adolescents and his or her family. The description of the at-risk family has been provided by numerous studies which show that families with a single parent, a parent out of work, a major loss or trauma, and few connections to school or community resources are at highest risk for all major social and emotional problems. The difficulty for health care workers is not in the description, but the identification of these families, since many have dropped out of the purview of agencies within the community. It requires a concerted effort on the part of community workers to find these families and bring them back into the system.

The at-risk adolescent is often one who may be difficult to approach. He or she may have withdrawn from friends, school, and family and may have retreated behind a wall of sadness and depression. This is not the adolescent who usually receives attention. However, school and community workers must be alerted to the "quiet" teenager and must be encouraged to reach beyond the defenses of withdrawal and disinterest to the lonely and sometimes desperate youth within.

Tertiary Prevention

Tertiary prevention requires the availability of a variety of sources to provide peer group support. The community may be willing to organize and train the volunteer crisis network composed of teen counselors, similar to the Samaritans, a voluntary self-help organization in England. Self-help groups, whether directly focused on suicide or not, will allow the adolescent an opportunity to express and work out troublesome feelings before they become critical. Some of these groups such as Alcoholics Anonymous, Al Anon, Narcotics Anonymous, Alateen, and Mental Health Anonymous can be found in most communities and provide a valuable resource to teenagers and families.

The roles and skills of the clinician providing crisis treatment and intervention to the suicidal adolescent and his or her family are similar to those of the clinician who provides good psychotherapy to any individual or family. Crisis intervention does, however, require a more active, involved, supportive position on the part of the clinician. The imminent needs and nature of crisis require a period of initial dependence on the part of the adolescent in terms of support and direction. This phase then moves into reestablishing coping skills with the family and adolescent. Important characteristics of the clinician include the ability to do the following:

1. Experience and express care and sensitivity to the client(s).
2. Elicit trust and rapport.
3. Identify, clarify, and mirror the family and individual issues presented.
4. Teach good parenting and interpersonal relations.
5. Move issues and experiences away from the realm of blame, evaluation, and anger and into the realm of understanding.
6. Establish good communication and listening skills within the family structure.
7. Provide hope, help, and the confidence to act and participate constructively in developing a caring, responsive family unit.
8. Promote the health and stability of the family unit.
9. Possess flexibility to deal with the vast range of moods and issues presented in even the normal adolescent process.
10. Be centered and stable enough to maintain perspective as to whether the adolescent and family dynamics are within the range of normal or may require further intervention.
11. Appreciate changes usually found within the adolescent's family, in which the parents are often in middle age and may be going through their own life changes and crises initiated by the adolescence process; many times both mother and father may be going through a "second adolescence" as they themselves review unopened doors, unmet needs, and unexplored potentials of their own youth. In their grieving process they may attempt to live through their own adolescence.
12. Help family members identify and separate their own problems from the adolescent's and take responsibility for their own actions.

13. Maintain an appropriate and good sense of humor. Adolescents, by their developmental nature, dramatize their problems onto a large screen. Many adolescents have also been well trained by the media, and particularly television, to distort the consequences of destructive and exaggerated behaviors. A sense of humor affords the adolescent, family, and clinician a perspective on others' behaviors which helps in riding out the difficult and seemingly tragic issues which await them.

14. Confront reality. Many adolescents and families are involved in addictions and abuses of various sorts. The clinician must have enough confidence and clarity to pursue his or her professional judgment to confront the family regarding these issues and to maintain clear limits.

Clinical Issues

The clinician offering crisis intervention to the suicidal adolescent and his or her family must be aware of the influence of relationships affecting the youth and contributing to a situation where suicide becomes a viable alternative. There are, of course, interactions and some overlap among these factors.

The Adolescent Developmentally

The developmental task of adolescence is one of identity formation requiring emotional and physical separation from the family. This is difficult at best and has been identified as one of the most intrapsychically stressful (Peck, 1968) stages of human development. Successful transition to adulthood depends on resolution of previous developmental tasks. If the adolescent's growth has been hindered through early loss, illness, or family disturbance, the stress of working through the identity issues will increase in intensity, placing the youth at considerable risk for depression and severe acting-out. One primary aspect of adolescent identity formation is *egocentrism,* a step in the necessary process of forming a distinct identity. During this process the adolescent retreats back into the self. As the adolescent becomes more self-absorbed there is considerable lack of perspective and a heightened sense of vulnerability. Events take on monumental importance while the adolescent swings from feelings of grandiosity to insignificance. Limited judgment leaves the adolescent open to impulsive acts which may prove destructive. The adolescent is attempting to find a "fit" for himself or herself in the world. The clinician must consider the adolescent's concept of death, which in suicide cases is characterized by a sense of lack of finality. Adolescent suicide attemptors have frequently said they believed they would be able to see the reactions and responses of others to their suicides. The suicide act is often seen as a heroic or grand sacrifice or gesture and often is an attempt to have an impact on others.

The Adolescent as Part of a Family System

Children often play a variety of roles and serve a variety of functions within the family. They may feel so minimized within the assigned role that they feel trapped and immobilized and can escape or fight back only through suicide. Minuchin (1974) described the family as a dynamic structure with covert relationship rules. He believed that if boundaries were too rigid the family members would disengage and isolate from each other, whereas if the boundaries were too diffused the family would appear enmeshed. An inflexible family structure is unable to respond and adapt to maturational and situational changes. Thus we may begin to see and understand the profile of both the "good" and the "bad" adolescent's suicide attempt.

In rigid families children often acquire labels in the process of growing up. Joey is lazy, Billy is handsome, Sharon is bright, Mary tells lies. Some children make a determined effort to play the "good" child with neat rooms, good homework, and pleasant manner. In essence, they create as little "trouble" as possible. At times this need to not get in the way can lead to leaving the family via suicide. Other adolescents are more defiant and may be scapegoated as the "bad" child—incorrigible, destructive, and unmanageable.

In healthy families there is a balance between the "bad" and the "good" child within each individual. In families which produce dysfunctional behavior, one or both adults and all of the children may be assigned roles inappropriate to their age, sex, and abilities. They may be treated as if they have only one characteristic—being stupid, lazy, selfish, dishonest, smart—instead of a wide range of human feelings and attitudes. In these families parents who are uncomfortable in accepting the dependence of their child may reverse roles with that child. The child may become overburdened with demands that he or she take care of underdeveloped parents and siblings and thus may never be given the chance to be a child in his or her own right. Boszormenyi-Nagy and Spark (1973) refer to this process as the "parentification of the child." This child, usually the one who is quiet, conforming, and "good," is frequently in a family in which depression, despair, and rage simmer unexpressed below the surface. This lack of expressivity may lead the child to hold on to feelings which escalate into an extreme cry for help, possibly in the form of a suicide attempt. Parents who have not themselves developed into responsible adults may abdicate their leadership responsibilities to the child. In doing so they justify their abandonment of the parental role, and the child, under the guise of permissiveness. These parents allow the adolescent to assume adult responsibilities before he or she can manage this lack of structure.

Characteristics of the family composition must also be considered. Parental loss at an early age through either death or divorce has been consistently identified as a salient factor in adolescent suicide (Garfinkel, Froese, & Hood, 1982; Husain & Vandiver, 1984). If these losses are not healed, the adolescent will be particularly vulnerable to the stress of additional losses. An example of this phenomenon is the devastating effect of a broken romance on an adolescent with previous unresolved losses. The cumulative grief experienced by the youth may precipitate suicide attempts as a means of escaping the overwhelming feelings.

Finally, the stress of the single-parent role may leave a parent, who often shoulders this struggle alone, with few emotional resources to respond to familial demands, and particularly those of the rebellious and difficult adolescent. The single parent may simply hit a "high water mark" and give up trying to cope with the demanding teenager.

The Adolescent as a Member of Society

Many dimensions of today's society serve to exacerbate the adolescent's struggle for individual identity. Our technological world, with its emphasis on competition, functionalism, and materialism, contributes to the objectification and reduction of all human beings to their functions and roles in society. This "technomaniacal" age has resulted in a lost sense of uniquely human "being" (May, 1983), a loss which is particularly salient to the adolescent's developmental task of identity formation. Associated with this technological age is the shadow of nuclear destruction, awareness of which brings all human beings, particularly the young with their unestablished psychological defenses, face-to-face with the precariousness of human life.

Perhaps as an escape from the pressures of society, the adolescent may turn to chemicals. Drug and alcohol abuse has reached epidemic proportions. This abuse can be tied to a perceived need to escape the world as it is—a strong and effective means of escape seen as necessary and desirable, at times to the point of suicide. Ishii (1981) interprets one dimension of the adolescent suicide attempt as "a silent indictment of society."

Assessment and Intervention

Given the many factors which may trigger an adolescent suicide, it is imperative that careful but swift assessment and intervention occur. The aim of such action is to reduce the immediate danger of a possible suicide by evaluating the potential for an additional suicide attempt.

Reducing the Immediate Danger

Certain criteria prove effective in assessing the suicide peril. These include:

1. The lethality of the current attempt. How serious was the intent? Did the individual take several aspirin or ten or more times the recommended dose of a drug?
2. Evidence of a history of multiple attempts. At what intervals and following what life events have the attempts occurred?

3. Evidence of drug or alcohol abuse. The onset and extent of such use is significant and any commitment to treatment must be noted.
4. Current stress levels and factors. What is happening in the adolescent's life that places him or her close to the edge? How realistic or exaggerated are these factors?
5. Emotional affect. Are there feelings of hopelessness and helplessness present? Are there strong signs of depression, ambivalence, or hostility apparent?
6. A suicidal plan. Does the adolescent share a strategy, and how defined is it?
7. Available resources. Who can give assistance, what assistance is available, and where can an adolescent go to find it? Does this include family members, friends, church, school, or agencies beyond the immediate professional helper? Is referral for hospitalization indicated, with necessary scrutinized medication? Assessment of immediate danger must include an evaluation of specific symptoms that lend evidence to a possible suicide attempt. These signs form a behavioral checklist to alert significant persons to an impending suicide crisis.

Behavioral Checklist for the Practitioner and Family

Part of the family intervention may involve the combined family efforts to identify and remain aware of the signs and signals which the adolescent attemptor displayed prior to the suicide attempt.

_____ Changes or shift in social behavior

_____ Emotional swings or shifts

_____ Changes in patterns of eating or sleeping

_____ Changes in academic standing and schoolwork

_____ Change in appearance, hygiene

_____ Giving away personal possessions

SPECIFIC BEHAVIORAL CHANGES NEEDED TO RESOLVE THE CRISIS

1. The entire family is expected to attend all counseling sessions they have agreed to attend.
2. All members of the family are expected to sit down to at least one meal together to discuss the day's coming events or what has transpired during that day. Priority is given to a specific dinner hour. Next in priority would be breakfast, and finally lunchtime. Part of the hour is devoted to a specific agenda, the rest in learning to talk together.
3. Parents are expected to set aside a daily time when they alone meet to discuss the day's events and progress in dealing with the entire family and the crisis that has occurred. Shifts in behavior of all family members are to be noted and brought to therapy sessions.

4. A chart is to be kept by all family members of the resentments and satisfactions each has experienced during the day relating specifically to family members and their involvement and interaction with one another. What contributed to their feelings within a particular situation, how these were communicated, and whether any resolution was reached is also to be noted.

5. The opening section of the counseling sessions is addressed by the clinician with a request for each member to go over her or his list. Family members are asked to respond to each other with the goal of opening and reinforcing communication of both positive and negative feelings and situations.

6. The clinician encourages seeking and arriving at constructive ways of handling the feelings and behaviors of each family member's concerns. Attention is given to ways such communication and behavioral shifts can have positive effects on all members—not just one particular person.

7. Of utmost importance will be the discussion of each member's role in the family and the expectations all have of one another working and living within the family structure. The risks and vulnerability that is concomitant with open communication must be addressed to avoid any member feeling "less than" or "not good enough" if anxious about sharing.

8. Finally, the meaning and place of choice, obligation, and consequences of each member's actions within the family framework must be delineated and organized around a defined plan to be outlined, followed, and reviewed at both the family meetings and those with the clinician. A follow-up plan of action must be available and made known as a backup should a break in communication or commitment occur. A family member is designated in the role of "guardian of progress" and given the authority to call the family together, suggest involving the clinician, and sound the alarm for immediate action. This role can rotate among all members and should include a weekly report at the family meeting.

These behavioral shifts are designed to bring about increased communication and honest attempts to find a high quality of commitment to standards and functioning within the family structure. They are concrete strategies for overcoming deficits in functioning and for substituting challenging paths not only to stay alive but to live more fully.

Stages in Family Intervention

The adolescent suicide attempt precipitates a crisis in the entire family. As soon as the danger of the suicide attempt is reduced, the family and the adolescent must be brought together by the clinician to express their feelings and begin to change. Here is an example of an interaction between therapist and parent:

> CLINICIAN Mrs. B., I know this has been a painful and confusing time for you.
> MRS. B. Yes, it has. I don't know why, we gave her everything she wanted.

> CLINICIAN Parents always wonder if they might have given more. In fact, there is something you can do now. Do you think you can get your entire family together for a meeting today at four o'clock with me and your daughter?
>
> MRS. B. Well, I don't know; my husband is so busy. He may not be able to get off from work.
>
> CLINICIAN If not, I'll be glad to talk to him or his employer. You see, this meeting is critical. Your daughter's suicide attempt is a family problem.
>
> MRS. B. Yes, I see. Well, I'll try.

In the interaction the clinician has offered understanding for the mother's feelings but has insisted that the family be brought together. In fact, the clinician has provided support by offering to telephone the husband or employer. It is only through the clinician's conviction that the family is intricately connected to the adolescent's behavior that change can occur.

When the family arrives the following goals must be kept in mind.

Hope and Direction Building.   During the early sessions the clinician must begin to develop trust and rapport with the family. Showing concern for the teenager and the family in a nonjudgmental manner will create an atmosphere in which others can share feelings without blame or fear of blame.

Sharing feelings with one another should be encouraged. For inhibited families the clinician may have to work harder to point out behavioral manifestations of feelings such as facial expressions, tone of voice, posture, and gestures, so that the family members can begin to identify their own feelings and express them to each other. For example:

> MR. B. I don't think there's anything we need to do. I think Karen will be just fine now!
>
> CLINICIAN When you say that, Mr. B., your voice seems a little shaky. What kind of feelings are you having?
>
> MR. B. I *have* to believe she will be just fine now. Otherwise, I don't know what I can do.
>
> CLINICIAN So you're feeling kind of helpless about what to do to help Karen. Karen, do you have some feelings about how your father might be helpful to you?
>
> KAREN Nothing! There is nothing he can do.
>
> CLINICIAN You sound angry and feel closed off with your arms crossed. Would you share what those feelings are about with us?

In order for hope to emerge, the family must reach into their cumulative pool of memories, connections, and caring for one another and allow the grief, anger, sadness, and love to be shown.

In the early sessions the family members will often express guilt over the adolescent's suicide attempt. The clinician can help them translate these feelings into a shared sense of responsibility. Rather than blaming, parents and siblings can begin to see how each may influence the others both positively and negatively.

> MRS. B. I know this is *all* my fault. I should have known that Karen was feeling this bad.
>
> CLINICIAN It sounds like you're taking on a lot of responsibility here.
>
> KAREN Yeah, Mom. I didn't tell you because I didn't want to upset or hurt you. And I just didn't think Dad would want to hear.
>
> CLINICIAN Is that how it feels to you, Mr. B.? That you don't want to hear?
>
> MR. B. No. I want to hear. It's just that I sometimes don't know the right thing to say to fix it. So I guess I don't encourage Karen to tell me.
>
> CLINICIAN Karen, do you feel that your Dad has to fix it for you?
>
> KAREN Well, not really. . . . What I really feel like I need is someone to just listen and care.

By the end of the first session a contract can be made with the family. The fact that the crisis counseling usually lasts from 8 to 12 weeks can be openly discussed, making the need for a commitment to this time period evident.

Assessment and Awareness of Current Family Dynamics.   Over the course of the meetings the clinician will have an opportunity to observe the following areas of family dynamics:

Communication and patterns including listening skills, blaming, and projection processes

Rigidity/flexibility of the family system

Individual roles and expectations

Identification of strengths, including previous positive coping strategies, positive feelings, and positive relationships

Identification of areas needing attention

Discussion of each family member's respective needs and developmental struggles

The Implementation and Support of New Behaviors and Roles.   After clarification and shared understanding of current family function, the family must identify and try out new, improved ways of interacting. The clinician is in the position of guiding and supporting the family's new behaviors and acting as a model of open and healthy care and communication. The following list details the clinician's role:

1. Help the family members discuss and reach consensus as to roles appropriate to age, sex, and ability. When a younger child is defining himself or herself in

an adult manner with no resistance from the family, the clinician may take on the child's perspective by saying, "If I were ten years old with those responsibilities, I would feel burdened. Do you?" or by addressing the parents: "Linda seems to be taking on a tremendous amount of responsibility in the family which I believe is more appropriate to you as the parents."

2. Encourage family members to try on new, more appropriate roles and express their attendant feelings. For example, when parents begin to assume abandoned parental roles they often feel overwhelmed and/or angry at the responsibilities. The clinician must validate these feelings *with* the support that there is something important to be gained in terms of the family's health.

> MRS. B. This is so hard. So much is being asked of us.
>
> CLINICIAN Yes, it is very difficult being a parent today and a lot of the ways we have been trying to enhance your growth and communication as a family feel like hard work.
>
> MR. B. Well, I guess not working hard as a family has caused us a lot of problems and pain too.
>
> CLINICIAN Yes, and even strong families have struggles. This counseling and the hard work costs, but I believe the health and new support in your family enriches all of your lives.

3. Voice and encourage a family attitude and atmosphere of commitment and respect for each family member. This care must be evidenced in behaviors such as good listening and communication skills. The movement should be toward coexisting, sharing, understanding, and working through different feelings both within and between family members.

4. Teach the family the difference between leaving the troubled person alone ("He or she doesn't want my company"), and offering care and interest actively while still allowing the person some space.

> MRS. B. I try so hard to talk to Karen but she doesn't seem to want to discuss anything with me, so I just assume she wants to be left alone.
>
> CLINICIAN Karen, do you want to be left alone?
>
> KAREN No! *That* is why I did it—I feel *so* alone!
>
> CLINICIAN Somehow your mom got the idea you wanted to be alone, but it sounds like you'd like something else from her. Do you have an idea what that might be?
>
> KAREN I'm not sure. I don't want her to get all upset or get mad or blame herself—then I still feel lonely and that I made things worse to tell her. I feel like it's really hard on Mom when I'm not happy.
>
> CLINICIAN Is that how it feels to you, Mrs. B.? That it's too hard for you to know what is going on with Karen?

MRS. B. Well, it feels hard because I really love Karen, but I know sometimes things just feel bad, and maybe I can't make it better, but I'd like to try to keep you company and listen when you're hurting, Karen.

The Coordination of Resources.   At the conclusion of the time-limited family crisis intervention, the family should recognize its troublesome patterns of communication and make advances toward establishing new means of living together. An attitude of hope and commitment should be evident. At this point the clinician is in a position to coordinate and make available resources which will aid the family in its continued efforts and to offer the continued support which is so important in maintaining new behaviors and growth.

This coordination involves the following:

1. Evaluate the need for continued family therapy. This consideration may be discussed with the family. The need for ongoing therapy will depend on assessment of the level of family dysfunction. It may be fair to say that a suicide attempt, even considering low lethality, represents significant family misunderstanding.

Often, after the crisis, family members are reluctant to seek continued assistance. In these instances, when the clinician believes additional assistance is important, this concern must be explored with the family:

CLINICIAN I'd like to discuss with you counseling resources which will allow you to continue the family growth you have just begun here.

MR. B. More counseling? Karen seems fine and says she won't ever do it again. Seems like the problem is solved.

CLINICIAN Yes. You have all done a lot of work in resolving the current crisis. Karen's suicide attempt, however, is really a symptom, not *the* problem. I believe continued counseling will support the development of some significant long-term goals which you have all discussed here for your family.

MRS. B. Well, we all agree some changes are needed, but I thought we went through all that.

CLINICIAN Yes, as a family you have identified some major areas of struggle in communication and understanding. The further exploration and implementation of these changes is a great challenge. I believe that additional support and assistance in this process will be of great value to all of you.

The clinician should make referrals which consider the family's location, financial situation, and the resources of the agency or individual providing therapy.

2. Develop and coordinate structures and support. Establish a support system which will be available to the attemptor and family, including contacts with schools, social systems, and friends.

3. Determine availability of resource lists, ranging from immediate assistance to long-term and social support agencies and individuals. Without sufficient referral and follow-up, many families become lost in the relief following a crisis. Clinicians must be willing to trace families to ensure that they have connected to resources that will help them prevent a recurrence of the suicide attempt. Prevention must, at last, be our primary goal.

Summary

A dolescent suicide is a malady which requires deep, comprehensive care. Integral to this care is therapeutic crisis intervention with the entire family unit. The movement toward resolution of family distress creates a family environment in which the adolescent may begin a personal healing process concurrently and interrelatedly with a family healing process. Family crisis intervention must involve attention to reducing immediate danger; offering support, hope, and direction; and identifying and offering individual and family growth in developmental, emotional, cognitive, and situational areas.

References

Aguilera, D. C., & Messick, J. M. (1984). *Crisis Intervention: Theory and Methodology.* St. Louis, MO: C.V. Mosby Co.

Boszormenyi-Nagy, I., & Spark, G. M. (1973). *Invisible Loyalties: Reciprocity in Intergenerational Family Therapy.* New York: Harper & Row.

Brody, J. (March 12, 1986). "Child Suicides: Common Ingredients." *The New York Times,* 42–43.

Cantor, P. (March 17, 1987). "Teenage Suicide: The Unheard Cry for Help." *The Los Angeles Times,* Part V, Page 1.

Corder, B. F., Page, P. V., & Corder, R. F. (1974). "Parental History, Family Communication and Interaction Patterns in Adolescent Suicide." *Family Therapy, 1*(3), 285–290.

Doyle, A. M., & Dorlac, C. (1978). "Treating Chronic Crisis Bearers and Their Families." *Journal of Marriage and Family Counseling, 4* (3), 37–42.

Garfinkel, B. D., Froese, A., & Hood, J. (1982). "Suicide Attempts in Children and Adolescents." *American Journal of Psychiatry, 139* (10), 1257–1261.

Hatton, C. L., & Valente, S. (1984). *Suicide: Assessment and Intervention* (2nd ed.), Norwalk, CT: Appleton-Century Crofts.

Honig, W. (1986). *Peer Counseling in California Public Schools: Summary of a Survey of Status & Scope.* Sacramento, CA: California State Department of Education.

Husain, S. P., & Vandiver, T. (1984). *Suicide in Children and Adolescents.* New York: Spectrum.

Ishii, K. (1981). "Adolescent Self-Destructive Behavior and Crisis Intervention in Japan." *Suicide and Life-Threatening Behavior, 11*(1), 51–61.

Kerfoot, M. (1980). "The Family Context of Adolescent Suicidal Behavior." *Journal of Adolescence, 3,* 335–346.

Langsley, P. G., & Kaplan, D. M. (1968). *The Treatment of Families in Crisis.* New York: Grune & Stratton.

Maris, R. (1985). "The Adolescent and Suicide Problem." *Suicide and Life-Threatening Behavior, 15* (2), 1018–1023.

May, R. (1983). *The Discovery of Being.* New York: Norton.

Mehr, M., Zeltzer, L. K., & Robinson, R. (1981). "Continued Self Destructive Behaviors in Adolescence." *Journal of Adolescent Health Care, 1,* 269–274.

Miller, J. (1980). "Helping the Suicidal Client: Some Aspects of Assessment and Treatment." *Psychotherapy: Theory, Research and Practice, 17* (1).

Minuchin, S. (1974). *Families and Family Therapy.* Cambridge: Harvard University Press.

Minuchin, S., & Barcai, A. (1972). "Therapeutically Induced Family Crisis." In C. J. Sager & H. S. Kaplan (Eds.), *Progress in Group Family Therapy.* New York: Brunner/Mazel.

Morris, J. (November–December, 1982). "Prevention Work With Students." *School Guidance Worker, 38* (2), 10–53.

Peck, M. (1968). "Suicide Motivations in Adolescents." *Adolescence, 3* (9).

Peck, M. (1984). "Suicide in Late Adolescence and Young Adulthood." In S. P. Husain & T. Vandiver, *Suicide in Children and Adolescents.* New York: Spectrum.

Pittman, F. S., De Young, C., Flomenhaft, K., Kaplan, D., & Lansley, D. (1966). "Crisis Intervention Therapy." *Current Psychiatric Therapies, 6,* 187.

Rosenkrantz, A. (1978). "A Note on Adolescent Suicide: Incidence Dynamics and Some Suggestions for Treatment." *Adolescence, 13* (50), 209–214.

Schafii, M., Carrigan, S., Whittinghill, J. R., & Derrick, A. (1985). "Psychological Autopsy of Completed Suicide in Children and Adolescents." *American Journal of Psychiatry, 142,* 9.

Seiden, R. H. (December 1969). *Suicide Among Youth: A Supplement to the Bulletin of Suicidology.* Public Health Service Publication, No. 1971, pp. 1–62.

Tishler, C. L., McHenry, P. C., & Morgan, K. C. (1981). "Adolescents' Suicide Attempts: Some Significant Factors." *Suicide and Life-Threatening Behavior, 11* (2), 86–92.

Valente, S. "Suicide in Children." (1984). In C. L. Hatton & S. M. Valente (Eds.), *Suicide: Assessment and Intervention* (2nd ed.). Norwalk, CT: Appleton-Century-Crofts.

Walker, B. A., & Mehr, M. (1983). "Adolescents Suicide—A Family Crisis: A Model for Effective Intervention by Family Therapists." *Adolescence, 18,* 70.

Chapter 4

Crisis Intervention in a High School: Lessons From the Concord High School Experiences

NORMAN M. SHULMAN, ED.D.

Introduction

On December 3, 1985, and January 28, 1986, Concord (New Hampshire) High School was struck with two tragedies which had significant emotional impact on most of its students, teachers, and administrators. The first incident involved a 16-year-old former student named Louis Cartier, who had recently dropped out of school. On December 3 he suddenly appeared at the school carrying a loaded shotgun. After pointing the weapon at school personnel in a threatening manner and taking two students hostage, he was mortally wounded in an exchange of gunfire with the local police.

Not two months later, Christa McAuliffe (the first teacher chosen for a mission in space) was killed in the space shuttle along with six others. Mrs. McAuliffe had been teaching at Concord High until her NASA appointment. When she died, most of the student body and faculty at the school were watching on television.

For both of these incidents, the Emergency Services Program of the Central New Hampshire Community Mental Health Services, Inc., in Concord was called to the school to provide consultation to the administration in the handling of these crises on a schoolwide level. These were unfortunate, but invaluable, opportunities to closely examine the effects on a school of traumatic events for which there was no preparation. They also served as tests for the school's ability to respond to crisis situations. As with a person coping with an individual crisis, these tragedies were opportunities the school could use for adaptive learning for the future.

Traumatic events which have emotional consequences for the entire school population seem to be increasing in frequency across the nation. It is therefore imperative that schools develop plans appropriate for handling potential tragedies in their own communities. Concord High School was not unique. Crises like these can and do happen anywhere.

As Emergency Services Program coordinator, I was closely involved in developing the school's response plans for these two events. In this chapter I want to convey what was learned about one school's reaction to crises of this magnitude and to describe the two detailed plans implemented to cope with them. Furthermore, at the end of the chapter I will make concrete pre-, inter-, and postvention suggestions emanating from these experiences that can be used by schools as models of response. I hope the lessons learned at Concord High will help other schools minimize the potential negative impact of tragedies such as these.

A Theoretical Construct for Human Response to Trauma

J ohn Bowlby's *attachment theory* (Farberow & Gordon, 1981) is one theoretical construct which can be used to help understand a person's reaction to precipitous loss and change. Attachment theory addresses the propensity of human beings for forming strong, affectional bonds with each other. Attachment behavior is especially apt to be aroused in times of stress or fear. At such times it is natural for people to search out the care and comfort of significant others, or even a place that offers a secure base.

The young, including adolescents, are especially prone to periods of distress, and during such times they naturally try to reach an attachment figure or a safe location (Farberow & Gordon, 1981). However, when this cannot be achieved and instead they feel separation, they respond with anxiety, regression, and other changes of behavior. Additionally, a longer term, negative consequence could be the reactivation of an adolescent's fears and anxieties from earlier stages of development.

During and following a major crisis (the acute disequilibrium period, which may last for several weeks) a group instinctively turns to recognized leaders for direction and guidance (Kafrissen & Heffron, 1975). If immediate and appropriate attachment is not formed, the troubled individuals may regress and develop maladaptive problem-solving behaviors. Furthermore, for those adolescents who suffer a second trauma very soon after the first one, as was the case at Concord High, their emotional plight may require even more active and supportive crisis intervention (McGee & Heffron, 1976).

Attachment theory may help explain the phenomenon of social supports acting as buffers in times of crisis. These supports and the security they provide directly moderate the negative effects of the experience and facilitate subsequent coping and adaptation. As a result, social supports protect individuals from both physical and mental disorder following exposure to crisis situations (Solomon, 1986).

Solomon (1986) found that exposure to negative events perceived as uncontrollable and/or unpredictable has been linked to adverse mental and physical outcomes. Attachment to positive social support networks influences health by enhancing the victim's perception of control over the environment. In fact, the predictability and controllability of social support may be of greater importance to well-being than interpersonal contact per se.

In the section later in this chapter about the reactions of the Concord High School community in the wake of its collective trauma, it may help to consider the significance of attachment theory in understanding the relative impact of the institutional intervention strategies. By doing this, it may be possible to better discriminate among the tactics and their applicability to situations specifically relevant to the reader's experiences or interests.

Psychosocial Reactions to Trauma: Myths and Realities

Many people assume that disasters produce extreme psychological and emotional reactions (Tierney & Baisden, 1979). When victims of a major traumatic event share this assumption, it may in fact have a self-fulfilling effect on their perception of what prevails and thereby impede crisis resolution. While evidence exists that serious psychological implications do result from disasters (Cohen, 1985), the belief that they trigger severe emotional and pathological reactions is one of the major myths about human response to extreme collective stress (Tierney & Baisden, 1979).

The reality is that while victims seem to undergo considerable stress and strain and do experience a wide variety of symptoms, disasters create little severe and chronic mental illness. Tierney and Baisden (1979) noted that most research assessing the effects of stressful life events on psychological functioning suggests that the individual's psychological reactions or symptoms resulting from such events may be as transient as the stress which induces them. In other words, once the extreme situation alters, the symptoms of disturbance will disappear.

Kafrissen and Heffron (1975) believed that most emotional responses associated with a severe crisis are quite normal and do not represent mental illness in the usual sense. Kennedy (1981) supported this contention by stating that while individuals and groups do lose their balance, are unable to function effectively during a crisis, and exhibit shock symptoms (low stimulation and activity levels, under-demanding-ness, and docility), they do not collapse.

Adolescents present their own unique crisis responses. Because adolescents' development is incomplete, tragedies may have a greater impact on them than on adults. As a result, when a negative life event occurs, special interventions are necessary for these victims to understand and accept their experiences.

Therefore, even though collective victims of a crisis do not necessarily develop symptoms indicative of severe emotional problems, treatment may be indicated for the symptoms which do emerge, both immediately and over a longer period of time. Symptoms requiring intervention can be prevented from causing any serious psychological damage if timely and appropriate crisis management techniques are employed. Before turning to a brief survey of suggested and applied interventions during incidents of major impact on large groups of people, it will help to examine some of these symptoms.

During the course of a disaster, victims find themselves in a general atmosphere of chaos and disorganization (Hoff, 1984). Cohen and Ahearn (1980) observed the major initial emotions of sadness, fear, and anger, which may be manifested in many forms and with a wide range of intensity. Mitchell (1981) listed many other reactions, some of which are manifested in the long term: insomnia, nightmares, memory disturbances, withdrawal, phobias, apprehension, shame, resentment, increased smoking and drinking, impotence, isolation, deteriorating relationships, unresolved grief, hypochondriasis, hopelessness, helplessness, and a sense of meaningless in life.

Compounding the problems of intervening therapeutically with these symptoms is that many victims with already vulnerable defenses, but who are able to remain initially symptom free, decompensate when another major crisis occurs within a short time after the initial disorder (Cohen & Ahearn, 1980). This observation, as you will see, is especially relevant to the Concord High School experiences. While this impressive array of traits and complicating variables is imposing, the crisis intervenor has the knowledge and techniques at hand to mitigate any potentially serious debilitating long-range consequences if intervention is conducted immediately and skillfully.

Therapeutic Responses to Large-Scale Trauma

T he literature is replete with examples of successful applications of crisis intervention strategies employed after a major traumatic event. Crisis workers called in to situations like these typically rely on at least three predictable responses of the victims to maximize therapeutic effectiveness.

First, following the initial shock phase, people will talk to almost anyone to relieve the emotional pressure of experienced incidents and events (Cohen & Ahearn, 1980). Second, Hoff (1984) noted the existence of greater cohesion among community members as they interpret tragedies as an occurrence beyond their own or anyone's control and attempt to account for the event from a common viewpoint. Consistent with this notion of community cohesion is the building of spirit and morale through social support (Solomon, 1986). However, as a result, the victims may resent outside intervention (Kennedy, 1981). Third, cognitive confusion and disorganization are apparent as people's general abilities to function decrease dramatically. These needs to ventilate, to be with others, and to understand what did and will happen to them are the underpinnings of appropriate intervention after traumatic events.

A primary treatment objective with victims of acute trauma is to help them develop an internal sense of order and perspective so that they will be able to recognize their environments as they process painful and powerful emotions. A second objective is to help the victim reach out, acquire, and build upon resources, especially social ones, which will help them develop a sense of comfort, security, and self-esteem (Cohen & Ahearn, 1980). A third objective is to render the intervention as close as possible to the time and place the client is experiencing the problem (Slaby, Lieb, & Tancredi, 1981). People in crisis need immediate, active, aggressive intervention (McGee & Heffron, 1976). An overall objective of trauma management is to minimize both immediate and long-range mental health problems triggered by such events.

There is general consensus regarding the best ways to achieve the objectives of intervention following major stressful events. Many of the basic principles of crisis management under these circumstances closely resemble those used when performing crisis intervention with individuals (see Chapter 1).

Major trauma intervention responses can be summarized as follows:

1. Obtain, disseminate, and update information about the details of the event.
2. Encourage ventilation about the experience in a warm, accepting, supportive environment to a concerned and sympathetic listener (or group), either professional or nonprofessional.
3. Strengthen awareness of the normalness of the victims' reactions, stressing that they should view themselves as normal individuals disrupted by severe stress.
4. Help the victim confront and accept the reality of the crisis and identify realistic causal relationships between events and reactions.
5. Arrange a group discussion and exchange of ideas about the impact of the event.
6. Resume concrete activity to help reorder life in the new context (as exemplified by time, space, and scheduling) established by the event.
7. Post-traumatically, make victims aware that certain distressing reactions are due to be expected and that these as well as the initial symptoms are normal.
8. Use existing community resources rather than creating new ones.

Wall and Viers (1985) reported on the application of some of these principles in a school which suffered the suicide of a popular teacher. They found that the group process in a classroom setting, later applied at Concord High School, was an effective way of helping students cope with sudden loss and understand that the grieving process is a healthy response to emotional injury. A naturalistic understanding of the event was emphasized to bolster coping.

Wall and Viers further reported that a free flow of information, group cohesion building, and acceptance of negative feelings were employed in the context of the classroom group meetings. The message conveyed in the group was that feelings were okay to talk about. The group meetings were also an opportunity to identify at-risk individuals who had not already received individual attention.

An interesting reaction supporting an earlier contention of the importance of disseminating information as quickly and as honestly as possible was the students' anger over the three-day delay from the time of the teacher's death to the actual announcement (Wall & Viers, 1985). A vital lesson was learned that prompt and open announcement of a tragedy appears to add credibility to efforts by school officials to intervene.

Other lessons Wall and Viers (1985) learned from this school's experiences included

1. The need for outside group facilitators to prevent the inadvertent suppression of feelings, thereby increasing the likelihood of indirect expression
2. The potential for an overwhelming demand for services to cope with a wide range of emotional struggles
3. The need for candid consultation between the crisis specialist and school representatives for the purpose of familiarizing the former with the school and the latter with the crisis intervention approach used

Crabbs (1981) emphasized the importance of a school being able to recognize the atypical and maladaptive responses of children exhibiting intense emotional and behavioral reactions. He advises that while stressful events can lead to serious emotional crises, children whose needs are responded to quickly using the lessons learned by Wall and Viers experience less severe and usually temporary reactions. The same may be said of adolescents. If left unchecked, atypical responses may continue until appropriate attention is provided. Unfortunately, this may not occur until months or even years later.

While only a small minority of children will develop severe or incapacitating reactions, opportunities to confront and deal with unresolved or unexpressed emotions or concerns must be made available to them. Crabbs (1981) reminded us that priority should be given to those students identified as manifesting unusual symptoms.

Before moving on to an examination of the application of the aforementioned responses to tragedies in the aftermaths of the Concord High School experiences, two other variables in the formula for determining therapeutic effectiveness should be mentioned: the press and nonprofessional crisis intervenors.

A specialized feature of disasters is the descent of the media, whose members are under great pressure, not to help the victims, but to file a story by deadline (Kennedy, 1981). They can often, if unwittingly, cause further dislocation and emotional harm. At the same time, it is seen as important to gather accurate information and disseminate it swiftly. Therefore, achieving a balance between using the media to aid in crisis resolution while limiting its intrusiveness must be emphasized.

The potential usefulness of employing nonprofessionals during times of acute trauma, such as students helping students, should not be undervalued. A major reason for both the attractiveness and supportive efficacy of nonprofessional social network members is that they do not attempt to maintain objectivity and distance, but rather involve themselves personally with the individuals in need (Solomon, 1986). Their interaction is reciprocal in that this kind of support allows the giver and recipient to alternate roles and receive esteem. Although professional help is usually perceived to be superior to that provided by the informal caregiver, there may be times when informal support is the treatment of choice.

Two Case Vignettes

Louis Cartier

After Louis Cartier was fatally wounded by the local police, classes were reflexively dismissed with little or no information disseminated at the time. The school administration was tied up with the media, many teachers left with the students, and guidance personnel were scattered throughout the building dealing individually with a few of the remaining students.

The only response made available to the student body to help them cope was an independently acting guidance counselor who offered to talk to students after dismissal. However, only a few students responded to this offer, most choosing to leave the school hurriedly. Nothing was made available to the staff. Disorganization, confusion, and ignorance reigned.

Since a basic crisis intervention principle, applicable to both individuals and groups alike, states that panic can be partially alleviated with information, it became obvious that the school needed to have the day's events reconstructed as soon and as fully as possible. In order to do this properly, staff first would have to be emotionally stabilized and informed before they could be expected to implement a crisis response plan for the students.

Assertive control of the situation had to be taken. As in any disaster aftermath, it was important that a person with a specific plan take charge and provide the structure necessary to ensure speedy crisis resolution. The school had no plan except to call me after the students had been dismissed. After arriving at the school, I requested that the principal inform school personnel, before any more could leave, that there would be a mandatory meeting for all personnel, including administrators, teachers, guidance counselors, and custodial staff.

Over 100 people with varying reactions and involvement in the crisis attended this meeting. It became readily apparent that prior to formulating a schedule of activities for the students covering the next few days, school personnel responsible for implementing such a plan would have to be given the opportunity to resolve their own feelings.

To initiate this process, school personnel with the most knowledge of the day's events related what they knew in detail and in chronological order. While doing this, the people most involved with the victim prior to and during the police intervention ventilated their feelings about what had happened. Since several others either had the loaded shotgun pointed directly at them or had offered to trade places with the student hostages during the brief negotiations, they were given the opportunity to talk firsthand about their experiences.

This ventilation stimulated several others to ask specific questions about the event, relate their own knowledge of the victim and the recent history leading up to his dropping out, and express their feelings as well. Having most of the staff together in one room was advantageous in that emotional support was readily available when needed. Further professional intervention was also offered.

Once the sequence of events became clear and feelings had been expressed, a structured plan was conceived so that students would be able to benefit from a similar opportunity to begin healing. It is important to note that my role as consultant, albeit essential in structuring the initial planning meetings, was not as the dominating expert. Once the meeting began, I encouraged the participants to offer specific suggestions regarding how to structure the students' time for the near future.

This tactic made sense, since the school personnel obviously knew far more about the students' needs and the inner workings of the school than I did. It would have been inappropriate for me to have imposed a plan of my own, even if I had one. My job as consultant was to organize the meeting and stimulate a discussion which would evolve into suggestions for a useful schedule of activities for the students.

Following is the outline of the overall schedule for crisis resolution on a schoolwide level in the wake of the Louis Cartier tragedy.

SPECIFIC INSTITUTIONAL CRISIS RESOLUTION PLAN I (LOUIS CARTIER)

  I. School personnel meeting (same day)
     A. Fact clarification and information sharing
     B. Affective discharge and support
     C. Identification of post-traumatic problems
     D. Planning of student activities
 II. Student general assembly (next day)
     A. Fact clarification by school administration
     B. Question and answer session with police present
III. Affective discharge (unlimited first period)
     A. Support offered and received
     B. Discussion of event led by teachers
 IV. Identification of post-traumatic problems (during first period)
     A. Outreach to symptomatic students, with special attention given to those
        students closest to the incident

    B. Referrals made to school guidance staff, mental health professionals, and
        local school psychologists
  V. School dismissal (after a half day; full day of classes to be held the next day)
 VI. Follow-up and evaluation
    A. Further psychological services for all staff and students made available
    B. Informal evaluation of interventions done with guidance staff

Christa McAuliffe

Throughout this account of Concord High School's response to Christa McAuliffe's sudden death, keep in mind the carryover effects of the earlier intervention and the school's handling of the Louis Cartier tragedy. Having already established a professional liaison as a crisis consultant with the school, I was summoned within minutes after the shuttle explosion. The lapse of time between this tragedy and the summoning of help was much less than the first.

Prior to my arrival, the principal had already decided that the students should go to their homerooms. By now the principal was aware that students have an overwhelming need in a time of crisis for as much information as possible. A rapid dissemination of information was thus facilitated, unlike during the Cartier incident, when students were prematurely dismissed and did not get the facts for 24 hours.

Because of a trusting relationship developed over the years and solidified during the tragedy a month before, the school was able to refuse national offers of assistance and turn instead to resources within its own community. A decision, later to be deemed a wise one, was made by the school administration that no outsiders would be included in the crisis response planning. At this time, I was considered to be very much an insider.

Following is the outline of the overall schedule for crisis resolution on a schoolwide level in the wake of the Christa McAuliffe tragedy.

SPECIFIC INSTITUTIONAL CRISIS RESOLUTION PLAN II (CHRISTA McAULIFFE)

   I. Suspension of classes (same day, Tuesday—press invited to leave school); students
      given freedom to stay or go at their discretion and asked to listen to news reports
      for further activity scheduling
  II. School personnel meeting (next day, Wednesday, A.M.); from experience gained
      in the aftermath of the previous crisis, sound decisions about future planning
      were made rapidly
  II. Press conference (next day, Wednesday, P.M.)
    A. Fact clarification of school's reactions and plans
    B. Question and answer session with press
 IV. Half day of shortened classes (Thursday)
    Students and teachers given choice of attending classes or going to designated
    mutual support areas, such as gym, cafeteria, and library (the "wake" area);

option left open for all to stay the entire day; peer counselors made themselves available

V. Memorial service (Friday)

    A. First three full periods held as usual

    B. Memorial service, 1 P.M., with no outsiders permitted

    C. Dismissal; special transportation arrangements made for those wishing to stay

VI. School resumed (Monday); personnel already aware from Cartier incident of signs of post-traumatic stress problems to look for and how to do appropriate outreach and referral

VII. Follow-up and evaluation

    A. Further psychological services for all staff and students made available

    B. Informal evaluation of interventions done with guidance staff

A week later I conducted a follow-up evaluation with the school's director of guidance to assess the effects of the plan on the resolution of the tragedy. Several interesting observations were made:

1. The shuttle disaster helped heal the trauma of the student's death the month before.
2. There was increased student respect for law enforcement, which assumed the role of protecting the mourners from the media.
3. The wisdom of not using any outside resources, but instead relying on internal and local external supports, was noted.
4. Much less consultation was required for the second tragedy, due to the learning which occurred during the first one.

To elaborate on this final observation, I was not utilized very much during the aftermath of the shuttle disaster. I experienced a sense of frustration and helplessness which many school staff must have felt during the hostage taking and subsequent shooting death. Only later, after I had gotten some distance from the tragedies and consultation of my own, was I able to recognize that it was largely as a result of the first active interventions that the school was able to respond so independently and efficiently during its second shared tragedy. The primary role of consultant helping others help themselves was clearly borne out.

Specific Roles of the Helper

W hile it is beyond the scope of this chapter to describe in detail how specific helpers may be utilized in the aftermath of particular crises of major proportion, a few general role descriptions will be offered. (For a more detailed outline of helping roles and their utilization during specific crisis scenarios, the reader is referred to Russman, 1988.) It should be noted that there is significant overlap between these role delineations and those played out during the Cartier and McAuliffe tragedies.

PRINCIPAL

The principal becomes the pivotal player during a crisis which has schoolwide impact. This person should be the first to receive a call from the outside about the incident and then should proceed to implement his or her school's crisis plan accordingly. This person does the following:

1. Calls in crisis team members—that is, those already designated to set the crisis plan in motion
2. Reviews the situation with the crisis team
3. Briefs the superintendent, school board members, and other essential personnel
4. Contacts other schools possibly affected by the incident and coordinates the development of ancillary critical care services to them
5. Calls a general staff meeting to obtain more information to be used in the dissemination of relevant data to others
6. Acts as liaison between the school and the press
7. Works wherever needed with other crisis team members

ASSISTANT PRINCIPAL

1. Assumes the duties of the principal in running the school during the crisis if the principal is unavailable
2. Provides normalcy and structure to help maintain the integrity of the school day

CRISIS TEAM MEMBERS

These people are usually volunteers, teachers, administrators, parents, civic leaders, or health service personnel who help formulate the school's individualized crisis response plan and are prepared on a moment's notice to help implement it. These people do the following:

1. Assess each other's abilities to carry out crisis response functions
2. Assist students, teachers, administrators, and guidance personnel involved in the crisis in carrying out tasks
3. Notify school support staff
4. Alert clergy
5. Coordinate and serve on telephone hotline
6. Help move students to designated areas
7. Plan logistics of upcoming events
8. Facilitate group discussions with students to process the event

GUIDANCE COUNSELORS

1. Identify students at risk
2. Contact parents for at-risk students
3. Open guidance offices at alternate safe meeting sites

4. Help run hotlines and facilitate discussions

5. Provide counsel and support for students and staff

SCHOOL NURSE

1. Identifies students at risk

2. Opens office for a safe place throughout crisis

3. Helps obtain information from such sources as hospitals, mental health affiliates, and emergency services

4. Contacts parents of students in extreme distress

TEACHERS

1. Disseminate information passed on to them by the crisis team

2. Help assess and identify students at risk

3. Move to and monitor students in designated areas

4. Provide normalcy and structure to help maintain the integrity of the school day

SECRETARIES

1. Assist administrator and crisis team members, as needed

2. Help identify students at risk

3. Handle the phones

4. Type, collate, and distribute specific crisis plans to facilitate the process

SUPPORT STAFF (CUSTODIAL, CAFETERIA, SWITCHBOARD)

1. Come to school to open the building and prepare space for such uses as planning meetings or process groups

2. Help identify students at risk

Proactive Consultation Suggestions

T he advantages of assuming a proactive stance and developing a crisis intervention plan to deal with tragedies which have schoolwide impact before they occur are obvious. The suggestions that follow emphasize the preventive aspect of school crisis management but also include intervention and postvention strategies that should be implemented by schools and their staff in the event that a tragedy does occur.

The suggestions are a compilation of strategies which have been found to be helpful by crisis consultants. They are also consistent with the theoretical premises and practical experiences which were discussed earlier in this chapter.

PREVENTION

1. Establish a relationship between the school and a local crisis intervention consultant which is consistent with a predetermined role.

2. Develop a well-defined, flexible, and adaptable crisis response plan upon which activities and strategies are implemented. Intervention strategies can be designed within a general framework, with alternate approaches available to meet any contingency.

3. Train school staff to identify the typical emotional reactions observed in trauma victims, and demonstrate the methods of intervention which are likely to be effective in coping with these symptoms, including the appropriate use of referral resources.

INTERVENTION

4. Demonstrate an interest and involvement in the situation.

5. Invite and encourage the school staff's participation and show consideration for their feelings.

6. Maintain and demonstrate respect for the skills and professionalism of the consultees.

7. Arrange for the rapid and complete dissemination of information and update it as soon as it becomes available.

8. Facilitate the adequate expression and management of the emotional concomitants of the crisis for staff before asking them to assist students.

9. Facilitate the adequate expression and management of the emotional concomitants of the crisis for the students.

10. Utilize trusted local mental health consultants and clinicians rather than outside experts.

POSTVENTION

11. Arrange for swift professional outreach and follow-up when symptoms of staff and students are noted.

12. Evaluate the effectiveness of the intervention of the school and crisis consultants working together shortly after the crisis is resolved to improve the school's response capabilities.

Summary

C onsulting to a school during the course of a traumatic event which affects the entire institution is very challenging in many ways. While there are definite similarities in working with large groups of people and separate individuals in crisis, the sheer magnitude of the group problem, among other major differences, can make consultations intimidating experiences.

However, rather than passively hoping that a large-scale trauma will not occur in local schools or doing difficult reactive consultations after the fact, it is far better to take a proactive position. There is a substantial body of literature which reflects the experiences of professionals and nonprofessionals on this subject. Unfortunately, all too many have had to learn the hard way by not having had the benefit of an understanding of the underlying principles of crisis response and management during such situations.

It is strongly recommended that school officials in positions of authority meet local mental health experts in crisis intervention to develop plans to cover a wide range of traumatic contingencies. These plans should strongly reflect an appreciation of the characteristics of people in crisis and a knowledge of the specific intervention strategies that will facilitate maximal resolution of a tragedy.

The advantages of developing such crisis response plans are so great when compared to the potential negative mental health effects on large numbers of students and others that it seems only logical for schools to assume a proactive, preventive posture within their communities. Let us learn our lessons and learn them well.

References

Cohen, R. E. (1985). "Crisis Counseling Principles and Services." In M. Lystad (Ed.), *Innovations in Mental Health Services to Disaster Victims.* Rockville, MD: National Institute of Mental Health.

Cohen, R. E., & Ahearn, F. L. (1980). *Handbook for Mental Health Care of Disaster Victims.* Baltimore and London: Johns Hopkins University Press.

Crabbs, M. A. (1981). "School Mental Health Services Following an Environmental Disaster." *The Journal of School Health, 3,* 165–167.

Farberow, N. L., & Gordon, N. S. (1981). *Manual for Child Health Workers in Major Disasters.* Rockville, MD: National Institute of Mental Health.

Hoff, L. A. (1984). *People in Crisis: Understanding and Helping* (2nd ed.). Menlo Park, CA: Addison-Wesley.

Kafrissen, S. R., & Heffron, E. F., with Zusman, J. (1975). "Mental Health Problems in Environmental Disasters." In H. L. P. Resnick & H. L. Ruben (Eds.), *Emergency Psychiatric Care: The Management of Mental Health Crises.* Bowie, MD: Charles Press.

Kennedy, E. (1981). *Crisis Counseling.* New York: Continuum.

McGee, R. K., & Heffron, E. F. (1976). "The Role of Crisis Intervention Services in Disaster Recovery." In H. J. Parad, H. L. P. Resnik & L. G. Parad (Eds.), *Emergency and Disaster Management.* Bowie, MD: Charles Press.

Mitchell, J. T. (1981). "Multi-Casualty Situations." In J. T. Mitchell & H. L. P. Resnik, *Emergency Response to Crisis.* Bowie, MD: Brady.

Russman, A. G. (1988). "Crisis Intervention Model Development." Unpublished manuscript.

Slaby, A. E., Lieb, J., & Tancredi, L. R. (1981). *Handbook of Psychiatric Emergencies*. Garden City, NY: Medical Examination.

Solomon, S. D. (1986). "Mobilizing Social Support Networks in Times of Disaster." In C. R. Figley (Ed.), *Trauma and Its Wake* (Vol. 2). New York: Brunner/Mazel.

Tierney, K. J., & Baisden, B. (1979). *Crisis Intervention Programs for Disaster Victims in Smaller Communities*. Rockville, MD: National Institute of Mental Health.

Wall, E. F., & Viers, L. A. (1985). "The Process and the Technique of Managing School-wide Tragedy." *NASSE Bulletin,* 69 (478), 101–104.

Chapter 5

Crisis Intervention at the College Campus Counseling Center

ALLEN J. OTTENS, PH.D., AND
LYNN FISHER-MCCANNE, PH.D.

T his chapter focuses on the delivery of crisis intervention services by college and university counseling centers. The prevalence and availability of these services reflect the integral role they fill. Whiteley, Mahaffey, & Geer (1987) found that 76 percent of the counseling center directors they surveyed reported crisis intervention as a center function. In another survey (Roney, Wiley, Croteau, & Gelwick, 1986), 46 percent reported that 24-hour emergency coverage was available on their campuses. These figures may increase as colleges strive to follow the standards and guidelines promulgated by the Council for the Advancement of Standards for Student Services/ Developmental Programs (1986, p. 33). The Council recommended that to fulfill its mission effectively, a counseling center must provide, either directly or through referral, "crisis intervention and emergency coverage, as appropriate."

The first part of this chapter surveys literature that underscores the appropriateness of crisis intervention for college students. Next, a framework is presented for practicing crisis intervention in college counseling centers. A crisis therapy model is then explicated and case material is presented that demonstrates the model in operation. The chapter closes with examples of outcome research of brief therapy/crisis counseling with college students and discusses a quality assessment model for determining treatment effectiveness.

Crisis Intervention and College Students: A Survey of the Literature

S tudent personnel workers have long recognized crisis intervention as a valuable and fitting counseling approach. Almost 25 years ago, Dr. James Paulsen, chief psychiatrist at Stanford University, commented that "at the time of the crisis, an hour or two with an empathic faculty member, a counselor, administrator, or psychiatrist may diminish the emotional intensity of the situation to a point where it can be easily handled by the student" (quoted in Farnsworth, 1966, p. 8). Today's campus crisis intervenor may only dream of a bygone era when crises could be patched up in such short order. However, crisis intervention remains compatible with the counseling needs of students due to the following factors.

Crisis Intervention and the Development Stage of the Young Adult

As the demand for skilled workers increases, more individuals decide to prepare for entry into the work force by pursuing higher education. Chickering (1969) argued that our increasingly complex world has created a new developmental stage encompassing the years 18 to 25 between adolescence and early adulthood which he calls "the young adult." Chickering postulated seven vectors or developmental tasks of this stage: achieving competence, managing emotions, becoming autonomous, establishing identity, freeing interpersonal relationships, clarifying purposes, and developing integrity. Thus, the young adult stage required individuals to develop personal values, emotional control, mental and physical competencies, self-confidence, independence, and relationship skills that are all crucial for successful entry into the adult world. These are significant developmental accomplishments that need to be achieved in a relatively short time.

In order to accomplish these tasks and achieve growth without undue risk or threat, students need a balance of environmental support and challenge (Sanford, 1962). When threatened, individuals attempt to maintain a kind of emotional homeostasis (Caplan, 1964), but this may be difficult, given the personal–social–cognitive demands of college and the problematic situations confronting students. Significant problems can arise that disturb this equilibrium and for which students may not possess adequate coping resources.

Crisis precipitants common to students are death of a parent (Werner & Jones, 1979); romantic relationship dissolution (Ottens, 1985), unwanted pregnancy/abortion (Boekelheide, 1978; Gould, 1980; McCarthy & Brown, 1974), physical assault/acquaintance rape (Bogal-Allbritten & Allbritten, 1985; Doweiko, 1981; Miller &

Marshall, 1987), and adapting to shared living environments (Waldo, 1984). An inspection of problem log data at our Counseling and Student Development Center during a recent semester revealed a varied list of precipitants, including spousal abuse, impending academic failure, hospitalization of a parent, sexual identity panic, and adverse financial circumstances. These problems lend themselves to a flexible, available, problem-focused intervention that can attenuate negative emotions and teach coping behaviors.

In many instances when developmental progress is thwarted, resulting hopelessness and confusion may spawn suicidal crises. Historically, suicide prevention has been a primary goal of college mental health workers (Raphael, Power, & Berridge, 1937), and it continues to be a raison d'être for college crisis intervention services (Weiss & Kapp, 1974). Research regarding the prevalence of suicide attempts among students yields some startling statistics. Mishara (1982) found that among 250 undergraduate students in psychology courses surveyed at the University of Massachusetts at Boston, 14 percent had made a suicide attempt. In an earlier study (Mishara, Baker, & Mishara, 1976) 15 percent of the surveyed students had made a suicide attempt within the previous five years. Crisis intervention may prevent problems from advancing to suicidal proportions.

Crisis Intervention Is Compatible with Students' Characteristics

There has been debate as to who is most appropriate for crisis-oriented or brief therapy (Ewing, 1978). In their review of the literature, Butcher and Koss (1978, pp. 725–767) summarized the types of patients considered best suited to brief techniques: (a) those in whom the behavioral problem is of acute onset, (b) those whose previous adjustment has been good, (c) those with a good ability to relate, and (d) those with high initial motivation. These characteristics seem generally descriptive of the college student.

Brief psychotherapy is also compatible with students because, as Pinkerton (1986) noted, students desire autonomy and control. A protracted therapeutic relationship is incompatible with students' developmental goal of striving for independence. Since crisis intervention involves a brief therapy encounter, swift problem resolution, and the teaching of coping behaviors, students are likely to emerge from it with a sense of mastery and self-control.

Crisis Intervention Matches Institutional Needs

College counseling centers are scrambling with their limited resources to meet almost overwhelming student needs. Clearly, the days of being "able to guarantee a school year of weekly sessions, about thirty, to 'all who need and can use it' " (Hanfmann, 1978, p. 6) are over. It is common practice at many colleges to limit most clients to 12 or fewer sessions during an academic year.

Efforts to limit sessions come at a time when counseling centers report increasing use of their services (e.g., Burral, 1985). Waiting lists of 250 have been reported

(Clack, Stone, & Thurman, 1984). Moreover, large universities (more than 10,500 students) must get by with unfavorable student-to-counselor ratios, such as 2,000:1 (Clack et al., 1984). Obviously, briefer therapies and alternative intervention strategies may be useful under these circumstances. Since crisis intervention is by definition brief, with a duration of 3 to 12 weeks (Patterson & O'Sullivan, 1979), it makes sense from an institutional standpoint to offer this form of treatment whenever indicated.

Practice Framework

H armon and Baron (1982) presented a model that classified all campus counseling centers into three *purposes* of intervention: crisis intervention, remediation, and development. Harmon and Baron operationalized the three purposes along three *levels* of intervention. Level I interventions focus primarily on the student and under some circumstances on those within the student's immediate environment. Level II involves the staff, faculty, and student leaders who interact with students. Level III includes the ecological factors and social systems that affect students' functioning. In this section we will illustrate how the model's three levels describe the delivery of a wide variety of crisis intervention services on college campuses.

Level I

According to Harmon and Baron, the goals of Level I crisis interventions are to (a) stabilize the person in crisis, (b) facilitate assistance and/or referral, and (c) provide support and/or counseling for those in the immediate environment affected by the student in crisis.

There are a number of strategies for accomplishing Level I goals: walk-in counseling, crisis teams, telephone counseling, and post-suicide support groups. Later in this chapter we will present a detailed model for the most typical Level I strategy, one-to-one crisis-oriented therapy. What follows is an overview of some other Level I strategies that are part of the crisis intervention effort at various colleges and universities.

Telephone Counseling.   It was mentioned earlier that many counseling centers offer 24-hour coverage. After-hours requests for assistance are typically forwarded from the infirmary, security office, or residence hall to the on-call clinician. Some colleges arrange to have after-hour calls handled by the local community crisis call-in service. Tucker, Megenity, and Vigil (1970) described an alternative implemented at a Colorado community college. Due to a shortage of counselors, volunteers from students, staff, and faculty staffed the phones to provide support, information, and referral. In another type of telephone alternative, Hill and Harmon (1976) and Thurman, Baron, and Klein (1979) described a University of Texas program that makes prerecorded telephone tapes available around the clock providing information about mental and physical health.

Often students prefer to turn first to their peer group for help during a personal crisis (Dana, Heynen, & Burdette, 1974). Many colleges are involved in peer counseling training in order to supplement campus helping resources and to capitalize on the frontline position peers occupy when crises occur. In a survey of college and university counseling center directors, 78 percent of the respondents indicated that their center provided peer counseling programs, and a third of these programs used peers in suicide and crisis intervention (Salovey & D'Andrea, 1984). Student-staffed telephone emergency hotlines are a valuable peer counseling service. At American University, a student-operated hotline received 7,000 calls each semester, handling problems related to drugs, sex, loneliness, and depression (Leventhal, Berman, McCarthy, & Wasserman, 1976).

Crisis Teams.   Some colleges have organized teams of staff members who mobilize during crises. Jones and Najera (1976) described a "helping network" at Brown University that consisted of key student services staff. This network facilitated the provision of care for the student in crisis as well as those affected by the crisis. More recently, Sprinkle and Matthews (1984) described the formation of an Emergency Intervention Team (EIT) at the University of Wyoming. The EIT was comprised of 10 two-member teams. When alerted to an emergency, a team contacted the student, assessed the situation, and took action such as referring the student to the appropriate campus service or escorting him or her to the hospital emergency room.

Postvention.   An additional Level I strategy involves providing assistance to those who have been affected by the crisis and its aftermath. Intervention is often useful for dealing with the post-crisis confusion, guilt, and grief and for dispelling rumors. Halberg (1986) outlined procedures which were implemented following the death, of natural causes, of a student at a small college: investigation at the scene of the incident, notification of appropriate people on campus, notification of next of kin, development of a press release, determining how to deal with friends, communication with legal counsel, treatment of grief after the funeral, and management of other procedures after the funeral (e.g., removing belongings from the room, taking care of the student's bursar accounts). Similarly, Hipple, Cimbolic, & Peterson (1980) suggested a seven-step postvention plan after a student suicide. Other postvention activities have been reported or suggested following a medical emergency (Katz & Viventi, 1976) and acute psychotic episode (Jones & Najera, 1976; Rockwell, 1986).

Level II

Interventions at this level are targeted toward staff, faculty, peer counselors, and student leaders (e.g., residence hall advisors) who work with students. Harmon & Baron (1982) enumerated three Level II goals: (a) communicating information about the symptoms experienced by students in crisis, (b) providing training in crisis intervention, and (c) consulting with those who work with students in crisis. Strategies suggested by Harmon and Baron to achieve these goals included case-centered consultation, workshops, presentations, and cooperative planning. We will present two examples of how Level II strategies have been applied in campus crisis intervention.

College Mental Health Consultation.   Consultation with faculty and staff who work with students is a way of extending the assistance of college mental health professionals. Not only does direct service (e.g., one-to-one counseling) reach few students, but it focuses on pathology or dysfunction, ignoring healthy aspects of development. Thus, if the counselor has knowledge and skills to benefit the institution and its members as a whole, direct service is an inefficient way to transmit them. Schwartz and Pierce (1976) made these points and commented on the incongruity of college counseling professionals failing to provide campus consultation:

> For college mental health workers specifically, the failure to give away their knowledge and skills appears out of keeping with their functioning in a setting where the elaboration and transmission of knowledge is the premiere reason for the existence of the institution (p. 163).

Schwartz and Pierce provided an insightful account of their failures and successes in trying to develop at the University of Rochester a consulting relationship with an academic department known for its demanding curriculum. Schwartz and Pierce felt their efforts were regarded as a threat to the department's administrators, who believed that improving student mental health might compromise academic excellence. With the arrival of a new, more flexible administrator, further consultative contacts were initiated. Schwartz and Pierce discussed their plans to help the administration understand student stress and to better equip faculty to be more effective sources of support.

Crisis Intervention Training.   After four students committed suicide during the 1977–78 academic year at Cornell University, a pilot program was initiated by the Psychological Services Clinic to train several key faculty and staff in basic crisis intervention techniques such as symptom detection and referral (White & Ottens, 1979). The pilot program was so successful that it was expanded and made available to the entire campus community. After five years, more than 200 student advisers, faculty, and staff had participated (Ottens, 1983). The program goals were to assist participants to (a) gain more knowledge about the campus crisis network, (b) understand how this network was organized to respond, (c) develop increased sensitivity to the psychological problems of those in crisis, (d) learn clues to attend to and questions to ask in assessing suicidal risk, (e) learn how to establish contact and rapport, (f) learn how to refer, and (g) practice these skills by role-playing hypothetical crisis situations. The overarching program goal was for participants to learn to respond proactively and knowledgeably so that they could be helpful to someone in crisis.

Level III

According to Harmon and Baron (1982), there are two main Level III goals: (a) identifying and remedying environmental factors that exacerbate student crises, and (b) advocating for environmental change to the present crises. Environmental design is a strategy suggested by Harmon and Baron to achieve Level III goals. We will present several examples from the literature which speak to Level III issues.

Residence Hall Crowding.   It is known that assigning three to a room affects the amount of time students spend in their rooms (Walden, Nelson, & Smith, 1981). In a study of students in double and triple rooms (Aiello, Baum, & Gormley, 1981), it was found that 31 percent of the students in triples felt left out by their roommates. No double-room resident felt left out. Triple isolates (ones who felt left out) were more likely to report residence hall life as hectic, to have problems with roommates, and to complain of noise and messiness. Thus, planning for adequate living space is a key strategy to reduce students' feelings of isolation and dissatisfaction.

Faculty–Student Interaction.   Pascarella and Terenzini (1976) found that the frequency of contact between freshmen and faculty was related positively to students' academic, intellectual, and personal growth. Subsequently, Terenzini and Pascarella (1980) obtained results which essentially replicated their earlier research and moreover found that discussing personal problems with faculty may help freshmen to alleviate some of their stress. More recently, Pascarella and Terenzini (1981) followed a group of 567 incoming freshmen. Four hundred ninety-three chose a conventional residence (CR); 74 chose an experimental living–learning residence (LLR). The living–learning residence combined students of all classes and faculty members in one residence hall where various courses, discussions, and contact with faculty and staff were offered. At the eight-month follow-up, the living–learning residence students had higher academic achievement and more positive attitudes toward their academic program than conventional residence students. These studies point to the desirability of colleges encouraging faculty contact with freshmen and designing environments where this can occur.

Role of the College Counselor in Environmental Design.   It has been noted that environmental design combines an environmental focus with a preventive purpose (Conyne et al., 1979). Examples of environmental design include scheduling mid-semester breaks to relieve student stress, making the campus accessible to physically handicapped students, housing student services in prominent campus locations, and implementing flexible programs such as providing emergency cash loans to students.

Conyne et al. (1979) proposed three broad design roles for counselors: environmental assessor, consultant and collaborator, and program evaluator. Regarding assessment, Corazzini, Wilson, and Huebner (1977) developed the Environmental Satisfaction Questionnaire (ESQ), which counselors can use to improve the fit between student needs and university resources. The questionnaire consists of two parts: The first attempts to uncover mismatches between student and environment; the second elicits environmental referent data—namely, what caused the mismatch, what the student has done to cope, and how the student could remedy the problem.

Clinical Issues

I n this section we will address the most typical Level I crisis intervention: individual, face-to-face counseling. Because this intervention is so common to the practitioner, we will explicate a detailed model for clinical practice. The model is based on the work of Charles Ewing (1978), who has identified the key stages of crisis intervention and coalesced them into a crisis-oriented therapy. This model is applied to the special concerns of the college student within a campus community context. This section closes with a case vignette which demonstrates how the model can be utilized as crisis-oriented therapy.

Ewing proposed six essential stages of crisis intervention: delineation of the problem focus, evaluation, contracting, intervention, termination, and follow-up. Ewing acknowledged that these stages overlap and are not clear-cut, chronological, or mutually exclusive. However, the stages are presented as discrete steps to illustrate more clearly the unfolding crisis intervention process. In this section, we will adapt Ewing's model to crises common to college students and identify specific therapist skills and roles that are relevant to this client population and setting. Finally, a clinical vignette demonstrates how stages can be integrated therapeutically.

Stage One: Delineation of the Problem Focus

In this stage, clinician and client collaborate to define a particular problem for intervention. To identify the problem focus, the clinician inquires as to why the student has sought help now. Clinician nonverbal behaviors (leaning forward, making eye contact, sitting across from the student) can encourage disclosure. Fortunately, college students are generally verbal and motivated and these minimal prompts are often sufficient to facilitate quick, specific problem articulation. In some cases there may be no obvious crisis precipitant, or the student may be unable to explain why he or she feels so bad. In that event, the clinician reviews recent experiences in the areas of schoolwork, social and sexual relations, living situation, employment, or family. The clinician must consider the major areas of the student's life in order to determine the main problem focus and the contributing or mitigating factors.

From the beginning, the clinician builds rapport and lays the foundation for productive therapy. This can be accomplished by providing the student with information and reassurance. For example, the clinician may provide information about the counseling center's services (e.g., confidentiality, short-term framework, weekly sessions) and differentiate the crisis from mental illness. Reassurance can be communicated by expressing optimism that the crisis is likely to be short-lived and to have a favorable prognosis; yet the clinician will want to leave open the possibility, if indicated, of longer term help.

Clinical Example. Trembling and tearful, Linda requests help with overwhelming feelings of anxiety and dread. You, as her clinician, begin by asking what brings her for counseling. At first she does not respond, but presently she says, "I don't know what it is. I looked around at everyone in class, and they seemed so friendly to each other. I felt so alone and so bad." She is distressed and struggles to describe her feelings. How do you proceed?

First, you begin to develop rapport with Linda. Normalizing her feelings is part of this step. You reassure her that her need for help does not mean she is crazy, and you inform her that her anxiety is exacerbated because she is not sure what she fears. Eye contact, encouraging nods, patient listening, and a brief touch on the arm communicate your caring and warmth. Your attending behavior elicits a cathartic release of emotion, and Linda weeps.

Next, you help Linda to determine the precipitant: "What happened today, Linda? Why do you need help now? How have you been feeling? When did things get worse?" As her story unfolds, you hypothesize about what she is experiencing and which developmental tasks have been thwarted. You inquire about major life areas: schoolwork, living situation, friendships, romance, family relationships, work. You recall the typical developmental tasks of an 18-year-old freshman—becoming autonomous, achieving competence, developing interpersonal relationships, establishing values. In fact, Linda discloses a number of current stresses (i.e., leaving home, breakup of a romance, roommate problems, and lack of college friends) that led her to consider suicide. The suicidal thoughts and feelings of loss of control frighten her, and she feels hopeless and guilty about failed relationships. Social isolation emerges as the problem focus. Also, attention must be paid to Linda's suicidal thoughts, not only because they engender considerable stress but because Linda regards suicide as a possible coping method.

The clinician plays several roles during the problem focus stage. She or he must be a *listener*, encouraging the outpouring of the client's feelings, beliefs, and personal history. As *nurturer*, the clinician provides the client with much-needed care, concern, and understanding. The clinician, as consummate *detective*, sifts through clues and helps the client make plausible connections. Always the *evaluator*, the clinician constantly weighs evidence, verbal and nonverbal, in order to generate hypotheses concerning the client. In the role of *teacher*, the clinician educates the client about his or her emotions and reframes the crisis in less catastrophic terms.

Stage Two: Evaluation

Careful evaluation is essential in crisis intervention. Evaluation begins in the first session and continues to some degree throughout treatment. In addition to the clinician's efforts at delineating the problem focus, evaluation will further determine the student's functioning, life situation, and ability to benefit from crisis intervention.

Following the Ewing model, the clinician should determine or obtain:

1. Basic demographic data (e.g., age, marital and family status, address, year in school).
2. Brief treatment history (e.g., circumstances surrounding the initiation and termination of previous therapy, and whether the student is receiving therapy elsewhere).
3. Present accessibility to evaluation. Serious interfering factors (e.g., intoxication, sedation, or extreme agitation) may necessitate detoxification and/or brief hospitalization.
4. Psychological functioning. The clinician should note the student's appearance and behavior. For example, is the student's attire appropriate? Are there any salient physical characteristics or handicaps? Is his or her affect congruent with experience? Does the student relate in a comfortable, strained, or detached manner? Does he or she speak openly and coherently? Also, for crisis-oriented counseling to be successful, the student should be reasonably capable of clear, organized thinking. Therefore, the therapist must informally assess intellectual capacity and note any formal thought disorder, delusions, hallucinations, or marked affect.
5. Precrisis adjustment. A major goal is to restore clients to at least their precrisis level of functioning.
6. Motivation. Good signs include self-referral and evidence of coping efforts prior to counseling.

Nearly every counseling center requires students to complete a basic demographic questionnaire. However, because of the need for rapid treatment and assessment of distraught clients, practitioners may find it inconvenient to use screening instruments. Nevertheless, brief paper and pencil measures should be available for evaluating depression, suicide potential, and adjustment.

There are several examples of brief measures that may be useful to the campus crisis clinician. Barrow, Talley, Miller, and Zung (1985) reported that the 20-item Zung Self-Rating Depression Scale is quickly and reliably scored and easy to complete, even for individuals in distress. Barrow et al. found that the scale was useful with university students, allowing therapists to spend more time on developing a trusting relationship and less on detailed interviewing to assess depression.

The Scale for Suicide Ideation (Beck, Kovacks, & Weissman, 1979) is a 21-item measure of the extent of the wish to die, the desire to make an active suicide attempt, details of any plan, internal deterrents, subjective feelings of control, and courage to make an attempt. The clinician completes the scale based on a semi-structured interview. Although developed as a research tool, its brevity, correlation with clinical ratings, sensitivity to changes over time, and measures of validity recommend the scale for evaluating suicide potential.

The Psychological Screening Inventory (Lanyon, 1973) is a 130-item true–false measure that can be completed in 15 minutes. Its alienation and discomfort scales are probably most relevant for the college clinician. A high score on alienation indicates similarity to psychiatric patients in responding and may therefore warrant more thorough evaluation. A high discomfort score may indicate the presence of debilitating anxiety.

The Bulimia Test (Smith & Thelen, 1984) may assist in the identification of bulimia, an increasingly common disorder on the college campus. The 36-item scale, which can be completed in 5 to 10 minutes, has been found to measure reliably and validly bulimic attitudes and behaviors.

Clinical Example.   George requests help with serious academic problems resulting from anxiety and inability to concentrate. You have already determined with George that the problem focus will be coping with his academic difficulties. You obtain some basic demographic data. George is 20 and a junior, living off campus. He has never had counseling. His minor study skills problems have worsened since he started upper level courses. He is alert, cooperative, and neatly dressed, but his anxiety is readily apparent as he describes his fear of failing courses and leaving school. However, you find no evidence of serious depression, and George's history is one of self-reliance, with a strong support system. He seems motivated, as exemplified by his precounseling coping efforts, which included talking to teachers, securing a tutor, and dropping a class. Thus, George seems a good candidate for crisis intervention, and his anxiety can be alleviated through learning assistance and realistic short-term planning to improve his academic functioning.

During the evaluation stage, the clinician plays four key roles. As in the problem focus stage, the clinician must be a *detective,* alert to verbal and nonverbal clues in the evaluation process; moreover, the clinician must look for any barriers to full participation in the crisis intervention process (e.g., substance abuse). As a *historian,* the clinician searches for trends or connections concerning historical data. The clinician also performs a *skeptic's* role, as she or he determines the client's accessibility to evaluation, level of motivation for treatment, and accuracy and completeness of the client's perspective. Of course, the clinician operates as an *evaluator,* making judgments about the data and assessing the client's condition.

Stage Three: Contract

Negotiating a treatment contract is the third stage of the Ewing model. The contract is an important element of crisis intervention because it structures the limited therapy time, establishes treatment as time-limited and focused, and offers the client a realistic idea of what to expect. Written or verbal, the contract should be explicit and understandable to the client. The minimum elements of the contract are a clear statement of the problem focus and treatment goals, time limits (e.g., maximum number of sessions), possible inclusion of others for information and/or treatment purposes (e.g., spouse, campus physician, residence hall adviser), and client/therapist responsibilities. Client responsibilities include keeping appointments, engaging in honest self-exploration, and implementing adaptive behaviors. The clinician may contract to keep appointments, listen attentively, maintain confidentiality, give feedback, suggest resources, and actively assist the client in self-understanding.

Clinical Example.   David is in acute distress when he seeks your help over his parents' recent divorce. Once you have identified David's situational distress as the problem focus and ascertained that his history, psychological functioning, and level of motivation do not preclude productive crisis intervention, you come to a verbal agreement with him. The agreement has four major points:

1. Crisis intervention will be initiated to reduce David's distress over the divorce and his father's alcohol abuse. This will be accompanied by *identifying David's feelings* (e.g., sorrow, anger, fear), by *cognitive restructuring* (e.g., rethinking David's belief about assuming responsibility for the divorce), by *using existing support systems* (e.g., friends, siblings), by *referring to additional support resources* (e.g., Al-Anon, campus clergy), and by *exploring ways to cope* with David's changing relationship toward his parents.
2. Within a five-week period, David will be eligible for five 50-minute appointments, with the option of two additional emergency sessions.
3. No one else will be included in the treatment.
4. David and you will keep all appointments or call in advance to cancel. David will work actively and honestly toward realistic and adaptive solutions. You will maintain confidentiality, especially if David's parents inquire. By providing feedback, insights, and alternatives, you will help David develop some realistic options.

For the contract stage, the clinician serves as *timekeeper* to establish parameters for time-limited treatment. He or she also functions as *negotiator* to develop the contract. As the *communication link,* the clinician assists the client to make use of helpful significant others.

Stage Four: Intervention

In Ewing's (1978) model, intervention occurs during every stage. Thus, delineation of the problem-focus, evaluation, and contracting qualify as interventions because they facilitate crisis resolution. Depending on the student's problems, needs, and resources and the clinician's judgment, skills, and creativity, additional interventions vary but typically include:

1. *Listening,* an effective intervention for building rapport, gleaning information, and permitting emotional release

2. *Utilizing interpersonal resources,* such as encouraging talking to a friend, parent, or faculty member
3. *Utilizing institutional resources,* such as academic advising, financial aid, and health services
4. *Advocacy,* when students need support to deal with institutional red tape
5. *Confrontation,* by therapeutically challenging students' discrepant feelings and behaviors or dysfunctional modes of thinking
6. *Giving information,* often pertaining to sexuality, drugs, and appetitive disorders
7. *Exploring alternative coping mechanisms,* such as relaxation or assertiveness
8. *Assigning "homework,"* such as behavioral recording or reading selected self-help literature

Clinical Example.   Susan seeks help for a roommate problem that has gotten "out of hand." She complains that she can no longer endure her roommate's "selfishness and insensitivity." (The roommate is black; Susan is white.) The problem escalated into a physical fight the previous night. Both roommates' schoolwork has suffered due to all the tension.

You and Susan determine that the problem focus is the emotionally draining relationship with her roommate. In your evaluation, you hypothesize that Susan, by virtue of certain behaviors and beliefs, may be creating problems with her roommate, and that she will resist exploring her role in the conflict. However, you negotiate a contract with Susan that includes examining her behavior as a factor in the crisis.

You develop rapport with Susan by listening and encouraging ventilation of feelings. You contemplate an intervention that would involve Susan receiving feedback from close friends who appear more tolerant than she. Using a combination of challenge and support, you confront Susan's prejudices against blacks—she grew up in an all-white neighborhood—and you explore with her the cooperative behaviors required of a shared living environment. As an only child, Susan never learned to room with another person, much less someone so "different" from herself.

As Susan tells it, she has tried everything to improve the living situation. You help her discover why some efforts have not worked, how some efforts might be applied more effectively, and what actual successes she has had, being careful not to offer advice she can reject. You assign Susan homework: compiling lists of similarities between herself and her roommate, specifying behaviors she wants her roommate to change (e.g., picking up dirty clothes), specifying behaviors her roommate would appreciate (e.g., playing radio softly). You have Susan perform assertive behaviors with friends which involve her getting practice in making appropriate requests and accepting feedback.

The clinician continues to play the roles of *listener* and *nurturer.* Additionally he or she may need to serve as *coordinator* to keep the client task-focused, *advocate* to facilitate the institution's responsiveness, *teacher* to convey essential information, and *explorer* to help the student discover alternative coping mechanisms.

Stage Five: Termination

When clinician and student reach the end of their contract or agree that their work is finished, the crisis intervention is terminated. Although the therapeutic relationship was brief, it was probably meaningful; therefore, the clinician must handle termination sensitively. In fact, the clinician may encourage discussion of termination during the last few treatment sessions.

The clinician must be alert to the student's reactions to termination. Some students terminate with a sense of competence and independence, which are desirable developmental goals. These clients need only validation of their positive feelings. However, some students see termination as a threat to the fulfillment of their needs, and they may feel sad, afraid, or angry at the prospect. They may try to prolong treatment by raising new problems or "backsliding." In these instances, the clinician should focus the student's attention on the feelings and question whether they represent efforts to prolong treatment. While empathizing with the student's feelings, the clinician nonetheless emphasizes the client's accomplishments and enforces the treatment contract.

If a student reacts impassively to termination, the clinician can still talk about possible feelings, thereby allowing the student a safe way to consider the event. If a student terminates prematurely, the clinician should follow up to encourage return if appropriate, to emphasize that assistance is available later, or to encourage discussion of termination-related feelings.

Clinical Example.   John is completing his six allotted sessions. In the last two sessions, you and he have discussed his feelings of relief and renewed confidence as well as fear that his distressing feelings may reappear. In his last session, he expresses appreciation for your help. You review his treatment progress and the strength of his coping skills. You encourage him to describe what he has learned about examining a crisis and how he has come to grow from it and develop new coping skills.

During termination, the clinician plays the role of *timekeeper,* establishing and maintaining a time schedule for the crisis intervention. The clinician completes the role of *nurturer,* preparing the student to leave with a sense of support, pride in her or his accomplishments, and optimism about the future. The therapist as *evaluator* monitors information and achievement and documents the student's progress.

Stage Six: Follow-Up

Follow-up is a last-chance intervention, and one that is too often neglected. A phone call one or two months after termination serves evaluative, educational, and clinical functions. With a call, the clinician can learn whether the intervention was effective and can acquire client feedback that may help the clinician hone his or her skills. In addition, the clinician can reinforce important aspects of the treatment and reevaluate any need for additional services.

Clinical Example.   You terminated crisis intervention with Liz six weeks ago and now call to see how she is doing. She tells you she is distressed at having "backslid," feeling unable again to cope with the breakup with her fiancé. Since they live in the same residence hall, they see each other daily. Because Liz seems to need more help, you suggest a therapy group dealing with relationship breakups.

The clinician resumes the role of *evaluator* as he or she attempts to assess the former client's progress. As an *educator,* the clinician may remind the former client of what he or she learned in therapy. Again, the clinician may serve as a *coordinator* by referring the former client to other support services or longer term or alternative treatment.

Case Vignette

CASE DESCRIPTION

Liz, a 21-year-old senior, comes to your office because she is depressed. She and her fiancé have just broken up and she feels unable to cope. She cries most of the day, feels agitated, and isn't sleeping or eating normally.
Liz expresses doubt about your ability to help, but she says she feels desperate.

You find that Liz, since beginning this relationship a year ago, has become socially isolated. Her family strongly disliked her fiancé, and her fiancé discouraged her from spending time with her friends.

Liz is from a large family, with parents who are very involved with the other children. She expects to graduate from college in a few months with a bachelor's degree in English. She doubts she

COMMENTARY

Delineation of problem-focus.   Is the breakup Liz's primary problem? Why did it occur? How was she functioning before the breakup? Before the relationship?
To establish rapport, introduce the concept of short-term crisis intervention, provide reassurance and optimism, and review the feelings associated with grieving.
Explore sexual relations, schoolwork, family dynamics, living situation, and job performance. How has the breakup affected these areas?

Identify the developmental tasks in question: establishing autonomy, competence, intimacy, and values. Liz's dependence on her fiancé, social isolation, "failure" at an intimate relationship, and struggle to identify her own rights and beliefs have left her feeling depressed and in crisis.
Evaluation.   What is Liz's current emotional state? Is she using alcohol or drugs? Is she thinking clearly? Is she ready to work at feeling better and

will find a job and is considering moving home. The thought of moving home and losing her independence as well as the breakup and lack of support system have immobilized Liz. She says that she has no intention of hurting herself, but she doesn't sound convincing. She drinks at night to get to sleep.

Liz won't agree to stop drinking at this time, saying it is the "one thing that keeps me going." She agrees to the time-limited approach and to working on her feelings of depression, but she has reservations about whether social isolation and dependence are issues for her. She consents to the suicide contract, although she expresses concern that six sessions may not be adequate.

Liz cut all her classes during the week prior to her first counseling session. She has not talked with friends or family about the breakup, but has "holed up" in her residence hall room. As she talks about her fiancé, she moves from glowing statements about him to more negative comments and memories.

By the sixth session, Liz is feeling more in control. She feels less depressed and has begun reaching out to friends and family for support. She has returned to classes and has stopped drinking. Her normal patterns of eating and sleeping have returned as well. Liz is able to talk about her ex-fiancé more easily, although she still cries

changing her behavior? Determine suicide risk by asking Liz if she has thought of hurting herself. Has she had suicidal thoughts or made an attempt? Consider administering the Zung Self-Rating Depression Scale (Zung, 1965) and/or the Scale for Suicide Ideation (Beck et al., 1979).

Contract.   Specify six sessions to work on Liz's feelings of depression, isolation, and dependence. Establish a suicide contract whereby she will call you or an emergency hotline if she feels suicidal or desperate. Also contract that Liz will not use alcohol during the duration of treatment. Reassure Liz that, should she need more help than the contracted amount of help, there will be provision for follow-up and possible referral.

Intervention.   Crisis intervention proceeds on several fronts. First, you encourage Liz to leave her room to attend classes, eat meals, and visit friends. You urge her to open up to friends and family about how she is feeling. Your listening encourages expression of her feelings about the fiancé and the breakup. You give Liz information about "normal" college relationships, the experience of developing and dissolving romantic relationships, grief, and starting over. You suggest she keep a journal to record her feelings, because writing has been an outlet for her.

Termination.   In the fourth session, you broach the topic of the upcoming termination. She seems comfortable with the idea and is able to review her progress. She expresses relief at not needing more extensive treatment.

from time to time. She reports feeling more optimistic about her future and has begun the process of job hunting.

When you call Liz a few weeks after termination, she sounds upset. She says she feels bad at having "backslid." She is again feeling unable to cope with the breakup because she and her ex continue to see each other daily in their residence hall. She reports problems with sleeping and eating, although she still is talking with her friends and getting to classes.

Follow-up.   When you learn that Liz is not doing well, you consider other treatment or service options. Among the services now offered at your counseling center is a semi-structured therapy group that aids students in recovering from broken relationships. You inform Liz about the group and refer her to it. You may meet with her personally or refer her directly to the group clinician.

Evaluation

T here are enormous difficulties with evaluating the effectiveness of any form of treatment performed in college counseling centers. The staff of Yale University's Mental Hygiene Clinic believed that evaluative research was impossible after facing some of these obstacles: (a) completing research protocols was a burden to overworked staff, (b) controlling for initial severity and chronicity of clients' problems was difficult, (c) positive treatment results could be attributable to "transference," (d) there was question as to whether clinician or client satisfaction should be the outcome variable (Arnstein, 1979). Moreover, research is barely a tertiary function at counseling centers, with most resources budgeted for direct service (Pinkerton, 1986).

These drawbacks are compounded by the special problems in evaluating crisis-oriented counseling. As McGee (1980) noted, this research is hampered by many factors, such as lack of specificity as to what constitutes a crisis and by a too broad definition of crisis intervention. For example, Butcher and Maudal (1976) make a distinction between crisis intervention and crisis therapy, the former being a method of case disposition.

Given these research impediments, evaluations of individual crisis-oriented counseling in college counseling centers are rarely reported. However, a number of studies have appeared which attempt to evaluate the effectiveness of brief or very brief individual counseling interventions. Many brief therapy contacts are precipitated by crises, and many counseling relationships are brief due to the acute situational and developmental crises common to students. Brief and very brief counseling interventions may represent the best available paradigm for evaluating Level I (Harmon & Baron,

1982) campus crisis intervention. However, the results must be viewed with caution since no study differentiates crisis from noncrisis therapy contact, and it is not known if the brief intervention was crisis-oriented therapy or some traditional therapy practiced in a time-limited framework.

Dorosin, Gibbs, and Kaplan (1976) discovered that 50 to 60 percent of the students served at Stanford University's Counseling and Psychological Services were seen three or fewer times. Dorosin et al. noted that their service emphasized crisis interventions and developmental concerns. They wondered if these "very brief interventions" meant dissatisfied therapy dropouts. Evaluation questionnaires were sent to a sample of former clients and a questionnaire return rate of 54 percent was achieved. Eighty percent of the respondents had a positive evaluation of the intervention. In fact, the students rated counseling as being more effective than did their clinicians. Haggerty, Baldwin, and Liptzin (1980) at the University of North Carolina replicated the Dorosin et al. research and obtained similar findings. Seventy-two percent of their very brief intervention clients expressed satisfaction; only 16 percent left dissatisfied. Haggerty et al. concluded that these interventions appear to be more often associated with rapid goal achievement than with client dissatisfaction.

Brown, Binder, and Johannessen (1980), using a questionnaire adapted from the Symptom Check-List, found significant self-rated improvement on major symptoms after brief individual therapy (from two to eight sessions). For students with anxiety neurosis, depressive neurosis, and adjustment reaction, improvement ranged from 81.8 to 88.4 percent. Again, self-reported improvement rates were higher than clinicians' estimates. More recently, Talley, Roy, and Moorman (1986) evaluated brief therapy performed at Duke University's Counseling and Psychological Services. They found that 70 percent of the students who received one to three sessions were "quite satisfied" with therapy; the figures for students receiving seven to nine sessions was 80 percent.

Thus, there is evidence that students endorse the effectiveness of brief treatment. Again, these studies cannot be construed as evidence of the effectiveness of crisis intervention per se with college students. Thorny methodological issues must be overcome (e.g., definition of crisis, agreement as to what constitutes crisis intervention therapy, and selection of relevant outcome criteria) in order to perform more finely tuned crisis intervention evaluation research.

Quality Assessment

Counseling centers cannot rely on length of waiting lists or popularity of particular clinicians as indicators of the quality of service provided (Whitaker, 1979). The need to assess the quality of counseling at the University of Massachusetts Mental Health Service led Sarnat (1979) to develop a problem list to document client improvement. The problem list form was devised to record changes in the problem(s) initially defined or focused on in therapy. Sarnat used resolution or nonresolution of problems as the

Figure 5.1   *Problem List Form*

Patient name _____   Intake date _____
Therapist name _____   Termination date _____

Problem	Date defined	ID'd by patient?	Target?	Code		Documentation (Intensity, Severity, Duration)	*Severity discomfort
					Initial		
					At term.		
						Difference:	
					Initial		
					At term.		
						Difference:	
					Initial		
					At term.		
						Difference:	

(use 2nd sheet to list any additional problems)   *Severity: 0 unappreciable
                                                                      1 mild
                                                                      2 moderate
                                                                      3 marked
                                                                      4 severe

SOURCE: From the *Journal of the American College Health Association*, vol. 28, December 1979, p. 135. Reprinted with permission of the Helen Dwight Reid Educational Foundation. Published by Heldref Publications, 4000 Albermarle St., N.W., Washington, DC 20016. Copyright © 1979.

outcome measure because the problem-oriented approach is relevant to brief/crisis-oriented counseling, which involves resolving specifically defined problems.

The problem list can be completed by the clinician at intake and termination. A brief statement of problems as specified in the problem focus stage of intervention, the date on which the problem was defined, and whether student or clinician initially date on which the problem was defined, and whether student or clinician initially identified the problem are entered in columns 1, 2, and 3. Column 4 asks if a particular problem is targeted for intervention. Column 5 allows for classifying the problem for later data analysis. In column 6 the clinician describes the problem and notes its intensity, severity, and duration. In the last column the clinician rates the severity of discomfort and impairment of functioning that each problem causes the student. Discomfort and impairment levels are rated at both intake and termination, and the different yields a measure of improvement. Sarnat's model could be expanded to include a third rating at follow-up.

Summary

C risis-oriented therapy is a valuable and appropriate intervention for a college student population. Campus crisis intervention consists of more than individual, face-to-face counseling in order to stabilize a client and should include consultative interventions targeted toward those who work with students as well as ecological interventions that can prevent crises. In this chapter a variety of examples were presented that illustrate how selected universities across the United States have implemented service delivery strategies at each of three levels of crisis intervention.

A goal of this chapter was to explicate a model for the clinical practice of crisis intervention and to present clinical examples and a case vignette to demonstrate how the model is applied to problems presented by college students.

Clinicians in college and university settings are all too often overwhelmed by the weight of their caseloads, and service delivery is of primary concern. Unfortunately, little time, energy, and budget are left for evaluating campus crisis services. Assessment of the effectiveness of brief/crisis-oriented therapies is a crucial but neglected undertaking. For an all inclusive discussion of appropriate methods and techniques for evaluating crisis services, see Chapter 15.

References

Aiello, J. R., Baum, A., & Gormley, F. P. (1981). "Social Determinants of Residential Crowding Stress." *Personality and Social Psychology Bulletin, 7,* 643–649.

Arnstein, R. L. (1979). "Psychotherapy Quality Assessment. Part Three: Discussion." *Journal of the American College Health Association, 28,* 131–139.

Barrow, J. C., Talley, J. E., Miller, K. H., & Zung, W. W. K. (1985). "The Zung Self-Rating Depression Scale as an Intake Screening Instrument." In J. E. Talley & W. J. K. Rockwell (Eds.), *Counseling and Psychotherapy Services for University Students* (pp. 50–61). Springfield, IL: Thomas.

Beck, J. C., Kovacks, M., & Weissman, A. (1979). "Assessment of Suicidal Ideation: The Scale for Suicide Ideation." *Journal of Consulting and Clinical Psychology, 47,* 343–352.

Boekelheide, P. D. (1978). "The Diagnostic/Therapeutic Preabortion Interview." *Journal of the American College Health Association, 27,* 157–160.

Bogal-Allbritten, R. B., & Allbritten, W. L. (1985). "The Hidden Victims: Courtship Violence Among College Students." *Journal of College Student Personnel, 26,* 201–204.

Brown, B. M., Binder, M., & Johannessen, K. (1980). "Brief Psychiatric Treatment and Symptom Improvement in University Students." *Journal of the American College Health Association, 28,* 330–335.

Burral, A. M. (1985). "Student Mental Health: A Survey of University Programs." Unpublished manuscript. University of Chicago.

Butcher, J. N., & Koss, M. P. (1978). "Research on Brief and Crisis-Oriented Therapies." In S. L. Garfield & A. E. Bergin (Eds.), *Handbook of Psychotherapy and Behavior Change* (2nd ed., pp. 725–767). New York: Wiley.

Butcher, J. N., & Maudal, G. R. (1976). "Crisis Intervention." In I. B. Weiner (Ed.), *Clinical Methods in Psychology.* New York: Wiley.

Caplan, G. (1964). *Principles of Preventive Psychiatry.* New York: Basic Books.

Chickering, A. W. (1969). *Education and Identity.* San Francisco: Jossey-Bass.

Clack, R. J., Stone, C. T., & Thurman, C. W. (1984). "Waiting Lists at University and College Counseling Centers: A National Survey." *Journal of College Student Personnel, 25,* 45–49.

Conyne, R. K., Banning, J. H., Clack, R. J., Corazzini, J. G., Huebner, L. A., Keating, L. A., & Wrenn, R. L. (1979). "The Campus Environment as Client: A New Direction for College Counselors." *Journal of College Student Personnel, 20,* 437–442.

Corazzini, J. G., Wilson, S. E., & Huebner, L. A. (1977). "The Environmental Satisfaction Questionnaire." *Journal of College Student Personnel, 18,* 169–173.

Council for the Advancement of Standards for Student Services/Developmental Programs. (1986). *Standards and Guidelines for Counseling Services.* Washington, DC: Author.

Dana, R. H., Heynen, F., & Burdette, R. (1974). "Crisis Intervention by Peers." *Journal of College Student Personnel, 15,* 58–61.

Dorosin, D., Gibbs, J., & Kaplan, L. (1976). "Very Brief Interventions: A Pilot Evaluation." *Journal of the American College Health Association, 24,* 191–194.

Doweiko, H. (1981). "Counseling the Victim of Sexual Assault." *Journal of College Student Personnel, 22,* 41–45.

Ewing, C. P. (1978). *Crisis Intervention as Brief Psychotherapy.* New York: Oxford.

Farnsworth, D. L. (1966). *Psychiatry, Education, and the Young Adult.* Springfield, IL: Thomas.

Gould, N. B. (1980). "Postabortion Depressive Reactions in College Women." *Journal of the American College Health Association, 28,* 316–320.

Haggerty, J. J., Baldwin, B. A., & Liptzin, M. B. (1980). "Very Brief Interventions in College Mental Health." *Journal of the American College Health Association, 28,* 326–329.

Halberg, L. J. (1986). "Death of a College Student: Response by Student Professionals on One Campus." *Journal of Counseling and Development, 64,* 411–412.

Hanfmann, E. (1978). *Effective Therapy for College Students.* San Francisco: Jossey-Bass.

Harmon, F. M., & Baron, A. (1982). "A Student-Focused Model for the Development of Counseling Services. *Personnel and Guidance Journal, 60,* 290–293.

Hill, F. E., & Harmon, F. M. (1976). "The Use of Telephone Tapes in a Telephone Counseling Program." *Crisis Intervention, 7,* 88–96.

Hipple, J. L., Cimbolic, P., & Peterson, J. (1980). "Student Services Response to a Suicide." *Journal of College Student Personnel, 21,* 457–458.

Jones, F., & Najera, G. A. (1976). "The Helping Network: Reaction and Actions Stimulated by Students' Acute Mental Illness in a University Community." *Journal of the American College Health Association, 24,* 198–202.

Katz, R. C., & Viventi, J. (1976). "Educational Intervention Following a Dormitory Crisis." *Journal of Consulting and Clinical Psychology, 44,* 877.

Lanyon, R. I. (1973). *Psychological Screening Inventory Manual.* Goshen, NY: Research Psychologists Press.

Leventhal, A. M., Berman, A. L., McCarthy, B. W., & Wasserman, C. W. (1976). "Peer Counseling on the University Campus." *Journal of College Student Personnel, 17,* 504–509.

McCarthy, B. W., & Brown, P. A. (1974). "Counseling College Women With Unwanted Pregnancies." *Journal of College Student Personnel, 15,* 58–60.

McGee, T. F. (1980). "Crisis Intervention." In M. S. Gibbs, J. R. Lackenmeyer, & J. Sigal (Eds.), *Community Psychology: Theoretical and Empirical Approaches* (pp. 239–266). New York: Gardner.

Miller, B., & Marshall, J. C. (1987). "Coercive Sex on the University Campus." *Journal of College Student Personnel, 28,* 38–47.

Mishara, B. L. (1982). "College Students' Experiences With Suicide and Reaction to Suicidal Verbalizations: A Model for Prevention." *Journal of Community Psychology, 10,* 142–150.

Mishara, B. L., Baker, A. H., & Mishara, T. T. (1976). "The Frequency of Suicide Attempts: A Retrospective Approach Applied to College Students." *American Journal of Psychiatry, 133,* 841–844.

Ottens, A. J. (1983). "Evaluation of a Crisis Training Program in Suicide Prevention for the Campus Community." *Crisis Intervention, 13,* 25–40.

Ottens, A. J. (1985). *Coping With Romantic Breakup.* New York: Rosen.

Pascarella, E. T., & Terenzini, P. T. (1976). "Informal Interaction With Faculty and Freshman Ratings of the Academic and Non-Academic Experience of College." *Journal of Educational Research, 70,* 35–41.

Pascarella, E. T., & Terenzini, P. T. (1981). "Residence Arrangement, Student/Faculty Relationships, and Freshman-Year Educational Outcomes." *Journal of College Student Personnel, 22,* 147–156.

Patterson, V., & O'Sullivan, M. (1979). "Three Perspectives on Brief Psychotherapy." *American Journal of Psychotherapy, 28,* 265–277.

Pinkerton, R. S. (1986). "Brief Individual Counseling and Psychotherapy With Students." In J. E. Talley & W. J. K. Rockwell (Eds.), *Counseling and Psychotherapy With College Students.* New York: Praeger.

Raphael, T., Power, S. H., & Berridge, W. L. (1937). "The Question of Suicide as a Problem in College Mental Hygiene." *American Journal of Orthopsychiatry, 7,* 1–14.

Rockwell, W. J. K. (1986). "Issues in Psychiatric Management." In J. E. Talley & W. J. K. Rockwell (Eds.), *Counseling and Psychotherapy With College Students* (pp. 113–122). New York: Praeger.

Roney, L. K., Wiley, M. O., Croteau, J. M., & Gelwick, B. P. (1986, April). "Psychological Emergencies on Campus: Standard of Care Issues." Paper presented at the meeting of the American College Personnel Association, New Orleans, LA.

Salovey, P., & D'Andrea, V. J. (1984). "A Survey of Campus Peer Counseling Activities." *Journal of the American College Health Association, 32,* 262–265.

Sanford, N. (1962). *The American College.* New York: Wiley.

Sarnat, J. E. (1979). "Psychotherapy Quality Assessment. Part Two: Psychotherapy Quality Assessment Via Record Review." *Journal of the American College Health Association, 28,* 133–137.

Schwartz, A. J., & Pierce, R. A. (1976). "College Mental Health Consultation: A Case Study." *Journal of the American College Health Association, 24,* 163–166.

Smith, M. C., & Thelen, M. H. (1984). "Development and Validation of a Test for Bulimia." *Journal of Consulting and Clinical Psychology, 52,* 863–872.

Sprinkle, R. L., & Matthews, T. E. (1984). "A Model and a Program for Emergency Student Services." *Journal of College Student Personnel, 25,* 476–477.

Talley, J. E., Roy, E. T., & Moorman, J. C. (1986). "What Components of Counseling Work Best With Whom and When: A Study." In J. E. Talley & W. J. K. Rockwell (Eds.), *Counseling and Psychotherapy With College Students* (pp. 142–170). New York: Praeger.

Terenzini, P. T., & Pascarella, E. T. (1980). "Student/Faculty Relationships and Freshmen Year Educational Outcomes: A Further Investigation." *Journal of College Student Personnel, 21,* 521–528.

Thurman, C. W., Baron, A., & Klein, R. L. (1979). "Self-Help Tapes in a Telephone Counseling Service: A Three-Year Analysis." *Journal of College Student Personnel, 20,* 546–550.

Tucker, B. J., Megenity, D., & Vigil, L. (1970). "Anatomy of a Campus Crisis Center." *Personnel and Guidance Journal, 48,* 343–348.

Walden, T. A., Nelson, P. A., & Smith, D. E. (1981). "Crowding, Privacy, and Coping." *Environment and Behavior, 13,* 205–224.

Waldo, M. (1984). "Roommate Communication as Related to Students' Personal and Social Adjustment." *Journal of College Student Personnel, 25,* 39–44.

Weiss, S. D., & Kapp, R. A. (1974). "An Inter-Disciplinary Campus Mental Health Program Specializing in Crisis-Oriented Services." *Professional Psychology, 5,* 25–31.

Werner, A., & Jones, M. D. (1979). "Parent Loss in College Students." *Journal of the American College Health Association, 27,* 253–256.

Whitaker, L. C. (1979). "Psychotherapy Quality Assessment. Part One: The Need for Quality Assessment." *Journal of the American College Health Association, 28,* 131–133.

White, W. C., & Ottens, A. J. (1979, May). "Crisis Intervention: The Cornell Plan." Paper presented at the meeting of the American College Health Association, Washington, DC.

Whitely, S. M., Mahaffey, P. J., & Geer, C. A. (1987). "A Profile of Staffing Patterns and Services. *Journal of College Student Personnel, 28,* 71–81.

Zung, W. W. K. (1965). "A Self-Rating Depression Scale." *Archives of General Psychiatry, 12,* 63–70.

Part III

CRISIS INTERVENTION WITH VICTIMS OF VIOLENCE AND THEIR ABUSERS

THE development of rapid assessment and crisis intervention programs for survivors of victimization and their abusers is a recent phenomenon. During the past decade, a proliferation of rape crisis centers, emergency shelters for battered women and their children, child abuse hotlines, and crisis-oriented treatment programs for abusive parents have emerged. The recent proliferation of programs for survivors of family violence, forcible rape, and other violent crimes came into being as an outgrowth of the women's movement, the crime victims' movement, and eventual federal and state legislation to fund these innovative crisis intervention programs.

By the late 1970s, rape crisis centers were developed as a result of federal funding from the now defunct Law Enforcement Assistance Administration and from the National Center for the Prevention and Control of Rape (of the National Institute of Mental Health). Emergency shelters and crisis intervention programs for battered women received substantial staffing support as a result of funding from the Comprehensive Employment and

Training Administration (CETA). Other funding sources for victim services were community development, ACTION, and state human service block grants. Most of these funding sources have been disbanded or significantly cut back as a result of the Reagan administration's fiscal cuts. During the early 1980s family violence and victim assistance programs in several states had difficulty staying open and those that could not locate alternative funding had to close.

The victims' movement is now thriving. In recent years, through state general revenue grants and innovative state authorized funding sources, family violence and victim assistance programs have received increased, stable funding. More specifically, 48 states now have provisions for the funding of domestic violence intervention programs. Thirty-four states have funding mechanisms for general victim service and victim/witness assistance programs at the local level. Twenty-five states have provided funding for local sexual assault crisis services. The primary state mechanisms for raising funds designated for family violence and victim assistance programs include the following:

Fixed penalty assessment on persons convicted of criminal and/or traffic offenses

Variable penalty assessments levied by judges on convicted felons

A surcharge on all criminal fines

State income tax check-offs

Bail forfeiture funding and marriage, divorce, birth, and death certificate surcharges

Wages earned by convicted offenders

Notoriety-for-profit laws

Alcohol taxes

Recognition of the need for and actual establishment of crisis intervention for survivors of the battering syndrome has increased dramatically since the mid-1970s. While there were only seven emergency shelters for battered women and four police-based crisis intervention programs in 1974, by 1987 there were more than 1,250 emergency shelters and crisis services for battered women and their children.

Chapter 6 begins by focusing on the nature of crisis assessments with battered women in both police victim assistance programs and hospital emergency rooms. It then discusses detection and assessment of batterment through the use of an adult abuse protocol which was developed by social workers at Harborview Medical Center in Seattle.

The chapter proceeds by presenting the step-by-step procedures and techniques used by the Marital Abuse Project of Delaware County, Pennsylvania, and Abuse Counseling and Treatment of Fort Myers, Florida. The innovative and structured procedures and guidelines for staff at these shelters should prove useful to staff working with battered women in crisis at other programs as well. Finally, Chapter 6 focuses on the psychosocial needs of the children of abused women. This discussion is based on the model crisis intervention programs developed by social workers at a mental health center in White Plains, New York; St. Martha's Hall in St. Louis, Missouri; Jersey Battered Women's Service in Morristown, New Jersey; and Haven House in Buffalo, New York.

Chapter 7 provides a format and model for using crisis intervention techniques with sexual assault victims. This chapter focuses on those assessment and crisis intervention strategies shown to be effective with both adolescent and adult female sexual assault victims. This chapter is further designed to familiarize graduate students and the practicing clinician with a variety of issues and processes involving sexual assault. Among these are current research findings; myths regarding sexual assault; symptom complexity and the sexual assault syndrome; cognitive, social, physiological and psychological sequelae; and program evaluation.

Chapter 7 includes a detailed discussion of the similarities and differences in the issues a sexual assault victim must cope with compared to victims of other types of life crises. These issues which impact on the severity of the crisis response include the preassault adjustment of the victim, the extent of violence and injuries, the response of the victim's social support system, the age of the victim, culture and religious beliefs, and attitudes held by both the victim and her family. The chapter concludes by briefly reviewing the research on crisis intervention with sexual assault victims. The authors recommend continuing empirical research in this area, particularly with regard to program evaluation and treatment efficacy.

Chapter 8 focuses on intervention with abusive parents. The short-term crisis intervention model that the authors describe is known as cognitive coercive group therapy. This chapter reports on group therapy—as required by the courts or other authorities—for physically abusive parents from 40 families. The threatened dissolution of the family by court action created a crisis for the parents and opened them up to change. Goal Attainment Scaling was used as both a therapeutic tool and as a means of evaluating outcome. The Holmes-Rahe Social Readjustment Rating Scale was also used to measure stress scores from change events upon entering and completing therapy. By the end of therapy, life change scores among the abusive couples had dropped significantly.

A Comprehensive Model for Crisis Intervention with Battered Women and Their Children

ALBERT R. ROBERTS, D.S.W., AND
BEVERLY SCHENKMAN ROBERTS, M.ED.

D o you know what some women get for their birthdays? A black eye, a punch in the ribs, or a few teeth knocked out. It's so frightening because it doesn't just happen on their birthday. It may be every month, every week, or even every day. It's so frightening because sometimes he abuses the kids, too. Or maybe she's pregnant and he kicks her in the stomach in the same spot where, just a few minutes ago, she felt the baby moving. It's so frightening because the woman doesn't know what to do. She feels so helpless. He's in control. She prays he'll come to his senses and stop. He never does. She prays he won't hurt their kids. He threatens to. She prays he won't kill her. He promises he will . . . (Haag, undated).

This description of the fear and anguish to which battered women are repeatedly subjected comes from a training manual for crisis clinicians prepared by the Domestic Violence Intervention Program of Brown County, Wisconsin. It is included in the manual to acquaint staff and volunteers with the painful history of the women they will be counseling. Increasingly, battered women are turning to emergency shelters and telephone crisis intervention services for help.

Recognition of the need for and actual establishment of crisis intervention for victims of the battering syndrome has increased dramatically since the mid-1970s.

While there were only seven emergency shelters for battered women in 1974 (Roberts, 1981), by 1987 there were more than 1,200 shelters and crisis intervention services coast-to-coast for battered women and their children (National Coalition Against Domestic Violence, 1988). Through crisis intervention, many women are able to regain control of their lives by identifying current options and goals and by working to attain those goals. The children of battered women may also be in crisis, but their plight has often been overlooked as the domestic violence programs focused their efforts on emergency intervention for the women. The progressive programs now incorporate crisis intervention for children (as well as for the mothers) in the treatment plan.

Battered women are usually subjected to a prolonged pattern of abuse coupled with a recent severe attack, so by the time the victim makes contact with a shelter she is generally in need of crisis intervention. Abused women are subjected to an extended period of stress and trauma which results in a continual loss of energy. The woman is in a vulnerable position, and when a particularly severe beating takes place or when other factors occur (e.g., the abuser starting to hurt the children) the woman may be thrust into a state of crisis (National Organization for Victim Assistance; *Nova,* 1983).

Effective treatment for battered women and their children in crisis requires an understanding of crisis theory and the techniques of crisis intervention. According to Caplan (1964), Aguilera and Messick (1984), and Janosik (1984), a crisis state can occur rapidly when the following four things happen:

1. The victim experiences a precipitating or hazardous incident.
2. The incident is perceived by the woman as threatening to her or her children's safety, and as a result tension and distress intensify.
3. The battered woman attempts to resolve the situation by using customary coping methods and fails.
4. The emotional discomfort and turmoil worsen and the victim feels that the pain or anguish is unbearable.

At this point of maximum discomfort, when the woman perceives the pain and torment as unbearable, she is in an active crisis state. During this time there is an opportunity for change and growth and some women are mobilized to seek help from a 24-hour telephone crisis intervention service, the police, the hospital emergency room, or a shelter for battered women.

The emphasis in crisis assessment is on identifying the nature of the precipitating event and the woman's cognitive and affective reaction to it. The three most common precipitating events which lead battered women in crisis to seek the help of a domestic violence program are (a) an acute battering incident resulting in serious physical injury, (b) a serious abusive injury inflicted on the woman's child, and (c) a temporary impairment of hearing, sight, or thought process as a direct result of severe batterment. Often the precipitating event is perceived by the woman in crisis as being the final incident or "last straw" in a long history of violence (Edington, 1987; Houston, 1987; Podhorin, 1987; and Schiller-Ramirez, 1987).

Crisis intervention with battered women needs to be done in an orderly, structured, and humanistic manner. The process is the same for victims of other violent crimes but it is particularly important to respond quickly to abused women because they may continue to be in danger the longer they remain in a place where the batterer can locate them. Crisis intervention activities can result in the woman either returning to her precrisis state or growing from the crisis intervention so that she learns new coping skills to use in the future.

This chapter will describe the following types of crisis intervention: early intervention by police-based crisis teams and victim assistance units; assessment and detection in the hospital emergency room; specific intervention techniques used by crisis hotlines and battered women's shelters; and short-term treatment for the children. The chapter will also discuss the importance of referrals.

Crisis Intervention by Police-Based Crisis Teams and Victim Assistance Units

S urveys of police departments around the United States indicate that approximately 80 to 90 percent of the police officers' time is spent on service calls, also known as order maintenance activities, for such incidents as assaults among family members, neighbor disputes, bar fights, traffic accidents, and individuals who are drunken and disorderly. The police may have the skills to intervene and resolve a dispute among neighbors, a bar fight, or a traffic accident, but they are rarely skilled to provide crisis intervention and follow-up counseling with victims of domestic violence.

In recognition of the large amount of time police spend responding to repeat family assault calls and their lack of clinical skills, several police departments have developed crisis intervention teams which are staffed by professional crisis clinicians and trained volunteers.

Victims often turn to their local city or county police department when confronted with the life-threatening danger posed by domestic violence. As a result of the Thurman case (in which a battered woman was awarded $2.3 million in her lawsuit against the Torrington, Connecticut, police department for its failure to protect her from her violent husband), more police departments are responding to calls from domestic violence victims. Police can respond quickly to domestic violence calls and can transport the victim to the local hospital emergency room or the battered women's shelter. In some cities, police receive backup from the crisis team, which arrives at the home shortly after the police. The first such crisis team began in 1975 at the Pima County District Attorney's Office in Tucson, Arizona. The acceptance of and growing reliance on this program by the Tucson Police Department is revealed by the significantly increased number of police referrals to the crisis team—there were a total of 840 police referrals in 1977 compared to 4,734 referrals in 1984. It should be noted that these figures reflect referrals for all types of crime victims, but most referrals are for domestic violence cases. Since violence in the home constitutes a considerable percentage of police calls, abused women are frequent beneficiaries of this innovative system.

The following descriptions of programs in Tucson and Houston will illustrate the intervention procedures utilized by victim assistance programs.

Tucson Program

The Pima County Victim Witness Program has received national recognition for providing immediate crisis intervention to battered women and other crime victims. It has served as a model for similar programs in other cities.

The program was initiated in 1975 with a grant form the Law Enforcement Assistance Administration (LEAA). The grant-funded program was so successful that, when the grant expired, the city and county officials agreed to pay for its continuation.

The crisis intervention staff uses two police vehicles (unmarked and radio equipped) to travel to the crime scene. The mobile crisis teams are on patrol every night between 6 P.M. and 3 A.M. At all other times they are contacted via a beeper system (Roberts, 1987).

Domestic violence cases are potentially the most dangerous for the crisis counselors. The staff members work in pairs, generally in a team of a male and a female. They are given an intensive training program in which they are taught self-defense, escape driving, and the way to use a police radio, as well as crisis intervention techniques.

Houston Program

In 1983, the Houston Police Department developed a program (modeled after the Tucson program) to provide immediate crisis counseling to victims of domestic violence, as well as victims of other violent crimes such as rape. The Crisis Intervention Team provides the following services: crisis counseling, advocacy, transportation to and from medical centers and shelters, and referrals to social service agencies. An estimated 40 percent of its clients are battered women (Hardman-Muye, 1985).

The Crisis Intervention Team staff are civilian employees of the Houston Police Department and all of the referrals come from the police. A crisis team (always working in groups of two) is notified of a crisis situation via the police radio, and the counselors meet the police at the crime scene. The police, after determining that the counselors will not be in danger, leave the home. The clinicians utilize a basic crisis intervention model of assessing the situation, discussing the options, forming a plan of action, and aiding the victim in implementing the plan. The Houston program has 12 full-time staff members and two to four graduate student interns each semester, and has recently recruited volunteer workers.

The program is funded by a state criminal justice grant and by the city of Houston. Initially all of the budget came from the state grant, but the city is expected to fund an additional 20 percent of the cost each year until it is totally city funded. In its first year, the program was budgeted at $159,000. This amount has increased to $351,000 in its third year of operation.

As of 1986, similar types of crisis intervention programs had been developed under the auspices of the police departments in many cities, including South Phoenix, Arizona; Santa Ana, California; Stockton, California; Indianapolis, Indiana; Detroit, Michigan; Omaha, Nebraska; Las Vegas, Nevada; Rochester, New York; Houston, Texas; and Salt Lake City, Utah. However, there are still many communities which have not initiated this type of crisis intervention program. It is hoped that the success of the newly developed programs will encourage other localities to establish a similar type of service.

Assessment and Intervention in the Emergency Room

A visit to the emergency room may provide the initial opportunity for some victims to recognize the life-threatening nature of the violent relationship and to begin making important plans to change their situations. At a growing number of large hospitals in urban areas, crisis intervention is being provided to battered women by emergency room staff.

A recommended way for emergency rooms to handle detection and assessment of batterment is through the use of an adult abuse protocol. Two of the pioneers in the development of these protocols are Klingbeil and Boyd of Seattle, who in 1976 initiated plans for emergency room intervention with abused women. The Social Work Department of the Harborview Medical Center in Seattle developed an adult abuse protocol which provides specific information on the assessment to be made by the involved staff—the triage nurse, the physician, and the crisis clinician. Using a protocol serves two purposes. First, it alerts the involved hospital staff to provide the appropriate clinical care; second, it documents the violent incident so that if the woman decides to file a legal complaint, "reliable, court-admissible evidence" (including photographs) is available (Klingbeil and Boyd, 1984).

Although this protocol was developed for use by emergency room crisis clinicians, it can easily be adapted for use by other health care personnel. The following case example describes the way in which the adult abuse protocol has been successfully used.

Mrs. J was admitted to the emergency room accompanied by her sister. This was the second visit within the month for Mrs. J and the emergency room triage nurse and social worker realized that her physical injuries were much more severe on this second visit. Mrs. J was crying, appeared frightened, and in spite of the pain, she constantly glanced over her shoulder. She indicated that her husband would follow her to the emergency room and that she feared for her life. The social worker immediately notified Security. . . .

Mrs. J indicated that she just wanted to rest briefly and then leave through another entrance. She was four months pregnant and concerned about her unborn child. She reported that this had been the first time Mr. J had struck her in the abdomen. The social worker spent considerable time calming Mrs. J in order to obtain a history of the assaultive event. Consent for photography was obtained and Mrs. J indicated that she *would* press charges. "The attack on my child" seemed to be a turning point in her perception of the gravity of her situation, even though Mr. J had beaten her at least a dozen times over the previous two years.

While the social worker assisted in the history taking, a physician provided emergency medical care: several sutures over the right eye.

With Mrs. J's permission, an interview was conducted with her sister who agreed to let Mrs. J stay with her and also agreed to participate in the police reporting. When Mrs. J felt able, the social worker and sister helped her complete necessary forms for the police who had been called to the emergency room.

Although the physician had carefully explained the procedures and rationale to Mrs. J, the social worker repeated this information and also informed her of the lethality of the battering, tracing from her chart her last three emergency room visits. Mrs. J was quick to minimize the assaults but when the social worker showed her photographs from those visits, documenting bruises around her face and neck, she shook her head and said, "No more, not any more." Her sister provided excellent support and additional family members were on their way to the emergency room to be with Mrs. J. When the police arrived Mrs. J was able to give an accurate report of the day's events. . . . She realized there would be difficult decisions to make and readily accepted a follow-up counseling appointment for a Battered Women's group (Klingbeil & Boyd, 1984, pp. 16–24).

It should be noted that all cases are not handled as easily as this one. The two aspects of Mrs. J's situation which led to a positive resolution were (a) the immediate involvement of emergency room staff and their discussion with the patient of her history and injuries, and (b) the availability of supportive relatives.

Before the woman leaves the emergency room, the crisis clinician should talk with her about whether to return home or to seek refuge with friends, with family, or at a shelter for abused women. The emergency room staff should be able to provide names and phones numbers of referral sources. It is helpful if the pertinent information is printed on a small business-size card (which would be easy to tuck away in a pocket or purse) and given to all abuse victims as well as to suspected victims (Klingbeil & Boyd, 1984). Even if a woman refuses to acknowledge that her current bruises are the result of batterment, she may keep the card for future use.

Merely having an adult abuse protocol does not ensure that it will be used. A study conducted by Flaherty (1985) at four Philadelphia hospitals found that the protocol was used selectively, mainly for victims who volunteered that they had been battered. The medical staff thus ignored the opportunity to help batterment victims who were not able to volunteer the information. The researchers cited the following reasons for underutilization of the protocol:

1. Some physicians and nurses did not regard battering as a medical problem.
2. Some of the emergency room staff believed that it would be an invasion of privacy to ask a woman questions about how she was injured.
3. Many viewed completing the protocol as an additional burden when they were already overworked.

Of those medical personnel who did recognize batterment as a legitimate problem, the intervention technique used most often was the tear-off list of referral sources which was printed at the bottom of the protocol.

There is a major difference between Flaherty et al.'s Philadelphia study and the procedures described previously by Klingbeil and Boyd (1984) in Seattle. The Philadelphia study requested the cooperation of nurses and physicians but did not involve medical crisis clinicians. In contrast, the Harborview Medical Center protocol was created and implemented by the hospital social work department. It emphasized a multidisciplinary team approach with the social workers taking the lead role in conducting screening and assessment, often talking to the victim while the physician provided medical treatment.

The information just presented would indicate that the involvement of medical social workers is advisable and perhaps necessary in successfully implementing a system for crisis assessment and intervention with battered women in the hospital emergency room.

Intervention Techniques Used by Telephone Hotlines and Battered Women's Shelters*

B attered women in crisis may reach out for help in any of a number of ways. The initial contact is generally by telephone, making the phone line a lifeline for many women. Violence often occurs late in the evening, on weekends, or holidays, and shelter staff are usually available 24 hours a day to respond to a crisis call. But a woman in crisis who has just been brutally beaten probably does not know the name or phone number of the local shelter. A frequent scenario is that of a woman and her children

---

*Parts of this section are adapted from Roberts (1988).

hastily escaping from home late in the evening and fleeing to a neighbor's home to make an emergency call for help. Not having the number of the local shelter, these women generally contact the police or the areawide crisis hotline (which aids people in all types of crisis). If the woman contacts the areawide hotline there is generally a brief delay while the worker gathers some basic information and then gives the caller the phone number of the closest shelter. An alternative is for the crisis intervenor to take the caller's phone number and have the shelter worker call her back.

When a battered woman in crisis calls a hotline it is essential that she be able to talk immediately to a trained crisis clinician—not put on hold or confronted with an answering machine. If she is not able to talk to a caring and knowledgeable crisis clinician she may just give up, and a valuable opportunity for intervening in the cycle of violence will have been lost. In these situations time is of the essence because if the violent male is still on the rampage he is likely to search for her, thereby endangering not only his mate but the neighbor as well.

Hotline workers distinguish between a *crisis call*—one in which the woman is in imminent danger or has just been beaten—and other types of calls in which the individual is not in immediate danger but is anxious or distressed and is seeking information or someone to talk to. The overriding goal of crisis intervention is ensuring the safety of the woman and her children. To determine whether the call is a crisis call, the worker asks such questions as

"Are you or your children in danger now?"

"Is the abuser there now?"

"Do you want me to call the police?"

"Do you want to leave and can you do so safely?"

"Do you need medical attention?'"

Programs have different policies regarding transporting women who need refuge but have no way to get there. While some shelters will send staff to pick up the woman at her home, it is more common for shelter policy to prohibit staff from doing so because of the possibility of the staff member being attacked by the abuser. In cities that have a crisis intervention team affiliated with the police department (such as those described earlier in this chapter), the shelter staff can contact the police, who investigate the situation and radio for the crisis clinicians to transport the victim and her children to the shelter. Sometimes the police themselves are prevailed upon to provide the transportation.

The Marital Abuse Project of Delaware County in Pennsylvania encourages battered women to call the police themselves, but there are circumstances in which they are not able to do so. In those cases, shelter clinicians call the police (with the woman's permission) and then contact the woman again. If the facility has two phone lines there may be times when it is advisable for the worker to keep the woman on the line while the clinician calls the police on the other line. Staff are advised to follow up on the woman's call to law enforcement by waiting a few minutes and then also calling the police to find out where they will be taking her (i.e., to the police station or hospital). If it is too soon for the police to have this information, the clinician asks the officer to call her back when they do know. If 30 minutes have elapsed without a call from the police, the clinician contacts the police department again (Roberts, 1981).

Once the urgent issues pertaining to the woman's physical safety have been resolved, the crisis clinician can begin to help the victim talk about her situation and discuss possible courses of action. Throughout this process it is important for the clinician to remember that he or she can present different alternatives but the client must make her own decisions.

The following is a step-by-step guide to intervention with battered women (originally developed by Jones, 1968) which is included in the training manual prepared by the Abuse Counseling and Treatment (ACT) program in Fort Myers, Florida. It is referred to as the A-B-C process of crisis management—the *A* referring to "Achieving contact," the *B* for "Boiling down the problem," and the *C* for "Coping with the problem."

A. *Achieving contact*
   1. Introduce yourself: name, role, and purpose.
   2. If a phone call, ask the client if she is safe and protected now.
   3. Ask client how she would like to be addressed: first name, surname, or nickname; this helps client regain control.
   4. Collect client data; this breaks the ice and allows the client and clinician to get to know each other and develop trust.
   5. Ask the client if she has a clinician or if she is taking any medication.
   6. Identify the client's feelings and ask for perception check.
B. *Boiling down the problem*
   1. Ask the client to describe briefly what has just happened.
   2. Encourage the client to talk about the here and now.
   3. Ask the client what is the most pressing problem.
   4. Ask the client if it were not for said problems, would she feel better right now.
   5. Ask client if she has been confronted with a similar type of problem before, and if so, how she handled it then. What worked and what didn't?
   6. Review with the client what you heard as the primary problem.
C. *Coping with the problem*
   1. What does the client want to happen?
   2. What is the most important need—the bottom line?
   3. Explore what the client feels is the best solution.
   4. Find out what the client is willing to do to meet her needs.

5. Help the client formulate a plan of action: resources, activities, time.

6. Arrange follow-up contact with the client.

Careful recruitment and thorough training of crisis intervention staff is essential to a program's success. It is also necessary for an experienced clinician to be on call at all times for consultation in difficult cases. In addition to knowing what to say, the clinicians need to learn about the tone of voice and attitude to be used while handling crisis calls. Crisis clinicians are advised to speak in a steady, calm voice, to ask open-ended questions, and to refrain from being judgmental.

A shelter's policies and procedures manual should include guidelines for crisis staff. For example, the ACT program in Fort Myers, Florida, has developed a 45-page training manual which includes sections on shelter policies and procedures, referral procedures, and background information on domestic violence which discusses both the victims and the abusers. The ACT manual explains the wide variation in the emotional reactions of the women who call for help. The client's speaking style may be "fast, slow, hesitant, loud, barely audible, rambling, loss of words, [or] normal." Her emotional reaction may be "angry, highly upset, hysterical, withdrawn, fearful, laughing, calm, icy, guilty, or a combination of these." (Houston, 1987). No matter what characteristics the caller exhibits, the crisis clinician's task is to try to help the victim cope with the immediate situation. However, the guidelines also advise crisis clinicians to avoid the pitfall of believing they need to provide the caller with immediate, expert solutions to her problems. Crisis clinicians should not subject themselves to guilt feelings if they cannot help an abused woman resolve her situation. If the clinician suspects child abuse or neglect, he or she is required to notify the supervisor and then report the suspected abuse to the appropriate agency (Houston, 1987).

Shelter staff are confronted with a dilemma when the caller is an abused woman who is under the influence of drugs or alcohol or who has psychiatric symptoms. Although such women are victims of batterment, they also have a significant problem which the staff are not trained to treat. Shelter policy generally requires crisis inter-venors to screen out battered women who are under the influence of alcohol or drugs, but there are exceptions. At Womanspace (in central New Jersey) women with drug or alcohol problems are accepted provided that they are simultaneously enrolled in a drug or alcohol treatment program (Podhorin, 1987). Likewise, it is the crisis clinician's responsibility to determine whether a woman's behavior is excessively irrational or bizarre or whether she is likely to be a danger to herself or others. If a woman is suspected of having psychiatric problems, she is generally referred to the psychiatric screening unit of a local hospital or to a mental health center for an evaluation.

Another policy issue relates to battered women in crisis who have no psychiatric or drug problems but who are denied admission to a shelter because they have a son aged 12 or older who needs shelter also. Many programs subscribe to the belief that by the time a boy from a violent family reaches the age of 12 he will have adopted his father's violent behavior patterns and they want to avoid the possibility of violent outbursts at the shelter. However, not all shelters have such a policy. There is a minority view that an abused woman in crisis should be helped regardless of whether or not she has a young adolescent son (Arbour, 1987).

Telephone Log

Battered women's shelters usually maintain a written record of all phone calls, whether or not they are crisis calls. In addition to seeking such routine information as name, address, phone number, marital status, and ages of children, the form may also include the following: (a) the questions "Are you in immediate danger?" "Do you want me to call the police?" and "How did you get our number?"; (b) action taken by crisis clinician; and (c) follow-up action (Podhorin, 1987). Shelters which are often over-crowded may also have a part of the form on which the counselor can indicate whether the family is able to be housed immediately, is to be referred to another shelter or safe home, or needs to be put on a waiting list.

Womanspace developed a one-page telephone log form which on the front asks many of the questions just listed and on the reverse side contains further screening questions and an explanation of their policies. An example is the following printed statement which explains the program's policy on weapons (Podhorin, 1987):

We do not allow weapons in the shelter.

We ask that you not bring a weapon or anything that may be used as a weapon with you.

Do you own a weapon?

If yes, do you agree to let us keep it in a safe place for you?

The advantage of printing this and other procedural statements on every telephone form is to ensure that all crisis workers impart the same basic information.

At the bottom of each form is a list of nine of the most frequently used telephone numbers, including those of three area police departments. The advantage of having those phone numbers on every form is that during a crisis, those numbers are always readily available and valuable time is not lost searching for them.

Group Therapy

Once the woman and her children have arrived at a shelter or other safe place and the immediate danger of further violence has passed, group counseling can be initiated. Rhodes and Zelman (1986) have developed group therapy sessions based on a crisis intervention model which are intended for mothers as well as their children. The sessions are provided for current and former residents of a spouse abuse shelter in White Plains, New York, and are led by staff from a local mental health clinic. The clinic staff believe that the families who come to the shelter are in crisis; therefore, group treatment focuses on crisis intervention principles. The group sessions emphasize (a) relieving feelings of isolation and alienation of persons in crisis, and (b) strengthening the relationship between the mother and children, which is viewed as the natural support group.

When the women come to the shelter, the group leader talks to them individually and develops a treatment plan for the woman and her children. The group sessions are one component of the treatment plan. The group leader is careful not to overlook the needs of the children during group sessions. As a result of the children's presence, special types of intervention are included, such as playing, educating parents, modeling appropriate parent–child interactions, and encouraging the children to facilitate an exchange of ideas and feelings.

The one-hour sessions are held at the shelter two afternoons a week. During the first 45 minutes of each meeting there is discussion, while the last 15 minutes are reserved for play activities the children have chosen.

Treatment for the Children

B attered women who seek temporary shelter to escape from the violence at home generally have children who come to the shelter with them. The children often feel confused, afraid, and angry. They miss their father and do not know if or when they will see him again. It is not uncommon for children to be misinformed or uninformed about the reason they were suddenly uprooted from their home, leaving their personal possessions, friends, and school to stay at a crowded shelter. Similarly, the children may not realize that all of the other children have come to the shelter for the same reason.

Moreover, large numbers of these children have at one time or another also been victims of physical abuse. The 1986 Annual Report from the Family Violence Center in Green Bay, Wisconsin, provided data on child abuse committed by the batterer. The center found that close to half (73) of the 148 abusers of the women had on one or more occasions also beaten their children (Prelipp, 1987).

The following is a true story written by a 10-year-old girl who came to a shelter after her father's violent attack on her mother.

My Life
by Lisa, a 10-year-old shelter resident

One day around two months ago my mom and dad got into a fight. First, my mom and I came home from the mall. We had a really nice time there. But, when we came home our nice time got to be terrible. I knew they were going to get into a fight so I went into my bedroom and did my homework. I knew he was going to talk to her about something, but I didn't know what. Then I heard my mom start screaming and I went to the door and asked what was wrong. My dad said, "Oh, nothing is wrong. Go do your homework." But I knew something was wrong so I went and prayed to God. My dad was really mean that night. I hated him so bad. My mom did not deserve to get hurt. I love her more than anything else in the entire world. Then I heard my mom scream something but I didn't understand what she said because my dad covered her mouth with his hand. Afterward she told me she said call the cops. Anyway, I went back to the door by the bedroom and told my mom I needed help on my homework, but I didn't. I just wanted my mom to come out of the bedroom because I was afraid. Then they both came out. And I hugged my mom and went to bed. Then my dad started to strangle my mom. So I went out and told my dad to stop. He told me to go back to the bedroom and go to sleep. So, I did. But I was so stupid. Then I heard my mom screaming. So I went back into the living room and he was kicking my mom. He wouldn't stop, he kept kicking her in her arm and legs. I told him to stop. He told me to go back to bed but I said, No! Then he took his guitar and was gonna hit her over the head. But I went on top of my mother. He told me to get off. But I said, No. So he put down the guitar, then he got her ice for her arm. Then I went to sleep crying. The next morning I didn't go to school and she didn't go to work. Then he called up the house and talked to her for a while. He threatened to kill her. So we left to go to the shelter. And here I am now. (*Disabuse*, 1986)

This girl was fortunate in that her mother brought her to the Jersey Battered Women's Service in northern New Jersey, which has a carefully developed counseling program for battered mothers and their children. Sadly, however, the majority of shelters offer only basic child care services; they do not provide the crisis counseling needed to help the children deal with the turmoil of recent events (Alessi and Hearn, 1984).

Nevertheless, innovative techniques for helping the children have been incorporated into the program of the more progressive shelters. At St. Martha's Hall, a shelter in St. Louis, Missouri, in addition to providing counseling for the children, the shelter requires mothers to participate in parenting classes and to meet with the coordinator of the children's program about establishing family goals and meeting the child's individual needs. The program also provides opportunities for mother and child to participate jointly in relaxing recreational activities (Schiller-Ramirez, 1987). Group therapy for mothers and children has been discussed. Two other types of intervention—coloring books and groups for children—will be described next.

Coloring Books as Part of an Individualized Treatment Approach

Some shelters utilize specially designed coloring books which discuss domestic violence in terms children can understand. Laura Prato of the Jersey Battered Women's Service in Morristown, New Jersey, has created two coloring books (Prato, undated)—one for children aged 3 to 5 entitled *What Is a Shelter?* and another for 6- to 11-year-olds called *Let's Talk It Over.* In addition to the children's books Prato has written two manuals for shelter workers which serve as a discussion guide for the counselors. The books contain realistic, sensitive illustrations which depict the confused, sad, and angry emotions the children are feeling. They are illustrated in black and white so that the children can color the pictures if they wish. Funding for preparation and printing of the books and manuals came from the New Jersey Division of Youth and Family Services.

The purpose of the coloring books and the way in which they are to be used is explained in the introduction to the counselors' manuals. The manuals state that the books are used as part of the intake and orientation process for all children who stay at the shelter. The stated objectives of the books are as follows:

To provide assurances of the child's continued care and safety

To encourage children to identify and express their feelings

To provide information needed for children to understand what is happening in their families

To provide information which will improve each child's ability to adapt to the shelter setting

To begin to assess the individual child's needs and concerns

The clinicians' manuals stress the importance of the way in which the book is presented to the child, as shown in the following passage:

> The process surrounding the use of the orientation books is extremely important. It is likely to be the initial contact between the counselor and the newly arrived family and one that will set the tone for future interactions. Consistent with the JBWS Children's Program philosophy, this initial meeting communicates respect for mother and child and acceptance of their feelings. (Prato, undated)

Before meeting with the child, the clinician meets privately with the mother to show her the book, explain its purpose, and ask for her permission to read the book to her child. The clinicians are advised to read any available intake information prior to meeting with the child so that the clinician is better able to "anticipate the individual child's special concerns and place the child's responses in a meaningful context" (Prato, undated).

The books have been prepared in a way that encourages the child's active participation. Throughout both books there are several places where the child is given the opportunity to write his or her thoughts on the page. For example, one of the pages in *Let's Talk It Over* focuses on a child staying at a shelter who misses her father. The caption under the picture states:

> Many children at the shelter think a lot about their fathers, and that's okay. You may not see your father for a while until everyone in your family has a chance to think about things carefully. The little girl in the picture is wondering about her father . . . What questions do you think she is asking?"

There is a place on that page for the child's response to the question. The response could be written by the child or dictated to the counselor, who would write it in the book. On the next page of the book is a large blank space and a caption which reads, "You may use this page to draw a picture of your father."

Books such as those developed by the Jersey Battered Women's Service are very appropriate in helping children cope with the crisis which has led to their staying at the shelter.

Group Treatment for Children

Another way to help children cope is through therapeutic groups such as the approach developed at Haven House, a shelter for battered women and their children in Buffalo, New York. Alessi and Hearn (1984) initiated the group approach when they observed the maladaptive ways in which the children reacted to the crisis they were experiencing. The children tended to be aggressive and attempted to resolve problems through hitting. They had considerable anxiety, "biting their fingernails, pulling their hair, and somaticizing feelings as manifested by complaints of headaches and 'tight' stomachs" (Alessi & Hearn, 1984). They had ambivalent feelings toward their fathers, loving them as well as hating them.

The two group leaders established a six-session treatment program for children ages 8 to 16 focusing on the following topics: "(1) the identification and expression of feelings; (2) violence; (3) unhealthy ways to solve problems; (4) healthy ways to solve problems; (5) sex, love and sexuality; and (6) termination and saying goodbye" (Alessi & Hearn, 1984).

To provide an indication of the scope of the group sessions, the following summarizes the content of the session on violence.

Violence.   The purpose of the session on violence is to give children an opportunity to explore and express feelings about the violence in their families and how it has affected them. This helps children break down their denial and minimization of the problem. It also gives children a chance to learn that other families have similar problems and that many families do not. The following questions are presented to each of the children for reflection and discussion:

1. Why did you come to Haven House?
2. Do you think it's right for a man to hit a woman or a woman to hit a man, and why?
3. Do you think it's right for a parent to hit a child, and why?
4. How do you think you've been affected by the violence in your family?
5. Do you think you'll grow up to be violent or accept violence in intimate relationships?

The children are always given homework to keep the session alive between meetings. For example, after the discussion on violence they are asked to develop a minidrama on family violence to be presented the next week. Following the session on healthy problem solving, they are asked to prepare a list of healthy ways of coping with their problems. (Alessi and Hearn, 1984.)

Referral

K nowledge of referral sources is essential. It is just as important for the police, hospitals, and human service agencies to know about and refer to programs helping battered women and their children as it is for staff at domestic violence treatment programs to refer clients to appropriate community resources.

It is frequently determined that the battered woman needs a variety of services, such as job training and placement, low-cost housing, day care, and ongoing counseling; therefore, referral should be made to the appropriate service providers. In its 1986 year-end report, St. Martha's Hall in St. Louis itemized the agencies to which their clients had been referred (Schiller-Ramirez, 1987). Most women were referred to three or more agencies and several clients were given nine or more referrals, depending on their individual needs. The most frequently used referral sources were as follows:

Legal aid

Medical care

Careers for Homemakers

Job Bank

Day care programs

Women in Need (WIN), long-term housing for single women

Alcoholics Anonymous

Women's Self-Help Center, providing counseling and support groups

St. Pat's, a Catholic social service agency that finds low-cost housing and provides classes in budgeting money and other life skills

Examples of other, less frequently used referral sources were

A shelter in another state

Alateen

Al Anon

Literacy Council

Big Brothers

Dental care

GED program

Crisis Nursery

Victim Services

Red Cross

There are two ways in which programs providing crisis intervention services can facilitate the referral process: (a) publicizing their services to the population at large and to other service providers, and (b) becoming knowledgeable about community services needed by their clients and in some instances accompanying them to the appropriate agencies.

Publicize the program through the following methods:
1. Print brochures that describe the program's services and have business cards which provide the program's name and phone number. They should be made available in large quantity to police officers, emergency room staff, and other potential sources of referral to the program.
2. Participate in interdisciplinary workshops and seminars on family violence so that the program can become widely known. In addition, this enables the staff to learn about appropriate programs to which their clients can be referred.
3. Attend in-service training programs for police officers, countywide hotline staff, emergency room staff, and others to discuss referral of abused women and to resolve any problems in the referral process which may have occurred.
4. Alert the public through newspaper articles and public service announcements on radio and television, with the program's phone number prominently mentioned.

Become familiar with community resources. Information for crisis clinicians on appropriate referral sources should be available in several ways:

1. The phone number of the most urgently needed agencies—such as the police, victim assistance program, drug/alcohol treatment programs, and psychiatric screening unit—should be readily available, preferably printed on each intake sheet or telephone log form.
2. The program's training manual should contain a section on the most frequently used referral sources. For example, the manual of the ACT program in Fort Myers, Florida, contains eight pages of often-used referral sources which list the address, phone number, office hours, and services provided for each source.
3. Most of the major metropolitan areas have a comprehensive resource guide (published by the local United Way or an affiliate such as Call for Action) which provides a comprehensive listing of all of the community services in that area. All programs serving abused women and their children should have a copy of and be familiar with their community's resources handbook.

The way in which referrals are made is extremely important, since it may affect the outcome. All too often, victims in crisis do not follow through in making the initial contact with the referral agency. Clinicians at St. Martha's Hall and other shelters provide support by accompanying the client to the agency in order to demonstrate how to obtain services. This is viewed as a positive alternative to the often intimidating and frustrating experience encountered by women who are given a referral but are expected to fend for themselves.

Summary

A number of important issues and techniques relating to crisis intervention with battered women and their children have been examined in this chapter. Specific methods for crisis intervention in different settings have also been discussed. As increased numbers of women in acute crisis seek help, crisis clinicians and victim advocates must be prepared to respond without delay. Crisis counseling for battered women and their children may do much to alleviate the emotional distress and anguish experienced by those exposed to the trauma of domestic violence. Because of their experience and specialized training, crisis clinicians and medical social workers can play a vital role in assisting women and children in crisis.

Law enforcement officers, victim advocates, hospital emergency room staff, and clinicians at areawide crisis lines and battered women's shelters often come in contact with abused women who are experiencing a crisis. Effective crisis intervention requires an understanding by these service providers of the value and methods of crisis intervention as well as the community resources to which referrals should be made.

Battered women are often motivated to change their lifestyle only during the crisis or post-crisis period. Therefore, it is important for service providers at community agencies to offer immediate assistance to battered women in crisis. With an estimated 2 million couples involved in battering episodes annually, policy makers and program developers should give priority to expanding urgently needed crisis-oriented and follow-up services for battered women and their children.

References

Aguilera, D. C., & Messick, J. M. (1984). *Crisis Intervention: Theory and Methodology.* St. Louis, MO: C. V. Mosby.

Alessi, J. J., and Hearn, K. (1984). "Group Treatment of Children in Shelters for Battered Women." In A. R. Roberts (Ed.), *Battered Women and Their Families* (pp. 49–61). New York: Springer.

Arbour, D. (1986, December). *Disabuse Newsletter,* p. 4. Morristown, NJ: Jersey Battered Women's Service.

Arbour, D. (1987, February 12). Director, Jersey Battered Women's Shelter, Morristown, New Jersey. Personal communication.

Caplan, G. (1964). *Principles of Preventive Psychiatry.* New York: Basic Books.

Edington, L. (1987, February 19). Executive Director, *Sojourner,* Indianapolis, Indiana. Personal communication.

Flaherty, E. W. (1985, February). *Identification and Intervention With Battered Women in Hospital Emergency Departments: Final Report.* Philadelphia, PA: Philadelphia Health Management Corp.

Haag, Rita. (Undated). "The Birthday Letter." In S. A. Prelipp, *Family Violence Center, Inc. Training Manual.* Green Bay, WI: mimeographed.

Hardman-Muye, M. (1985, December). Director, Crisis Intervention Team, Houston Police Department. Personal correspondence and response to victim assistance survey.

Houston, S. (1987). *Abuse Counseling and Treatment, Inc. (ACT) Manual.* Fort Myers, FL: ACT.

Janosik, E. H. (1984). *Crisis Counseling.* Belmont, CA: Wadsworth Health Sciences Division.

Jones, W. A. (1968). "The A-B-C Method of Crisis Management." *Mental Hygiene, 52,* 87–89.

Klingbeil, K. S., & Boyd, V. D. (1984). "Emergency Room Intervention: Detection, Assessment and Treatment." In A. R. Roberts (Ed.), *Battered Women and Their Families: Intervention Strategies and Treatment Programs* (pp. 7–32). New York: Springer.

National Coalition Against Domestic Violence (1988). *Directory of Shelters and Services for Battered Women.* Washington, DC: Author.

National Organization for Victim Assistance [N.O.V.A.] (1983). *Victim Services: A Guide to Action.* Washington, DC: Author.

Podhorin, R. (1987, February 12). Director, Womanspace, Inc., Lawrenceville, New Jersey. Personal communication.

Prato, L. (Undated). *What Is a Shelter?; Let's Talk It Over; What Is a Shelter? A Shelter Worker's Manual;* and *Let's Talk It Over: A Shelter Worker's Manual.* Morristown, NJ: Jersey Battered Women's Service.

Prelipp, S. (1987, February 13). Director, Family Violence Center, Green Bay, Wisconsin. Personal communication.

Rhodes, R. M., & Zelman, A. B. (1986, January). "An Ongoing Multi-Family Group in a Women's Shelter." *American Journal of Orthopsychiatry, 56,* 120–130.

Roberts, A. R. (1981). *Sheltering Battered Women: A National Study and Service Guide.* New York: Springer.

Roberts, A. R. (Ed.) (1984). *Battered Women and Their Families.* New York: Springer.

Roberts, A. R. (1987). *National Survey of Victim Service and Witness Assistance Programs: Final Report.* Indianapolis, IN: Indiana University School of Social Work.

Roberts, A. R. (1988). "Crisis Intervention: A Practical Guide to Immediate Help for Victim Families." In A. Horton & J. Williamson (Eds.), *Abuse and Religion* (pp. 60–66). Lexington, MA: D. C. Heath.

Schiller-Ramirez, M. (1987, January). *St. Martha's Hall Yearend Report 1986.* St. Louis, MO: St. Martha's Hall.

Schiller-Ramirez, M. (1987, March 4). Executive Director, St. Martha's Hall, St. Louis, Missouri. Personal communication.

Chapter 7

Assessment and Crisis Intervention with Rape and Incest Victims: Strategies, Techniques, and Case Illustrations

Patricia Petretic-Jackson, Ph.D.,
and Tom Jackson, Ph.D.

T his chapter is designed to provide a format for working with sexual assault victims using crisis intervention techniques. The chapter will be limited to assessment and crisis intervention strategies shown to be effective with adolescent and adult female sexual assault victims. This includes women experiencing compounded rape reaction (e.g., retrospective adult victims of incest) and unresolved sexual trauma (e.g., unreported victims). Such women often come to the attention of crisis clinicians after a rape or some other life crisis/events that have made them aware of a previously undisclosed, unresolved assault. Although many of the assessment and intervention strategies discussed can be used in crisis work with children or male sexual assault victims, a discussion of the unique needs of these groups is beyond the scope of this chapter. This chapter is further designed to familiarize the practicing clinician with a variety of issues and processes involving sexual assault. Among these are current research findings; the sexual assault syndrome; cognitive, social, physiological, and psychological sequelae; and program evaluation.

In considering the problem of sexual assault it is important to keep in mind first that in the process of her adjustment to sexual assault, a victim will experience many of the same symptoms and issues as do individuals faced with other life crises. Similar problems are faced by both rape and incest victims. Independent of the particular type of assault, the clinician can estimate the severity of the crisis response by considering four variables: (a) the preassault adjustment of the victim, including social, intellectual, and occupational adjustment and prior victimization experiences; (b) the specific nature of the assault experience, including the extent of injuries, prior relationship with the offender, and the amount of violence involved; (c) the response of the victim's social support system; and (d) the coping strategies and skills of the victim during and after the assault.

There are other issues concerning sexual assault that the clinician should keep in mind. The nature of the acute crisis is often self-limiting, and many women show adequate post-assault readjustment. However, for others the cognitive, physiological, and behavioral sequelae of assault are long-lasting and potentially severe. Also, in light of the specific symptoms which characterize the response to sexual assault, problem-specific assessment and interventions have proven of greatest use. Clinicians must be sensitive to the effects of age and situational variables on assault victims and should use a developmental perspective in assessment and intervention. Similarly, clinicians must be aware of how beliefs regarding sexual assault impact on behavior. Therefore, clinicians must examine their own values and attitudes regarding sexual assault prior to their work with assault victims and should not underestimate the impact of the beliefs held by both the victim and the members of her family or social support network on her recovery. Last, research on assessment and treatment of sexual assault victims is relatively recent. There is a need for continuing empirical research in this area, particularly regarding program evaluation and treatment efficacy.

Brief Review of the Research Literature on Sexual Assault

We will review three areas of research within the sexual assault literature: definitional and epidemiological issues; the effects of attitudes and beliefs on symptoms and treatment outcome; and delineation of the symptom picture and course of the sexual assault syndrome.

Definitions

Gathering information concerning its victims requires a coherent definition of the term sexual assault, a task that is much more difficult than one might suspect. Definitions vary among legal authorities, mental health clinicians, society, and the individuals involved. Much of our early information regarding incidence and prevalence rates came from victimization studies which sampled individuals and based estimates of assault on a victim's likelihood to report herself as a victim of sexual assault. This approach defines victimization in such a way that the woman is identified as a victim if she reports having experienced an assault which meets the legal criteria for rape—for example, the Federal Bureau of Investigation's criteria for forcible rape as "the carnal knowledge of a female forcibly and against her will" (U.S. Department of Justice, 1985, p. 13). Within this framework, *incest,* typically a felonious sexual offense, is commonly defined as sexual contact between two people too closely related to marry legally. Additionally, one of the individuals involved is typically under the age of majority. The definitions of rape and incest both include the use of force or coercion or indicate the incapacity or unwillingness of the victim to provide informed consent for the activity as an essential feature.

While such definitions have legal utility, they often lack clinical meaning. Legal victimization studies fail to consider that sexual victimization can include a range of sexual assault experiences. Findings from more recent research on rape, conducted by mental health researchers (Koss, 1983; Koss, Gidycz & Wisniewski, 1987; Koss & Oros, 1982), have indicated that women often fail to identify themselves as rape victims despite the fact that their assault experience meets legal criteria. This is even more likely to be the case when the victim knows the perpetrator (Williams, 1984), which is of special concern, given that 75 percent of rape victims know their assailants (Bateman, 1982). Societal attitudes also may serve to inhibit the reporting and treatment seeking of sexual assault victims. Burt (1980) indicated that many individuals subscribe to rape myths which blame the victim and reduce responsibility for the perpetrator. Surveys of high school (Goodchilds & Zellman, 1984) and college students (Sandberg, Petretic-Jackson, & Jackson, 1987) indicate that young adults hold similar views. These distortions are more common when rape victims have a prior acquaintance or relationship with the perpetrator, or when alcohol is involved in the incident.

Prevalence Rates

How likely is a woman to be sexually assaulted? The FBI Uniform Crime Reports for 1987 estimate that 90,434 forcible rapes occurred in 1986, an increase of 3.2 percent from the 1985 estimate of 87,671. While this statistic may seem high, many feel it is a serious underestimate of the actual frequency of sexual assault, given that rape is thought to be the most underreported of violent crimes. Many sexual assaults may go unreported by victims due to fear of retribution, embarrassment, denial, victim mislabeling, and insensitive treatment by legal and health professionals (Jackson & Sandberg, 1985; Kilpatrick, 1983; Koss, 1983). Estimates of the actual number of rapes range from 2.5 times (Chappel, 1976) to as high as 10 times the nationally reported number of cases (Koss, 1983).

The percentage of women reporting some form of sexual victimization has been addressed by recent surveys. Koss (1983) reported that 37 percent of 2,016 women surveyed reported prior assault experience. Kilpatrick (1983) reported a 14.5 percent sexual victimization rate from a sample of 2,004 women. Sandberg et al. (1987) reported that 22 percent of their college-aged female sample reported meeting legal criteria for rape in a dating context, and that 54 percent of the women reported being held or kissed against their will at some time in their dating history. In a recent national college study Koss et al. (1987) reported that 26 percent of their sample experienced some form of sexual assault.

Estimates of sexual assault in a marital context are difficult to determine. Several investigators place the rate of forced sex among married women at between 10 and 12 percent (Finkelhor & Yllo, 1983; Russell, 1982). Russell (1982) reported that the rate of reported marital rape was twice that of stranger rape in her sample of over 900 women. Still, these numbers are an underestimate of true rates of sexual assault within marriage, since many women do not perceive forced sex with a spouse as rape.

When forced sexual contacts between adults and children are examined, the literature has reported dramatically changing prevalence rates as attention has increasingly focused on this form of sexual assault. Justice and Justice (1979) maintain that incidence figures for incest were one per million in 1940, one per hundred in 1950, and one per twenty in 1970. A conservative estimate is that as many as one in four females in the United States has become a victim of sexual abuse and molestation by the time she reaches the age of majority (Forward & Buck, 1978). Rates for males may be as high as one in seven. While the female-to-male ratio of victims in reported cases has been 9:1, currently it is thought that a more accurate estimate is 5:1 (American Humane Association, 1981; National Center on Child Abuse and Neglect, 1981). Also, despite the stereotype that most child molesters are seedy strangers luring children into cars, current estimates by researchers have suggested that 75 percent of child sexual assault victims are acquainted with their assailants and nearly 50 percent have been assaulted by a family member.

Attitudinal Research

The investigation of attitudes concerning sexual assault has been an area of growing interest for researchers in the last several years. Several authors have proposed the view that prevalent attitudes toward rape and incest contribute to the underreporting of such crimes (Brodsky, 1976; Jackson & Ferguson, 1983; Resick & Jackson, 1981; Schwendinger & Schwendinger, 1974; Spencer, 1978).

Symptom Picture and Course of the Sexual Assault Syndrome

There is currently a substantial body of literature delineating the nature, course, and symptom picture of sexual assault, most of it describing instances of stranger rape. Included among the common sequelae are depression (Atkeson, Calhoun, Resick, & Ellis, 1982), anxiety (Burgess & Holmstrom, 1974a), lowered sexual satisfaction (Feldman-Summers, Gordon, & Meagher, 1979), rape-related and more generalized fears (Burgess & Holmstrom, 1974a; Kilpatrick, Veronen, & Resick, 1979), sexual dysfunctions and heterosocial adjustment difficulties (Becker & Skinner, 1983; Burgess &

Holmstrom, 1979), and anger and hostility (Burgess & Holmstrom, 1974a). Investigations of symptom course have underscored the importance of the time since an assault in determining therapeutic focus. Frank and Stewart (1983) suggest that depression emerges slightly later than fear and anxiety, with depression peaking at two weeks to three months after the assault (Atkeson et al., 1982). Symptoms of assault-induced fears and anxiety may diminish after the three-month post-trauma period (Kilpatrick et al., 1989). Impairment in social functioning generally remits within four months, while impairment in occupational/work functioning can last for considerably longer (Resick, Calhoun, Atkeson, & Ellis, 1981). While many symptoms are subject to remission within the first year after the assault, symptoms in any of the categories can persist. Becker, Skinner, Abel, and Treacy (1982) found evidence of sexual dysfunctions lasting as long as 35 years.

While few studies compare victims' responses in different forms of assaultive experiences, some tentative distinctions are suggested. Ellis, Atkeson, and Calhoun (1981) found that victims of stranger rape had a much higher initial fear level than victims who knew the perpetrator. However, victims who knew their offender experienced greater levels of anger. Research with incest victims has suggested that consanguinity of the perpetrator, number of assaults, and degree of legal involvement all hinder the victim's adjustment. Clinical reports further suggest that the type of offense (e.g., fondling, penetration) does not predict the degree of initial distress or the process of later adjustment. The positive support of significant others in both extrafamilial child sexual assault and incest appears to help the victim adjust. Problems reported by adult women who were sexually victimized as children include depression, anxiety, poor self-esteem (Boatman, Borkan & Schetky, 1981), substance abuse, self-destructive behavior (Carper, 1979; Nakashima, 1979), and a greater likelihood for sexual revictimization.

Practice Framework

Key Concepts in Crisis Intervention and Brief Treatment: Crisis Theory, Requests, and Emphasis

The crisis facing the sexual assault victim can be characterized as an interaction between the external crisis imposed by the assault and the internal, developmental crisis facing the individual. This implies that the effects of the assault will vary with the victim's particular developmental stage in the life cycle. Using Erikson's (1963) developmental tasks, we can identify concerns specific to different life stages. For example, the adolescent, concerned with developing a sense of identity, may have great difficulty recounting the assault experience for an adult in the face of concern about developing independence from the adult world. The young adult, now concerned with developing intimacy, may have difficulty establishing trust in new relationships and may have separation/independence problems with her family of origin. There may also be a sense that she "should have known better" if the perpetrator was an acquaintance, and she may experience considerable self-reproach. The middle-aged assault victim, faced with developmental tasks of generativity and caring for the next generation, may be concerned with how the rape will affect others in her care. A middle-aged married woman may experience problems getting emotional support from her spouse, who may be experiencing his own midlife crisis. For the older adult victim who faces the developmental task of ego integrity, the major issue is concern for her physical safety, not necessarily the sexual aspects of the assault. Of primary importance for her is dealing with the strong feelings of vulnerability and fear of death engendered by the assault. Social views about sexuality in the older adult may make a discussion of sexual concerns more difficult for both the victim and clinician. Thus, by examining the impact of an individual's age and life circumstances, the clinician should consider the impact of personal and developmental variables as well as the specific problems created by the external crisis of the assault.

The time that has passed since the assault should also be considered by the clinician. For example, a rape victim in crisis intervention is typically seen immediately following the assault. Severity of symptomatology is often quite intense, yet ongoing medical and legal intervention may mediate the stress level. In contrast, an adolescent incest victim seen in a crisis intervention setting typically will not be seen in the immediate post-assault period. More likely the crisis precipitating the intervention with the clinician will be associated with detection of the assault relationship by the authorities. The victim's crisis responses may focus on the family relationship and separation concerns. After many years an incest victim's crises may involve the stress of a confrontation with the perpetrator, sharing information after many years with a family member or current partner, a flashback experience, her own child's assault which serves to exacerbate guilt and anxiety at her inability to protect her child, or entry into therapy for another presenting problem and dealing with unresolved assault issues.

For effective crisis intervention, several approaches or emphases concerning the nature of sexual assault should be examined. The first approach, derived from Lazare (1971), focuses on meeting the victim's crisis requests. The victim is viewed as a highly active participant in the intervention process and is considered normal (e.g., showing adequate preassault functioning). Viewed as a customer requesting specific emergency services, she is assumed to know best what she needs. Typical client requests may include the need for medical intervention, police intervention, psychological intervention, and/or control (e.g., if in an incoherent state due to drugs, alcohol, or a prior psychiatric condition).

Another approach is adherence to a crisis model of intervention. Rape is identified as the external crisis. Intervention is not considered psychotherapy and any of the victim's previous problems which are not associated with assault (e.g., family problems, alcohol/drug abuse, psychiatric history) are not a priority issue in this view.

Outside referral may be made if such problems exist, given the possibility of an exacerbated reaction to the rape.

An associated approach to sexual assault crises is on intervention which is time-limited (short-term) and problem-specific. The rape incident and recovery strategies are the focus of intervention in the initial interview. The counseling goal here is to facilitate a return to the victim's preassault lifestyle.

The crisis-oriented approach to sexual assault intervention views the counselor's role as an active one. There is an emphasis on assisting the victim in regaining a sense of autonomy and control over her life. Treatment focus is on developing crisis-related problem-solving skills (e.g., preparation for medical and possible legal procedures, evaluation of options) and identifying a personal social support network for the victim.

A final goal in the crisis intervention model is victim education. The clinician can help the victim adapt to the rape or incest experience by changing the way she views it. This is accomplished by reframing the sexual assault in terms of societal issues and shifting self-blame to the perpetrator.

Case Vignettes

The two case vignettes that follow illustrate a cross-section of victim experiences, symptom patterns, adjustment levels, and social support networks. The first case is an instance of acquaintance rape.

Case 1

Laura, an 18-year-old college freshman, first contacted a clinician at the local rape crisis intervention center four days after her assault. She did so on the recommendation of the attending physician who had examined her at a local hospital immediately after the assault and at the urging of the friends she had confided in after returning to her dorm following the incident. Her friends had initially insisted that Laura report the assault to the police, despite her initial reluctance to do so. The police accompanied her to a local hospital for a physical examination after she filed her report.

In her meeting with the crisis clinician, Laura's manner was subdued, eye contact was poor, and her voice was barely audible. She seemed a pleasant, passive, moderately unassertive, and psychologically naive young woman. She told the clinician that she had experienced an attempted rape by a young man in his twenties she had recently met. She appeared ambivalent about her experience being a "legitimate" assault, pointing out that the police officer referred to it as an assault and not a rape. She reported that both law enforcement and medical personnel had been supportive and had recommended prosecution of the assailant and counseling for her.

Her manner was subdued as she told the clinician she was uneasy receiving services, since she felt the man had "only attempted" to rape her and she had been "stupid enough to get in the car with him" despite all the warnings her mother had given her in the past about "going with strangers." She said she was with friends and met the man for the first time on the evening of the assault. Both were mildly intoxicated when he suggested that the two of them drive to another bar in a different part of town. She said with some embarrassment that she had found the man attractive and did not protest when he parked the car in a dark alley or when he made initial sexual advances. She said he tried for several seconds to have intercourse with her, but stopped when she protested verbally. They then talked a while and he again tried to have intercourse with her. At this point she actively resisted and he held her down, bruising her thighs, torso, and arms in the process. She then reported that he stopped. After further questioning she admitted that actual penetration had occurred but the man had not ejaculated. She said that the two of them talked for a while and then he took her home.

Laura said she was angry at herself, not only for getting into the situation, but also for not more actively resisting or confronting the man. In addition to the guilt, she said she was experiencing moderate depression, concentration problems, and mild social anxiety. Although she felt she had no somatic symptoms, her roommate had said she had been crying and shouting in her sleep every night since the rape.

In the initial intervention, the focus was on legitimizing the assault and pointing out that forced sexual contact is not appropriate when a woman says no or wants to stop sexual activity, that forced intercourse is rape even if the victim knows the man involved. Initial intervention also dealt with her cognitive distortions and negative self-statements, modifying her statement that "I am stupid and all to blame. I should have physically fought him off or yelled" to "I ignored my discomfort with him, thinking this guy was nice and it was okay to go with him. I probably made a mistake but it still doesn't give him the right to physically force me to have intercourse if I don't really want to. I have a right to refuse sexual contact and have my wishes be respected." The initial intervenor also described common symptoms of women who experience assault by dates, provided bibliotheraphy, and assessed Laura's plans about pursuing the matter legally (she had chosen not to) and about getting further medical contact. She was encouraged to meet with a clinician for follow-up in one week and to determine at that time if she wished to be referred to therapy for assertiveness training, one of the things she had indicated she wanted to get from mental health contact.

In follow-up Laura scheduled and failed to meet with a clinician on two occasions before coming in. At that time she stated her ambivalence in talking about the matter due to her guilt, even though she said she wanted to talk to someone. Further assessment and specific planning was done. The crisis clinician saw her on two more occasions and maintained monthly telephone contact. Laura had also been referred to a clinician for the assertiveness training she requested. At the six-month post-assault contact she reported overall good adjustment and was asymptomatic.

The next vignette describes a more complicated stress reaction.

Case 2

Nancy, a 22-year-old married graduate student in education, attended a midwestern university. The clinician's first contact with the case was during a visit one afternoon by several law enforcement officers who were seeking a consultation. They had just interviewed Nancy, who had reported a sexual assault by a stranger earlier that morning. Because of concerns they had about the case, they asked the clinician to contact and interview Nancy. Their concerns were that Nancy was "not acting like she had been raped" and that her report of the details of the assault did not match physical evidence. They felt that she might have been assaulted by her husband or other acquaintance and was trying to protect that individual.

Before an interview was scheduled, the clinician received a call from the young woman. She came to the office accompanied by her husband, who along with one of Nancy's girlfriends had encouraged her to talk to a clinician following the assault. Initially Nancy seemed controlled. She showed little affective expression, her voice was flat, her tone was monotonous, and generally she held her body stiffly. When asked about her concerns, Nancy said she feared the police doubted her story because she had lied to them. At this point in the interview she became very distressed and said her assailant had threatened that he would come back and kill her if she told the police exactly what had happened. He had then provided details of her schedule (where she worked, what she had worn the day before) which indicated that he had been observing her for several days. He had then provided a story she was to tell the police (which she had) and told her he knew some local police and that he could check to see if she had told the right story. She asked whether the clinician felt this was true and whether Nancy could trust the police.

Nancy said the attack occurred when the assailant was waiting for her with a knife when she went to her car. She was upset that she had not noticed him approach her (although it was from the rear) and that she had not been able to run away or scream. After detailing the circumstances of the assault (in which the assailant was impotent and unable to complete intercourse), she said that following her release she went home and changed her clothes (which he had shredded with the knife). She said that although she "knew better" she had scrubbed her body to "get clean." She then called a friend, who accompanied her to a local hospital, where she was interviewed by the police. She felt angry that her assailant would probably hurt someone else because of her "stupidity" in lying to the police, who would probably not further investigate the case. Nancy reported symptoms of nausea, gastrointestinal distress, general malaise, and obsessive thoughts concerning the assailant and the events of the assault.

Nancy's social support system (her husband and girlfriend) were reported to be supportive. In taking Nancy's history, the clinician found that she had been assaulted by a stranger while an undergraduate attending another university. She had reported the incident to the authorities, who identified her assailant as a known serial rapist. Following educational strategies, Nancy decided with the clinician that she and her husband would stay with a relative in a nearby town until they could decide what to do about moving back into their home. A follow-up session was set for the next day. Subsequently Nancy was in daily contact with the clinician for three weeks following the assault.

Nancy reported nightmares, flashbacks, and continued appetite disturbance. As time progressed she became more depressed, although the severity of most of her other symptoms had lessened. She reported continued difficulty concentrating on her classwork and subsequently withdrew from her classes for the semester. She reported increasing anger and annoyance with her husband, who she felt was "just being nice because he felt sorry for me" and indicated that she was considering divorce. Her husband attended counseling sessions. Nancy was referred to another clinician for treatment of her continuing depression. Telephone contact was maintained on a weekly basis for three additional months, then monthly until one year after the assault. At that time she had returned to school and reported she and her husband were doing well. Fifteen months after her assault her assailant was caught following another rape in a nearby community.

Problems Complicating Crisis Intervention with Sexual Assault Victims

As can be seen from the preceding vignettes, a number of problems can complicate the crisis intervention process with sexual assault victims, including behaviors, emotions, and attitudes on the part of the client or the clinician. Burgess and Holmstrom (1979) refer to such problems as "stalls" in the intervention process. They note that often clinicians will get a "gut feeling" that something is going wrong in the intervention process when a "stall"—which serves to stop the progress of the interview—is about to occur. Warning signs that the clinician should be aware of include personal discomfort, a sense that the interview is "getting nowhere," a change in the victim's attitude or unexplained hostility toward the clinician, or the clinician's sense of his or her own withdrawal or emotional distancing from the client. But more importantly, what specific circumstances can interfere with the therapeutic process?

Client Issues

Ambivalence. Perhaps the greatest obstacle to successful intervention is ensuring that the victim finds and contacts mental health service providers. The difficulty in this is partially explained by victims' ambivalence. Only 1 in 10 victims will use some type of crisis intervention service such as a rape crisis center or hospital. As few as 1 in 20 adult female rape victims will seek out a clinician during this period. Of those women identified through the crisis intervention process as appropriate candidates for counseling, less than half will consent to enter short-term therapy. Most victims of acquaintance rape are unlikely to seek treatment at all.

With adolescent incest victims there is less certainty of the numbers receiving immediate intervention because of the vast number of undetected cases assumed to exist. Given their legal status as minors, most identified adolescent assault victims are referred for some type of mental health intervention through the court or social service system. While referral is more likely to occur in detected cases of adolescent assault, the same issues of concern that exist with adult rape victims and retrospective incest victims are present.

Intervention is less successful when externally motivated rather than self-motivated. Most clinical interventions in the immediate post-assault stages end prematurely due in part to client ambivalence or denial. A client may be anxious in the presence of the clinician when discussing the assault, even though the clinician is supportive or empathic. However, the clinician also has positive value. The victim simultaneously desires therapeutic contact while experiencing negative, therapeutic-distancing anxiety associated with discussing the assault experience (Kilpatrick, 1983). While this ambivalence is most intense during the initial contact, it can continue to be a factor.

Ambivalence is often expressed in apparently inconsistent behavior. For example, the client may urgently request a meeting with the clinician and then not attend. It is important that the clinician understand the dynamics of such behavior. The clinician must avoid taking the inconsistencies personally and responding with anger or concluding that such behaviors indicate a lack of motivation for therapy.

Trust.   Particularly salient with adolescent and adult retrospective incest victims is the issue of trust. Trust is often related to family issues such as power, control, sexism, and intimacy, and may be expressed in counseling as an unusual concern with confidentiality. The clinician may note in such victims a confusion of sex with affection, expression of sex roles in a stereotyped manner, or poor self-management skills due to expressed feelings of powerlessness and lack of control.

Emotional Detachment.   Emotional expressiveness may be related to a client's early learned coping strategies. For example, the child/adolescent assault victim may learn to detach himself or herself from feelings as a survival strategy. Such detachment strategies are difficult to overcome, but allowance for expressions of fear and anger with the clinician may facilitate coping. At times, as women discuss an assault experience with a clinician, they may experience extreme physical reactions such as vomiting and fainting or more common responses such as crying and body tremors. Clinician permission for such expression facilitates the intervention goal of emotional catharsis, in which facing and working through feelings relating to the sexual assault are encouraged as opposed to denying or repressing such feelings.

Self-Blame.   Self-blame involves not only self-esteem issues, but the view of "specialness" and self-abuse as well. The client who engages in self-blame may ask the question "Why work with me?" both directly and indirectly. Self-blame issues are related to the intervention goal of client self-management. Several clinician strategies can be used successfully in working with self-defeating, self-blaming victim attitudes. They include a focus on client strengths and the use of cognitive techniques such as client self-monitoring of negative self-statements while substituting positive self-statements. For example, a client may be encouraged to replace statements such as "What a dumb person I was to not try harder to get away; I should have fought harder" with statements such as "I did what I thought was best at the time and kept myself alive. That's what's really important." To counteract the self-perception of "specialness" as related to self-blame for the assault (e.g., "If only I hadn't decided to go to the store then. I shouldn't have worn shorts"), the clinician can anticipate high-probability thoughts, feelings, and behaviors that the victim is likely experiencing early in the therapy process. The clinician can then include in interaction with the client statements such as "Frequently, women who were incest/rape victims say they experience a problem with trust, expressing anger, and so on. You may or may not have similar feelings, but if you do, recognize that they are not unusual, given the circumstances."

Clinician Issues

Gender.   The issue of clinician gender has received considerable attention in the literature. While we don't hold the view that males are incapable of being effective interventionists with female victims of sexual assault, we would suggest caution in this regard in one-on-one work immediately following the assault. At this stage many female victims have strong negative reactions to males and some will express a strong preference for a female clinician. That request should not be ignored, despite the fact that highly skilled male clinicians may be available. Perhaps during the initial crisis period a male clinician is more valuable in acting as a resource and model for the victim's male partner, if there is one. In fact, the concept of the male–female crisis intervention team should be given strong consideration when both male and female clinicians are available. It also appears that the issue of gender becomes less of a concern after the initial acute crisis period has passed.

A major obstacle facing the male clinician dealing with rape victims is coping with his own anxiety about victim acceptance of him in the helping role. Such anxiety may cause the male clinician to alter his clinical style and employ behaviors which could be interpreted as either seductive (e.g., he uses a softer tone, increased touching, and physical proximity to convey a caring attitude) or distancing (e.g., he is technical, hypervigilant to body boundaries, "stiff") in his effort to demonstrate to the victim that not all males are "bad." A male clinician can also err by being overzealous in proving his effectiveness with rape victims. This could result in a patronizing, oversolicitous attitude. Another, more subtle error a male clinician should be aware of is a focus on the sexual aspects of the assault to the exclusion of its violent aspects.

What appears to be of greater importance than clinician gender are the values and attitudes the clinician subscribes to regarding victims and victimization. Gender may interact with values; some male clinicians will have difficulty validating the experiences of a victim if they identify with the male offender, while female clinicians can be prejudicial and blame women for their victimization (e.g., believing only certain kinds of women get assaulted). But gender alone will not necessarily determine intervention success or failure. A male clinician who is nonjudgmental and validating would be preferable to a female clinician who ascribes to stereotyped views regarding sexual assault, victims, and victim blame.

Clinician Values.   Before beginning work with sexual assault victims, a clinician should have carefully examined his or her own biases and prejudices associated with sexual assault. This self-awareness, termed *autodiagnosing* by Burgess and Holmstrom (1979), ensures that the clinician continually assesses feelings and possible prejudices concerning each particular client to avoid contributing to the client's revictimization. Such revictimization occurs when the clinician places himself or herself in the role of assessing whether a reported rape or incest experience was "real," or whether the client was "provocative," "overreacting," "self-destructive," harbored "incestuous longings," or "enjoyed the experience" and is now expressing "guilt." Usually it is easy for clinicians to have positive feelings about child and elderly victims. However, prejudices may surface in the case of prostitutes, women with a history of substance abuse or other psychiatric problems, and victims who report multiple rapes. Prejudicial attitudes also tend to go hand in hand with victim labeling. Labeling occurs when the clinician is thinking, "She's just a crazy/prostitute/professional victim, etc." When labeling and prejudicial values exist, there is a risk that the client's basic rights of being taken seriously and carefully listened to will not be met.

Rescue Fantasies.   Both male and female clinicians can be less than effective with sexual assault victims if they overidentify with the victim or lose perspective and become too active. Subsequently a clinician will feel angry or manipulated by a client, primarily because he or she was not actively listening to the client's requests.

Clinician Feelings: Subjectivity and Burnout.   Crisis intervention work with sexual assault victims is often emotionally draining. Feelings of rage, disgust, or even sexual arousal are commonly experienced by clinicians working with victims. While the clinician's empathic expression of anger over client victimization can be quite thera-peutic, it is not therapeutic to burden the client with excessive expression of anger or rage. The client needs to work with a professional who is in control of his or her own emotions despite the intensity of the situation. When a clinician loses perspective, he or she can experience a heightened sense of personal vulnerability. The victim's experience can bring the frightening awareness of how easily we are all vulnerable to such assault. Blaming or rejection of the client can result. Statements like "She must have done something" serve to dichotomize the world into victims (them) and non-victims (us). If bad things can't happen to good people (like us), perhaps the victim somehow precipitated her assault. Such thoughts can also precipitate clinician anxiety and depression.

The stress in working with victims can also be exacerbated by frustrations inherent in working with the "system" and institutions involved in assault. To reduce the risk of burnout, it is vital that the clinician build a strong professional support network.

Target Systems

Family System

A family-based intervention is crucial to the optimal adjustment of the assault victim. Detailed guidelines for working with the assault victim's partner or significant other and the members of her family of origin and nuclear family are provided elsewhere (Benedict, 1985). The family as well as the victim should be educated concerning assault reactions and attitudes. The family members should also be prepared for common victim responses. The need for family availability is important, as is support for the victim's ability to mobilize her own coping strategies. Family can also provide an environment in which it is safe for the victim to express her emotions and thoughts (i.e., the concept of containment). Family responses which hinder the adjustment of the victim should be avoided. These include avoidance, attack, indifference, and overprotection. The rape is conceptualized as a shared life crisis the entire family must face. Since the victim requires support, empathy, and reassurance from her family at this time, ventilation of family members' own emotional responses should occur when the victim is absent.

Professionals

It is important that the clinician know about appropriate medical, police, and judicial processes. Educating a victim about what to anticipate in her interactions with professionals in these areas helps reduce anxiety and facilitate decision making. Several sources detailing procedural aspects of forensic and medical services are available to the crisis worker (Benedict, 1985; Burgess & Holmstrom, 1979; Halpern, 1978).

Clinician Roles and Skills

A lthough the topic of clinician roles and skills has been discussed in the context of crisis intervention philosophy and potential problems (i.e., values, biases, lack of objectivity), this section will provide a listing of suggestions or techniques to consider in the course of intervention.

The following are useful attitudes and behaviors:

1. Present a calm, professional, and supportive demeanor.
2. Develop a supportive relationship with the victim through reassurance and empathic listening. Indicate that you believe her story, and do not convey a sense of suspiciousness or doubt ("Why did you park there?" "Did it really happen that way?").
3. Respond to the victim's unique immediate concerns and needs by attending to verbal and nonverbal cues. Answer her questions. Don't offer false reassurances (e.g., "This can never happen to you again if you get a new job").
4. Let the victim set the tone and pace of the intervention. Resist the impulse to push her to discuss topics too soon. Allow her to retain a sense of control in the interaction.
5. Anticipate a variety of physical and emotional victim responses. Remember that a woman's response is a function of her personal style interacting with the circumstances of the assault.
6. Attend to the victim's symptom phase. While individuals vary, placement within a particular phase of the sexual assault syndrome provides a conceptual framework from which to direct assessment and intervention strategies.
7. Be aware of your feelings toward the victim. You may experience rage, disgust, or even sexual arousal. Guard against responding with defensiveness or per-

sonalization to a victim's maladaptive behaviors such as ambivalence about help-seeking, power issues, sexism, and attempts to sexualize the therapeutic relationship. Particularly with respect to the issue of sexuality, the clinician must recognize that such a personal relationship would be unethical.

8. Focus on immediate affective experiences. Use reflection of the victim's emotional responses.

9. Provide validation for the victim's feelings and thoughts. Let her know that her responses are not abnormal given her experience, and that they are common to many women who have undergone similar trauma.

10. Use techniques of clarification, labeling, and generalization to convey an understanding of the victim's situation. Statements can be prefaced with comments such as "Some women who have been assaulted are concerned about . . . [identify a specific issue]."

11. Encourage victim decision making and planning to allow her to regain a sense of control. Use the techniques of clarification and selective interpretation to evaluate alternatives in decision making. Avoid a controlling style; don't make decisions for the victim or attempt to "rescue" her. Let her know you will support her decisions.

12. Set the stage for the development of a survivor mentality. The victim's distress can then be more effectively normalized. Begin to set the stage in the initial interview for self-recovery by sharing successful coping strategies used by other assault victims. Remind the victim that while she has experienced a trauma, it has made her use a variety of coping skills which demonstrate that she possesses many strengths. Emphasize what she did "right" in the situation, not what she did "wrong." Her survival skills will allow her to reach recovery goals of autonomy and control. Facilitate acquisition of coping and mastery skills through the techniques of rehearsal and anticipatory guidance.

13. Offer hope and realistic reassurance. Suggest that the victim will feel in greater control of her life as time progresses. Use the concept of life crisis to explain her thoughts, feelings, and attitudes. It is useful to remind her that although she has undergone a severe trauma, the assault does not preclude her from being able to function normally in the future.

The following are specific task-oriented strategies:

1. Progress from a general to a more specific focus in gathering information during the interview. Avoid listening pitfalls. Use open-ended questions. Avoid emotionally charged words or doubled-edged questions (e.g., "Don't you . . . ?"). Put potentially embarrassing questions about sex in context (e.g., "I need to know about . . . because . . . "). Probing questions should be avoided, except those dealing with issues of suicide, depression, psychiatric history, and the victim's ability to control her own behavior.

2. Assess psychosocial functioning. Also, take a crisis history to assist the victim in anticipating possible reactions. Consider issues of specific life stage and the nature and specifics of her assault.

3. Be a good observer and document impressions and findings. Include victim comments and such nonverbal clues as appearance, facial expression, her characteristic communicative style, and any physical findings such as bruises. Notes provide a baseline on victim behaviors and may be useful if the clinician is subpoenaed for later court proceedings.

4. Educate the victim regarding the following:
   a. The various legal and medical procedures, to reduce anxiety about the unknown and allow her to consider alternatives and make informed decisions.
   b. The various physiological and psychological/emotional sequelae she may encounter. Bibliotherapy may be useful (Benedict, 1985; Los Angeles Commission on Assaults Against Women, 1983).
   c. Common myths concerning sexual assault and victims. Identify positive victim self-attitudes and appropriate blame attribution to the perpetrator.

5. Use anticipatory guidance and rehearsal to reinforce educational principles. In this way the victim can anticipate, plan for, and better cope with many post-assault situations and problems.

6. Be problem oriented. List the various options open to her and the things she must attend to in the near future. Encourage her to prioritize events. Partialization (Holmes, 1984), in which the totality of the assault is divided into manageable parts to facilitate task identification, evaluation, prioritization, and management, is a useful technique.

7. Be future oriented. In the initial session encourage her to make a schedule or a detailed plan of her activities for the next several days, scheduling hour by hour if necessary.

8. Identify and use the victim's social network to facilitate her recovery. Offer services and information to concerned family members and friends.

Clinical Issues

Stages/Phases

The sexual assault syndrome has been conceptualized as having two (Burgess & Holmstrom, 1979), three (Sutherland & Scherl, 1970), or four (Symonds, 1980) post-assault phases, depending on the theorist. Whatever the model, there appears to be general agreement that an initial acute phase exists. This *acute* or *impact phase* is characterized by disorganization. Somatic, emotional, and cognitive symptoms are evident. The victim exhibits one of two primary styles of emotional response: expressed or controlled. In the *expressed style* the individual shows emotions of anger, fear, and/or anxiety and behavioral signs of tension and restlessness. The *controlled style* is characterized by masked emotions and behavior that appears calm, composed, and subdued. The time frame for this phase varies, with most immediate symptoms lasting several days to several weeks.

Some clinicians have posited an extra stage of denial and repression following the acute stage. During this *denial and repression stage* the victim appears well adjusted but is actually repressing anger over the loss of control the assault represents. This is followed by a final phase in which the focus is the task of reorganization. During this *reorganization stage* there are lifestyle concerns in four primary areas: physical (e.g., gynecological problems), psychological (dreams, nightmares, and phobias specific to the assault), social (changing residence and telephone numbers, visiting family, getting away), and sexual (fear of sex, disruption of an ongoing relationship). Despite the fact that the victim is gaining additional coping skills, this phase is characterized by depression and a working through of the emotional issues involved in the assault (Burgess & Holmstrom, 1979; Lenox & Gannon, 1983). Occasionally this stage is further delineated into two substages. The first is an *early recoil phase* in which the symptom picture decreases due to an increase in coping strategies. However, the rape trauma has not yet been resolved (Bassuk, 1980). There are concerns with dependency, self-worth, and the need for an effective support system. Since feelings about the rape may be masked at this time, the desire for continued counseling typically diminishes. The recoil phase is followed by a *reconstitutive phase,* in which the victim deals with the meaning of the rape. The ultimate resolution and integration of the rape is a long-term process, lasting as long as two years in some cases.

Some research (Williams & Holmes, 1981) has suggested a change in the preceding conceptualization of rape as crisis. It indicates that the disequilibrium present in the acute stage may not end within a two-month period. Instead, victims may be left with a variety of residual crisis effects, what is referred to as a *prolonged crisis.* Thus, while a clinician should be aware of the stage the victim is in, it is important to recognize that the specific symptoms presented may vary with time for a given individual, as it will vary among individuals, and may vary with the type and nature of the sexual assault. A clinician must be knowledgeable about the varied symptom picture in order to know what to look for in clients, remembering that individuals differ substantially in their expression of this symptom picture and in the severity of the syndrome's features. Symptom patterns also tend to be complex. Symptoms may appear in a straightforward time sequence or may incubate for several years before emerging. This last point is relevant to correct diagnosis of the sexual assault victim. The typical *DSM-III-R* diagnosis applied to sexual assault victims is post-traumatic stress disorder. The issue of symptom incubation is salient in regard to post-traumatic stress disorder, in that it is not uncommon for symptoms to emerge after a latency period of months or years following the trauma (American Psychiatric Association, 1987, p. 237).

Victim Reactions

Physical.   Victims report a wide range of physical/somatic concerns. Many victims describe a general soreness or malaise, others indicate pain specific to an area that was a focus of the assault. Somatic symptoms in the acute phase can be classed as disturbances in sleep (e.g., onset insomnia, early morning awakenings, nightmares, disturbed sleep with muscle tension); disturbances in eating (e.g., marked decrease in appetite, nausea, stomach pains, gastric upset); and symptoms specific to the assault (e.g., bruising, rectal pain and bleeding with anal sex, irritation to the mouth with oral sex, venereal disease, pregnancy).

Emotional. The most common emotional response is fear. Victims report concern with body integrity during and after the assault—fears that they would be killed or physically injured. Other emotional responses range from shock, shame, disbelief, guilt, embarrassment, and helplessness to self-blame, anger, and desire for revenge. There may be emotional overreaction and irritation with others that appears out of proportion, given the situation. Accompanying this may be a sense of extreme emotional isolation from others. Many women report feeling out of control and powerless. They may fear they are going crazy. Mood swings and feelings of paranoia may also occur. Signs of depression will emerge later than fear or anxiety, usually two weeks to three months after the assault.

Cognitive. Following an assault a victim may spend considerable time trying to undo the experience and imagining what she could have done to avoid the assault. Recurrent thoughts of the assault are common, as are efforts to block such thoughts from consciousness. Most efforts at blocking are unsuccessful. Recurring thoughts of the assault may be accompanied by flashbacks. The victim may make negative self-statements and reveal cognitive distortions similar to those associated with depression. A sense of disorientation and problems in concentration are common. Incest victims may also report feelings of dissociation.

Behavioral. Common immediate physical responses to assault in the acute phase include crying, shaking, rocking, staring, fidgeting, chain smoking, or emotional lability. These responses characterize a woman who is responding in an expressive mode. If the victim appears calm and composed, she may be responding using a controlled coping style. The clinician should assess whether this response style is typical for the woman. Later in the acute phase the woman may engage in what appear to be risk taking behaviors (e.g., visiting the scene of an assault, driving around looking for her assailant) as an attempt to regain control over her life.

Self-Issues. Self-issues may involve cognitive, behavioral, and physiological reactions. Included in this category are concerns pertaining to identity and self-esteem ("How am I going to go on?" "What is going to happen to me?"), as well as physical ("My body is disgusting") and sexual functioning. Adolescent and retrospective adult incest victims also may have a sense of being powerful in a "malignant" way or just "different." They may experience amnesia for the period in which the incestuous relationship occurred. Feelings of inadequacy related to parenting skills are common.

Psychosocial.   Relationship issues encompass concerns with relationships in general (e.g., trust, isolation, sexism), with a current partner, and with the family of origin and the nuclear family. Relationships in general may be characterized as empty, superficial, conflictual, sexualized (in the case of incest victims), and lacking in trust. The relationship with a significant other/partner is often impaired in terms of general trust (a function of global negative feelings toward men) and impaired sexuality. It is not uncommon for the adult partners of incest victims to be seen as either overvalued as a protector or abusive or neglectful. A family-of-origin issue with rape victims is overprotection, dependency, and infantilization. The relationship between an incest victim and the members of her family of origin may range from mistrust, ambivalence, and an inability to relate in positive ways or receive nurturance to fear and a sense of hatred and betrayal. Parent–child relationship issues (adequacy in the parental role, ability to protect children) are particularly salient in the case of incest victims.

Assessment

Assessing the Incident(s)

Jackson, Quevillon, and Petretic-Jackson (1985) provided the Sexual Assault Victim Interview Guide, which was designed to identify a range of issues relevant to sexual assault victims.

Expanding from the outline of Jackson et al., the following material should be assessed in interview:

I. The nature and circumstances of the assault
   A. Circumstances (who, what, when, where, how).
   B. Attribution of blame (victim's perception of the "why" of assault; self-evaluation of how she might have acted differently).
   C. Degree of familiarity or consanguinity with the assailant.
   D. Number of assaults (single versus multiple assaults and prior history of unwanted sexual experiences).
   E. Type of coercion (verbal threat, physical force).
   F. Nature of assault (fondling, penetration).
   G. Level and nature of violence (threats of death, use of a weapon, battering).
II. Post-Assault Interactions
   A. Professional contacts (legal, medical).
   B. Time line between assault and help-seeking (self-care: Did victim clean self, change clothes? Who did she talk to? Who determined that she would seek help?).
   C. Initial contact. (Who did you tell first? How did they react?)
   D. Social support system (partner, friends, family of origin, children).

      1. Partner. (If victim is involved in a relationship at time of assault, assess partner's reaction: sensitivity, levels of support and blame.)
      2. Family of origin/children (style of family coping; allowance for victim control, dependency issues, levels of support and blame).
      3. Friends (levels of support and blame).

III. Victim's initial reaction
    A. Self-Perceptions. ("In your own words, describe your initial reaction. What were your thoughts, your feelings?")
    B. Symptoms. (Refer to the categories of physical, cognitive, emotional, psychosocial, and self-issues listed earlier; assess fear and vulnerability; evaluate congruence between self-reported problems/symptoms and test data; assess changes in vegetative function: sleep, appetite, weight, menstruation, elimination.)
    C. Sex history (cf. Pomeroy, Flax, & Wheeler, 1982).
    D. Initial changes in daily functioning (job performance, relationship, social life, maintenance of place and circumstances of residence, need to visit relatives, future plans).
    E. Mental status changes: judgment; orientation to person, place, time; memory; affect; cognitive functions.
    F. Changes in personality or behavior reported by others. (Examine congruence between reports of victim and significant others; evaluate anger directed at family members, particularly spouse/partner.)

IV. Current status
    A. Evaluate mental status.
    B. Coping efforts and strategies, such as life changes, reorganization efforts, and cognitive/affective coping. (Assess intellectual insight with/without emotional working-through. For example, does the victim report that she knows "in her head" that it wasn't her fault, but still has problems "in her gut" believing she was not to blame?)
    C. Symptom expressivity/issue of prolonged crisis. (Is there more to come? What other personal or social factors can exacerbate stress symptoms?)
    D. Self-reported nightmares, fears, sexual acting-out, sexual dysfunctions, depression, anxiety, hostility, heterosocial impairments.
    E. Ability to self-evaluate (self-perceived strengths and weaknesses).
    F. Changes in lifestyle, life events, social surroundings.
    G. Social/political context (current feminist perspective).
    H. Behavioral coping (self-defense courses, new locks, changing of telephone number, moving).

V. Course
    A. Presence/absence of premorbid psychological history (previous psychiatric treatment, hospitalization, medications, depressions, and suicide attempts).

B. Social functioning (friendships, dating/relationship status, assertiveness, trust level).

C. Educational, occupational, social, and familial adjustment.

D. Symptom fluctuation. (The use of a graph to chart the symptom course may be useful.)

VI. Attributions

A. Attribution of blame (self, situation, offender).

B. Self-efficacy rating. ("How well do you feel you are doing? Do you feel it is taking too long to get readjusted? What had you anticipated? Are you pleased or disappointed at where you are now in terms of gains?")

C. Attributions to legal/medical/psychological community. ("Were professionals supportive? accusing? What could have been done to facilitate your coping? Was there a sense that professional contacts resulted in a 'second assault'?" (Williams & Holmes, 1981)

VII. Future orientation

A. Short-term plans and goals.

B. Self-statements (ability to reinforce gains made: "I did the best I could. At least I kept myself alive, which is the most important thing.")

C. Optimism regarding relationships and own recovery. ("I can recognize that sometimes I am responding to my partner not for what my partner is doing, but because I'm thinking about the assault. If I keep that in mind, I'll eventually be able to react to my partner and separate him from my assailant. I am a survivor. I've made gains and will eventually be back to normal in time. I can regain control of my life."

Tests/Instruments

P ractical considerations dictate primary use of multiple, brief, problem-specific tests. If there is a concern with preexisting problems (e.g., a compounded rape reaction), more global personality functioning can also be assessed. For the majority of clients, the following instruments provide the most relevant information without taxing the client in terms of time requirements for completion.

Beck Depression Inventory (BDI)

The BDI (Beck, Rush, Shaw, & Emery, 1979) is a 21-item scale assessing the cognitive and somatic components of depression. One question specifically assesses suicidal risk. Scores of 11 to 20 indicate mild to moderate depression, while scores over 20 imply severe depression. The BDI is recommended because of its wide use with assault victims (norms) and its sensitivity to change, which allows its use to monitor changes in depression over time.

Derogatis Symptom Checklist (SCL-90-R)

The SCL-90-R (Derogatis, 1977) is a 90-item scale in which symptoms are rated for severity of discomfort they have caused in the past week. The test yields separate scores for somatization, obsessive-complusive feelings, interpersonal sensitivity, depression, anxiety, hostility, phobic anxiety, paranoid ideation, and psychoticism. Its advantages are the relevance of many subscales to sexual assault symptomology and the ability to provide a quick screen for more severe problems associated with compound rape reactions.

Veronen-Kilpatrick Modified Fear Survey (MFS)

The MFS (Veronen & Kilpatrick, 1980) is a 120-item scale based on the original Fear Survey Schedule of Wolpe and Lang (1964), modified specifically for use with assault victims. Respondents rate stimuli on a five-point scale of severity (i.e., whether these objects or experiences produce fear or unpleasant feelings). The 42 new items yield a rape subscale to augment preexisting animal, interpersonal, tissue damage, failure/loss of self-esteem, classical phobia, and miscellaneous fears subscales. The test is thorough and has a good research base with rape victims.

Attribution of Rape Blame Scale (ARBS) and Jackson Incest Blame Scale (JIBS)

Twenty-item scales, the ARBS (Ward & Resick, 1980) and JIBS (Jackson & Ferguson, 1983) can be used as clinical assessment devices, although clinical norms are still in the process of being established. Each scale provides four blame scores consisting of offender, societal, situational, and victim blame attribution. They can be of use in highlighting treatment issues when given to the client (e.g., to assess self-blame) and to significant others (to assess the victim's environmental support), and can serve as a means of counselor self-assessment. Ongoing work has produced a number of samples for normative comparison.

Minnesota Multiphasic Personality Inventory (MMPI)

The routine use of the MMPI is strongly encouraged with women who have a suspected or confirmed compounded rape reaction. Despite the considerable administration time involved, its clinical utility makes it worthwhile. Variability in profiles may reflect differences in current symptom phase, premorbid adjustment, time since assault, type of assault, and overall level of post-traumatic stress.

Steps in the Crisis Intervention Model

First Contact

There are several goals to be accomplished in a clinician's first intervention session with the assault victim. After an introductory rapport-building phase, the clinician conducts the basic assessment in the working phase of the interview. This is followed by a closing phase in which specific planning strategies are established. The clinician needs to be flexible about where and when she or he meets with the victim, but it should be somewhere private, quiet, and with no interruptions. The clinician should fully identify himself or herself (e.g., name, professional role, purpose of interview, information about research aspects if relevant). Establishing a therapeutic alliance at this point can be facilitated by active listening (What is important to the victim in terms of primary concerns?), treating the victim with respect, responding in a calm and professional way, and putting her at ease. The clinician should have a sense of what the victim's stated concerns are, her positive coping skills, and the meaning of the assault for her before beginning the working/assessment phase of the session. The working/assessment phase is designed to assess the nature and impact of the assault and develop immediate coping alternatives. The goal of assault assessment is to gain as much knowledge as possible about the assault itself and what has happened since. Then the "rape work" (Bassuk, 1980) should focus on discussing options, evaluating alternatives, and developing a specific plan for the next 24 to 48 hours. Before the victim leaves, the clinician should establish a follow-up plan. Agree as to who will make the next contact (client or clinician), obtain at least two telephone numbers (home, that of a good friend or family member), schedule a time for either the follow-up telephone call or a subsequent appointment, and agree to what identification the clinician can use in contacting the victim.

Follow-Up

Several options for follow-up services are available. Each crisis intervention system/clinician will choose to establish a follow-up program that best fits agency resources and philosophy. A good guide for those interested in telephone follow-up is provided by Halpern (1978). Others may prefer face-to-face contacts during this period, particularly with victims whose assaults involve complicating factors (e.g., compounded rape reaction, intrusive imagery, unresolved sexual trauma). Ideally, follow-up should occur within 24 hours of initial contact, again within 48 to 72 hours, at one week, at four to six weeks, at three months, at one year, and/or whenever the victim or her support system require assistance.

Short-Term Counseling

If a short-term counseling intervention is desired, clinicians can also employ the Brief Behavioral Intervention Procedure (BBIP; Kilpatrick, Veronen, & Resick, 1980), a multicomponent treatment package combining both behavioral and feminist treatment strategies. The program requires four to six hours of client contact and consists of an induced affect interview, an educational component (e.g., assault myths, origin of assault fear, description of common victim reactions), and training in specific coping skills (e.g., techniques of deep muscle relaxation and deep breathing, guided self-dialogue, and strategies for coping with avoidance responses).

Short-term interventions are most useful when focused on fears and phobias, depression, and/or sexual dysfunction. A useful treatment package for clients who have resolved many assault-related problems yet continue to exhibit severe fear responses involves stress inoculation training (SIT). A cognitively and behaviorally based anxiety management approach, SIT is designed to assist the client in actively coping with target-specific, assault-related anxiety. The general procedure (Veronen & Kilpatrick, 1983) is based on Meichenbaum's (1977) model of self-control. While some clinicians promote systematic desensitization (SD) as the optimal treatment for rape-induced fears and anxieties, the technique is best used when the client's fear and anxiety cues can be clearly specified. For more global fears and anxieties, cognitive techniques (Beck et al., 1979) may be useful. Thought-stopping procedures are effective for treating victims' feelings of guilt, shame, and self-blame concerning the assault.

Cognitive techniques have proven useful for treatment of depression accompanying both rape and incest (see descriptions by Frank & Stewart, 1983, 1984). The approach allows the victim to develop confidence that she can control her thoughts and, through them, her feelings and behaviors. Promoting such a sense of control in sexual assault victims can be highly therapeutic. Since the approach works with anxiety or fear as well, an intervention plan using these techniques has consistency and continuity. It is also a direct, active treatment in which the mechanisms for change are made explicit at the onset of therapy. Each treatment session reinforces the client's knowledge of how the treatment works.

A sophisticated, time-limited behavioral treatment package appropriate for use with a wide variety of sexual dysfunctions for both incest and rape victims has been developed by Becker and Skinner (1983, 1984). Their approach is highly flexible, can be used in individual or group formats, and appears to be effective in symptom relief.

Evaluation of Crisis Intervention

I f crisis intervention services for assault victims are to effectively achieve their objectives, efforts must be based on a systematic plan and evaluation of the program's stated goals. Unfortunately, program planning, coordination with other disciplines, and program evaluation have not been given the necessary attention, despite what appears to be provision of quality care in many programs.

If one examines the results of research which has focused on short- and long-term adjustment and symptom course in rape victims using crisis services, it appears that the majority of victims report improved adjustment. However, research is hindered by failure of many clients to complete even short-term intervention programs. It appears that the crisis model proves to be the best immediate treatment in cases of rape (Burgess & Holmstrom, 1985). However, it is important to allow for a flexible approach when considering time limits for intervention. The possibility that many women may experience residual effects long after their assaults suggests the need to provide education and an environment that supports help seeking. Evaluation of the adequacy of crisis services as well as information regarding victim adjustment should be obtained at all follow-up contacts with clients. Evaluation of client satisfaction with short-term intervention should be obtained at the end of the brief treatment course along with client post-test. In both cases clients can be asked to complete a brief client satisfaction questionnaire on which they rate the usefulness of specific strategies, the overall perceived level of utility of services, the adequacy of educational information provided, availability of services, and clinician skills (listening, support), as well as suggestions for program changes and the need for additional services. Such a form can be provided to women in a packet along with self-help information. For telephone follow-up, such information can also be obtained at the end of the contact.

Summary

T his chapter has attempted to dispel some of the myths regarding sexual assault and acquaint the crisis intervention clinician with the symptom complexity involved in the sexual assault syndrome. In addition, the chapter has presented what are felt to be current and effective approaches to assessment and treatment of the sexual assault victim. The chapter would not be complete, however, without a call for the continued collection of data and dissemination of results in this critical area of crisis intervention.

References

American Humane Association. (1981). *National Study on Child Neglect and Abuse Reporting.* Denver, CO: Author.

American Psychiatric Association. (1987). *Diagnostic and Statistical Manual of Mental Disorders (DSM-III-R).* Washington, DC: Author.

Atkeson, B., Calhoun, K., Resick, P., & Ellis, E. (1982). "Victims of Rape: Repeated Assessment of Depressive Symptoms." *Journal of Consulting and Clinical Psychology, 50,* 96–102.

Bassuk, E. (1980). "A Crisis Theory Perspective on Rape." In N. F. McCombie (Ed.), The Rape Crisis Intervention Handbook: A Guide to Victim Care (pp. 121–129). New York: Plenum.

Bateman, P. (1982). *Acquaintance Rape: Awareness and Prevention*. Seattle, WA: Alternatives to Fear.

Beck, A., Rush, A., Shaw, B., & Emery, G. (1979). *Cognitive Therapy of Depression*. New York: Guilford Press.

Becker, J. V., & Skinner, L. J. (1983). "Assessment and Treatment of Rape-related Sexual Dysfunctions." *The Clinical Psychologist, 36,* 102–104.

Becker, J. V., & Skinner, L. J. (1984). "Behavioral Treatment of Sexual Dysfunctions in Sexual Assault Survivors." In I. Stuart & J. Green (Eds.), *Victims of Sexual Aggression: Treatment of Men, Women & Children* (pp. 211–233). New York: Van Nostrand Reinhold.

Becker, J. V., Skinner, L. J., Abel, G. G., & Treacy, E. C. (1982). "Incidence and Types of Sexual Dysfunctions in Rape and Incest Victims." *Journal of Sex and Marital Therapy, 8,* 65–74.

Benedict, H. (1985). *Recovery.* New York: Doubleday.

Boatman, E., Borkan, E. L., & Schetky, D. H. (1981). "Treatment of Child Victims of Incest." *American Journal of Family Therapy, 9,* 42–51.

Brodsky, S. (1976). "Sexual Assault: Perspectives on Prevention and Assailants." In M. Walker & S. Brodsky (Eds.), *Sexual Assault: The Victim and the Rapist* (pp. 1–8). Lexington, MA: Lexington Press.

Brownmiller, S. (1975). *Against Our Will: Men, Women, and Rape.* New York: Simon & Schuster.

Burgess, A., & Holmstrom, L. (1974a). "Rape Trauma Syndrome." *American Journal of Psychiatry, 131,* 981–986.

Burgess, A., & Holmstrom, L. (1974b). *Rape: Victims of Crisis.* Bowie, MD: Brady.

Burgess, A., & Holmstrom, L. (1979). "Sexual Disruption and Recovery." *American Journal of Orthopsychiatry, 49,* 648–657.

Burgess, A. & Holmstrom, L. (1985). "Rape Trauma Syndrome and Post-Traumatic Stress Response." In A. W. Burgess (Ed.), *Rape and Sexual Assault: A Research Handbook* (pp. 55–60). New York: Garland.

Burt, M. (1980). "Cultural Myths and Supports for Rape." *Journal of Personality and Social Psychology, 38,* 217–230.

Carper, J. M. (1979). "Emergencies in Adolescents: Runaways and Father–Daughter Incest." *Pediatric Clinics of North America, 26,* 883–894.

Chappel, D. (1976). "Forcible Rape and the Criminal Justice System: Surveying Present Practices and Projecting Future Trends." In M. J. Walker & S. J. Brodsky (Eds.), *Sexual Assault: The Victim and the Rapist* (pp. 9–22). Lexington, MA: Lexington Press.

Courtois, C. A., & Watts, D. C. (1982). "Counseling Adult Women Who Experienced Incest in Childhood or Adolescence." *The Personnel and Guidance Journal, 60,* 275–281.

Derogatis, L. R. (1977). *SCL-90: Administration Scoring and Procedures Manual.* Baltimore, MD: Johns Hopkins University.

Dixon, J., & Jenkins, J. (1981). "Incestuous Child Sexual Abuse: A Review of Treatment Strategies." *Clinical Psychology Review, 1,* 211–222.

Ellis, E., Atkeson, B., & Calhoun, K. (1981). "An Assessment of Long-term Reaction to Rape." *Journal of Abnormal Psychology, 90,* 263–266.

Erikson, E. (1963). *Childhood & Society* (2nd ed.). New York: Norton. (Originally published 1950).

Feldman-Summers, S., Gordon, P. E., & Meagher, J. R. (1979). "The Impact of Rape on Sexual Satisfaction." *Journal of Abnormal Psychology, 88,* 101–105.

Finkelhor, D. & Yllo, K. (1983). "Rape in Marriage: A Sociological View." In D. Finkelhor, R. Gelles, G. Hotaling, & M. Straus (Eds.), *The Dark Side of Families: Current Family Violence Research.* Beverly Hills, CA: Sage.

Forward, S., & Buck, C. (1978). *Betrayal of Innocence: Incest and Its Devastation.* New York: Penguin Books.

Frank, E., & Stewart, B. (1983). "Treating Depression in Victims of Rape." *The Clinical Psychologist, 36,* 95–98.

Frank, E., & Stewart, B. (1984). "Physical Aggression: Treating the Victims." In E. Bleckman (Ed.), *Behavior Modification With Women* (pp. 245–273). New York: Guilford Press.

Giarretto, H. (1982). "A Comprehensive Child Sexual Abuse Treatment Program." *Child Abuse and Neglect, 6,* 263–278.

Goodchilds, J. D., & Zellman, G. L. (1984). "Sexual Signaling and Sexual Aggression in Adolescent Relationships." In N. M. Malamuth & E. Donnerstein (Eds.), *Pornography and Sexual Aggression* (pp.234–243). Orlando: Academic Press.

Halpern, S. (1978). *Rape: Helping the Victim.* Oredale, NJ: Medical Economics.

Harrison, R., & Beck, A. (1982). "Cognitive Therapy for Depression: History, Concepts and Procedures." In P. Heller & L. Ritt (Eds.), *Innovations in Clinical Practice: A Source Book* (Vol. 1, pp. 37–52). Sarasota, FL: Professional Resource Exchange.

Herman, J. (1981). "Father-Daughter Incest." *Professional Psychology, 12,* 76–80.

Jackson, T. L., & Ferguson, W. (1983). "Attribution of Blame in Incest." *American Journal of Community Psychology, 11,* 313–322.

Jackson, T. L., Quevillon, R. P., & Petretic-Jackson, P. A. (1985). "Assessment and Treatment of Sexual Assault Victims." In P. Keller & L. Ritt (Eds.), *Innovations in Clinical Practice: A Source Book* (Vol. 4, pp. 51–78). Sarasota, FL: Professional Resource Exchange.

Jackson, T. L., & Sandberg, G. (1985). "Attribution of Incest Blame Among Rural Attorneys and Judges." *Women and Therapy, 4* (4), 13–22.

Justice, B., & Justice, R. (1979). *The Broken Taboo: Sex in the Family.* New York: Human Sciences Press.

Kilpatrick, D. (1983). "Rape Victims: Detection, Assessment and Treatment." *The Clinical Psychologist, 36,* 92–95.

Kilpatrick, D., Veronen, L., & Resick, P. A. (1979). "Assessment of the Aftermath of Rape: Changing Patterns of Fear." *Journal of Behavioral Assessment, 1,* 133–148.

Kilpatrick, D., Veronen, L., & Resick, P. A. (1980, November). *Brief Behavioral Intervention Procedure: A New Treatment for Recent Rape Victims.* Presented at the annual meeting of the Association for Advancement of Behavior Therapy, New York, NY.

Kilpatrick, D., Veronen, L., & Resick, P. A. (1981, November). *Rape-Induced Fear: Its Effect Upon Behavior and Lifestyle.* Paper presented at the 15th Annual Convention of the Association for Advancement of Behavior Therapy, Toronto, Canada.

Koss, M. P. (1983). "The Scope of Rape: Implications for the Clinical Treatment of Victims." *The Clinical Psychologist, 36,* 88–91.

Koss, M. P., Gidycz, C., & Wisniewski, N. (1987). "The Scope of Rape: Incidence and Prevalence of Sexual Aggression and Victimization in a National Sample of Higher Education Students." *Journal of Clinical and Consulting Psychology, 55* (2), 162–171.

Koss, M. P., & Oros, C. J. (1982). "The Sexual Experiences Survey: A Research Instrument Investigating Sexual Aggression and Victimization." *Journal of Consulting and Clinical Psychology, 50,* 455–457.

Lazare, A. (1971). The Walk-In Patient: A Reformulation. Paper presented at Grand Rounds, Massachusetts General Hospital, Boston, February 16, 1971.

Lenox, M. C., & Gannon, L. R. (1983). "Psychological Consequences of Rape and Variables Influencing Recovery: A Review." *Woman and Therapy, 2,* 37–49.

Los Angeles Commission on Assaults Against Women. (1983). *Surviving Sexual Assault.* New York: Congdon & Weed.

Martin, R. (1982). "Primer on Stress Inoculation." In P. Keller & L. Ritt (Eds.), *Innovations in Clinical Practice: A Source Book* (vol. 1, pp. 112–125). Sarasota, FL: Professional Resource Book Exchange.

Meichenbaum, D. (1977). *Cognitive-Behavior Modification.* New York: Plenum.

Nakashima, I. (1979). "Incestuous Families." *Pediatric Annals, 2,* 29–42.

National Center on Child Abuse and Neglect. (1981). *Study Findings: National Study of Incidence and Severity of Child Abuse and Neglect.* Washington, DC: Department of Health, Education and Welfare.

O'Hare, J., & Taylor, K. (1983). "The Reality of Incest." *Women and Therapy, 2,* 215–229.

Pomeroy, W., Flax, C., & Wheeler, C. (1982). *Taking a Sex History: Interviewing and Recording.* New York: Free Press.

Prentice, R., & Jackson, T. (1984, May). *Attribution of Incest Blame by Metropolitan Police Applicants and Sworn Officers.* Presented at the annual meeting of the Midwestern Psychological Association, Chicago, IL.

Resick, P. A., Calhoun, K. S., Atkeson, B. M., & Ellis, E. M. (1981). "Social Adjustment in Victims of Sexual Assault." *Journal of Consulting and Clinical Psychology, 49,* 705–712.

Resick, P. A., & Jackson, T. L. (1981). "Attitudes Toward Rape Among Mental Health Professionals." *American Journal of Community Psychology, 9,* 481–490.

Russell, D. (1982). *Rape in Marriage.* New York: Macmillan.

Sandberg, G., Petretic-Jackson, P., & Jackson, T. (1987). "College Students' Attitudes Regarding Sexual Coercion and Aggression: Developing Educational and Preventive Strategies." *Journal of College Student Personnel, 28,* 302–311.

Schwendinger, J., & Schwendinger, H. (1974). "Rape Myths: In Legal, Theoretical and Everyday Practice." *Crime and Social Justice, 1,* 18–26.

Spencer, J. (1978). "Father-Daughter Incest: A Clinical View from the Corrections Field." *Child Welfare, 57,* 581–590.

Sutherland, S., & Scherl, D. (1970). "Patterns of Response Among Victims of Rape." *American Journal of Orthopsychiatry, 40,* 503–511.

Symonds, M. (1980). "The Second Injury to Victims of Violent Crime." *Evaluation and Change.* Minnesota Medical Research Foundation (Special Issue: "Services to Survivors").

Tsai, M., & Wagner, N. (1978). "Therapy Groups for Women Sexually Molested and Children." *Archives of Sexual Behavior, 7,* 417–427.

U.S. Department of Justice (1987). *Crime in the United States: Uniform Crime Reports for the United States* (Item No. 722). Washington, DC: Author.

Veronen, L., & Kilpatrick, D. (1980). "Self-reported Fears of Rape Victims: A Preliminary Investigation." *Behavior Modification, 4,* 383–396.

Veronen, L., & Kilpatrick, D. (1983). "Stress Management for Rape Victims." In D. Meichenbaum & M. Jaremko (Eds.), *Stress Reduction and Prevention* (pp. 341–374). New York: Plenum.

Ward, M. A. (1980). *Attribution of Blame in Rape.* Unpublished doctoral dissertation, University of South Dakota, Vermillion, SD.

Ward, M. A., & Resick, P. A. (1980). *Attribution of Rape Blame Scale.* Unpublished dissertation, University of South Dakota, Vermillion, SD.

Williams, J., & Holmes, K. (1981). *The Second Assault: Rape and Public Attitudes.* Westport, CT: Greenwood Press.

Williams, L. (1984). "The Classic Rape: When Do Victims Report?" *Social Problems, 31* (4), 459–467.

Wolpe, J., & Lang, P. T. (1964). "A Fear Survey Schedule for Use in Behavior Therapy." *Behavior Research and Therapy, 2,* 27–30.

Chapter 8

Crisis Intervention with Abusing Families: Short-Term Cognitive Coercive Group Therapy Using Goal Attainment Scaling

Rita Justice, Ph.D., and
Blair Justice, Ph.D.

T om and Susan had been married 13 years. They had three children. Bobby, age 8, was the first son and the middle child. He was a good little boy who tried to please his parents. One summer afternoon, while Tom was driving his truck down the freeway, he exploded in rage at Bobby and began to beat him with his fist. That night, the police arrived at Tom and Susan's home and took Bobby into protective custody.

Life had been chaotic for Tom and Susan for a long time. Early in their marriage, Tom had hit Susan when he lost his temper, but that had stopped after a few months. Lately there had been a lot for the family to handle. Tom had just gone back to work after having been laid up for six months from having had his shoulder pinned between two trucks at work. This was the most recent of several on-the-job injuries for Tom in the last few years. The family had moved to a new city only a month before Tom was injured. They had impulsively decided to move one night, took their children and $75, and left. Their house was without furniture for several months because they could not afford to have it moved. This was their third move in eight months. On the day Tom beat Bobby, he had taken five 10-milligram doses of Valium, four Tylenol #4, and had consumed eight or nine beers. He had smoked marijuana twice that week.

Tom and Susan had either tolerated or coped with these myriad problems for years without considering the need for outside help, other than medical treatment. When Bobby was taken from their home, Tom and Susan had a crisis they had to face.

A crisis, like stress, in large part depends on the eye of the beholder. Recent research on crisis intervention points up the fallacy of defining a crisis solely in terms of the actual event (Auerbach, 1986). This is especially true in dealing with families in which child abuse occurs. Abusive families often live in a state of chronic distress and violence that nonabusive families would certainly define as crisis. But to people who have grown up in violent homes, violence is not a crisis but rather a painful part of relationships (Justice & Justice, 1976).

This perception that parent–child violence is the norm makes it unlikely that abusing families will voluntarily seek professional or community support. Another factor working against these families' being open to intervention is the basic distrust that comes from having been abused as a child. Child-abusing parents were in almost every instance themselves abused children and therefore experienced others as a source of pain, not comfort and sustenance. Isolation from people became a survival adaptation, one not easily relinquished.

The combination of a high tolerance for violence and fear of reaching out for help means that abusing families are not likely to seek therapy even if the life or health of their children is at risk. This makes coercive therapy essential if there is to be successful intervention with these families (Justice & Justice, 1982). The term *coercive therapy* is usually used when the client is under some outside pressure to seek therapy. Consequences do play a role in a person's choice. With abusive families, it is often necessary to impose consequences that are unacceptable to the parents. For many, only the threat or actual removal of the children from the family or the threat of imprisonment are sufficient coercion for abusive parents to seek therapy.

In effect, the threatened dissolution of the family creates a situation that the abusing family defines as a crisis. Violence may be acceptable but imprisonment or the loss of their children is not. Even these coercions are not sufficient to induce all abusive families to leave their protective walls of isolation and seek therapy, but many will. The fact that some families will relinquish their children rather than seek help points out how the concept of coercion in psychotherapy is somewhat misleading. No matter what the external pressure, each individual makes the choice to present himself or herself for therapy. The person's presence, under whatever conditions, is evidence of willingness to change something about his or her life.

It was in that spirit that the parents in 40 families in which there had been physical abuse were treated by us in group therapy over a six-month period. The parents were referred by child-protective agencies in Houston, Texas. In 75 percent of the cases there had been a court order removing the couple's child from the home, thereby creating a crisis to which these families chose to respond. The parents were coerced in that they were told that their chances of getting the child or children back would be greater if they were in therapy. In the remaining 25 percent of the families, the children's remaining in the home was conditional on the parents' seeking psychological help.

The coercion was not enough to sustain the motivation for all the families. Six of the couples dropped out of therapy and subsequently lost custody of their children.

In the remaining 34 families, there was only one reported case of a recurrence of abuse. Those who completed therapy attended an average of 15 sessions over a six-month period.

Just as important as the cessation of the abuse were the changes in family dynamics that made it possible for them to interact differently. These changes were measured using an evaluative technique called Goal Attainment Scaling (GAS; Kiresuk & Sherman, 1968). GAS involves identifying the main problem areas for each family, setting goals to be attained in therapy, and measuring change in each problem area. Measurement of change was also reflected in lower scores on the Holmes and Rahe (1967) Social Readjustment Rating Scale. While the number of life event changes a person experiences in a given period of time is not in and of itself sufficient to predict crisis (Felner, Rowlinson, & Terre, 1986), the abusive parents described here consistently were in a state of what Holmes and Rahe (1967) called "life crisis." Even though the parents may not have defined their lives as being in crisis until the family unit was threatened with dissolution, the flood of changes they experienced at any one time put them at risk of chronically going over the edge and losing control with their children.

The Extent of the Problem

T he number of children affected by their parents' losing control and maltreating them is increasing steadily. The National Incidence Study funded by the federal National Center on Child Abuse and Neglect (1986) estimated that more than 1 million children, or 16.3 per 1,000, are abused or neglected annually. This figure represents a 66 percent increase over the number of children identified as maltreated in a similar study conducted in 1980. The 1986 study projected that 1,100 children died in 1986 as a result of child abuse, 10 percent more than were identified in 1980.

Intervention in the lives of most of these families will be by the police, protective service workers, and physicians. Those who do get into treatment often do not have the financial resources or motivation for long-term psychotherapy. Short-term group therapy is a model that is well suited to the enormous problem of treating millions of abusive families. While there are no accurate figures on the extent of the use of this treatment approach for child abuse, the model is easily adapted to most treatment settings and as such has been employed widely.

Crisis Theory

B ecause these families live with potentially explosive stress, they are like other populations that face recurring crises, such as prisoners of war or concentration camp survivors, in terms of the time scheme of symptoms and problems (Ursano,

Boydstun, & Wheatley, 1981; Eitinger & Strom, 1981). Physical, psychological, or behavioral symptoms of the abusive system may show up before, during, or even years after the actual intervention by outsiders into the family system. Some or all of the problems to be discussed in this chapter may be apparent at the time the family is initially seen by the clinicians, but with time most of the symptoms characteristic of abusive families emerge.

With some families the severity of the effects of the abuse and outside intervention will be greater than with others, just as with other types of crises (Brenner, Roskies, & Lazarus, 1980). The experienced stress or crisis is a result of interaction between the person and environment, including the person's expectations of his or her ability to control the situation, basic attitudes, and the context that shapes these beliefs (Auerbach, 1986, p. 15). Success in dealing with the current crisis depends in part on how past crises have been handled (Hiroto & Seligman, 1975). Since abusive parents have had remarkably little success in handling their children or their lives satisfactorily, the goal of crisis intervention group therapy is to offer a repertoire of concrete coping skills for familial and interpersonal interactions.

Key Concepts

W hat can be expected to happen in short-term crisis therapy with these seriously dysfunctional families? Basically, the problem-solving model of crisis intervention (Burgess & Baldwin, 1981) and the concepts of brief therapy (Haley, 1977) are most useful in conceptualizing what is possible under the time constraints. Both emphasize the value of being able to enter a system when it is in crisis. Brief therapy is based on the premise that a system in crisis is more open to change and that certain critical and often brief interventions into the system when it is unstable can result in lasting changes in how the system functions. Because these abusive families are open to intervention, however unwillingly, the family system is open to changes that may permanently alter how the family functions in the future. At the very least, the clients are exposed to a helping model and may experience caring relationships that will serve as a positive reinforcement for seeking additional help. If they are successful in learning new coping skills and improving family relationships, the parents discover that negative motivators (such as having a child removed by the protective service agency) can have a positive outcome (the child is returned and the family gets along better). Perhaps most important of all, the child management/development information the parents are exposed to gives them tools for more effectively coping with their children.

Certain changes are *not* likely to happen in this brief therapy with abusing families. The parents are dealing with deep wounds from childhood. Healing wounds from an abusive childhood is a slow and painful process. It cannot happen in a few months. One consequence of an abusive past is addictive behavior. Drugs, alcohol, work, food, or codependent relationships are all efforts at numbing the rage and pain from childhood. Short-term crisis therapy can do little in addressing these addictions, even though there are important problems in the abusive family system that this approach can and does address. Psychotic or psychopathic parents are also not likely to be helped with brief therapy, but only a small percentage of abusive parents fall into those categories (Justice & Justice, 1976, pp. 47–50).

Major Areas of Concern in Abusing Families

U sing the Goal Attainment Scale makes it easier to keep a clear focus on what problems the clients and clinicians have agreed to address and offers a tool for setting contracts and measuring change. Each goal level bears a numerical designation, and each problem area carries a relative numerical weight. The numerical goal levels, scale weights, and the changes the parents make between entry into the group and follow-up are plugged into a formula to compute the composite goal attainment score. This process removes some of the subjectiveness in assessing change and helps everyone involved know what the goals are and what has or has not been accomplished. Staying focused is essential when dealing with these families that seem to be facing a never-ending wave of problems. The six problem areas most critical to change in an abusing family are symbiosis, isolation, marital communication, temper/impatience, child development and management, and employment.

Symbiosis

Symbiosis is a physical or emotional attachment for the purpose of survival. An infant must depend on its mother or a mother surrogate in order to survive. If that early dependence is insufficient or contaminated by rejection or suffering, an emotional hunger persists. Abused children grow up longing for a symbolic "good mother." They pick mates hoping their partners will make up for the lack of love they received as children. Those unrealistic expectations inevitably lead to disappointment. In their disappointment, they put their unrealistic hopes on their own children, who end up in turn not getting their needs met. In abusing families there is a constant struggle to be the nurtured one—a perpetual shifting symbiosis. Violence is an attempt to force a mate or child into caretaking.

In addressing the problem of symbiosis in abusive families, the goal is teaching new coping skills for getting emotional needs met. Rather than struggling for nurturance through passivity or violence, the parents are taught communication tools that enable them both to be more effective in getting what they want from each other. By using these tools, they relinquish to some extent the fantasy that their partners can or will magically know and meet all their emotional needs, as a good mother might for her infant. Rather, these parents come to terms with their responsibility and ability to meet their own needs.

Isolation

As a result of having experienced people as hurtful, abusive parents are usually cut off from others both socially and emotionally. Even if they do decide to turn to others in times of distress, it is unlikely that they will have anyone other than family to call on or that they will know how to effectively use the community resources available to them.

Participation in group therapy is an important first step in breaking up the isolation of these parents. Once a week, for one and a half hours, they experience other people as being helpful and caring instead of punitive, giving rather than exploiting. Their concept of what is possible in human relationships begins to expand, and trust slowly builds.

Using the positive group experience as a starting point, the members begin to take risks that further break down the walls of isolation. The risks may seem small—meeting a neighbor, applying for a job, getting a telephone—but each step out of isolation builds a road to greater openness.

Marital Communication

There are no abusive families that have a positively rewarding marital foundation. This is hardly surprising, since the partners have so few skills at positive social interaction and such poor marital role models from their childhoods. The most common complaints of the couples entering our group are "We don't communicate" or "He/She never talks/listens to me." People who have been unsuccessful in getting their needs met as children enter marriage with an unconscious expectation that again they will be emotionally disappointed. Almost invariably, they are. Both mates are battling to be nurtured, and neither has any pool of nurturance from which to draw. Teaching communication skills is a first step in enabling these husbands and wives to be more effective in problem solving and attaining emotional, spiritual, or physical satisfaction with each other. They learn that marriage need not be a win/lose proposition.

Temper/Impatience

It is understandable that people who were emotionally and/or physically abused as children would have problems in handling their own and others' anger. The rage stored from childhood either explodes or is turned into depression. Typically in abusive families, one or both mates are "rage-aholics." As in an alcoholic family system, the addictive behavior is reinforced by either submissiveness or negative attention. Rageful acting out and the family's adaptation to it was witnessed by these individuals as children, and they repeat the pattern with their own families.

A variety of approaches to handling the temper are necessary. They range from "no hitting" contracts to relaxation training. It is essential to define clear limits for rage-aholics, since no one may have ever done that before in their lives. Limit setting and contracting for expressing anger in appropriate ways enhance the parents' growing awareness of their ability to effectively manage their emotions.

Child Development and Management

Abusive parents are woefully ignorant of what babies and children need at different ages and stages and how to respond to those needs. Just as most of us do, these mothers and fathers draw on their own experiences of being parented. Since those experiences were frequently abusive, they have few healthy guidelines to follow naturally. Also, the emotional demands of their children serve as chronic, unconscious reminders of the parents' own unmet childhood demands. The combination of not knowing the right thing to do, knowing the wrong thing to do, and not wanting to do any of it makes for an explosive combination.

A large portion of each group session must be devoted to giving information on developmental stages of children, appropriate parental responses, nonviolent behavioral management, and other basic skills essential to even minimal success in parenting. The teaching is typically in response to the parents' immediate concerns about their children's behavior, such as bedwetting, lying, nightmares, or school problems. The information given in group therapy is supplemented with assigned readings geared to the educational level of the parent.

The readings range from *TA For Tots* (Freed, 1973) to Dreikurs' (1964) *Children: The Challenge*. In group therapy, Smith and Smith's (1966) *Child Management* and Gordon's (1970) *Parent Effectiveness Training* are used to teach concepts such as consistency and positive reinforcement.

Employment

Problems with employment are usually symptomatic of dysfunctional interpersonal skills. For example, a young mother stays home alone watching soap operas, waiting for the protective service agency to somehow magically return her child. Her refusal to look for a job is primarily because of fear of rejection. A man gets fired from his fourth construction job in a year because he blew up at the foreman or started a fight with another worker. A couple works opposite shifts because they find they fight less only if they see each other little.

All employment problems are addressed from both a practical and a psychological perspective. While it is helpful to give information about where the community unemployment office is located, it is of even greater value to give the group members an opportunity to learn new skills in handling relationships at work. The 16-year-old mother who refused to look for a job came from a large family that emotionally neglected all the children and seemed to notice them only when they made mistakes.

She got pregnant by and married the first young man who showed any interest in her. By contracting to apply for three jobs she was not to accept, she was relieved of any possibility of rejection while taking the risk of actually looking for a job. She came back to group therapy the week following the assignment having accepted the first job she was offered. The construction worker was both abused and neglected as a child. He carried with him great rage, which erupted both within the family and at work. By inviting him to look at what sets him off gave the man an opportunity to think before he reacts and to use more effective, nonviolent coping behavior. He was able to hold off his outbursts and discuss any upsetting incident in group therapy, thus saving him from being fired from any more jobs or harming his family. Both the husband and wife working opposite shifts came from alcoholic and rage-aholic families. By slowly learning to communicate and deal with their feelings, they could stop withdrawing from problems and each other.

Behind all these six problem areas (symbiosis, isolation, marital communication, temper, child development and management, and employment) and other problems that abusive families face lie belief systems that sustain the tension, conflict and disharmony. Albert Ellis (1973) described these beliefs as *erroneous thinking*. In working with these abusive families what must be addressed are their erroneous belief systems. The following seven beliefs are those that most commonly contribute to the abusive system.

1. If my child cries, misbehaves, or does not do what I want, he or she does not love me and I am a bad parent.
2. My child should know what I want and want to do it.
3. My child should take care of me like I took care of my parents.
4. My husband/wife should know what I want and meet all of my needs.
5. If I have to ask, it does not count and I am a failure.
6. You cannot trust anyone.
7. People are out for what they can get.

The focus of crisis intervention with abusive parents is to shake their certainty in these beliefs. When they have an experience in group therapy of being supported and even nurtured, their beliefs about all people being untrustworthy and selfish are shaken a little. Learning that asking directly for what one wants is the most effective way of getting it goes against the belief that it is a weakness to ask. Bit by bit, their armored view of the world relaxes, letting in the light and warmth of human caring and compassion.

Clinicians' Roles and Skills

W hat is required of the clinician for successful crisis intervention with abusive families? Perhaps it is more important to say what is not required. The effective clinician working with abusive parents and their children must not be a rescuer, in the sense of a knight on a white horse. It is essential that the clinician set clear limits with the parents about what the clinician can and cannot do to help. This helps avoid unrealistic expectations on both sides. For example, the clinician can help the parents learn new child management skills that may convince the protective service worker or a judge that the children are not likely to be abused again. The clinician cannot guarantee that the children will be returned. Humility is a necessary ingredient in working with these families, and the invitations for rescuing are ever present.

Just as there are temptations to be a rescuer, at times it is equally tempting to be a persecutor. A certain amount of initial anger is natural, but if that anger is ever unleashed on the parents, the therapeutic alliance is irreparably shattered. Any clinician who was emotionally or physically abused as a child needs to address his or her own pain and rage before working with abusive parents. In addition to resolving one's own therapeutic issues, it is helpful in mitigating the anger to remember that all abusive parents were once and still are suffering and abused children.

As much as abusive parents are victims, they too can be persecutors. The wise clinician guards against becoming a victim to these parents. The most prudent means of doing so is by taking care of oneself. This entails clear limit setting as to availability, behaviors that will not be tolerated in or outside group, and general self-care (e.g., good diet, exercise, a support group). Working with a co-clinician is very helpful in avoiding victimization. At times when all the parents seem to be ganged up against the clinician, it is comforting to have at least one other human being in the room who is an ally. Ideally, the group sessions ought not to deteriorate into confrontations, but if that happens, it can be very lonely not to have someone on one's side.

Finally, to work effectively with these families it is essential to understand the abusive system—that is, the characteristics of the parents, children, and the environments in which they live, the psychological dynamics and tensions between and within the family members, and the typical problems. These are challenging families with which to work, and it is foolhardy to enter their world without a map of the territory and a knowledge of the rules by which they live.

Case Vignettes

G oal Attainment Scaling (GAS) is the primary tool for identifying problems and evaluating progress, but for getting the parents to make initial disclosures about their concerns, the simple checklist in Figure 8.1 works almost every time.

All new group members are given this checklist the first night they come to group therapy and are asked to check any problems they are having. This is a nonthreatening way for each person to say something about what worries him or her without having to be self-disclosing verbally right away. The checklist also allows the parents to avoid dealing immediately with the guilt-laden problem that brought them to group—the abuse of their children. A willingness on the part of the clinicians to deal with what the parents choose to say are problems allows the parents time to test

Figure 8.1   *Goal Attainment Scaling Checklist*

Which of the following are areas of concern to you?

(Check here)

_____ Low Self-Image—low opinion of self, think you're no good, can't do anything right.

_____ Don't Have Friends—stay to self a lot, isolated from others, feel alone.

_____ Temper and/or Impatience—have a "short fuse," blow up easily, or get impatient with nearly everyone.

_____ Dependent—depend heavily on spouse, can't make decisions yourself, can't make it without spouse or some other relative; often irresponsible.

_____ Little Support from Spouse—have to do most of decision making yourself, can't depend on spouse to help with kids or to give "moral support," or to say nice things.

_____ Stress—feel under pressure all the time from job, kids, house, finances, or other reasons.

_____ Child Development and Needs—don't know much about the needs of babies and children at various ages and what to expect.

_____ Sex—little or no sexual satisfaction in marriage; frustration, arguments over sex.

_____ Trust—can't trust anyone, always being let down, look at people with suspicion.

_____ Depression—feel down and hopeless; have trouble getting things done and making decisions; life looks bleak.

_____ Child Is Disappointment—child isn't loving or doesn't do what you expect or seems different from other children.

_____ Child Care and Management—need to know much more about what to do for and with baby or child ar various ages, and how to get child to "behave."

---

the safety of the group and the clinicians. Once trust starts to build, they are more willing to address the more painful issues.

Once the parents are "hooked"—that is, engaged in the therapeutic process by declaring some problem(s)—the GAS is constructed for each group member. Client and clinician mutually arrive at goals to be reached within a three-month period in each area of concern. As more problems surface, they are added to the GAS, and additional goals are set. At the end of each three-month contract period, change is

Make sure you have checked all the problems that are of concern to you.

Now look at the list of problems again and RANK them in terms of which are bigger problems and which are smaller problems.

For example, if Temper and/or Impatience is your biggest problem, put the number 1 by it in the list below. Then go down the list and see what is your second biggest problem. If Trust is the second biggest, put a 2 by it.

Put numbers by all the problems that are of concern to you so you will rank them according to importance. If two are of EQUAL weight or importance, put the same number by each of the problems.

(Rank problems by putting number by each concern)

_____ Low Self-Image

_____ Don't Have Friends

_____ Temper and/or Impatience

_____ Dependent

_____ Little Support from Spouse

_____ Stress

_____ Child Development and Needs

_____ Sex

_____ Trust

_____ Depression

_____ Child Care and Management

_____ Child Is Disappointment

---

evaluated and recorded by both the parents and their clinician, in the group setting. This encourages accountability and discourages grandiosity in goal setting.

The same guide is used during follow-up interviews after the parents leave group therapy. For successful terminations from therapy, each parent must reach the expected level of success as defined by the contract in each of the six major problem areas: symbiosis, isolation, marital communication, temper, child development and management, and employment. If all six areas are not problems for any particular parent, change scores are based on identified problems. (For more details on scoring GAS, see Justice & Justice, 1976, pp. 114–130). A recommendation is made that the child be returned to the parents when both parents have made sufficient changes in these six problem areas and have shifted their erroneous belief systems enough for them to parent appropriately and relate to the world and each other from a more positive stance.

While it is both possible and necessary to define problems and goals in a somewhat orderly fashion, reaching the goals is far from a linear process. Crisis intervention therapy with abusive families is much more akin to dancing to atonal music than performing a graceful minuet: At times it is hard to know what beat will come next. The only solution is to stay flexible.

Dianne and Al were one couple that demanded such flexibility. Their symbiotic relationship was almost classic in the controlling mother–guilty son roles they adopted. Dianne not only instructed Al on how to behave, she even answered questions addressed to him in group therapy. While she rigidly functioned in the parent role most of the time, the deprived child in her would periodically erupt in a rage, screaming at Al that he and their children were worthless, hated her, and that if he loved her at all, he would beat the children into obedience (which he would then attempt to do). This vignette reflects how both Al and Dianne held all the erroneous beliefs that support the abusive system.

Symbiosis. Dianne and Al both had an unspoken understanding that she knew what Al needed (to say, to wear, etc.) better than he did. Both discounted his ability to think for himself. The arrangement worked until Dianne would feel too much strain from always being the responsible one. When she expressed her neediness in the form of rage, she was actually railing against the fact that Al had failed to "know what I want and meet all my needs." The children also failed her by not being able to "know what I want and do it." The arrangement was a no-win double-bind. The lock on this emotional prison was the belief that "If I have to ask, it does not count, and I am a failure." Dianne could not allow Al to take responsibility for asking for what he wanted, and she herself would not ask to have her needs met.

Isolation. Dianne and Al's family was virtually a closed system. They had no friends and only occasional visits with relatives. Unfortunately, because their relationship with the relatives was usually discordant, the relatives were not inclined to be helpful or they extracted a high psychological cost for being so. This oft-repeated scenario reinforced for Al and Dianne their feelings of failure for having to ask for help and their beliefs that "you cannot trust anyone" because "people are only out for what they can get."

Marital Communication. Not surprisingly, a controlling mother–guilty son relationship does not make for very satisfying marital interchanges. As in most abusive families, communication is limited to either the basic exchanges necessary for daily living or ones negative in tone or content. In this family, Al generally spent his free time addictively glued to the television set. He complained, quite truthfully, that he was too tired to play with his children whenever they asked him to do so. He said little to Dianne when they or the family were together. Dianne did almost all the talking, which consisted primarily of nagging and criticism.

Temper. Dianne lost her temper easily, both with her children and at work. Her explosions at work left her jobless on more than one occasion. When she would burst out in anger and pay a severe price either in guilt or lost employment, she would remind herself, "If I say what I want, it does not work, and I am a failure." Al, on the other hand, held in his anger and responded to the world (and his family) with passivity. His only expressions of anger were when he beat his two young daughters with a belt, which was basically a compliant response to try to please and placate Dianne.

Child development and management. Both parents were essentially unaware of their children's psychological needs or any technique of discipline other than physical punishment. Underlying their ignorance was the basic belief that the children should know what their parents wanted them to do and should comply voluntarily (as Al did much of the time). Dianne, more than Al, saw her daughters' unhappiness and misbehavior as evidence of their lack of love for her and her failure as a parent. Since both Al and Dianne as children had been in caretaking roles with their parents, they expected the same of their daughters and reacted punitively when the children failed to meet these unrealistic expectations.

Employment. Al complained about the pressure, long hours, and his supervisor's "unfair" treatment at work. Dianne, because of her fear that she would lose her temper on the job, refused to look for employment even though she was extremely bored and restless at home after the childrens' protective service authorities removed the children from the home. Because they both saw others as persecutors and themselves as victims ("You cannot trust anyone. People are only out for what they can get"), it was virtually guaranteed that the workplace would be a source of stress for them.

The first step in confronting Al and Dianne's symbiosis was to contract with them that each would answer the questions in group addressed to him or her. It was difficult for Dianne to be quiet and let Al talk for himself, but the more he did the more they both realized that he could think for himself and the less she felt obliged to do so for him.

The second step was to teach them the appropriateness, necessity, and techniques of making requests of each other and the children. Role-playing in group and home-work assignments (e.g., asking your spouse to do something personal for you once a day) were useful in shaking the belief that asking invalidated the response and indicated failure. Contracting for "forbidden" behaviors is an effective way to bring to light the unconscious beliefs and resistances. By role-playing in group, the couple gets useful feedback from other members about how they appear to their spouse and what they might be doing that is interfering with their requests being fulfilled.

Similarly, isolation can be broken down by contracting with the couple to meet the neighbors, start attending church, or take on some activity that will enable them to test their belief that all the world is untrustworthy. If things go wrong in the encounters they attempt, the group and the clinician are available to help analyze what went wrong and what could be done differently next time. Dianne and Al agreed to begin attending church services and to meet one new couple a month there. Within a few months, they had a small but growing support group and, more importantly, were learning how to use people for support with guilt feelings.

To begin a positive flow between themselves, Al agreed to limit the hours of television he watched and Dianne agreed to listen to him without criticizing and interrupting his budding efforts at communication. In group therapy, they practiced saying positive statements to each other and were surprised at how often negativity was embedded in what was ostensibly a positive stroke.

During their eight months in group therapy, Dianne and Al were exposed to a great deal of information on basic developmental needs of infants and children and nonviolent techniques of child management. The more they learned, the more they realized that their expectations of their children were unreasonable. Dianne stopped interpreting their daughters' noncompliance as nonlove. Sometimes another group member would role-play a child in their family and Dianne and Al would try to get the "kid" to comply. The information from the group member on how it was to be parented in that way gave valuable insight. As Al and Dianne began to nurture each other more, they stopped turning to their children for nurturance. They also saw the fallacy in expecting their children (or each other) to read their minds about what they wanted, and to make clearer requests.

Relaxation training at the end of each group meeting, accompanied by an assignment of repeating the exercise several times a week at home, helped Dianne keep her rage in check. Instead of waiting until she was out of control, she would remove herself from the children when she first sensed that she was getting very angry. By knowing techniques to use to help her calm down, she could avoid outbursts both at home and at work. Also, since she was getting her needs met by Al and the girls more regularly, she had less need to escalate to a violent rage. Al also found the relaxation exercises useful in alleviating his depression.

Once Dianne felt confident that she would not lose control of her temper, she was willing to look for work and got a more rewarding job than she had ever had previously. As Al's confidence grew, he was less passive at work and felt less victimized there. He also aired his grievances more quickly and kept resentments from building up.

By the time Al and Dianne left the group, they had reached or surpassed all the goals they had set using the GAS. Their daughters were returned to them, and there were no further incidences of abuse. They had learned to be supportive of each other and nurturing to their children. Above all, a belief in the goodness of people and themselves was slowly replacing the erroneous beliefs that sustained their abusive family system.

Clinical Issues

Early Stages

The initial stage of crisis intervention with abusive families is one of mutual "sizing up." The clients are consciously and unconsciously protecting themselves from whatever harm or duress they imagine the clinician might inflict on them. Simultaneously, the clinician is trying to measure the extent of the clients' commitment to change. It is a period of mutual distrust and mutual hopefulness. Each is hoping the other means well. Neither believes that completely.

When parents come to therapy, the clinician must make it clear that he or she does not have the authority to return the children or have charges dismissed. The clinician's role is to facilitate and report psychological and behavioral changes in the parents that indicate a reduced likelihood of further abuse. It is also the job of the clinician to make it clear to the parents that mere attendance at group sessions is insufficient for there to be a report of positive change. This is where the GAS becomes so helpful in helping parents see the necessity of making concrete, observable, reportable changes.

Once the parents understand the role of the clinician and their own responsibility for change, the process of therapy can begin. It may be necessary to get past protests by the parents that they were wrongly accused of abusing their children. One effective reply is to point out to the parents that the one problem they will certainly admit to having is that the authorities have intervened in their lives and that therapy can be a means for getting the authorities *out* of their lives. They are usually then willing to fill out the checklist and begin discussing problems checked.

At this point in the intervention process, the group itself serves an important role in breaking down distrust. The "old-timers"—that is, clients who have been in group therapy a few weeks or months—share with the newcomers how they felt when they first came to the group, what they feared, what they erroneously believed, and how their lives have improved since starting treatment. It is important to have an ongoing group for just this purpose. With an ongoing group, there will be people who have made sufficient changes to have had their children returned or charges dropped against them, and they serve as powerful role models for parents who have just lost their children and are filled with fear and rage.

As trust begins to build, there is inevitably a period of testing. Clients may fail to show up without calling to explain their absence, a violation of one group rule. Or they may report hitting their children or each other. In this stage, as well as in the initial stage of intervention, they may lie. However, having both parents in a group makes it more likely that one or the other will report the "bad" behavior of their spouse or give off cues when their spouse is lying. This is the period in which it is crucial that the clinician be a fair but firm "parent." Lying and broken agreements must be confronted but without hostility or shaming. Each problem becomes an opportunity for a client to learn more about himself or herself and also to learn that he or she can make a mistake without being attacked or banished. This testing stage may continue almost the entire time clients are in the group.

The final stage deals with issues of separation. Once the clients commit to group therapy, it becomes an important source of strokes, support, learning, and social contact. Not surprisingly, many of the parents are reluctant to leave the group even after the court or the child protective agency has returned their children or closed the case. In order to facilitate the process, parents go through a "graduation" ceremony. As part of the ceremony, parents give a little speech summarizing their accomplishments in the group, and they are awarded a certificate of completion that is suitable for framing. Afterward, the whole group shares in the celebration with cake and congratulations. This ritual helps the parents feel better about leaving, and the certificate serves as a visible reminder to them of all they have accomplished to make their lives and the lives of their children better.

To make the pain of separation a little easier, parents are given permission to come back to the group at any time they feel their lives are getting out of control. About 10 percent do return at some later date for another month or two of therapy.

Psychosocial Symptoms and Physiological Reactions

P arents entering group therapy bring with them all the psychosocial problems that they carry in the rest of their lives: manipulativeness, distrust, hostility, fear, a lack of boundaries. They are often depressed emotionally and many are ill physically. Since they live with chronic distress, it is hardly surprising that they often suffer from colds, lung infections, chronic aches and pains, injuries, and obesity. Any or all of the behavioral and physical problems can be addressed once a contract is agreed on using the Goal Attainment Scale.

While any problem the abusive parent presents can become the therapeutic focus, by addressing the six most common problem areas discussed earlier, the other problems usually clear up. For example, once the parents begin communicating better and break out of their isolation, their depression starts to lift. When they feel more stroked and acknowledged by each other, they are less likely to use food for strokes and nurturance. Their immune systems are able to function with less strain when they are not chronically *awful*izing and *should*ing about all the life events they face (Justice, 1987). Stress management and better coping skills help relieve most of the physical complaints (Justice, 1988).

Assessment and Determination of Abuse

I t is both unwise to proceed too hastily in labeling parents as abusing and unsafe for the children in delaying too long in so doing. Fortunately for the clinician, that decision is more often in the hands of the child protective service worker and the courts than in those of the clinician. Once a decision is made that there is evidence of abuse, the case worker may work with the parents to use community resources to lessen the stress in the family, or the child or children may be removed until the parents participate in therapy and the clinician reports there is no further risk of abuse. If the parents do not chose to go to therapy, the children may be removed and parental rights may be terminated if the risk of continued abuse is sufficient.

When the clinician is asked to determine the likelihood that abuse has taken place, it is necessary to put together a gestalt impression, using the six typical problems discussed in this chapter as an outline. When either or both parents have been abused as a child and there are three or more of the six problems present, in particular symbiosis, it is virtually assured that the family system is abusive. Some test instruments have been developed for assessing the abusive profile, and they are proving to have some validity (Abidin, 1983; Milner, 1986). But use of the instruments needs to be supplemented with clinical observations.

When is it safe for the children to be returned or for the parents to terminate therapy? Clinical impressions are necessarily subjective. The Goal Attainment Scaling allows for a precise measurement of change, based on mutually agreed-on contracts. Follow-up studies on group members since 1973 have confirmed that when clients obtain a GAS score of 55 or more, the danger of further abuse to the children is minimal and termination is appropriate. In order to reach a score of 55, the parents must have reached or surpassed the stated expected level of success in all six problem areas. When they have changed their behavior with respect to all six major areas of concern, the children return to parents who not only are no longer abusive but are more understanding and giving.

By the time parents are ready to terminate successfully, they have made the following changes:

1. Their symbiotic relationship has changed from one of struggling for nurturance to mutual support and personal responsibility for their own needs.
2. Isolation has been replaced with healthy and appropriate social interactions and interdependence.
3. Marital interactions are positive more than negative and communication skills are sufficient for problem resolution.
4. They are using nonphysical methods of discipline and are responsive to the developmental needs of their children.
5. Problems at work are not a major source of stress to either parent.

Using these criteria, only one of the 36 couples who completed therapy was determined to have again abused a child, as assessed by the child protective service workers.

Crisis offers an opportunity for positive change in the abusive family system. The system is a closed one that imprisons all the family members. Unless society breaks into the system by requiring the parents to seek help, the cycle of abuse continues unrelentingly. Actual or threatened removal of a child from the parents creates a crisis that opens the locked system to growth and learning skills for effective coping.

Since physically abusive families live in a chronic state of stress punctuated by explosive episodes, a crisis to them is not the outbreak of violence or the inability to cope with other pressing problems. The crisis comes when authorities step into their lives and remove a child from the family and/or force the parents to enter therapy. It is this step that presents clinicians with an opportunity for crisis intervention that can result in greater growth and health for the family. *Coercive therapy* is the term that has been applied to the psychological treatment of parents required by the courts or other authorities to enter therapy. The threatened dissolution of the family by court action creates a crisis that the parents define as such and opens them up to change.

Table 8.1 *Distribution of Life Change Scores for Abusing and Nonabusing Parents*[a]

	Life-change scores			
Parent group	No crisis 0–149	Mild crisis 150–199	Moderate crisis 200–299	Major crisis 300+
Abusers				
(N = 35)	4	9	14	8
$\bar{X}$ = 233.63				
Nonabusers				
(N = 35)	25	5	3	2
$\bar{X}$ = 123.62				
[a]x^2 = 25.69, p < .001; $t$ind = 4.28, p < .001.				

SOURCE: From Justice and Justice (1976), p. 29.

Summary

I n our study of parents from a total of 40 families, the average length of time in therapy was six months. Six of the couples dropped out of therapy and lost custody of their children. Among the remaining couples, there was only one reported case of recurrence of abuse.

Goal Attainment Scaling was used as both a therapeutic tool and a means of evaluating outcome. GAS requires the identification of problems to be addressed in therapy and the specification of goals to be reached in three-month time frames. The Holmes-Rahe Social Readjustment Rating Scale was also used to measure stress scores from change events at the time of entering and completing therapy. At entrance, the scores of abusive couples were significantly higher than those of a matched group of nonabusive parents (see Table 8.1). By the end of therapy, life change scores among the abusive couples had dropped dramatically.

Although the parents in our study achieved important behavioral changes and abuse of their children ceased, brief therapy cannot be expected to overcome a number of other problems rooted in the parents' own experiences as children and their own physical and emotional mistreatment. As noted earlier, six important areas of concern were worked on and showed significant improvements: symbiotic behavior by the parents and in the family system, isolation, marital communication, temper and/or impatience, little knowledge of child development and management, and job or unemployment stress. Underlying many of the problems and much of the stress were seven faulty beliefs:

1. If my child cries or misbehaves, he does not love me and I am a bad parent.

2. My child should know what I want and need.

3. My child should take care of me emotionally.

4. My spouse should know what I need and want.

5. If I have to ask for what I want or need, it does not count and I am a failure.

6. I cannot trust anyone.

7. People are out for what they can get.

To be successful with such parents, the clinician must be careful to be nurturing but not to serve the role of rescuer. It is essential to set limits with the parents about what the clinician can and cannot do to help. This minimizes unrealistic expectations. The clinician must also resist the occasional temptation of becoming a persecutor and responding with anger and rage to the passive-aggressive behavior that the clients will exhibit. A third role the clinician must avoid is that of victim. The most effective means of avoiding such a role is by taking care of oneself, by setting limits as to availability, by being clear about what behaviors will not be tolerated, and by following good practices in diet, exercise, and social support systems.

Stages with the group therapy in our study included an initial distrust and testing by the parents, the socialization of newcomers to the group by seasoned members, the development of trust and friendships, and finally "graduation" from the group and separation. Although parents who made the necessary changes and had their child returned by authorities graduated from the group, they were invited to return any time they felt their lives were getting out of control.

In keeping with crisis intervention theory, the majority of the couples demonstrated that growth, greater strength, and more effective coping can be the outcome of therapy for abusive families—even when that therapy is mandated and is, by definition, coercive.

References

Abidin, R. R. (1983). *Parenting Stress Index Manual.* Charlottesville, VA: Pediatric Psychology Press.

Auerbach, S. M. (1986). "Assumptions of Crisis Theory and a Temporal Model of Crisis Intervention." In S. M. Auerbach & A. L. Stolberg (Eds.), *Crisis Intervention With Children and Families* (pp. 3–37). Washington, DC: Hemisphere.

Brenner, P., Roskies, E., & Lazarus, R. S. (1980). "Stress and Coping Under Extreme Conditions." In J. E. Dimsdale (Ed.), *Survivors, Victims, and Perpetrators: Essays on the Nazi Holocaust.* Washington, DC: Hemisphere.

Burgess, A. W., & Baldwin, B. (1981). *Crisis Intervention Theory and Practice: A Clinical Handbook.* Englewood Cliffs, NJ: Prentice Hall.

Dreikurs, R. (1964). *Children: The Challenge.* New York: Hawthorn.

Eitinger, L., & Strom, A. (1981). "New Investigations on the Mortality and Morbidity of Norwegian Ex-Concentration Camp Prisoners." *Israeli Journal of Psychiatry and Related Sciences, 18,* 173–195.

Ellis, A. (1973). Rational-Emotive Therapy. In R. Corsini (Ed.), *Current Psychotherapies.* Itasca, IL: Peacock.

Felner, R. D., Rowlinson, R. T., & Terre, L. (1986). "A Critical Examination of Crisis, Stress, and Transition Frameworks for Prevention." In S. M. Auerbach & A. L. Stolberg (Eds.), *Crisis Intervention With Children and Families* (pp. 39–63). Washington, DC: Hemisphere.

Freed, A. (1973). *TA for Tots.* Sacramento, CA: Jalmar.

Gordon, T. (1970). *Parent Effectiveness Training.* New York: Wyden.

Haley, J. (1977). *Uncommon Therapy: The Psychiatric Techniques of Milton H. Erickson.* New York: Norton.

Hiroto, D. S., & Seligman, M. E. P. (1975). "Generality of Learned Helplessness in Man." *Journal of Personality and Social Psychology, 90,* 311–327.

Holmes, T. H., & Rahe, R. H. (1967). "The Social Readjustment Rating Scale." *Journal of Psychosomatic Research, 11,* 213–218.

Justice, B. (1987). *Who Gets Sick: Thinking and Health.* Houston: Peak Press.

Justice, B. (1988). "Stress, Coping and Health Outcomes." In M. Russell (Ed.), *Stress Management for Chronic Disease* (pp. 14–29). New York: Pergamon Press.

Justice, B., & Justice, R. (1976). *The Abusing Family.* New York: Human Sciences Press.

Justice, B., & Justice, R. (1982). "Etiology of Physical Abuse of Children and Dynamics of Coercive Treatment." In J. C. Hansen & L. R. Barnhill (Eds.), *Clinical Approaches to Family Violence.* Rockville, MD: Aspen.

Kiresuk, T. J., & Sherman, R. E. (1968). "Goal Attainment Scaling: A General Method for Evaluating Comprehensive Community Mental Health Programs." *Community Mental Health Journal, 4,* 443–453.

Milner, J. S. (1986). *The Child Abuse Potential Inventory: Manual* (2nd ed.). Webster, NC: Psyctec.

National Center on Child Abuse and Neglect (1986). *Study of the National Incidence and Prevalence of Child Abuse and Neglect.* Washington, DC: National Clearinghouse on Child Abuse and Neglect (P.O. Box 1182, Washington, DC 20013).

Ursano, R. J., Boydstun, J. A., & Wheatley, R. D. (1981). "Psychiatric Illness in U.S. Air Force Viet Nam Prisoners of War: A Five-Year Follow-up." *American Journal of Psychiatry, 138,* 310–314.

Part IV

CRISIS ASSESSMENT AND INTERVENTION IN HEALTH-RELATED AND MENTAL HEALTH–RELATED CRISES

HEALTH and mental health professionals frequently encounter persons in crisis. Individuals in crisis are seen in hospital emergency rooms, crisis units at mental health centers, and inpatient and outpatient units of hospitals and mental health facilities. Examples of frequently occurring crisis precipitants include bad drug reactions and/or drug overdoses, violent crime victimization, severe depression, illness, or debilitating injuries due to an accident. Since acute and overwhelming crisis events occur at all hours of the day and night, it is imperative that crisis intervention services be available 24 hours a day, seven days a week. These services should be easily accessible to all members of the community wherever they are located. They should be well publicized and staffed by crisis intervention specialists.

Cocaine is a commonly abused drug that is very addicting both psychologically and physiologically. Some consequences of cocaine use include depression, paranoia, marital disharmony, social isolation, impaired occupational functioning, financial ruin, and legal problems. Cocaine addicts often appear in crisis only after a number of psychosocial consequences have accumulated. Chapter 9 describes crisis intervention with this population and includes a profile of cocaine users, information on obtaining a drug history and medical and psychiatric data, and guidelines for making appropriate intervention. The chapter describes clinical issues, steps in the crisis intervention model, and evaluation of the crisis intervention. It also includes information on assessment and treatment of the family members.

Emergency room visits are often made by persons grappling with a combination of a psychological crisis and a physical injury or illness. Chapter 10 describes the importance of staffing the hospital emergency room with professional social workers who can provide patients in crisis with immediate assessment and crisis intervention. The chapter illustrates the multidimensional nature of practice in an emergency room. A large part of the chapter is devoted to a discussion of the intervention methods used most frequently by clinicians in emergency room settings: advocacy, case coordination, counseling, education and referral, and mobilization of resources.

Chapter 11 points out that clinicians who provide crisis intervention services for Hispanic-Americans must be very knowledgeable about the way in which the clients' cultural values affect access, assessment, and treatment. Certain crises may have special significance for Hispanics because of their cultural values. For example, because of Hispanic sexual mores, hysterectomy and rape are particularly traumatic for the Hispanic woman. A crisis often involves an intergenerational conflict between first-generation rural Hispanic parents and their second-generation urban Americanized children. The chapter emphasizes that the Hispanic focus on the present, dependency on the "expert," and a fatalistic attitude can be used positively in helping the Hispanic in crisis.

Infertility is experienced as a reproductive crisis by 15 to 20 percent of all couples in America. Infertility shifts the individual or couple from the anticipation of parenting to an unknown state. Couples often experience feelings of loss of control in the resolution of their infertility crisis. Chapter 12 discusses provision of services to infertile couples, with the emphasis of the intervention on the preferred outcome, pregnancy. Couples may experience the medical interventions negatively, especially when cognitive distortions occur. Intervention strategies focus on challenging distorted thinking and helping the individual or couple take control of their responses. By using cognitively structured exercises, cognitive distortions can be identified and challenged.

Chapter 13 provides an introduction to the problems associated with erectile difficulty among men and the short-term treatment of those problems from a crisis intervention perspective. The chapter explores erectile difficulty as a phenomenon, identifies and discusses the relevant terminology, and reviews the etiology and prevalence of erectile difficulties among men. A crisis theory model is then applied to the onset and development of these difficulties. The second half of the chapter addresses the processes of crisis intervention and short-term treatment of erectile difficulties. The chapter then presents guidelines for information gathering and assessment/diagnosis and discusses useful intervention procedures.

During the past decade, mental health professionals have taken a more active role in a team effort to provide crisis intervention services following natural disasters such as a tornado or earthquake. They have joined emergency relief teams (whose primary purpose has been the immediate provision of food, shelter, and medical help) to serve as mental health crisis team members and provide crisis services to disaster victims. Chapter 14 focuses on the issue of developing and mobilizing resources for crisis intervention. This includes a discussion of the phases of post-disaster behavior. The chapter then identifies the necessary crisis-oriented techniques and services most responsive to disaster victims and links them with a multilevel mental health emergency relief program. The chapter includes specific implementation guidelines for crisis intervention teams. The final section addresses the clinical skills and techniques needed in post-disaster crisis assessment, intervention, and recovery.

Chapter 9

Recognition and Crisis Intervention Treatment with Cocaine Abusers: The Fair Oaks Hospital Model

JAMES A. COCORES, M.D.,
AND MARK S. GOLD, M.D.

C ocaine is a commonly abused drug that is very addicting both psychologically and physiologically. Some consequences of cocaine abuse include depression, paranoia, marital disharmony, social isolation, impaired occupational functioning, financial ruin, and legal problems. Whether cocaine is snorted, smoked, or injected, its physiological effects include rapid heart rate, hypertension, increased respiration, elevated body temperature, increased blood sugar, dilated pupils, and hyperactivity. Some fatal consequences include suicide, stroke, and heart attack. Cocaine addicts appear in crisis only after a number of psychosocial consequences have accumulated. These abusers have much denial of illness and tend to minimize the amount of cocaine and other drugs used. They also minimize the psychosocial consequences they have accumulated as a result of their cocaine abuse. Obtaining a brief but complete recent drug history is essential because most cocaine addicts are polydrug abusers and frequently require detoxification from drugs other than their drug of choice.

Although the cocaine addict and his or her family appear in crisis, they may be ambivalent and hesitant to finish the intervention partly due to their own denial and minimization of illness. It is therefore important to keep the intervention moving in order to avoid idle time lapses. Medical and psychiatric emergencies are first stabilized in an intensive care unit, medical unit, or neuropsychiatric evaluation unit. Inpatient rehabilitation of cocaine addiction requires daily structure for both the addict and the family member. Cocaine users not in need of hospitalization must follow a highly structured outpatient treatment plan which should begin on the day of intervention and should be continued daily. Family members frequently are in crisis along with the cocaine-dependent individual. The significant other in the abuser's life, usually the spouse or a parent, is sometimes referred to as the *codependent*. Codependents often develop psychological and physical problems as a direct result of being in an intimate relationship with the active substance abuser. For example, affective disorders such as major depression and dysthymic disorder are quite common in codependents. Therefore, the codependent also requires rapid treatment along with the cocaine abuser.

This chapter discusses the practice framework as it pertains to crisis intervention with cocaine abusers. This section covers the profile of cocaine abusers; obtaining a drug history, psychological history, and medical and psychiatric data; and guidelines to making the appropriate intervention. Assessment and treatment of the family members is also discussed. Case vignettes and clinical illustrations will further exemplify the way in which cocaine abusers present and the intervention method. This section will also examine clinical issues, suggested steps in the crisis intervention model, and evaluation of the crisis intervention.

Rapid recognition of the cocaine abuser and crisis intervention treatment requires swift but precise assessment by the clinician. Concurrent recognition and treatment of codependency not only results in stabilization of the family member but also improves the prognosis of the recovering cocaine abuser.

When we first met Alan B., he was 5 feet 10 inches tall, weighed only 106 pounds, and looked like someone out of a concentration camp. He had a hole through the center of his nasal septum the size of a quarter and was coughing up large quantities of dark-colored sputum. He had chest pain and heart irregularities. He became sloppy about his personal hygiene and his clothes were worn and dirty. He said he had been freebasing day and night for weeks with just a few hours off for sleep and almost no time to eat. His chest pain persisted and intensified and he became frightened. His mother rushed him to the hospital, where an electrocardiogram continuously monitored marked irregularities of the upper heart and less frequent arrhythmias of the lower heart.

Alan's case history is in no way atypical. Cocaine abuse is an equal opportunity disease that affects people from all walks of life. He was not a deprived inner-city kid looking to escape or forget his terrible environment. Alan was brought up in an intact, functional, churchgoing family by his biological parents. He earned a more than adequate living in the family's very successful restaurant business. His mother was a dedicated homemaker who also worked in the family business. His older, 33-year-old married brother lived in the same town and a younger brother commuted to college. Alan had been an above-average high school student, enjoyed team sports, and had friends of both sexes. He had tried beer and marijuana socially during high school but was not a habitual user.

After high school he began working in the restaurant business and within a few years had proved to be a very competent chef and manager. By the age of 26 he was earning over $30,000 a year. He gradually began indulging in "the finer things in life," such as fancy restaurant meals, Caribbean vacations, casinos, Broadway shows, and fast cars. His immediate peer group began changing, and it was not long before Alan was introduced to cocaine. His initial exposure to cocaine was pleasurable, but he convinced himself he could "take it or leave it." He continued to snort cocaine occasionally, but only when it was available through his friends. Eventually he felt he was leeching cocaine and decided to occasionally buy it himself for social gatherings. He began enjoying the high more and more and the new acquaintances cocaine would attract.

Within six months Alan was buying about $100 worth each week and would pool this with his friends' supplies on the weekends. By this time he had already tried smoking crack. The crack high was much more rapid and intense. It also seemed less expensive. Alan slowly transformed from a social snorter to an isolated weekend crack user.

Gradually the crack use began invading weekdays. The drug use was no longer of recreational proportions. During the drug-free periods he was haunted by preoccupations and ruminations of continued cocaine use. The drug became more important than family, friends, job, and his own sanity. He began feeling deep depression and even entertained thoughts of suicide. The only practice that would temporarily alleviate his social and psychological discomfort was more cocaine. He would find himself wanting to stop cocaine and at the same time having increasingly more intense cravings for the drug. He slowly became irresponsible at work and socially isolated. All he could think about was getting more cocaine. He found that he had no money left and began stealing from the family business and waitresses. He began missing time at work. He began drinking more alcohol when cocaine was not available. His appetite had decreased and he developed frequent insomnia. Alan began lying and cheating. He was becoming paranoid and tremulous. After two weeks of almost nonstop cocaine use he was having severe chest pain and believed that he was dying.

It had taken Alan about two years to get from that first innocent snort to daily crack addiction. Cocaine abstinence will probably reverse most of his psychological and social problems in time. Two weeks of extensive cardiac monitoring revealed irreversible cardiac damage. He will probably have to take a heart medication for the rest of his life. That is relatively easy, considering that there is no pill for the disease of cocaine addiction. A rehabilitation program is the only hope for Alan's long-term recovery from cocaine addiction. The problem is whether Alan will be able to admit that he has a chronic illness with a high probability of future cocaine cravings and relapse.

Introduction

C ocaine is a commonly abused drug extracted from the coca plant, *erythroxylum coca,* which is indigenous to the eastern Andes of South America. The drug causes anesthesia and potent central nervous system stimulation. The drug is very addicting both psychologically and physiologically. The distressed cocaine abuser and his or her significant other(s) in crisis often seek professional direction following the accumulation of numerous social and psychological consequences. Rapid assessment, intervention, and treatment goals are the clinician's objective for cocaine abusers and their family members.

It has been estimated that cocaine's anesthetic and central nervous system stimulant properties were recognized by inhabitants of South America as long ago as 1500

B.C. The Incas incorporated the coca plant in many of their religious rituals. Coca leaves have been chewed by natives of Bolivia and Peru for thousands of years and the practice continues in South America today. It was not until the mid-1800s that cocaine was popularized in Europe. One of the first cure-all elixirs to emerge, Vin Mariani, consisted of a combination of wine and cocaine. The wine was endorsed by many influential leaders of the time. Over 50 cocaine-containing drinks and elixirs were available to the public by the turn of the nineteenth century. The detrimental effects of cocaine became apparent and by 1906 cocaine tonics were severely restricted in the United States (Gold, 1986). Cocaine has a high abuse potential and, despite myths to the contrary, is very addicting.

South America clearly generates the largest volume of coca leaves, although the plant is also cultivated in Southeast Asia, the United States, and Europe. Cocaine leaves are processed into a light brown paste which is further refined into a white sugarlike powder. The drug is usually insufflated, or snorted, into the nasal passages, where it is absorbed into the bloodstream. Cocaine powder, or cocaine hydrochloride, is sniffed and cannot be smoked. Cocaine is also changed from its hydrochloride form to freebase by freeing the alkaloid from the hydrochloride form. Freebase can be ignited and smoked. When freebased, the drug is rapidly absorbed through the lungs into the bloodstream in very high concentrations approaching those achieved by injecting cocaine.

Crack is cocaine (Chatlos, 1987). Crack is smoked and comes in the form of small pellets or rocks that are usually sold in small vials. Crack is already prepared, ready-to-use cocaine freebase. While cocaine snorting leads to a high after two or more minutes, crack enters the lungs and bloodstream within seconds because it is smoked. Smoking crack usually results in a higher cocaine blood level than that achieved by snorting. Crack seems less expensive than cocaine powder because it is sold in small amounts and at a low price (three or four rock salt–like pellets are sold for about $15). But crack abusers use more frequently and crack can be ultimately more expensive than cocaine powder. Because of the larger amounts generally used and the higher blood level usually achieved, crack is rapidly addicting. Cocaine cravings during abstinence are usually more intense in the crack abuser than in the cocaine powder addict. The use of cocaine in any form is highly addicting and characterized by frequent and often intense cocaine cravings. The crisis intervention process is usually identical when treating cocaine or crack addicts.

Scope of the Problem

I t has been estimated that almost 25 million people have experimented with cocaine and the number continues to rise. About 3,000 adolescents and adults try it for the first time every day. Over 1 million Americans are so dependent on cocaine that they cannot stop using the drug no matter how destructive it is to their health, their families, and their careers. The majority of cocaine abusers are between the ages of 25 and 40, with the average age being 30. About one out of three cocaine users is a woman and the number of women cocaine abusers continues to rise. The majority of cocaine abusers are white, well educated, and make less than $25,000 per year (Gold, 1984).

Surveys conducted on the national hotline, 800–COCAINE (Washton & Gold, 1986; Washton, Gold, Pottash, & Semlitz, 1984), revealed some startling statistics concerning adult cocaine abusers. Some leading physical problems were chronic insomnia (82%), chronic fatigue (76%), severe headaches (60%), nasal and sinus infections (58%), and sexual dysfunction (55%). Cocaine-induced seizures with loss of consciousness were reported by 14 percent of the sample. Psychological problems commonly reported by the callers were depression (80%) and anxiety (80%). Paranoia and difficulty concentrating were each reported by more than 60 percent. Cocaine-induced suicide attempts were reported by 9 percent. Other personal and social problems were also reported. For example, 45 percent had stolen money from their employers and family to support their cocaine habit. Thirty-six percent said they had dealt drugs to support their habit, 26 percent reported marital/relationship problems ending in divorce or separation, 17 percent lost a job due to cocaine, 12 percent had been arrested for cocaine-related problems, and 11 percent reported a cocaine-related automobile accident. Similar problems were reported by adolescent cocaine abusers. Seventy-five percent had missed school days, 69 percent said their grades dropped significantly, 48 percent had disciplinary problems, and 31 percent were expelled because of cocaine-related difficulties. Thirty-one percent were stealing money and 62 percent used lunch or travel money or income from part-time jobs to buy drugs. Other problems reported by adolescents were brain seizures (19%), auto accidents (13%), suicide attempts (14%), and violent behavior (27%).

It is believed that the cocaine addict originally uses the drug for a number of reasons, including peer pressure, boredom, curiosity, and recreation. Cocaine delivers a physiological reward and repeated use occurs as a means of again achieving pleasure. This repetitive, self-defeating pattern can be seen in the tendency of experimental animals to self-administer cocaine to the point of central nervous system seizure or death. Euphoria is the driving force leading to repetitive cocaine use. A dysphoric state rapidly follows which cocaine users describe as "crashing" from the cocaine. The dysphoric phase ironically includes a cocaine craving. The crash is a negative reinforcer that also contributes to continued cocaine use. Although abrupt cocaine withdrawal lacks the severe physical withdrawal seen in other drug addictions (i.e., opiate dependence), it is characterized by equally if not more severe craving. Due to cocaine's more specific action on the physiological reward system in the brain, it may possess a greater positive reinforcement property. The process of cocaine addiction is an interplay between positive and negative reinforcers. Central nervous system addiction to cocaine is best conceptualized in terms of neurotransmitter-induced physiological reinforcement, rather than the presence of physical abstinence symptoms (Dackis & Gold, 1985b).

Practice Frameworks

8 00–COCAINE is a national drug abuse treatment referral and information service based at Fair Oaks Hospital in Summit, New Jersey. The calls come from virtually every state and geographic region in the United States. The hotline provides immediate access to information, advice, and treatment referral (if needed) anywhere in the 50 states. In addition to providing easy access to information and assistance, the hotline has served to heighten public awareness of the epidemic of cocaine use. The hotline has been operating 24 hours a day since May 6, 1983, and handles over 1,200 calls daily, or over 400,000 calls annually. It is staffed by 40 members who have had at least one year of counseling and crisis intervention training under the supervision of a highly respected team of medical professionals, including two psychiatrists specializing in substance abuse. Family members frequently call for information and cocaine abusers are referred to treatment programs throughout the country, including inpatient, outpatient, and self-help groups.

Cocaine addicts exhibit much denial of illness and tend to minimize the amount of cocaine and other drugs used. They also minimize the psychosocial consequences they have accumulated as a result of their cocaine abuse. It is therefore useful to have a family member present and/or signed consents to contact significant others or employers when possible.

There are certain key concepts to consider when embarking on cocaine crisis intervention. One is a rapid but careful cocaine history. Cocaine addicts often will have difficulty presenting an accurate and detailed history. It is therefore wise to request average frequency of cocaine use over the past three months (e.g., daily or biweekly). This often enables the clinician to estimate the extent and level of progression and the extent of addiction. The day and time the patient last used cocaine is useful in determining extent of motivation for treatment, risk of medical complications, and amount of cocaine-induced paranoia, anxiety, and depressive symptomatology. A urine or serum cocaine level is often useful in confirming the estimated time of last cocaine use. Asking how the drug is administered is also crucial, as the route of administration can help the clinician determine the stage of cocaine addiction. The individual who snorts cocaine usually has lower cocaine blood levels than people who chronically freebase or inject. Although both methods lead to rapid addiction, freebasers become dependent on cocaine and develop psychosocial consequences faster. To summarize, it is important to consider the route of administration, average frequency of use, and time of last use during the intervention.

Obtaining a brief but complete recent drug history is essential because most cocaine addicts are polydrug abusers and frequently require detoxification from drugs other than their drug of choice. Alcohol and marijuana are the drugs most frequently abused by cocaine addicts. Alcohol, marijuana, and other drugs are often used by the cocaine addict to help alleviate the dysphoria or crash that follows the stimulant phase of cocaine intoxication. Cocaine addicts frequently minimize their alcohol consumption history despite the fact that most abuse alcohol during the cocaine crash. It is not unusual, therefore, for cocaine addicts to become defensive while being questioned about alcohol or other drugs. Nevertheless, it is important to obtain a complete drug history in order to avoid seizures and other dangerous withdrawal symptoms. Concurrent alcohol dependence is common and in many instances requires inpatient hospitalization for detoxification. A comprehensive urine drug screen is useful in alleviating any suspicions the clinician may have about the polydrug abuse.

A brief psychosocial history is an integral part of the crisis intervention. Cocaine addicts appear in crisis only after a number of psychosocial consequences—such as financial, marital, family, employment, and legal problems—have accumulated. Specific problems in these areas must be assessed. It is useful to review the psychosocial consequences with the abuser, linking each in an empathetic fashion with the cocaine abuse. This helps the clinician penetrate deeper into the addict's denial system and can facilitate compliance with future treatment recommendations.

The clinician also needs to be aware of any prior treatment attempts. Consent form and time permitting, the clinician can consult with the previous rehabilitation center, hospital, or clinician if further clarification is needed. The patient's own attempts at correcting the addiction are also useful to review. A reminder that the patient's own attempts at stopping or decreasing cocaine use have failed can also increase the probability that the addict will follow the treatment plan.

Highlights of the addict's medical history are important to obtain from the cocaine addict or family member. Physical illnesses such as seizure disorder or hypertension are aggravated by cocaine and immediate medical attention may be required. The clinician should also be aware of any prescribed medications the addict might be taking. The interaction of cocaine with the prescribed medications must be considered for proper patient management. A complete physical and neurological examination is essential in all cases. Recent cocaine use in an addict or first time cocaine user can result in severe physical problems or death. Any acute physical problems must first be stabilized.

A brief, well-structured treatment plan can begin to be formulated and initiated after medical complications have been stabilized or ruled out (Figure 9-1). Hospitalization may be required if acute medical or psychiatric problems persist. Major depression, suicidal tendency, detoxification, and overwhelming cocaine cravings may warrant continued inpatient treatment. Cocaine abusers are often reluctant to enter inpatient treatment despite the fact that they are in crisis. A brief review of how cocaine has affected their lives is sometimes convincing enough. Education on the progression of cocaine addiction and how it worsens without treatment is also useful in convincing the patient to enter treatment. A general rule applies here: The larger the amount and intensity of psychosocial consequences, the easier the cocaine abuser enters treatment. Financial problems are the most common precipitating factors motivating the cocaine addict to agree to enter treatment.

Chronic cocaine abuse often leads to major depression and other life-threatening psychiatric disorders. A large array of psychiatric symptomatology often slowly abates

Figure 9.1 *Intervention Flow Chart for the Cocaine Abuser*

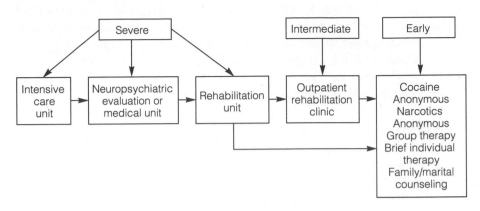

after two to three weeks of cocaine abstinence, but at the time of assessment or intervention it is difficult if not impossible to determine if the cocaine caused the symptoms or the symptoms antidated the cocaine use. In any case, a brief psychiatric assessment is useful to rule out any current psychiatric emergency. Some cocaine abusers have persistent psychiatric symptoms well after an adequate cocaine abstinence period and may fit the self-medication hypothesis of cocaine addiction (Khantzian, 1985).

Cocaine users not in need of hospitalization must follow a highly structured outpatient treatment plan, which should begin on the day of intervention and be continued daily. Cocaine abusers should be advised to immediately avoid people, places, and things associated with their cocaine abuse—that is, they must stay away from friends who use cocaine, stay away from clubs or other places where they used cocaine, and avoid things that may induce cocaine cravings, such as cocaine documentaries and cocaine paraphernalia. The patient should also be advised not to continue using other drugs, including alcohol, because they alter mood and judgment, which may lead to cocaine relapse. A minimum of biweekly urine drug screens should be obtained and the patient should initially attend daily or evening group sessions. The structured outpatient rehabilitation program also encourages integration into self-help groups such as Cocaine Anonymous or Narcotics Anonymous on the days the abuser does not attend the clinic. Consent forms should be signed by the patient allowing the clinician to give progress information to a significant other and/or employer. The patient must also be aware that a positive urine drug screen could result in confirmation that inpatient treatment is required. Having the patient sign a contract describing these points is essential.

Family members frequently are in crisis along with the cocaine-dependent individual. Codependents sometimes develop psychological and physical problems as a direct result of being in an intimate relationship with the active substance abuser.

Codependents develop a maladaptive reaction consisting of continued investment of time and energy in order to control actions and behaviors of the substance abuser despite repeated adverse consequences. They assume many of the responsibilities held by the substance abuser and are preoccupied with problems that have evolved from the abuser's addictive behavior and actions (e.g., social, financial, legal, child abuse, and employment). The repetitive efforts of codependents to curtail or stop the addict from using cocaine frequently result in almost daily feelings of defeat, frustration, inadequacy, helplessness, anxiety, depression, and anger. Codependents often develop stress-related medical conditions such as hypertension and skeletomuscular and gastrointestinal symptoms and often suffer from insomnia, appetite disturbances, and tension states. Major affective disorders such as major depression and dysthymic disorder are quite common in codependents (Cocores, 1987).

The codependent also requires rapid treatment in the form of reassurance and guilt removal. Codependents often blame themselves for the addict's rapid progression into chemical dependency. They also feel guilty about having led the abuser to a treatment facility. Brief education is indicated stressing that addiction is a family illness and that recovery is also a family affair. The importance and need for treatment must be conveyed to the codependent. Figure 9-2 illustrates some common referral tracking. Most inpatient and outpatient cocaine rehabilitation centers provide therapy for the codependent in the form of education, small group therapy, and integration into the appropriate self-help groups (Narcotics Anonymous, Tough Love, or Families Anonymous).

The clinician's role is a rapid and precise recognition of the extent of cocaine addiction. Obtaining a recent general drug and alcohol history is also of paramount importance. Recent major psychosocial stressors, physical status, and mental status must be assessed and the appropriate crisis intervention treatment must be firmly instituted. Similar involvement and assessment of the codependent is important. A signed consent form to speak to the employer or to employee assistance personnel is good practice when possible. One of the greatest motivating forces known in cocaine rehabilitation is job jeopardy.

Figure 9.2 *Flow Chart for Family Members of Cocaine Abusers in Crisis*

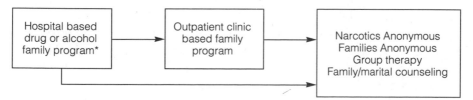

*There also are inpatient treatment programs for codependency.

The clinician must rapidly develop a therapeutic alliance with a good trust level. A nonthreatening, nonjudgmental, empathetic but firm approach is important during the process. Familiarity with the jargon used by cocaine addicts helps avoid disruptions in the assessment process. The clinician must have a strong understanding of addiction as a disease and must view the individual not as a street urchin but as someone who is physiologically and emotionally handicapped. Some clinicians have parents who are alcoholics and substance abusers and others are married to active substance abusers. When this is the case, the clinician's own personal feelings regarding addiction should be recognized, as they often can influence clinical judgment and further enflame an already volatile crisis intervention situation.

Case Vignettes and Clinical Illustrations

T he following case is about a young cocaine addict who arrived for assessment typically after some social pressure. He also had a problem with depression and needed detoxification from alcohol.

Case 1

Mr. R., a 28-year-old self-employed male, was seeking assessment on an emergency voluntary basis because of impaired functioning due to cocaine abuse. He was referred by his business partner and was accompanied by his wife. His chief complaint was that he was using too much cocaine and wanted help to stop. Mr. R. began using cocaine intranasally four years ago and used cocaine initially only when it was conveniently available. His cocaine use gradually escalated and he began freebasing about six months ago. Mr. R.'s use rapidly escalated to a daily frequency over the past month. He described himself as a social drinker during his early twenties and said that he did not have a problem with alcohol. When questioned further he revealed that he had been drinking about two six-packs of beer per day but that this was only to alleviate the cocaine crash. He denied any other recent drug use, although he had experimented with a large variety of drugs during high school.

Physical examination revealed tremors, increased reflexes, and high blood pressure. Mr. R.'s nasal septum was perforated and his lungs were congested. His heart rate was rapid and at times irregular. A urine drug screen revealed the presence of cocaine, alcohol, and marijuana.

Mr. R. was severely depressed and was not certain how serious he was about the suicidal plans he had told Mrs. R. about earlier in the day. He had been suffering from insomnia and had lost over 30 pounds. He said that he had been under a lot of pressure at work and at home, that he had been spending most of his salary on cocaine, and that it was time to cut down.

Mrs. R. said that over the past few months there were times when he would be missing for hours, would come home late, would hit the children, and would mistreat her because he had been under a lot of pressure at work. She had been worried about Mr. R. to the point of suffering from insomnia, tension states, and decreased appetite herself. Mr. R.'s partner was contacted and confirmed poor performance and judgment on the job. His partner added that he was considering dropping Mr. R. for a new partner because he was now forced to do the work of two.

Mr. R. became ambivalent about entering the neuropsychiatric evaluation unit. He wanted to think about it overnight and also consider outpatient treatment. The need for immediate treatment was agreed on after the consequences of his cocaine addiction were again reviewed. Mrs. R. reluctantly agreed to attend the family program, making it clear that she would attend only for Mr. R.'s benefit.

The next case illustrates a cocaine addict who was arrested for possession of marijuana and whose wife threatened to leave him if he did not accompany her to the intensive care unit.

Case 2

Mr. A., a 31-year-old married employed male, was seen in crisis intervention because of complaints of being unable to stop cocaine binging episodes. He was accompanied by his wife, who was most influential in getting him to the assessment.

Mr. A. had been snorting cocaine about two or three times a week. He would go out with his friends, who would periodically indulge in cocaine binges. He last used cocaine five days earlier. He denied ever smoking cocaine but drank an occasional beer or smoked marijuana when binging, and he denied any other recent drug use.

Mrs. A. said Mr. A. was recently caught with possession of marijuana and legal action was pending. She added that this was the last straw. He had been having terrible mood swings, bouts of depression, insomnia, tardiness, was neglecting chores and calling in sick to work, and provided elaborate stories justifying missing funds.

Mr. A.'s physical examination was essentially normal except for nasal congestion. The comprehensive drug screen revealed traces of marijuana. He appeared tense, angry, and defeated. He agreed halfheartedly to begin the outpatient program that same evening with Mrs. A., who refused to attend that evening but agreed to pick him up and attend in the future when babysitting arrangements could be made. She insisted that Mr. A. begin that night.

The next case illustrates an adolescent mixed substance abuser who was accompanied by her mother. The student was referred to the early intervention program.

Case 3

M., a 17-year-old student, was brought by her mother, Ms. H., for assessment of a possible cocaine problem. M. appeared very angry and reluctantly entered the assessment area. She answered questions with one-word responses. Ms. H. said she had found a mirror, a razor blade, and cocaine wrapped in aluminum foil in the adolescent's bedroom dresser. She had suspected that something was wrong with M., as the student had recently begun hanging around with the wrong bunch, had been neglecting chores around the house, and had been failing courses in school. M. said she had not used any drugs in over two weeks and that she did not have a problem with drugs. Her drug history revealed experimentation with other substances like marijuana, Doriden, and mescaline. She denied alcohol use.

M.'s physical examination, including a comprehensive drug screen, was normal. She had no significant psychiatric history. On the contrary, M. had many friends, was quite responsible, and did well in school up until about two years earlier.

It was not clear whether M. was an early cocaine abuser or an adolescent experimenter who might "grow out of it." M. was admitted to our early intervention program and attended educational and group sessions biweekly. M. completed the program following eight weeks and 16 negative urine drug screens. Ms. H. continued to develop coping skills and become educated about cocaine in the weekly parent groups and Families Anonymous.

The next case illustrates a self-employed crack addict who was highly motivated for treatment despite his young age and few psychosocial consequences.

Case 4

Mr. S., a 23-year-old employed male, came to the assessment center seeking help because of uncontrollable crack use. He said no one suggested that he seek help and that it was all his idea. Mr. S. had started snorting cocaine off and on about three years ago. His cocaine use gradually escalated to weekend use and by one year ago he was snorting daily. About six months before assessment he first tried crack. Mr. S. initially confined his crack use to weekends, but over the past few months this increased to daily use. He often would stay up all night smoking cocaine. He began neglecting his landscaping business and customers were complaining. He also began drinking large amounts of beer and found that he could drink more than usual while high on cocaine.

A physical examination revealed high blood pressure, increased reflexes, occasional heart irregularities, a cough, and shortness of breath. The urine drug screen was negative.

Mr. S. said that he stopped using cocaine five days ago and that he currently had intense cocaine cravings and was afraid he could not finish the day without using cocaine. He said he had managed to stop for as long as one week on several occasions but had learned that he could not stop alone and needed help.

Mr. S. was admitted to the neuropsychiatric evaluation unit for observation of possible withdrawal and a cardiology consult. He agreed to enter the inpatient rehabilitation program after the evaluation.

Clinical Issues

T he cocaine abuser may arrive for treatment in any phase of addiction. Most cocaine addicts have a history of other substance abuse problems prior to their initial experimentation with cocaine. Alcohol and/or marijuana abuse are common predecessors. We have seen many recovering heroin addicts become addicted to cocaine as well.

In any case, the majority of cocaine addicts are initially exposed to cocaine in a social setting. It is almost always first snorted. Cocaine abuse casually continues until the abuser feels obligated to buy and share his own supply or buys cocaine out of desire for a personal supply. Days, weeks, or months pass before the addict graduates to regular "social" weekend use. Cocaine use gradually infiltrates into the weekdays, usually after work and/or at lunch break. A denial system begins forming in parallel with increased cocaine use. Despite prior claims, cocaine proves to be highly addictive and tolerance and dependency escalate rapidly during this intermediate phase. Cocaine rapidly becomes a daily habit. It is frequently in the intermediate or advanced stages of cocaine snorting that freebase experimentation or crack use begins. Others begin by freebasing. Many freebasing experimenters continue and very rapidly develop further tolerance and dependency. An average time period for the cocaine snorter from experimentation to crisis is two years. The time span for a freebaser is about six months.

The cocaine addict develops antisocial personality traits by virtue of purchasing and using the illicit substance. Often, however, these traits antidate the cocaine addiction and are part of a cluster of traits commonly referred to as the addictive personality. Cocaine addicts also exhibit impulsiveness to a large extent. Marked behavioral changes cycling from hyperactivity and elation to marked depression and social isolation are the rule. The cocaine abuser begins to resent responsibility and begins believing that his or her cocaine use is a result of an unhappy marriage or job. The addiction continues to breed frustration, anguish, anxiety, and anger. The Dr. Jekyll and Mr. Hyde presentation of the alcoholic also applies to the cocaine addict. The promises the addict has made to himself or herself about stopping cocaine are gradually directed toward the codependent, and with each broken promise comes increasing amounts of frustration and depression. Consequences begin piling up in the meantime. Marital disharmony, separation, divorce, child neglect, child abuse, parental arguments, late mortgage payments, unpaid parking tickets, overdrawn checks, larceny, gambling, lost time at work, unemployment, legal problems, incarceration, and death are some of the consequences of cocaine addiction.

Whether cocaine is snorted, smoked, or injected, its physiological effects include rapid heart rate, hypertension, increased respiration, elevated body temperature, increased blood sugar, dilated pupils, urges to urinate, anorexia, hyperactivity, and altered muscle control. These physiological reactions are primarily a product of cocaine's stimulating influence on the central nervous system. Cocaine increases the release of the brain's natural stimulators. Some of these natural brain stimulators are norepinephrine, dopamine, and epinephrine. Cocaine use increases the neurotransmitter conduction, which leads to stimulation for a brief period of time (for snorting, about 30 minutes; for freebasing, about 15 minutes). What follows is a temporary state of brain stimulator depletion, which contributes to the depression of the cocaine crash. These euphoric and dysphoric chemical changes in the brain directly influence other body organ functions. Cocaine also creates direct physical damage to parts of the body. Cocaine addicts develop medical problems which include nasal damage, chronic sinusitis, nasal septum perforation or necrosis, bronchitis, productive coughs, hypertension, ruptured brain vessels, seizures, heart irregularities, and heart attack (Gold and Estroff, 1985).

Cocaine exerts a major influence on brain neurotransmitters. Alterations in certain neurotransmitters can induce physical problems such as hypertension and can also lead to psychiatric problems. Alterations in ratios of neurotransmitters do result in dramatic changes in psychological, cognitive, and behavioral status. Cocaine addicts in crisis treatment often meet criteria for major affective disorders. Psychosocial consequences and cocaine-induced biochemical imbalances contribute to major depression, while recent cocaine use can make a person look manic. Chronic cocaine-induced neurotransmitter disequilibration also produces marked paranoia and psychotic symptomatology. Depletion of stimulator neurotransmitters such as dopamine contributes not only to depression but also to difficulties concentrating and preoccupation with cocaine urges or cravings (Dackis & Gold, 1985b). Dopamine depletion is also present in children with attention deficit disorder. Some cocaine addicts develop the poor attention span, inattentiveness, and impulsiveness seen in children with attention deficit disorder (Cocores, Patel, Gold, & Pottash, 1987). The active cocaine user may also appear to be suffering from a panic disorder or other major anxiety disorder.

Cocaine addicts can mimic many psychiatric disorders. It is therefore wise to refrain from making any psychiatric diagnoses until a psychiatric evaluation can be performed after a few weeks of cocaine abstinence. In most cases the psychiatric symptoms abate with cocaine abstinence. It can take up to three weeks for the neurotransmitters to stabilize. However, some cocaine-induced or exacerbated psychiatric problems need immediate attention. The two most common examples are psychosis and major depression. The physical and mental condition of the cocaine addict must be rapidly assessed, as lethal consequences are not uncommon.

Crisis Intervention Strategies

E arly assessment of danger to self or others is a priority in most clinical settings that deal with cocaine abuse. Frequently the cocaine addict will seek help when the cocaine supply is depleted and the euphoric effects of the drug begin diminishing. The cocaine "crash" that ensues is frequently accompanied by anxiety, depression, and suicidal thoughts. Most individuals who call the cocaine hotline or the outpatient recovery centers do not, however, have discrete suicidal plans and are not seriously considering a suicidal gesture. The crisis clinician should decrease the danger of the situation in cases of suicidal, homicidal, or violent cocaine addicts.

Another crisis counseling step involves rapidly establishing rapport with the client. Cocaine addicts often become frustrated when they feel the clinician is being judgmental and nonaccepting. Cocaine addicts are often quite perceptive about others and may easily detect defensiveness, a feeling of being overwhelmed, anger, insecurity, or naïveté on the part of the crisis clinician. The clinician should have a clear understanding of the disease of cocaine addiction and should be pleasant, self-confident, and hopeful.

The clinician should examine the recent precipitants which led the cocaine addict to seek help. Some common preceding events include discovery of the addiction by a spouse, the employer confronting the addict, cocaine-related legal problems, or cocaine-induced health or psychological problems. Where appropriate, the clinician should explore ways in which the client coped or lacked coping skills with similar problems in the past. The clinician should also identify the danger of the event(s). For example, a client was recently confronted at work because of increased conflicts with fellow employees, decreased job performance, increased forgetfulness, and moodiness. The employee assistance person at work asked the cocaine addict many questions about drug abuse. The client told the crisis clinician, "I want to get help for my cocaine problems before the boss finds out or I lose my job. I was questioned at work yesterday afternoon and used cocaine last night. I have tried to stop on my own before and I have been successful, but not for long periods of time."

The addict's feelings should also be identified. The cocaine addict who has recently been confronted at work may feel afraid, ashamed, sad, and guilty. Even after being frightened by confrontation, the addict may be temporarily positive he or she will never use cocaine again but may find himself or herself using the drug anyway a few hours later. The resulting feeling of powerlessness and hopelessness is important for the addict to recognize. It is important through education to link this powerlessness to the disease concept of cocaine addiction. This often reduces anxiety, denial, and self-blame.

Briefly evaluate the addict's adaptive, less adaptive, and inadequate coping mechanisms by asking how he or she has handled certain specific situations (e.g., prior confrontations, relapses, or cocaine-related depression). If crisis is the result of collapse of the usual problem-solving mechanisms, then the crisis intervention clinician should identify and alter the addict's coping behavior.

Many cocaine addicts have a preconceived idea of what may be proposed by the clinician to cope with the crisis at hand. The crisis clinician may need to modify the addict's preconceptions and/or present the various alternatives. It is useful to explore with the addict the consequences and feelings associated with the various alternatives such as inpatient detoxification and rehabilitation, outpatient rehabilitation, educational assignments, individual sessions, and self-help group involvement.

The cocaine addict needs to be given a clear and realistic outline of the events that led to the cocaine-related crisis. It is important to review with the client how the crisis clashes with his or her future expectations and to simply state that recovery from cocaine addiction is priority number one. The crisis clinician then needs to replace maladaptive coping mechanisms, myths, and misconceptions with rational beliefs and new cognitions. This may involve cocaine addiction education, reading assignments, referral to self-help groups, or inpatient or outpatient referral.

An open-door policy is needed for the cocaine addict to encourage his or her return if further crisis evolves. The addict may find the alternatives and treatment suggestions excessive and may begin believing again that the crisis is not as severe as initially perceived. A follow-up call by the clinician may reveal that seeing a clinician and being advised to seek rehabilitation instilled enough fear that the addict feels rehabilitation is no longer needed. The addict may say, "You really scared me. Since I saw you I haven't wanted to use cocaine and everything is fine." Leaving the door open for future contact in a case such as this is essential. The addict is then able to call for help a month later if, for instance, he or she is fired from a job.

SUGGESTED STEPS IN THE CRISIS INTERVENTION MODEL

1. Interview family member if present and/or obtain consent to call significant other(s) while the cocaine addict undergoes a physical examination. The physical examination should include a comprehensive drug screen.
2. Conduct a brief psychiatric evaluation focusing on symptoms which would constitute a psychiatric emergency.
3. Complete the assessment with both the addict and codependent when possible. Prior treatment attempts, drug and alcohol history, psychosocial history, and knowledge of the major environmental consequences of the addiction are essential components of the assessment.
4. Integrate all the information, execute an intervention, and firmly present the treatment plan.

Evaluation of the Crisis Intervention

A lthough the cocaine addict appears in crisis, he or she may be ambivalent and hesitant to finish the intervention, partly due to denial of illness. It is therefore important to keep the intervention moving in order to avoid idle time lapses. The waiting or unattended cocaine addict will begin minimizing the crisis situation and may believe that his or her problems can be resolved another day. Failure to be sure the recognition and crisis intervention process flows smoothly and rapidly may result in the patient leaving the center with increased cocaine cravings and continued cocaine abuse. The time elapsing from the moment the cocaine addict enters the crisis intervention area until the time a contract is signed and the treatment plan is formulated rarely should exceed two hours. The procedure is often accomplished in about one hour.

Medical and psychiatric emergencies are first stabilized in an intensive care, medical, or neuropsychiatric evaluation unit. When necessary, the patient should begin the rehabilitative program during detoxification in the form of cocaine or drug

groups. This serves two purposes: (a) It reminds patients who have been in treatment for a while what they were like in crisis, and (b) if the patient lies in a hospital bed without education and therapy he or she may develop a false sense of what rehabilitation entails and may leave treatment right after medical or psychiatric stabilization. Once medically or psychiatrically stabilized, the patient should be transferred to a cocaine rehabilitation unit. The rehabilitation service provided should include: skilled drug and alcohol counselors as primary clinicians; nursing and associate staff knowledgeable about substance abuse disorders; medical and psychiatric support for coexisting problems; extensive psychological testing and psychosocial evaluations; family counselors; and clinicians trained in systematic methods of treatment, including reality therapy, transactional analysis, Gestalt therapy, behavior therapy, stress management, and activity therapy. Other components include systems therapy (especially with employers and a strong family component), family- and peer-oriented aftercare, and a strong Narcotics Anonymous orientation. Most inpatient cocaine rehabilitation units successfully integrate the addict into aftercare programs, Narcotics Anonymous, and marital/family therapies within six to eight weeks.

Outpatient rehabilitation of cocaine addiction requires daily structure for both the addict and codependent and a signed contract. The contract should include but not be limited to the following:

1. Because of my significant history of cocaine abuse, I will not use alcohol or any illicit substance.
2. I understand the importance of attending and actively participating in all educational sessions and therapies. I commit myself to rigid attendance, further understanding that failure to do so may result in extension or immediate discharge from the program.
3. During the first six to eight weeks of the program, I will be expected to attend Cocaine Anonymous or Narcotics Anonymous on the weekends or days I do not attend the clinic.
4. I understand that because of my history of cocaine abuse, a relapse will leave me no alternative other than inpatient rehabilitation.
5. I understand that at the discretion of the staff and at least biweekly I may be asked to submit to random supervised cocaine and drug screens. Failure to agree to submit to random drug screens will be interpreted as a relapse.

Signed consent forms allowing the staff to give progress updates to employers or significant others often results in a better prognosis for the cocaine abuser. Parents and spouses are also encouraged to attend separate educational and group therapies for family members. Family members are also expected to attend Families Anonymous or Narcotics Anonymous on weekends and evenings that they do not attend the clinic. Multifamily groups and codependent/addict groups are also useful. Both inpatient and outpatient programs should include aftercare programs. Patients should meet one to two times a week for at least one year and should be expected to continue attending

self-help groups. Marital, individual, and psychopharmacological therapies should continue during the aftercare period when indicated.

The clinician should also be aware of less intensive outpatient programs in cases of early addiction, preaddiction, or uncertainty. These programs are especially useful with adolescents and young adults. Individual, group, and educational sessions meeting twice a week for two months help clarify the situation. Weekly drug screens are also a must in this type of program.

In summary, the cocaine assessment should include notes on consent for treatment, client description, medical/psychiatric clearance, negative physical and psychological effects of cocaine use, referral source, prior treatment, event(s) precipitating crisis, cocaine history, level of cocaine dependence, brief drug and alcohol data, brief family history, and the Michigan Alcoholism Screening Test (MAST) or its drug equivalent, the DAST. Consent for systems therapy and contract should be signed. The codependent should also be briefly assessed. Areas to explore with the codependent include sleep disturbances, appetite problems, anxiety symptoms, depression, alcohol/drug use, psychosocial functioning, signs of physical abuse, medical/psychiatric history, verification of the cocaine addict's history, and prior attempts to help the addict curtail his or her cocaine abuse.

Summary

C ocaine addiction is a major epidemic in our society. Experimentation with cocaine is rampant. Experimentors often become "social users" and the transition to addiction is cunning, gradual, and often invisible to the addict. Cocaine addiction also ushers in addictions to other substances such as alcohol and marijuana. It leads to rapid and progressive social and occupational dysfunction. Cocaine addiction produces problems in areas of physical status, mental health, finance, employment, and the law. Cocaine addiction is not isolated to the individual. The hazards of cocaine addiction rapidly spread to family members and detrimentally influence their mental and physical well-being. Significant others can be severely affected by remaining in an intimate relationship with the active cocaine abuser.

Rapid recognition of the cocaine abuser and crisis intervention treatment require rapid but precise assessment by the clinician. Concurrent recognition and treatment of codependency not only results in stabilization of the family member but also improves the prognosis of the recovering cocaine abuser.

References

Chatlos, C. (1987). *Crack: What You Should Know About the Cocaine Epidemic.* New York: Putnam.

Cocores, J. A. (1987). "Co-dependence: A Silent Epidemic." *Fair Oaks Hospital, Psychiatry Letter,* 5 (2), 5–8.

Cocores, J. A., Patel, M. D., Gold, M. S., & Pottash, A. C. (1987). "Cocaine Abuse, Attention Deficit Disorder and Bipolar Disorder." *Journal of Nervous and Mental Diseases, 175* (7), 431–432.

Dackis, C. A., & Gold, M. S. (1985a). "Bromocriptine as Treatment of Cocaine Abuse." *Lancet,* 1151–1152.

Dackis, C. A., & Gold, M. S. (1985b). "New Concepts in Cocaine Addiction: The Dopamine Depletion Hypothesis." *Neuroscience Biobehavioral Review, 9,* 469–477.

Gold, M. S. (1984). *800-COCAINE.* New York: Bantam Books.

Gold, M. S. (1986). *The Facts About Drugs and Alcohol.* New York: Bantam Books.

Gold, M. S., & Estroff, T. W. (1985). "The Comprehensive Evaluation of Cocaine and Opiate Abusers." In R. C. W. Hall & T. Beresford (Eds.), *Handbook of Psychiatric Diagnostic Procedures* (pp. 213–230). New York: Spectrum.

Khantzian, E. J. (1985). "The Self-medication Hypothesis of Addictive Disorders: Focus on Heroin and Cocaine Dependence." *American Journal of Psychiatry, 142,* 1259–1264.

Washton, A. M., & Gold, M. S. (1986). "Recent Trends in Cocaine Abuse: A View From the National Hotline, 800–COCAINE." *Advances in Alcohol and Substance Abuse, 6* (2), 31–47.

Washton, A. M., Gold, M. S., Pottash, A. C., & Semlitz, L. (1984). "Adolescent Cocaine Abusers." *Lancet,* 746.

Chapter 10

Assessment and Crisis Intervention with Clients in a Hospital Emergency Room

HOWARD J. HESS, D.S.W., AND
PAMELA L. RUSTER, M.S.S.W.

Ms. Martinez arrived unescorted late Friday afternoon at the emergency room (ER) of a Catholic hospital in a large midwestern city. She complained of faintness, chest pains, and shortness of breath and became increasingly agitated during the waiting period. Her complaints and demand for service escalated. Emergency room staff doubted the full validity of Ms. Martinez' claim that she was experiencing a medical crisis. They complained that they were unable to understand her rapid, mixed use of English and Spanish. In addition, the emergency staff remembered that Ms. Martinez had previously presented similar symptoms that subsided shortly after the medical examination. Earlier examinations had not revealed the presence of any physical illness. Due to the potential for disturbance in the waiting room, the staff requested an immediate consultation from the hospital social worker assigned to the emergency room.

In interviewing Ms. Martinez the crisis clinician noted the patient's level of distress. Ms. Martinez said she had come to the hospital out of desperation and confusion, hoping that someone would help her. She described having walked the streets to locate an apartment for herself and her five children, aged 3 to 13. She and her children were the only occupants left in a three-story walk-up that had been abandoned by its owner. The electricity and heat had been disconnected. Some water pipes had frozen and burst. She had obtained electricity by running an extension cord across the alley to the next building. The only source of heat was the gas oven. Ms. Martinez had followed up on every affordable apartment advertised in the newspaper without success. She was now attempting to locate a vacant apartment by walking the streets in subfreezing wet conditions, had not eaten since morning, and was quite fatigued. She had vowed not to go home until she had located an apartment and now was feeling quite desperate. She told the clinician that she had considered walking in front of oncoming traffic but decided to come to the hospital instead.

The clinician was faced with the dilemma of quickly assessing the risk and responding appropriately to Ms. Martinez within the limits of the hospital and community resources and the timing of the service request.

Although all patients seen by crisis clinicians in emergency rooms do not necessarily present such complex psychosocial problems, the task of casefinding, assessing, and intervening in very brief time frames requires a highly specific knowledge and skill base, particularly in the area of crisis intervention theory and techniques. This chapter presents a model for crisis intervention service in emergency rooms. This model defines the unit of attention broadly and requires active decision making within brief time frames.

Review of Relevant Literature

Crisis Intervention in the Emergency Room

The literature supports the importance of placing crisis clinicians in the hospital emergency room, asserting that "bodily illness is a reality problem with a large social and emotional component" (Bartlett, 1961). A number of sources suggest the roles clinicians might play in the emergency room. For example, Strinsky (1970) proposed that clinicians remain flexible and complete those essential tasks not assumed by others. Bennett (1973) described clinicians in this setting intervening with patients with serious social and/or psychological problems and with families and patients requiring follow-up.

Bergman (1976), Groner (1978), Krell (1976), Moonilal (1982), and others have emphasized the combinations and versatility of clinicians' roles in the emergency room. The major roles delineated by Soskis (1985) are staff education, patient/family service, crisis intervention, and "filling in the gaps."

Social work literature also stresses the range of patient biopsychosocial problems brought to the emergency room. Examples of medically induced crises described include myocardial infarction (Sokol, 1983), cancer (Oppenheimer, 1967), and miscarriage (Soskis, 1985). Crisis intervention with persons experiencing a range of biopsychosocial emergencies is described, including cancer patients (Berger, 1984), premature and stillborn infants (Hancock, 1976; Stringham, Riley, & Ross, 1982), and persons with conversion disorders (Swartz & McCracken, 1986). Intervention with patients' families is identified as a crucial component of crisis intervention (Epperson, 1977). Studies support the contention that a large proportion of emergency room patients present nonemergency medical and secondary psychosocial problems and/or primary problems that are psychological in nature (Grumet & Trachtman, 1976; Healy, 1981).

Other researchers note the severity of psychosocial problems seen in the emergency room. For example, Clement and Klingbeil (1981) point to the increased linkage of the emergency room with the criminal justice system. Victims of family violence, child abuse, rape, criminal attack, and attempted suicide are seen and in fact are often identified as such by emergency room staff.

The emergency room is also described as an important treatment resource for victims of traumas (Grossman, 1973), the critically ill and dying (Floren, 1981; Weinberg, 1985), substance abusers (Rund, Summers, & Levin, 1981), persons with psychiatric emergencies (Jacobsen & Howell, 1978), children (Meier, 1981), the elderly (Gerson & Skvarch, 1982; Wilson, Simpson, Duncan, & Lloyd, 1982), and the homeless (Friedman, 1983). Particularly in low-income urban areas, the emergency room is the major health care provider for large populations (Soskis, 1980).

Crisis intervention is identified as a major component of hospital emergency room practice. In her discussion of the use of crisis intervention theory in hospitals, Sands (1983b) identifies not only illness but also hospitalization and treatment procedures as patient crises. More recent literature provides crisis intervention protocols and criteria for emergency room practice (Clement & Klingbeil, 1981; Holland & Rogich, 1980; Segal, Watson, & Nelson, 1985).

Crisis Theory

The literature emphasizes the high potential for problem solving during crises. For example, Golan (1978) noted that the word *crisis* is derived from the Greek word for "decision," or more broadly, "a turning point." She emphasized that the Chinese ideograph for crisis can be interpreted both as a "danger," in the sense that it threatens to overwhelm the individual and may result in serious consequences, and as an "opportunity," since during such periods one tends to become amenable to outside influences (p. 61).

The matter of timing is generally considered very important in crisis intervention. Caplan, Mason and Kaplan (1965) observed that crises tend to evolve through four phases:

Initial rise in tension due to precipitating stress

Increased tension in response to coping skill failure

Crisis reaction with high tension levels

Crisis resolution or functional breakdown

According to Smith (1976), it is critically important to intervene prior to the final phase, when breakdown may be difficult to prevent. Patient reactions during a crisis are often infused with high levels of anxiety, depression, and helplessness (Sands, 1983a, p. 253). It is in part the intensity of these feelings that can overwhelm the person in crisis.

Crisis theorists have long emphasized the importance of a rapid and skillful response from helping professionals (Rapoport, 1965, 1970). While pointing to conceptual weaknesses in "crisis theory" (Lukton, 1974), theorists agree that crisis intervention requires unique, identifiable skills. For example, Smith (1976) asserted that crisis work must have a very sharp focus. The clinician must complete an accurate assessment based on an understanding of the normative reactions that tend to characterize particular crises (p. 170). Holland and Rogich (1980) discussed timing. They advised that the clinician treating the family of a deceased or critically ill patient withhold full disclosure until meeting the family in the emergency room. In working with rape and child abuse victims, Soskis (1985) recommended against asking "why" questions that might reinforce self-blame.

As documented in Chapter 1 of this handbook, the literature supports goal-directed interventions within the context of a supportive, reassuring style. Crisis clinicians should be aware that often the patient is in a state of high expectancy regarding the clinician's ability to help. Consequently, patients in crisis are likely to comply with clinician advice and suggestions (Haffen & Peterson, 1982; Golan, 1978; Parad, 1965). Patient readiness allows a highly productive working alliance to develop rapidly. This patient–clinician bond and the parallel bond that develops between crisis clinicians is described often and positively in the literature. For a thorough review of the basic tenets of crisis theory and the steps in the crisis intervention model, see Chapter 1 of this handbook.

Practice Framework

T he crisis intervention approach proposed for the emergency room is consistent with the ecological model of practice for health settings. As delineated by Germain (1977, 1984), this model emphasizes the interaction and balance between person and environment through a series of exchanges of resources, including information. The exchange of resources acts to reduce or limit an individual's level of stress. Germain's person–environment balance is similar to the equilibrium that is disturbed by a crisis. Coulton (1979) has proposed that one can measure the nature of the person–environment fit through studying a series of variables, including social relationships, level of activity, and financial resources. Ecological theorists suggest specifying the sources of current imbalance as a preliminary step to reordering the equilibrium. Coulton (1981) specifies that to restore balance, the intervention targets and goals may be directed at either the person or environment. The ecological approach provides both a frame of reference and a value base for emergency room crisis intervention.

Value/Ethical Base of Emergency Room Practice

The crisis clinician in the emergency room is often asked to assist the hospital in transferring or removing "undesirable patients" who represent financial liabilities, behave in unacceptable ways, or present biopsychosocial problems that frighten caregivers. In the current environment of cost containment and enhanced profitability, it is sometimes difficult to evaluate the extent to which hospital decisions are made to support organizational survival or enhance profitability. The literature discusses the importance of maintaining a balance or equilibrium between these organizational goals and patient care (Friedman, 1982a, 1982b; Satin & Duhl, 1972).

Clinicians must maintain a clear focus and commitment to the well-being of their emergency room clients, even when this stance results in appearing to work at cross-purposes with the employing hospital (Mannon, 1976). However, as indicated in the *Code of Ethics* (National Association of Social Workers, 1980), the clinician is responsible for retaining primary focus on client well-being, as illustrated in the following vignette.

A 77-year-old black woman, Mrs. Morgan, had come to the emergency room on several occasions complaining of dizziness. Her medical record repeatedly indicated the determination that she was out of compliance with her medical plan from the adjoining family practice center. The emergency room triage nurse prepared to refer her back to family medicine for a medical examination. Due to the multiple risk factors of age, minority status, social isolation, and poverty, the clinician prevailed upon the triage nurse to arrange for medical examination by emergency room staff, to be followed by a clinical assessment. The medical examination revealed a decubitus ulcer with hospitalization indicated. The clinician learned from the patient that she had serious difficulties in obtaining prescribed medications and could not read the prescription or written doctors' orders. Although she said yes to directions given by medical staff, she claimed that she rarely understood what was being directed. After arranging for appropriate care, the clinician conferred with emergency room and family practice center staff to help them address the multiple sources of this patient's noncompliance.

Multidimensional Nature of Emergency Room Practice

Emergency room practice is multidimensional in terms of the populations served, the units of attention, and the methods used. Figure 10.1 suggests the multiple choices.

The Multidimensional Approach Within the Emergency Room

The multidimensional approach moves from the ecological metaphor to specific prescriptions for practice which reflect the highly fluid interactive emergency room environment. Multiple clinical decisions are made rapidly with limited information. The following guidelines provide direction in application of the multidimensional approach:

1. Crisis intervention services provide a unique and necessary component of emergency room care. Consequently, crisis clinicians must be given sufficient *autonomy* to locate and intervene with psychosocially at-risk patients, set case boundaries and

Figure 10.1 *Multidimensional Nature of Emergency Room Practice*

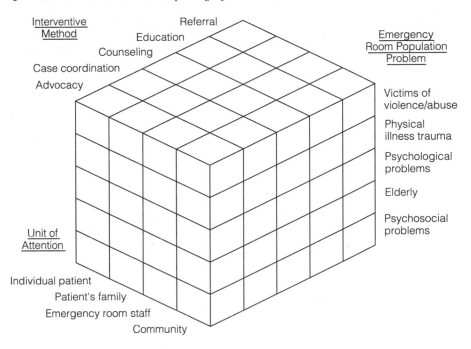

intervention goals, and provide time-limited but comprehensive psychosocial care. Clinicians providing crisis services in the emergency room must tolerate a conflicting set of directions without losing sight of their primary responsibility to the patient.

2. The nature of practice in the emergency room is very much focused on the *person in situation*. The unit of clinician's attention often includes the patient's family and the emergency room health team as well as the individual patient. By targeting interventions at multiple points, crisis-resolving resources are orchestrated to positively reinforce one another. For example, it is well understood that vulnerable patients in crisis are susceptible to suggestion from helping professionals and family members. Should messages from family members and emergency room staff prove nonconfirming or contradictory, patient helplessness and confusion are reinforced. Therefore, crisis intervention in the emergency room often includes emergency room crisis management.

3. The importance of clinical *case assessment* cannot be overemphasized. In the assessment process, clinicians are responsible for establishing a primary diagnosis that includes, but is not limited to, the presenting medical problem. Soskis (1985) provides a helpful example: "A young woman's presenting problem may be a broken arm, but after talking with her, the [clinician] may make a primary diagnosis of spouse abuse. The approach of the whole medical team, not just that of the [clinician], will be different because of this knowledge" (pp. 23–24).

4. Clinicians assigned to emergency services must possess the *requisite set of practice knowledge and skills* to support autonomous practice. The emergency room crisis clinician must intervene rapidly with patients in crisis without lead time to prepare. Consequently, the clinician's knowledge and skill base must be strong and versatile. Credibility within the health team and effectiveness with patients relies on a working knowledge of the hospital and surrounding community resources. Clinicians must be able to access all necessary resources while working with patients in the emergency room.

5. A working knowledge of *crisis concepts* is a feature of emergency room practice. In some instances, patients are experiencing physical and/or psychological crises that require immediate care. These patients and their families will often be in a state of acute crisis and will present the crisis symptoms described in the literature. Patients in other instances are experiencing what might be called *psychosocial crises.* These crises are characterized primarily by psychosocial problems such as homelessness, extreme social isolation, and unmet primary care needs which may contribute to physical and psychological trauma and illness. Although viewed in some hospital settings as controversial and undesirable, these emergency room patients must be appropriately served by crisis professionals.

6. Five clinician roles are central to crisis intervention practice in the emergency room: *advocacy, case coordination, counseling, education,* and *resource mobilization and referral.* Advocacy on the client's behalf may occur with the patient's family, community resources, and emergency room staff. Because of the complexity of the emergency room, crisis clinicians frequently provide case coordination in which multiple crisis responses and interventions are managed. Counseling is often required to deal with anxiety, depression, grief, anger, and other reactions associated with crisis. Crisis counseling assists with retrieval and use of pertinent information, anticipatory guidance, and reframing patients' perceptions. In the role of educator the clinician teaches new information and skills to both patients and emergency room staff. Resource mobilization provides linkage to problem-solving resources during and after the current crisis. Such resources potentially include public and private social service, and voluntary and self-help resources. The task of linking patients with appropriate resources is deceptively complex.

Dimensions of Practice Model

A multidimensional approach to emergency room practice recognizes a range of intervention choices within a three-way matrix of patient characteristics, unit of attention, and interventive method. This normative model assumes that people experience a range of pressing life problems, many of which may be presented in the hospital emergency room. Therefore, with the exception of a subset of patients whose major presenting problem is psychiatric in nature, the crisis clinician's assessment does not emphasize the clinical diagnosis. Instead, the multidimensional approach defines and assesses current patient crisis, determines patient and family strengths and risk factors, and structures an intervention plan that maximizes patient, family, clinician, hospital, and community strengths and resources. This process begins with an initial psychosocial triage to determine the extent to which patients require immediate and decisive clinician response. For example, the arrival of a critically ill emergency room patient should result in immediate efforts by the crisis clinician to both locate and begin anticipatory grief counseling with the patient's family.

The Nature of the Patient Population and Problem

Identifying the nature of the patient population and of the presenting problem typically is the entry point into the multidimensional matrix. The normative nature of psychosocial issues associated with specific patient categories provides initial direction to the crisis intervention efforts. Once the patient population/presenting problem is identified, salient psychosocial treatment issues can be anticipated. Thus, important themes with several representative emergency room populations can be identified.

KNOWLEDGE BASE	PROBABLE NEEDED CRISIS INTERVENTION SERVICES

Population/Problem: Victims of Violence and Abuse (Child Abuse, Spouse Abuse, Elderly Abuse, Rape, and Criminal Assault)

Patients/families will be ambivalent about full disclosure of relevant data and history.	Intervention must be skillfully managed with an emphasis on data collection and avoidance of a "blaming the victim" focus.
Patients/families will most likely require help in processing reactions to the abusive incident and its consequences.	Anticipatory guidance encourages ventilation through active listening, education about future reactions, and referral with follow-up to appropriate community resources, including shelters, victim/perpetrator programs, and legal resources.
Victims and perpetrators will require assistance initiating and managing interactions with law enforcement and public welfare personnel.	Initial reporting by hospital is often mandated in many instances. Social workers will need to be skillful in contacting and linking patients with reporting agencies.

Population/Problem: Victims of Physical Illness and Trauma

While physically ill and traumatized patients are receiving medical care, families are often experiencing high levels of stress. Families may be quite isolated while dealing with their reactions.

The crisis clinician should assess the degree of stress of the patient's family and intervene by providing appropriate information, support, and referral to community resources.

Many patients and their families have great difficulty integrating important information about the illness/trauma and consequently experience stress due to the hospital and treatment procedures as well as the illness itself.

The crisis clinician can directly provide helpful information; interpret, explain, and repeat information provided by others; and assist in beginning integration of the crisis experience.

In instances of actual or potential death, patients and their families need crisis counseling to reduce the toxic impact of the loss.

Counseling provided in the emergency room can be quite intense. A bond may form quickly which allows the clinician ready access to important client fears and concerns. Counseling should be appropriately supportive and should emphasize the normalcy of client reactions and the importance of expressing these reactions as well as challenge self-recriminations. Appropriate referral and follow-up is imperative.

Problem: Psychological Problems

The emergency room is a frequently used resource for persons with a very broad range of psychological problems and symptomatology, including high levels of anxiety, agitation, and/or depression.

A crisis clinician can help establish an accurate differential diagnosis and treatment plan. In particular the clinician should access psychosocial information about the patient's current life situation in order to sharpen the assessment process. Knowledge of the *DSM-III-R* (APA, 1987) is essential.

Patients presenting psychological problems often require rapid disposition with incomplete available data. The risk for suicide or danger to others might be high. Also common are high levels of distress and somatic complaints. At the

It is very important to develop and utilize assessment tools and protocols for managing patients presenting psychological problems. The crisis clinician often provides leadership in obtaining voluntary or involuntary same time patients may be combative, passive, or difficult to manage.

Assessment of patients with psychological problems should be broadened beyond the clinical diagnostic interview with the identified patient. The clinician should obtain a thorough history of previous and current treatment received as well as an emergency room family assessment.

Emergency room staff often find patients with psychological problems difficult to treat. Staff may require clinician support and consultation while providing patient care.

commitment, involving or distancing law enforcement personnel, and providing case coordination. This role requires excellent skills in health team networking. Follow-up is particularly crucial with this population.

The crisis clinician needs to formulate a thorough psychosocial assessment that integrates clinical diagnosis and relevant history with a current social work analysis. Whenever possible, emergency room discharge plans should incorporate use of the patient's resource network. Follow-up after emergency room discharge is desirable, as it stimulates network activity.

Crisis clinicians should possess team-building skills that facilitate the appropriate ventilation and management of stressful responses to this patient population. In addition, clinicians should educate staff regarding symptomatology and dispositional options.

Population: The Elderly

Among the elderly, medical and psychological problems are closely related. For example, eating habits are closely associated with a range of medical illnesses.

The elderly must be viewed as high-risk patients with respect to social isolation and inadequate social resources. Screening mechanisms should be employed in the emergency room to identify at-risk elderly. Typically, elderly living alone with severe chronic or acute illness who are 70 years of age or older would be automatically screened by the emergency room clinician (Rehr, Berkman, & Rosenberg, 1980).

The elderly may be prone to either underestimate or overestimate their self-reported difficulties. Therefore it is necessary to carefully explore the elderly

Crisis clinicians can access and contribute important information about an elderly patient's housing, eating and sleeping habits, self-care, income, and patient's biopsychosocial situation. Elderly patients often require a unique approach to emergency room interviewing and examination. They are sometimes less likely to communicate relevant data precisely and to retain directions given at discharge.

The elderly population is vulnerable to being underserved in the emergency room and to having difficulty in obtaining necessary resources such as medication and follow-up medical care.

general social relationships. This information is often necessary for case disposition.

In serving elderly patients the crisis clinician must be skillful in advocacy and follow-up. Resources must be developed both within and outside the hospital for use with elderly patients who cannot afford care or qualify for funding.

Population: Patients with Other Psychosocial Problems*

Given the current climate of cost containment, many hospitals encounter patient populations that are having difficulty obtaining crisis services outside the hospital. The question of how to employ limited hospital resources with this population is perplexing.

Some patients will be labeled by hospital emergency room staff as malingerers, inappropriate users of service, and generally undesirable. Socially marginal populations such as the chronically mentally ill will often be categorized this way.

Crisis clinicians are responsible for addressing and resolving the ethical questions related to a patient's right to care. Primary focus must be maintained on the responsibility to meet the patient's needs and advocate for care. Skills required include fact finding, conflict resolution, mediation, and advocacy.

The crisis clinician is in a unique position to monitor the nature of emergency care provided to "difficult" patients. Clinicians can ensure that a complete understanding of a patient's behavior and motivation is sought. In addition, the clinician should contribute information and understanding of the patient's psychosocial situation to be considered in the decision-making process.

---

*This category refers to those patients not previously discussed whose presenting medical problems appear to be associated with serious psychosocial dilemmas, including homelessness, chronic mental illness, and AIDS.

When a particular emergency room is unable or unwilling to provide care, adequate referral and follow-up rather than "patient dumping" is mandated.

Adequate referral is based on a thorough knowledge of available resources, knowledge about methods of access, and when necessary, skill in mediation and advocacy. In addition, post-referral follow-up is necessary to verify that appropriate service is provided.

The nonmedical problems associated with patient care of this population are often massive. Referral for financial assistance, food, clothing, housing, and social support are necessary.

The crisis clinician must be skillful in locating and connecting patients with psychosocial services, identifying gaps in community service, and providing leadership in resource creation.

Understanding of each patient population and problem area provides a basis for predicting both patient risk and specific biopsychosocial concerns. Screening devices and protocols can help the crisis clinician best use available time for skillful crisis intervention.

Units of Attention

Often in the course of serving one patient the crisis clinician has multiple simultaneous or sequential targets or units of attention and may move from patient to family to emergency room staff in the midst of an unfolding crisis. The nature of intervention with each unit of attention will be discussed separately.

Individual Patient

The individual patient is the standard unit of attention, as the central goal of emergency room services is to stabilize the individual patient medically and prevent physical deterioration and death. The crisis clinician's role is to both support achievement of that central goal and to attend to the psychosocial aspects of the crisis. The following activities are examples of clinician interventions with individual patients:

Prepare for the arrival of the individual patient at the emergency room by contacting family members, helping emergency room staff anticipate the nature of the biopsychosocial crisis, and arranging for necessary professional resources such as chaplains to respond to individual patient needs during the crisis.

Obtain and transmit to those providing crisis medical care accurate nonmedical information from ambulance drivers, families, or others who might have observed the onset of the crisis and subsequently brought the patient to the emergency room.

Provide leadership in the psychosocial assessment of the patient following resolution of the immediate medical crisis. Clinicians should also assure that psychosocial problems are sufficiently addressed in the emergency room treatment plan.

Act as liaison and mediator between hospital emergency room staff, the patient, and other resources needed while care is being provided, such as law enforcement and child welfare personnel.

Provide emergency room discharge planning and follow-up to link patients with appropriate resources and to verify that appropriate care has been offered and accepted.

Advocate for individual patients whose vulnerability or other characteristics might result in their receiving inadequate care or no care at all.

Patient's Family

The family is often neglected by emergency room medical staff in the press to respond to the emergency crisis. Sitting for long periods in the waiting areas, families are left to sort out their own complicated responses to an often unexpected crisis. The crisis clinician's potential role with the patient's family includes doing the following:

Contact the family and ask them to come to the emergency room. Avoid overwhelming them at this time with distressing information about the crisis.

Share, and arrange for other emergency room staff to share important information with the family in a timely and appropriate manner.

Help the family participate as much as possible in the patient's experience at the emergency room. This includes retrieving important information from family members, facilitating their participation in treatment decisions, arranging for them to see and/or visit the patient when possible, and providing them with private space when needed.

Provide crisis intervention counseling. This process can be intense, involving expressions of anxiety, guilt, denial, rage, and grief.

Assure active involvement with the family concerning discharge planning and referral to other resources. When possible, families should be involved in developing and implementing discharge plans.

Emergency Room Staff

Emergency room staff are likely to experience a constant press of multiple demands and must organize patient care in a manner that causes many patients to wait for long periods of time. Even when care is immediate there are times when treatment is unsuccessful or the nature of trauma particularly disturbing. Injuries and deaths of children are often very difficult. One of the crisis clinician's most important roles is to help emergency room staff deal with their own reactions as caregivers in order to improve their ability to practice competently. The following are several ways in which crisis clinicians can intervene with emergency room staff:

Provide opportunities for emergency room professionals to ventilate, explore, and integrate their own reactions while in the process of providing patient care.

Participate as consultant in creating and maintaining an interdisciplinary team. Through the team, help emergency room staff increase their mutual reliance and support.

Educate emergency room professionals regarding the psychosocial component of care. Encourage staff to screen patients for psychosocial risk and make appropriate referrals to social services.

Provide educational opportunities for staff in crisis intervention, work with families, and other related topics.

Larger Community

The primary focus of the emergency room clinician is within the hospital emergency department. There are also times when the community itself is the target for change.

Organize the community to respond to unmet needs apparent to emergency room medical and social work staff. For this purpose, it is important to routinely document unmet resource needs.

Mobilize the hospital and the larger community to recognize and deal with inadequate and inappropriate responses on the part of community agencies, funding sources, and other hospitals. Documentation is important in this area as well.

Participate in community coalitions that can improve the quality of patient referrals and follow-up, and help monitor changes in funding patterns, eligibility requirements, and special projects.

Methods of Emergency Room Intervention

C onsistent with the person in situation formulation, multiple methods are often used in the same case to improve service outcomes. This approach specifies advocacy, case coordination, counseling, education, and referral and mobilization of resources as the most central emergency room methods.

Advocacy

Advocacy is particularly vital when practicing with the elderly, indigent patients, and other oppressed groups. The role of advocate presumes a firm alignment by the clinician with the emergency room patient. As an advocate, the clinician is responsible for promoting competent care within the least restrictive environment. As much as possible the clinician is to perform a watchdog function to assure that emergency room patients are provided timely medical care while being given accurate information about alternative procedures and levels of risk. Further, this information should be provided in a manner the patient can understand and recall. It is recognized that the clinician is not in a position to supervise medical care, nor should he or she assume that care can be error-free. However, in those instances where the press of time or the caregivers' bids about particular patient populations cause emergency staff to undercut quality care, the clinician is mandated to intervene.

Intervention should use adversarial techniques only when less conflictual mechanisms have been attempted. Often an assessment suggests that the clinician should perform a mediating role. Information and opinions are gathered, refined, and processed with patient, family, and staff. This process allows for perceptions and behaviors to change. In some situations supervisors, attending physicians, and service administrators will need to be consulted in an attempt to reverse unacceptable decisions. There are also times when the clinician must refuse to participate in an unacceptable care plan. For example, Soskis (1985) proposes that if an unjust and potentially harmful decision is made to transfer a patient the clinician may well need to refuse to assist in arranging transportation.

In the case of Mrs. Morgan, described earlier, emergency room staff were preparing to prematurely discharge the patient. The patient's risk was not fully explored due to staff frustration regarding her lack of compliance. Her age, income level, and minority status also contributed to the staff's biased perception of Mrs. Morgan as uncooperative, intellectually limited, and generally an undesirable patient. Fortunately, the clinician accurately assessed Mrs. Morgan. as a socially isolated, medically at-risk patient. The clinician's intervention was not adversarial. However, the clinician raised sufficient question with both the triage nurse and the examining physician to warrant a patient examination. The failure to examine and treat Mrs. Morgan at that time might have resulted in further deterioration and more costly and painful treatment at a later time.

Case Coordination

Patients in crisis frequently present complex biopsychosocial problem constellations which are only partly resolved through managing the medical crisis. Often a case manager is required who can cross programmatic and discipline lines to ensure patient care. The crisis clinician's knowledge, skills, and psychosocial orientation provide a useful framework for approaching this role. The following case exemplifies the case management role:

A stat request for a crisis clinician to report to the emergency room was received at 1 P.M. A mother and her four children were being evaluated following a one-vehicle accident. The children had not yet been identified. Assistance was requested in obtaining collateral information regarding this family as well as in providing for a flow of information throughout the triaging/treatment of the patients while in crisis.

Mr. Barnes, spouse/father of the patients, arrived within half an hour and provided historical information on the family members. Shortly thereafter, other significant family arrived. The clinician provided support and information to the family regarding the planned treatment of each family member as reported by the emergency room staff. The injuries ranged from facial lacerations to serious internal trauma and orthopedic fractures.

Emergency room staff refused Mr. Barnes' request to see his family. The reason provided was the severity of their trauma. His wife was scheduled for emergency surgery, as was his 10-year-old daughter prior to a planned transfer by helicopter to a trauma center 50 miles away. The clinician intervened and advocated for Mr. Barnes to see his other children while the more severely injured patients were undergoing emergency care. Mr. Barnes then was allowed to see both his daughter and spouse prior to their surgery. During the next five hours the clinician remained with Mr. Barnes as the various family members were relocated throughout the hospital. The 5-year-old and 7-year-old had suffered facial lacerations, required orthopedic consultations for possible fractures in their extremities, and were taken to intensive care prior to scheduling casting. The 8-year-old son was relocated to pediatrics.

Mr. Barnes had five family members in three distinct areas of the hospital. During this time the crisis intervention focused on maintaining communication with the various nursing units regarding newly scheduled surgeries and room transfers. When the oldest daughter had been stabilized sufficiently to warrant transfer to a trauma center, her father was escorted to surgery to be able to accompany her to the helicopter and to meet the medical team who came to provide transport. This was met with disfavor by nursing personnel, who were concerned about the patient's critical status and felt that since the patient had directly come out of surgery she was not "cleaned up" enough for her father to see her. The father was able to tell his daughter good-bye on the helicopter pad, not knowing if he would see her alive again. Arrangements for extended family members to meet the daughter at the second hospital were then completed. During this same time the plastic surgeons prepared to begin surgery on the 7-year-old daughter, and Mr. Barnes' wife was completing one surgical procedure and beginning another.

Without clinician intervention, Mr. Barnes would have been unable to follow the course of his family's treatment. Emergency room administration, surgeons, and nursing supervisors were consulted by the clinician to allow Mr. Barnes to remain involved with his family. Mr. Barnes was enabled to remain in touch with all five family members in addition to being provided crisis counseling to assist in the processing of the trauma which had devastated his world.

Counseling

As a component of almost all patient interventions, counseling activities assist patients in preparing for, coping with, and learning from the crises that cause them to come to the emergency room. The counseling may consist of advice, supportive reassurance, active listening, and confrontation. Patients may be challenged to view the situation differently or be reassured that their perceptions and reactions are normal. Although brief in duration, counseling of emergency room patients in crisis is often very intense. Patients express powerful emotions, including grief, anger, denial, anxiety, and confusion. On occasion, the counseling, case coordination, and referral activities are provided simultaneously. The following illustrates a mixture of counseling and other activities:

A crisis clinician was called to the emergency room to meet with the spouse of a patient brought by ambulance. The patient, Mr. Parker, 67, was diagnosed as having had a fatal myocardial infarction. The family physician had requested a crisis clinician to be with him while notifying the family. Mrs. Parker, a son, and a daughter were present. Mrs. Parker experienced an appropriate, acute grief response. The family was invited to view Mr. Parker's body in the examining room and the clinician accompanied them. Mrs. Parker initiated contact with her husband by attempting to awaken him. After several unsuccessful attempts, she began shouting at him to wake up. Her son and daughter made attempts to interrupt her behavior and divert her attention. They were uncomfortable with her behaviors, as were the nursing personnel. The clinician supported Mrs. Parker in experiencing her acute grief reaction and reassured the son and daughter that their mother's behavior was not to be interrupted. Mrs. Parker then sobbed and acknowledged that her husband was dead. The daughter and son joined her with their father's body. They were encouraged by their mother to hold his hand, noticing how cold it was, and to kiss him.

When the family members were ready to leave the examining room they were escorted back into the nursing supervisor's office to discuss funeral arrangements. Discussion ensued regarding Mr. Parker's whereabouts at the time of the myocardial infarction. The ambulance report was shared with them. Upon learning the location at which he was found, Mrs. Parker experienced a dramatic shift in affect. She flew into a rage. It became evident that the grieving widow had been transformed into a scorned wife. She revealed that Mr. Parker had been involved in an extramarital affair a few years earlier, and according to his wife had terminated that relationship. The address where his car was to be retrieved was the home of his former lover. Mrs. Parker continued to be intensely angry and agitated. She made serious threats against the other woman.

The clinician assumed a counseling role throughout this interchange, appropriately encouraging ventilation, reassuring the daughter and son that the reactions were normal, and exploring reactions to Mr. Parker's presumed infidelity. At the point that Mrs. Parker made threats against the other woman, the clinician challenged the plan and suggested that Mrs. Parker delay any actions until she had had time to more fully explore and understand her own reactions. In addition, the clinician made a referral to a local counseling agency and asked the attending physician to reconfer with the family due to his long-standing knowledge of the patient and of the Parkers' marital discord.

The clinician also made the judgment that considerable risk did exist for Mr. Parker's former lover. After consultation with emergency room staff the decision was made to contact the household where Mr. Parker had experienced his myocardial infarction and warn the resident of the threats against her life. Given that Mrs. Parker remained angry and threatening as she left the hospital, the police were notified of the situation, including the possibility of a disturbance when Mr. Parker's car was retrieved.

This case provides an example of crisis counseling in which the clinician works quite intensively with a family while also coordinating emergency room and community response.

Education

The clinician engaged in an educational intervention attempts to teach patients, families, or staff new information or skills that will be useful in coping with a biopsychosocial crisis. This activity differs from counseling in that the emphasis is on cognitive learning rather than mastery of the crisis on an affective level. The purpose of an educational intervention is twofold: first, to enhance the probability of recovery from the current crisis and to prevent later crises through better self-care; second, to counteract the patient's and family's sense of helplessness within the hospital emergency room. Educational interventions focus on specific manageable content and provide opportunity for rehearsal when new skills are being learned. As previously discussed, educational interventions are used frequently with emergency room staff to improve their knowledge and skills when working with patients in crisis. The following case example demonstrates the use of educational interventions:

Mrs. Riley, 73, was seen in the emergency room complaining of dizziness, blurred vision, and difficulty in standing. Physical examination indicated elevated blood pressure and an electrolyte imbalance. In the course of the medical examination Mrs. Riley commented that she periodically ate "uncooked ground round steak." Emergency room staff understood her to say that she was eating raw hamburger and referred her for possible psychiatric hospitalization. Upon completing a social history, the clinician learned that Mrs. Riley's family had come from a part of Europe where ground round steak was frequently eaten uncooked as a delicacy. The opportunity was used to educate emergency room staff regarding the importance of cultural differences and the tendency to make false assumptions about members of other cultural groups. Upon further evaluation of this patient it was learned that her diet was deficient in potassium. With the aid of a hospital dietician a series of educational interventions resulted in a substantially improved diet and a reduction in diet-related health problems.

Referral and Mobilization of Resources

It is extremely difficult for patients in crisis to locate needed but unfamiliar resources. Many of the patient's available psychosocial resources will have been mobilized to deal with the current crisis. Expert assistance in locating and accessing additional resources greatly enhances the likelihood of crisis resolution. As a general principle patients should be encouraged to take as much initiative as possible in obtaining services. Activities inherent in referral and resource mobilization include developing a resource network, assessing the patient situation in order to select the proper resource, helping patients access the resource, and following up to verify that the resource was appropriate and was used. In the following case patient needs were limited:

Mr. and Mrs. Randolph are residents of a neighboring state. On their vacation they were involved in an accident on the interstate and were brought to the emergency room for services. Neither required admission to the hospital. However, they were detained for several hours. Their car was not drivable, and crisis intervention staff were summoned to provide assistance to them in retrieving their belongings from their vehicle, which had been towed to another location. They had little cash on hand and were unable to obtain transportation. The clinician arranged for transportation to their vehicle and helped remove their belongings. They were then transported to a rental car dealer in order to facilitate transportation for their return home. Upon return to their home community, the Randolphs wrote a letter to the clinician and enclosed a check for her services. They said they could never repay the kindness with which they were met and hoped that this would enable others to continue to have assistance when in crisis.

In other instances the need is for concrete resources:

The emergency room staff called the social service department to request help for a young mother who presented her 18-month-old daughter with earaches. The child was diagnosed as having bilateral otitis media and was given a prescription for antibiotics. The mother informed staff that she had applied for Aid to Families with Dependent Children (AFDC) upon moving into the community but had not yet received approval. The clinician arranged for emergency funds for the medication and evaluated other needs relative to food, housing, and general social support. The patient did not appear at risk in any of these areas.

In still other instances the clinician may call for emergency psychiatric services.

Mark, 24, was brought to the emergency room by his parents at 5:30 in the evening. He said that he was afraid he would kill himself. He was an electrician and had shocked himself two times in the last day at work. His wife, 12 years his senior, left him two weeks ago. The crisis clinician was asked to see the patient. He said that he had been "holding myself together" for the past two weeks while at work but not at home. He was unable to sleep at night, had tremors, and found himself crying at all hours of the day and night.

He indicated that he knew how much voltage it would take to kill himself and that he hadn't "made those mistakes yet." The precipitating factor for his marital separation centered on a disagreement with his wife regarding the knowledge that her 15-year-old daughter was pregnant. During the interview Mark experienced muscle tremors, was emotional labile, had difficulty concentrating, and said he did not know how he could go on without his wife. He was encouraged to accept referral to a nearby psychiatric hospital. He voluntarily agreed to do so and was transported directly by ambulance from the emergency room.

Ron, 27, presented himself to the emergency room of the local hospital with gastrointestinal complaints coupled with an inability to concentrate. The physician on staff found no physical abnormalities and contacted the crisis clinician, who evaluated his social functioning. Ron revealed that this episode was triggered by a recent contact with his ex-wife and 4-year-old child. Upon returning from a weekend visit, his son proceeded to call the male at his mother's home "Daddy" in Ron's presence. Ron reported that at that instance he lost control of himself, immediately left the premises, and began driving aimlessly. He found himself three hours later in a state park, his car parked by a lake. He then left and checked into a motel in a nearby town. He did not leave his motel room for three days except on two occasions to eat. It was following this that he arrived at the emergency room and reported that he was experiencing somatic discomforts. He reported that he was not able to face anyone or return to his employment. He requested a referral to an inpatient psychiatric program. Following consultation with an emergency room physician a referral was made to a nearby psychiatric hospital.

As the preceding case vignettes have demonstrated, the crisis clinician's role in the emergency room is diverse in terms of patient population, intervention target, and method used. In all instances, the crisis intervention provided by the clinician had the purpose of helping to meet the immediate biopsychosocial needs that had caused the visit to the emergency room.

Clinical Issues

I n the practice of crisis intervention in the emergency room both time frame and setting are important dimensions of practice.

Time as Focus of Crisis Intervention

The emergency room provides an exceptional opportunity to intervene in a biopsychosocial crisis before functioning permanently deteriorates. The high level of patient vulnerability provides a receptivity and often a willingness to address the immediate crisis-related problems. The crisis experience itself stimulates many patients and their families to have more than the usual amounts of energy for problem resolution. In addition, anticipatory guidance in the emergency room helps reduce the harmful impact of both the crisis and its associated medical treatment. In many respects crisis intervention in the emergency room epitomizes the model of service delivery that attempts to position crisis services where they are most needed and most readily accessible.

In discussing the issue of time, certain features of emergency room crisis intervention should be emphasized:

Early identification of patient risk and casefinding in the emergency room in order to initiate crisis intervention quickly and decisively

Provision of crisis services in a manner that articulates well with the medical treatment being provided

Inclusion of pertinent information and guidance in a manner which encourages patients to remain aware of the crisis reality without being overwhelmed

Mediation between individual patient, family, and emergency room staff which minimizes helplessness and passivity

Referral and follow-up of patients to community and self-help resources that when necessary will provide continuing crisis intervention

Crisis intervention in the emergency room could range in duration from a few moments to a number of hours and could include one or multiple interviews. In general, crisis services in the emergency room support patients in the initial or most acute phase of their crisis but are not sufficient to enable many patients to reestablish a new equilibrium. When provided effectively, emergency room crisis intervention is useful in assisting patients with the initial crisis response and in differentiating those patients who require follow-up from those who do not.

Emergency Room Setting as Focus of Crisis Intervention

The emergency room is a normative setting for crisis intervention. It does not require that patients identify or label themselves as crisis intervention clients. Rather, the crisis intervention is offered routinely as a part of emergency room services. In this way the need for assistance in coping with a crisis is normalized.

Having normalized the crisis, it is important for the crisis clinician to mobilize helpful responses from patient, family, emergency room staff, and the community. When providing crisis intervention in the emergency room the clinician engages not only in crisis intervention but in crisis management. Consequently the clinician *must* be cognizant of the entire emergency room system as a potential unit of attention. During crisis intervention the emergency room clinician continually assesses, intervenes with, and manages multiple systems simultaneously.

Evaluation

Crisis intervention in the emergency room is a highly specific and focused activity. Screening mechanisms (Rehr et al., 1980) and protocols for specific patient populations have been developed (Soskis, 1985). Both kinds of instruments provide structure for the practice of crisis intervention in the emergency room. A minimum acceptable level of care is established which provides the basis for subsequent evaluation review of the services provided. The more specific and well developed the protocols, the greater the clarity provided about the clinician's crisis intervention activities. The Social Work Department of Harborview Medical Center in Seattle, Washington, has developed a series of emergency room protocols for use with all patients presenting problems of child abuse, domestic abuse, grief reactions, and sexual assault (Soskis, 1985) or requiring psychiatric evaluation. The protocol for psychiatric evaluation provides criteria to determine case involvement and a specific series of sequential steps to gather necessary information, assess the patient's needs, and implement the case plan (Clement & Klingbeil, 1981).

Similarly, in a protocol developed for use at Harborview Medical Center with critically ill patients and their families (Holland & Rogich, 1980), the clinician's activities with patient, family, and staff are very carefully specified. Choices can be made based on the circumstances of the case.

Evaluation of the crisis intervention provided is possible by comparing the nature of actual service provided with the service standards set in the protocol. According to Dockhorn (1982), the quality of all hospital-based social work services must be regularly evaluated. Crisis intervention in the hospital emergency room is routinely included in this review. As outlined by Berkman and Weissman (1983), there are several approaches to quality assurance. A peer review system can be devised whereby a preset proportion of randomly selected cases can be reviewed. Quality assurance can also be achieved through the use of ongoing and systematic monitoring activities. According to the Division of Education and Division of Accreditation, Joint Commission on Accreditation of Hospitals (1986), the focus of quality assurance is the promotion of "contemporary standards of good practice." The appropriateness and efficacy of patient care is also emphasized. Monitoring and evaluation activities are implemented through the identification of patient care quality indicators, outcome measures, and associated measurement criteria. For example, criteria can be used to evaluate adherence to protocols, patient satisfaction, successful discharge, and the quality of crisis intervention documentation. Berkman and Weissman discuss in considerable depth the relationship between quality assurance and applied social work research in health care.

Summary

C risis intervention in the emergency room has been discussed in terms of both the pertinent literature and an ecological approach to practice. This approach emphasizes an active multidimensional professional response to crisis and encourages versatility with respect to intervention target and method. To assure the quality of emergency room crisis intervention, this approach recommends the use of screening mechanisms and protocols. The approach places emphasis on the clear responsibility to provide crisis intervention to patients experiencing biopsychosocial difficulties, even if the employing hospital is ambivalent about their care, and the importance of health team participation and patient advocacy during crisis intervention.

References

American Psychiatric Association (1987). *Desk Reference to the Diagnostic Criteria from DSM-III-R*. Washington, DC: Author.

Bartlett, H. (1961). *Social Work Practice in the Health Field*. New York: National Association of Social Workers.

Bennett, M. (1973). "Emergency Medical Services: The Social Worker's Role." *Hospitals,* 47, 111, 114, 118.

Berger, J. (1984). "Crisis Intervention: A Drop-in Support Group for Cancer Patients and Their Families." *Social Work in Health Care, 10,* 81–92.

Bergman, A. (1976). "Emergency Room: A Role for Social Workers." *Health and Social Work, 1,* 32–44.

Berkman, B., & Weissman, L. (1983). "Applied Social Work Research." In R. Miller & H. Rehr (Eds.), *Social Work Issues in Health Care* (pp. 221–251). Englewood Cliffs, NJ: Prentice-Hall.

Caplan, G., Mason, E., & Kaplan, D. (1965). "Four Studies of Crisis in Parents of Prematures." *Community Mental Health Journal, 2,* 149–162.

Christopherson, L. (1976). "Cardiac Transplant: Preparing for Dying or Living." *Health and Social Work, 1,* 58–72.

Clement, J., & Klingbeil, K. (1981). "The Emergency Room." *Health and Social Work, 6* (Supp. 2), 83–90.

Coulton, C. (1979). "A Study of Person-Environment Fit Among the Chronically Ill." *Social Work in Health Care, 5,* 5–17.

Coulton, C. (1981). "Person-Environment Fit as Focus in Health Care." *Social Work, 26,* 26–35.

Dhooper, S. (1984). "Social Networks and Support During the Crisis of Heart Attack." *Health and Social Work, 9,* 294–303.

Division of Education and Division of Accreditation, Joint Commission on Accreditation of Hospitals. (1986). "Monitoring and Evaluation of the Quality and Appropriateness of Care: A Hospital Example." *Quality Review Bulletin, 12,* 326–330.

Dixon, S. (1979). *Working With People in Crisis.* St. Louis: Mosby.

Dockhorn, J. (1982). *Essentials of Social Work Programs in Hospitals.* Chicago: American Hospital Association.

Epperson, M. (1977). "Families in Sudden Crisis." *Social Work in Health Care, 2,* 265–273.

Floren, T. (1981). "Death and Dying in the Emergency Setting." *Emergency Medical Services, 8,* 38, 40, 42, 45.

Friedman, E. (1982a). "Access to Care: Serving the Poor and Elderly in Tough Times." *Hospitals, 56,* 83–90.

Friedman, E. (1982b). "The Dumping Dilemma: The Poor Are Always With Some of Us." *Hospitals, 56,* 51–56.

Friedman, E. (1983). "Homeless Represent Major Health Problem." *Hospitals, 57,* 21.

Germain, C. (1977). "An Ecological Perspective on Social Work Practice in Health Care." *Social Work in Health Care, 3,* 67–76.

Germain, C. (1984). *Social Work Practice in Health Care: An Ecological Perspective.* New York: Free Press.

Gerson, L., & Skvarch, L. (1982). "Emergency Medical Service Utilizations by the Elderly." *Annals of Emergency Medicine, 11,* 610–612.

Golan, N. (1978). *Treatment in Crisis Situations.* New York: Free Press.

Groner, E. (1978). "Delivery of Clinical Social Work Services in the Emergency Room: A Description of an Existing Program." *Social Work in Health Care, 4,* 19–29.

Grossman, L. (1973). "Train Crash: Social Work and Disaster Services." *Social Work, 18,* 38–44.

Grumet, G., & Trachtman, D. (1976). "Psychiatric Social Workers in the Emergency Department." *Health and Social Work, 1,* 113–131.

Haffen, B., & Peterson, B. (1982). *The Crisis Intervention Handbook.* Englewood Cliffs, NJ: Prentice-Hall.

Hancock, E. (1976). "Crisis Intervention in a Newborn Nursery." *Social Work in Health Care, 1,* 421–432.

Healy, J. (1981). "ERs and Psychosocial Services." *Health and Social Work, 6,* 36–43.

Holland, L., & Rogich, L. E. (1980). "Dealing With Grief in the Emergency Room." *Health and Social Work, 5,* 12–17.

Jacobsen, P., & Howell, R. (1978). "Psychiatric Problems in Emergency Rooms." *Health and Social Work, 3,* 88–107.

Krell, G. (1976). "Hospital Social Work Should Be More Than a 9–5 Position." *Hospitals, 50,* 99, 100, 102, 104.

Levy, R., Durgin, J., & Thayer, S. (1980). "An Integrated Data Management System for Social Work Services." *Quality Review Bulletin, 6,* 21–28.

Lukton, R. (1974). "Crisis Theory: Review and Critique." *Social Service Review, 48,* 384–402.

Mannon, J. (1976). "Defining and Treating Problem Patients in a Hospital E.R." *Journal of Medical Care, 14,* 1004–1013.

Meier, E. (1981). "The Pediatric Emergency Patient." *Emergency Medicine, 13,* 29–32, 36.

Moonilal, J. (1982). "Trauma Centers: A New Dimension for Hospital Social Work." *Social Work in Health Care, 7,* 15–25.

National Association of Social Workers (1980). "Code of Ethics." *Social Work, 25,* 184–187.

Oppenheimer, J. (1967). "Use of Crisis Intervention in Casework With the Cancer Patient and His Family." *Social Work, 12,* 44–52.

Parad, H. (1965). *Crisis Intervention: Selected Readings.* New York: Family Service Association of America.

Rapoport, L. (1965). "The State of Crisis: Some Theoretical Considerations." In H. Parad (Ed.), *Crisis Intervention: Selected Readings* (pp. 22–31) New York: Family Service Association of America.

Rapoport, L. (1970). "Crisis Intervention as a Model of Treatment." In R. Roberts & R. Nee (Eds.), *Theories of Social Casework* (pp. 307–311). Chicago: University of Chicago Press.

Rehr, H., Berkman, B., & Rosenberg, G. (1980). "Screening for High Social Risk: Principles and Problems." *Social Work, 25,* 403–406.

Rund, D., Summers, W., & Levin, M. (1981). "Alcohol Usage and Psychiatric Illness in Emergency Patients." *Journal of the American Medical Association, 245,* 1240–1241.

Sands, R. (1983a). "Crisis Intervention and Social Work Practice in Hospitals." *Health and Social Work, 8,* 253–261.

Sands, R. (1983b). "Identity and the Experience of Crisis." *Social Casework, 64,* 223–230.

Satin, D., & Duhl, F. (1972). "The Hospital Unit as Community Physician." *Medical Care, 10,* 248–260.

Segal, S., Watson, M., & Nelson, L. (1985). Application of Involuntary Admission Criteria in Psychiatric Emergency Rooms." *Social Work, 30,* 160–165.

Smith, L. (1976). "A General Model of Crisis Intervention." *Clinical Social Work Journal, 4,* 162–171.

Sokol, B. (1983). "Intervention With Heart Attack Patients and Families." *Social Casework, 64,* 161–168.

Soskis, C. (1980). "Emergency Room on Weekends: The Only Game in Town." *Health and Social Work, 5,* 37–43.

Soskis, C. (1985). *Social Work in the Emergency Room.* New York: Springer.

Stringham, J., Riley, J., & Ross, A. (1982). "Silent Birth: Mourning of a Stillborn Baby." *Social Work, 27,* 323–327.

Strinksky, C. (1970). "Medical Social Worker." *Hospital, 44,* 58–61.

Swartz, M., & McCracken, J. (1986). "Emergency Room Management of Conversion Disorders." *Hospital and Community Psychiatry, 37,* 828–832.

Weinberg, N. (1985). "The Health Care Social Worker's Role in Facilitating Grief Work: An Empirical Study." *Social Work in Health Care, 10,* 107–117.

Wilson, L., Simpson, S., Duncan, M., & Lloyd, M. (1982). "Emergency Services and the Elderly: The Role of the Social Worker." *Health and Social Work, 7,* 59–64.

Chapter 11

Crisis Intervention with Hispanic Clients in an Urban Mental Health Clinic

ELAINE P. CONGRESS, D.S.W., A.C.S.W.

A crisis intervention model which specifically focuses on the needs and problems of Hispanics who enter the mental health system should be utilized in working with this client population. In order to implement this model, crisis clinicians and other mental health professionals who treat this minority must have cultural awareness of differing utilization patterns of seeking and following through with mental health services.

Barrier Theory

H ispanics especially have been reported as underutilizing mental health services (National Institute of Mental Health, 1980). Yet this population, which experiences geographic dislocation, economic poverty with its concurrent problems, and continuing language difficulties, would seem to frequently need and be able to benefit from mental health services. The barrier theory has been proposed as one explanation as to why Hispanics* underutilize mental health services. This theory maintains that

---

*The terms *Hispanics* and *Puerto Ricans* are used interchangeably throughout this chapter.

the structure, policy, and program of many mental health centers do not take into account the language, culture, and social class systems of the clients they service (Abad, Ramos, & Boyce, 1974).

The cause of the need for crisis intervention treatment has been defined as a hazardous event which places the client in a vulnerable state (Golan, 1978). Yet many clinicians view the need for crisis intervention services quite differently than their clients. The following case vignette illustrates differing interpretation of crisis by a Hispanic client and a clinician:

Mrs. Sanchez quite tearfully presented herself with her very frightened 7-year-old son late one June afternoon. She had just learned from her son's teacher that he would have to repeat first grade. She was told by the intake worker that she and her son could not be seen for intake that day, that it was too late in the day, and anyway school problems were never considered an emergency. The next available intake appointment she could be given was in early August.

Despite research on the nonadvisability of waiting lists in programs for mental health clients who are poor, differing methods of delaying treatment do exist, especially during this era of economic cutbacks and staff shortages in human services (Levine, 1964). Most mental health centers, however, do attempt to treat crisis as it arises. Yet in the example just given, being held back in school was not interpreted as a crisis.

The mental health policy decision about the definition of crisis in the example of Mrs. Sanchez and her son fails to consider the tremendous importance of children in the Hispanic community. As with other newly arrived immigrant groups, Puerto Ricans are very concerned about the welfare of their children. Parents who believe that their own progress in America has been impeded by their language difficulties, educational deprivation, and economic poverty perceive that their children are more quickly assimilated and are hopeful that they will be more successful in the new country. Thus a failure in school presents a major crisis in the life of this family and certainly warrants immediate attention from the mental health clinic that purports to treat them.

Alternative Resource Theory

T he alternative resource theory proposes that Puerto Ricans underutilize mental health services because they usually turn first to extended family, then friends and neighbors—the *compadrazgo* (coparent) system—and spiritualists before they approach a mental health center (Rogler, 1983). Frequently, even after Hispanic clients begin treatment at a mental health center, these various support systems continue to exert immense influence on their lives. The mental health professional can utilize these various support systems in treatment of Puerto Rican clients, especially in crisis intervention treatment which is time-limited.

The following case vignette illustrates how the presence and utilization of these alternative support systems can be very foreign to the white, middle-class clinician:

Mrs. Medina came for her intake appointment accompanied by her 18-year-old daughter, her daughter's godmother, and her downstairs neighbor. When the intake clinician asked the identified patient to come into her office, all four stood up and began to follow the intake clinician into the office.

Schooled in the medical model of diagnosis and treatment of the individual patient, and educated in psychoanalytic practice that families often create psychiatric problems in the identified patient, the clinician's first approach is often to see the designated patient alone. Yet this is often counterproductive with the Puerto Rican client in crisis, as families often provide important diagnostic information as well as emotional support throughout the treatment process (Canino & Canino, 1980).

The utilization of family is essential, especially when the client is unable to provide any information about his or her situation, as in the following example:

Mrs. Santiago was brought to the mental health clinic by her two teenage daughters and her sister. She was shaking all over, grinding her teeth, clenching her fists, and seemed not to recognize those around her. Mrs. Santiago did not move under her own volition, but did allow herself to be guided by her daughters.

Those who have worked in a mental health clinic which treats Puerto Ricans will recognize that this woman was suffering from what has been called the Puerto Rican Syndrome, an *ataque* (Fernandez-Marina, 1961). This conversion reaction expressed in extreme hyperkinetic behavior is often quite frightening for both family and clinician and has been frequently misdiagnosed by the inexperienced as a schizophrenic episode. This very dramatic, hysterical behavior, however, can best be understood as a severe reaction to stress, often related to repressed anger or sexual tension. Anger is often discharged through this behavior without the patient remembering it later, and there is much secondary gain in terms of attention from concerned family and friends.

All models of crisis intervention begin with a rapid assessment process and treatment with immediate focus on the crisis situation. As supervisors frequently instruct their social work students, the clinical social worker should initially concentrate on the here and now, and this principle is most important in working with the client in crisis. In order to help the client, it is essential to elicit the precipitating event which led to the client's appearance at the clinic. If the client in the case vignette just given only presents herself behaviorally, the clinician especially must use the family as an important resource for information about the events that led up to the clinic appearance.

While the *ataque* is an extreme form of physiological reaction to stress, often the Hispanic client appears at the mental health clinic with milder somatic reactions to stress. For many Puerto Ricans the body and mind are perceived as two very different systems. This is one reason many Hispanics first consult the medical doctor for physical symptoms such as headaches and stomachaches which seem to be clearly related to emotional stress (Garcia-Preto, 1982).

Mind–Body Split

T he first task of an intake clinician with a Hispanic client who has somatic complaints is often a psychoeducational one. The client often has to learn that the body and mind are interrelated. Only then can the client explain and begin to understand what led to the current state of crisis.

Part of the reason for this mind–body split for many Hispanics relates to the stigma of being considered *loco*. A *loco* (crazy) person does not belong to the community; he or she is considered outside the traditional values of Puerto Rican society. In rural Puerto Rico a *loco* relative might be hidden in the back room of the house to prevent others from knowing that the family has a mentally ill member. Thus many Hispanics resist seeking services at the mental health clinic, lest they be considered *loco*. Also, emotional reaction to stress is seen as a sign of weakness, with the implication that a person could choose not to present these emotional symptoms if he or she so desired. Thus many Hispanics often seek mental health services only after all other forms of help have been pursued, and when they do appear for mental health treatment they frequently present symptoms in physical terms which are viewed by them as more acceptable.

Active Role of the Clinician

I n general the role of the clinician in the initial stages of crisis intervention is usually a passive one. The main task of the clinician is to set the stage so that clients can tell in their own words the circumstances which precipitated their appearance in crisis at the mental health clinic. With Hispanics who come to the mental health center in crisis, however, it is frequently necessary for the clinician to be more active (Inclan, 1985). First, the client must be reassured that this is an appropriate place to go, given the problem. Those with physical symptoms may think they should go to a medical doctor, while those with spiritual (nonphysical) problems may feel they could be better helped by a spiritualist. The mental health clinic must be described as a service which helps people with all kinds of physical and emotional problems ranging from minor to more severe.

The clinician must also assume an active role in educating Puerto Rican clients as to the mind–body interrelationship, which many professionals erroneously assume is understood by all clients. Only then can many Hispanics move beyond the somatic complaint to a greater comprehension of emotional stress causing somatic disorders.

Thus a psychoeducational model is often most useful during the initial stages of crisis intervention treatment of Hispanics.

Crisis treatment has been classified into treatment of six main areas (Baldwin, 1978):

1. Dispositional crisis
2. Anticipated life transitions
3. Traumatic stress
4. Maturational/developmental crisis
5. Psychopathological reactions
6. Psychiatric emergencies

In all crisis intervention it is essential to understand the meaning of this crisis to the individual. Reaction to crisis, however, is usually defined from a white, middle-class orientation. In working with Hispanics and other minorities, it is important to understand cultural values which influence the client's definition and reaction to a crisis situation.

Dispositional Crisis

Dispositional crisis may be very intense for many Puerto Ricans if the nature of the crisis has special meaning for the client. Earlier the case vignette of a mother with a child who had failed in school was presented. The mother should not have to wait for the usually lengthy child evaluation process which would thoroughly clarify the situation and then refer the child for appropriate school placement. Immediate attention and support may be needed for the Hispanic client with such a dispositional crisis.

Anticipated Life Transitions

Anticipated life transitions include marriage, pregnancy and impending parenthood, and career changes. The role of the crisis intervention clinician is to help the client gain a full understanding of the upcoming change and to provide anticipatory guidance to help the client cope with change. The Hispanic client may have a very different interpretation of the crisis than the clinician, as the following case vignette illustrates:

Mrs. Garcia and her 16-year-old daughter, Ana, a sophomore in high school, were referred by the gynecology (GYN) clinic after the daughter was found to be eight weeks pregnant. Mrs. Garcia and her daughter were on welfare, as Ana's father had abandoned the family shortly after Ana's birth.

The social work student assigned to this case came to the interview with information about abortion services. Although she knew the importance of self-determination in working with clients, the student thought that abortion was the best alternative, given the age and financial dependency of Ana. Furthermore, she had read in extensive social work literature about the problems teenage mothers face, both in terms of their own development and that of their children. When Mrs. Garcia and her daughter were interviewed, however, they had already worked out a plan by which Ana would have her baby and be able to continue in school.

The student in this example clearly had not anticipated the importance of children in the Hispanic culture. Even though the pregnancy was unplanned, now that it had occurred both mother and daughter eagerly awaited the birth of the child. Also, both mother and daughter believed that abortion was a sin. Most Hispanics are either Catholic or Pentecostal, two religions which oppose abortion as an intervention for unplanned pregnancy. Finally, the family had already worked out a plan by which Ana could have her baby and return to school.

Extended family is often very available as a child-caring resource for the pregnant Puerto Rican adolescent. In fact, to place a child for adoption or in a foster home is often taboo for the Hispanic family. The poor nonworking Hispanic grandmother is often eager to assume the role of caretaker for grandchildren, especially if she is struggling with her own "empty nest" syndrome. For the poor Hispanic woman with limited education and language barriers, the options for a second career in the paid work force seem limited. Thus the teenage daughter's transition from adolescence to parenthood is often paralleled by the middle-aged Hispanic woman's transition from primary parenthood to secondary parenthood as grandmother and chief caretaker of her daughter's children.

Traumatic Stress

Traumatic stress can be defined as stress resulting from an event such as a devastating fire, serious illness, rape, or major operation. Poor Hispanics who live in substandard housing are often very vulnerable to catastrophic loss by fire. It is not unusual to encounter, in clinic practice with the poor, families who have survived several fires. Apart from the physical threat of death and disfigurement, the fire victims often endure total physical loss of all their belongings as well as their residence. Extended family often emerges as a helping resource which is utilized much more often than social service disaster agencies such as the Red Cross.

Many first-generation Hispanics have already experienced a dislocation from their homes. Many of them, even without a fire, have scanty documentation that would be required to receive needed social services; fire frequently destroys what little evidence the poor Hispanic may have been able to assemble for interactions with the complex bureaucracy of social service agencies. This factor often increases the traumatic effect of a fire crisis on the Hispanic client.

Different ethnic groups have been noted as responding differently to the stress of serious illness. Hispanics are often viewed as being more dramatic and hysterical in their reactions to the crisis of serious illness (Devore & Schlesinger, 1986). Unlike many people who when faced with a serious illness will use denial as their first defense mechanism, many Hispanics will tell clinicians on first contact that they feel they may die as a result of their illness. This stems in part from the essentially fatalistic Hispanic world view (Inclan, 1985). The Hispanic may feel helpless to confront the powers of fate in the face of serious illness. One of a clinician's first tasks when seeing a Hispanic patient with serious illness may be to encourage the patient to follow through on prescribed medical treatment, as the patient may be pessimistic about the possibility of cure.

Crisis for Women: Rape and Hysterectomy.   Rape is often very traumatic for a Puerto Rican woman and her family. Most Hispanic families highly value the virginity of their adolescent girls (Garcia-Preto, 1982). In fact, often an adolescent who becomes sexually active is encouraged to marry early, as marriage is seen as the only viable solution for loss of virginity. There is fear that her lack of virginity will prevent her from finding a good husband, which increases the trauma of rape for the unmarried girl and her family.

Married Hispanic women are also especially traumatized by rape, as the married woman is expected to be strictly monogamous. Husbands and other extended family often question the rape victim's participation in the rape, which may have serious negative consequences for the marital relationship and the victim's position in the community. Crisis intervention with the Hispanic rape victim often involves counseling for the husband and other extended family members about the blamelessness of the victim.

An operation which produces much emotional stress for the Hispanic woman is the hysterectomy. In previous years this operation was frequently performed for a variety of gynecological complaints. Yet the nature of this operation is most traumatic for Hispanic women, as many believe that this operation signals not only the end of their reproductive lives, but also their sexual lives. Some women opt not to tell their husbands about the operation, as they fear they will be abandoned for "real women." A psychoeducational approach is essential in working with Puerto Rican women who are anticipating or have had a hysterectomy. Still, despite crisis intervention treatment, many Hispanic women still adhere to deeply entrenched beliefs about the meaning of this operation.

Maturational/Developmental Crisis

Crisis can occur at transitions between developmental phases, as when children become adolescents and later young adults. These transition periods may be particularly traumatic for the Hispanic family when there is a clash of values between first- and second-generation Hispanics, as in the following case vignette:

Mrs. Cruz came to the mental health clinic with severe symptoms of anxiety and insomnia. She had had an argument with her 14-year-old daughter, who wanted to go on a movie date with a boy she had met in school. Mrs. Cruz thought her daughter was too young to date. She also knew nothing about the boy her daughter was planning to see. In exploring details of Mrs. Cruz' own adolescence, the clinician learned that Mrs. Cruz had married, at 16, the son of a neighborhood family she had known all her life.

In the United States there is a period of prolonged adolescence, usually extending from 13 to 21, during which adolescents pursue education and have multiple dating experiences before making a vocational and a marital choice. Furthermore, urban living often necessitates that adolescents travel to high schools far away from their home communities. In contrast, in rural Puerto Rico a generation ago, such a phenomenon of extended adolescence was virtually unknown. Young adolescents often left school at 12 or 13 to work in agriculture or care for younger siblings. Adolescent girls frequently married young, often their first boyfriend, who lived in the same community and was well known to their parents.

How can the clinician help the Hispanic family that is experiencing a clash of values and traditions, as in the case vignette just given? As in all crisis intervention treatment, the clinician must help the clients identify and clarify the crisis situation. The clients need to become more aware of the different value systems in conflict. The clinician must help each client accept that each belief is right in accordance with his or her background and social context. For instance, once both mother and daughter learn to accept and understand different value orientations, the groundwork is laid for further compromise and adaptation (Inclan, 1985). In the case vignette, after four sessions of crisis intervention treatment, Mrs. Cruz did permit her daughter to go out on a movie date with a boy she had met in school, after the boy had once come over for a visit.

Psychopathological Reactions

Psychopathological crisis reactions can occur even with minor stress, especially if there are severe underlying emotional problems, as in the following example:

Mrs. Santos appeared at the mental health clinic and reported much anxiety and agoraphobic symptoms during the previous week. Furthermore, she had not let her two children go to school during that time. In exploring the situation, the clinician learned that Mrs. Santos had recently seen the brother of her ex-husband in the neighborhood. Also, she said she had had two psychiatric hospitalizations for paranoid symptoms.

Crisis intervention theory advises that the clinician try to support Mrs. Santos and help her return to her previous level of adaptive functioning, and then, because of Mrs. Santos's psychiatric history and extreme reaction, refer her for long-term psychotherapy (Baldwin, 1978). The clinician, in assessing the client's inadequate adaptation to a crisis situation, should first determine whether the client's symptoms indicate a more severe psychopathology, to avoid treating only by short-term crisis intervention more severe personality and emotional disorders which warrant long-term treatment.

Hispanics, however, often are overdiagnosed, not underdiagnosed. Many Puerto Ricans, because they present at the mental health center with dramatic symptomatology such as *ataques,* are frequently misdiagnosed as having severe psychological illness and thus needing lengthy mental health treatment (Abad et al., 1974). Yet the situation is often a crisis in nature and the client's adaptation is within normal limits, given the cultural context. This is why many Hispanics do not continue with long-term therapy after the crisis has abated. In a classic case of blaming the victim, mental health clinicians further stigmatize the Hispanic client by labeling him or her as unmotivated and incapable of sustaining a long-term therapeutic relationship, when in reality the initial treatment choice was inappropriate because it was based on a faulty diagnostic assessment of adaptation to stress.

Psychiatric Emergencies

In working with a Hispanic client population, the clinician often encounters suicidal gestures by pill ingestion as a severe reaction to stress. Often this type of behavior spans generations, as the intake clinician frequently learns that the suicidal client had a parent who attempted to cope with stress by multiple suicide attempts.

Many Hispanics have well-developed support systems of immediate and extended family members who can be called on to help prevent further suicide attempts. Family can be involved in keeping dangerous medications unavailable for clients at risk for suicide, supervising the identified client's activities, and providing needed support and concern for the suicidal patient during a crisis period. Often a decision can be made not to hospitalize a patient for suicidal intention because of the presence of a strong family support system.

Time-Limited Crisis Intervention

Understanding Hispanic values and traditions is very important in assessing the nature of the crisis and the coping skills of Hispanic clients during crisis intervention treatment. First, the immediacy and short-term nature of crisis intervention treatment is more acceptable to Puerto Ricans than more traditional long-term therapeutic models. Puerto Ricans are often very present oriented (Inclan, 1985). They want symptom relief now, not years later following extensive psychotherapy. This present orientation rather than concern for the future is very akin to crisis intervention theory, which focuses on the immediate problem more than on past issues or future plans.

Some clinicians, however, fail to clarify with Hispanic clients the short-term nature of the intervention and don't focus appropriately on the problem at hand, as in the following example:

Mrs. Roman came to the mental health clinic because of conflict with her husband's 20-year-old daughter from an earlier marriage, who had just moved in to live with them. She reported that her husband paid more attention to this girl than to her.

After first hearing about the problem, the clinician immediately tried to link this with Mrs. Roman's own oedipal problems, as Mrs. Roman had been abandoned by her father when she was very young. Parallel communication between clinician and Mrs. Roman went on for three sessions, with Mrs. Roman complaining each week about new problems the girl presented (dropping her dirty laundry on the floor, eating everything out of the refrigerator) and the clinician trying to link Mrs. Roman's anger with her unresolved oedipal conflicts.

Finally, after three sessions, Mrs. Roman did not return. When the clinician called, she learned that Mrs. Roman saw no reason to return, as the girl had left their home and moved back to Puerto Rico.

In this example, Mrs. Roman presented a clear-cut problem for which she needed short-term crisis intervention treatment. The clinician, however, failed to concentrate on the immediate problem and instead tried to engage the client in long-term therapy about how her past conflicts contributed to her present problem. Mrs. Roman left after three sessions, as she felt the problem had been resolved (without much assistance by the clinician) when the girl moved out.

Many Hispanics want short-term therapy focused on specific issues, which lends itself well to a crisis intervention model. The contract for the nature and type of intervention should be explicit between clinician and client from the very beginning of therapy. Otherwise, the mental health clinic may be faced with many "unexplained" dropouts after only a few sessions.

Fatalism Versus Self-Determination

A fatalistic approach to life crises is often apparent in working with Hispanic clients, who often believe that whatever will happen will happen and that they can do little to control their fate. This is antithetical to most theories of crisis intervention, which stress the self-determination and efficacy of the individual client. Often one of the first tasks in crisis intervention treatment with Hispanic clients is to help them see that they have the ability and also the right to make important decisions for themselves.

Directive Approach in Crisis Intervention

Frequently coupled with the fatalistic approach to crisis is a dependency on the expert, the authority figure (Inclan, 1985). Hispanics may not come to the mental health clinic directly, as they first consult family, friends, godparents, and often spiritualists before they seek professional mental health treatment. Once they decide on mental health services, however, Hispanics often look to the clinician for expert advice, which they readily accept. This may be quite foreign for the clinician who has been schooled in permitting clients to make their own choices and told not to offer advice.

Yet in short-term crisis intervention direct suggestion, if used carefully and appropriately, is advantageous in engaging and helping the Hispanic client resolve an immediate crisis, as in the following example:

Mrs. Negron came to the mental health clinic because her 10-year-old son had "suddenly" developed a phobia about attending school. There had been no problems with him going to school previously. In fact, in the past he often woke up early in anticipation of going to school.

The previous week, however, two 12-year-old boys had accosted him on the way to school and had taken his lunch money. He had not been physically hurt, but had returned home and had not gone to school since. Mrs. Negron was very upset and asked the clinician how to handle this problem.

After exploring and accepting the feelings of anxiety and fear expressed by both the mother and child, the clinician advised Mrs. Negron to send the child back to school the next day, even if she had to personally accompany him. The client seemed to readily accept the clinician's suggestion in handling this school phobia.

In this case vignette direct suggestion was used to help a client handle a crisis situation. Mrs. Negron had brought the child into the clinic for crisis intervention services because she felt powerless and unknowledgeable about how to handle the crisis situation. She readily accepted the expert's advice and was then engaged in therapy to help with further aspects of the problem.

Yet the clinician must be cautious about giving direct advice and guidance, even when clients appear helpless and demonstrate maladaptive behavior in handling their problems. Because Hispanic clients are so dependent on expert opinion and are in a vulnerable position during a crisis, the clinician must give advice most carefully and judiciously.

An inexperienced social work student once presented the following case vignette to her supervisor:

Mrs. Gonzalez came to the mental health clinic with severe symptoms of anxiety, which had become most acute during the last week since her mother-in-law came to visit. I interpreted the client's anxiety as stemming from her mother-in-law's visit and advised the client that the latter's anxiety would probably dissipate if the mother-in-law curtailed her visit. I then did some role-playing with the client as to how she could tell the mother-in-law to leave early.

The next week I expected to see the client much improved, as I had heard the problematic mother-in-law had left over the weekend. Instead the client was more anxious than before. The client had followed my instructions exactly, but now felt very guilty that she had offended her mother-in-law. Also her husband was very angry at her and there was increased marital conflict.

Although the Hispanic client may look for immediate expert advice, premature and inappropriate advice, especially when it negates the Hispanic concern and respect for family, is counterindicated both for crisis intervention and long-term therapy.

"Confianza" Essential in Treatment

Development of basic trust is seen as essential in the beginning phases of all models of social work treatment. With crisis intervention this is even more essential, as the client is very vulnerable and in need of immediate support. Furthermore, the process of developing basic trust has to be accelerated, as the whole therapeutic process is short-term. Sometimes it is difficult for clients to develop trust in a clinician they have met for the first time, without the benefit of weeks and months of therapeutic acceptance and support.

For the Hispanic client, *confianza* (trust) is an important value in all human relationships. *Confianza* in family members and friends who have helped in the past comes more easily to the Hispanic than *confianza* in a distant, middle-class white clinician who does not speak the same language or share the same values, and who has a history of association with public assistance institutions which have demoralized and deprecated Hispanics. Yet the Hispanic highly values *confianza,* and clinicians who attempt crisis intervention treatment with Hispanics must quickly help their clients develop trust in them.

In order to develop trust, the clinician must act in ways which seem trustworthy to Hispanic clients. Writing notes during an interview and asking too many personal questions, especially of sexual behavior, is usually counterproductive during first interviews with Hispanic clients. The clinician must immediately discuss issues of confidentiality and actively disclaim association with the public assistance, court, and child welfare system. In developing basic trust with the Hispanic client the clinician must be honest and consistent. The client has the right to know the limits of confidentiality—for example, that child abuse must be reported to the appropriate state agency. If the Hispanic client is not able to develop trust in the clinician, it is questionable whether he or she will return for treatment beyond the first session.

"Personalismo" Important in Therapy

Hispanics frequently demonstrate more trust in the individual person than in the larger institution (Rogler et al., 1983). This value of *personalismo* is most advantageous in crisis intervention with Hispanics. The Hispanic client is very receptive to the individual attention of the clinician. Once the Hispanic has made the decision to approach the formidable institution, he or she can best be helped by speedy assignment and follow-through by a specific clinician.

Crisis intervention treatment is most effective when the same clinician helps the client from intake through treatment. Many Hispanics will frequently try to personalize the relationship with the clinician, often by making "small talk" about the weather or how the clinician looks that day, especially at the beginning of the interview. Hispanics are very sensitive to what they perceive as the clinician's rejection of them— for example, not wanting to speak to the client about any other issue than the presenting problem. When kept within appropriate limits, Hispanics' attempts to personalize their clinician should not be discouraged, as it is essential for the development of *confianza* in the clinician.

"Respecto" in Crisis Intervention

Respecto (the value of respect which is intrinsically owed to another person) is seen as a guiding principle for Hispanics in their relationships with others (Rogler et al., 1983).

This concept is often difficult for non-Hispanics to understand, especially the way *respecto* is interpreted in family relationships. Each family member is obligated to respect the others and to receive respect, depending on specific role, age, and gender distinctions. The prevailing U.S. interpretation of respect is that it must be earned, and certain behaviors are seen as causing an individual to lose respect for another. For Hispanics, *respecto* is a constant, not easily disregarded, even in the wake of negative behavior.

Crisis intervention clinicians who work with Hispanics have heard abused women report that they still respect their husbands, as they are the fathers of their children. Unfaithful husbands will claim that they respect their wives, proving it by never bringing any of their girlfriends home. The cultural value of *respecto* is very important to most Hispanics and the crisis intervention clinician is ill advised to try to change this value system, as the following case vignette illustrates:

Mrs. Colon had been physically abused by her husband several times when he was drinking. Yet she told the clinician she must respect him, as he is the father of her children. The clinician then began to lecture the client that the husband had done nothing to earn her respect. The client finally said the clinician just didn't understand and left the office, never to return.

The crisis intervention worker lost the client, who was certainly in need of continued treatment, because of an inappropriate attempt to change the Hispanic client's value of *respecto*.

Sometimes the loss of *respecto* can produce a crisis which leads the Hispanic family into treatment, as in the following example:

Mr. and Mrs. Rivera, their neighbor who was already a patient at the clinic, and the Riveras' tearful 10-year-old son arrived at the mental health clinic late one spring afternoon. Apparently the son, Reynaldo, had wanted to go out to play baseball with his friends, but his mother did not want him to go to the park because she had heard of recent drug sales there. Reynaldo was trying to persuade his mother when Mr. Rivera came home from work and Reynaldo began to ask him.

When Mr. Rivera also refused, Reynaldo began to question Mr. Rivera's authority, finally retorting that, as Mr. Rivera was not his real father, he did not have to respect him. Then Mr. Rivera hit Reynaldo very severely. A neighbor finally encouraged them to bring this problem to the mental health clinic.

Many crises which bring Hispanic families into mental health clinics arise because of intergenerational conflicts between first-generation rural Puerto Rican parents and their second-generation Americanized offspring. Respect for parental figures is an important value for traditional Hispanics. In rural Puerto Rico there may be various permutations of the nuclear family, including a stepparent, stepsiblings, half-siblings, godparents, and sometimes an *hijo de crianza* (an adopted child whose adoption is not necessarily legal; Garcia-Preto, 1982). *Respecto* is accorded to each family member, especially adult authority figures, and even more so male authority figures. The nuclear family pattern of natural mother, natural father, and children is most common in the United States, though this pattern has changed somewhat in recent years. Each family member has more of an egalitarian voice in the United States, unlike the traditional Hispanic hierarchical family structure.

The crisis intervention clinician treating the Rivera family's problem described in the vignette would first clarify individual differences in values as expressed by this family. The needs of each family member—the father to receive respect as the male head of household, the mother to protect her child from the dangers of urban life, and the son's desire to be accepted by his peers—must be recognized and acknowledged as important to the respective members. Though it may be contrary to his or her beliefs and orientation as a middle-class American, the clinician who wants to effectively help this Hispanic family in crisis must work toward a meaningful compromise on conflicting values. For example, the father's role as authority figure could be substantiated. Yet closer bonding between father and son could be promoted and more appropriate discipline methods reintegrated. The goal for this family could be a change to a slightly more egalitarian model, but nevertheless in keeping with the Hispanic hierarchical family structure (Garcia-Preto, 1982).

"Machismo" Redefined

Frequently maligned and often misunderstood by clinicians who treat Hispanics is the important Hispanic value of *machismo* (Garcia-Preto, 1982). Feminists especially have objected to the top hierarchical position of the Hispanic man within his family and the larger community. A corollary of *machismo* is that the man is not supposed to show emotions, as this is perceived as a sign of weakness. This is why the adult population of many mental health clinics which service Hispanics is predominantly female.

The Hispanic man may not make use of the mental health system unless he is severely *loco,* has suffered a major upset in terms of family values (as with the child who did not show respect), or has suffered a major loss as financial head of the household. Often the Hispanic man does not at first come to the mental health clinic. The wife in crisis may arrive instead and ask for the authority of the clinician to help in bringing her husband into treatment. Hispanic men are much more likely to cope with the psychological stress of economic and social dislocation by substance abuse, however, as the increasing numbers of Hispanic men in alcohol and drug treatment programs indicate.

When the Hispanic man does present in crisis at the mental health clinic, it is often because his sense of *machismo* has been threatened by his experiences in the urban United States. Often the education and skills he brought from rural Puerto Rico may be inadequate for him to find employment in an urban environment, and thus he fails as financial provider. Furthermore, his wife as caretaker of their children may find it much easier to receive financial and social services, which may further emasculate him and threaten his traditional role as head of household.

The crisis intervention clinician must recognize the tremendous loss of status the Hispanic man in such crises has experienced and the psychological effects of this loss. His important role in the family as husband and father must be acknowledged, despite his inability as financial head of household.

Very often in crisis intervention treatment, clinicians focus more on Hispanic women and children as victims and ignore the Hispanic men, who are often seen to be at fault. If the Hispanic man does appear at the mental health clinic, he has taken a tremendous step in asking for help. His self-esteem and sense of competency is at a low ebb, which may have led him to extreme behavior that often merits the clinician's disdain. By acknowledging this man's pain, however, and supporting the importance of his role as husband and father, the clinician with an understanding of the *machismo* value in Hispanic culture can help the man function at a much more effective level. Furthermore, this will have beneficial effects on both the women and children in his nuclear and extended family.

Summary

C linicians who provide crisis intervention services for Hispanics must be knowledgeable about how Puerto Rican cultural values affect access to services as well as crisis intervention assessment and treatment. Many Hispanics underutilize the mental health system, as they first seek alternative resources such as family, godparents, friends, and spiritualists. When Puerto Ricans do come for treatment they often encounter barriers to receiving crisis intervention services, including different interpretations of crisis and waiting lists. It is necessary to recognize *ataques,* somatization, and fear of being *loco* in crisis intervention assessment with Puerto Ricans. Often the client's family can be utilized as a source of information and a provider of additional support for the client in crisis.

The role of the clinician may be more active with Hispanics than with other ethnic groups. Crises such as life transitions and traumatic stress may have special meaning for Puerto Rican clients due to their cultural background. For example, because of Hispanic sexual mores, hysterectomy or rape is particularly traumatic for the Hispanic woman. Often crisis occurs when there is a clash of values between first-generation rural Puerto Rican parents and their second-generation urban Americanized children. Finally, dramatic symptoms of Hispanics such as the *ataque* syndrome may lead to erroneous overdiagnosis of adaptation to crisis.

Understanding of Hispanic values is important not only in the assessment of the nature of the crisis and its effect on the client, but even more so in crisis intervention treatment. The Puerto Rican focus on the present, dependency on the expert, and even a fatalistic attitude can be used positively in crisis intervention. The values of *confianza, respecto, personalismo,* and *machismo* must be accepted and understood in order to effectively provide crisis intervention services for the Hispanic minority.

References

Abad, V., & Boyce, E. (1979). "Issues in Psychiatric Evaluations of Puerto Ricans: A Socio-Cultural Perspective." *Journal of Operational Psychiatry, 10* (1), 28–30.

Abad, V., Ramos, J., & Boyce, E. (1974). "A Model for Delivery of Mental Health Services to Spanish Speaking Minorities." *American Journal of Orthopsychiatry, 44* (4), 584–595.

Baldwin, B. A. (1978). "A Paradigm for Classification of Emotional Crisis." *American Journal of Orthopsychiatry, 28* (3), 538–551.

Canino, I., & Canino, G. (1980). "The Impact of Stress on the Puerto Rican Migrant: Some Treatment Considerations." *American Journal of Orthopsychiatry, 50* (3), 232–238.

Devore, W., & Schlesinger, E. (1986). *Ethnic-Sensitive Social Work Practice.* Columbus: Merrill.

Fernandez-Marina, R. (1961). "The Puerto Rican Syndrome: Its Dynamics and Cultural Determinants." *Psychiatry, 24,* 79–82.

Garcia-Preto, N. (1982). "Puerto Rican Families." In M. McGoldrick, J. K. Pearce, & J. Giordono (Eds.), *Ethnicity and Family Therapy.* New York: Guilford Press.

Golan, N. (1978). *Treatment in Crisis Situations.* New York: Free Press.

Inclan, J. (1985). "Variations in Value Orientations in Mental Health Work With Puerto Ricans." *Psychotherapy, 22* (2), 324–334.

Levine, R. A. (1964). "A Short Story on the Long Waiting List." In F. Riessman, J. Cohen, & A. Pearl (Eds.), *Mental Health of the Poor.* New York: Free Press.

Lum, D. (1982). "Toward a Framework for Social Work Practice With Minorities." *Social Work, 27* (3), 244–249.

Miranda, M. R. (1976). *Psychotherapy With the Spanish Speaking: Issues in Research and Service Delivery.* Los Angeles: Spanish Speaking Mental Health Research Center.

National Institute of Mental Health. (1980). *Hispanic Americans and Mental Health Facilities: A Comparison of Hispanic, Black, and White Admissions to Selected Mental Health Facilities, 1975* (Series CN, No. 3, DHHS Publication No. ADM 80-1006). Washington, DC: U.S. Government Printing Office.

Parad, H. J. (Ed.). (1965). *Crisis Intervention: Selected Readings.* New York: Family Service Association of America.

Rogler, L. H., (1983). *A Conceptual Framework for Mental Health Research on Hispanic Populations.* New York: Hispanic Research Center.

Chapter 12

Time-Limited Cognitive Therapy with Women in Crisis of Reproductive Failure

DIANE B. BRASHEAR, PH.D., A.C.S.W.

Donna and Jim were married at age 25 and now at age 29 wanted to have children. Although they knew their chances of getting pregnant were somewhat decreased because they were older, each assumed there would be no problem. Both had sexual experiences before their marriage. Donna had had some minor infections but nothing to cause any alarm or worry. When they finally decided to try, nothing happened. During the first several menstrual cycles, little was said. After all, it does take time. Finally, after six months, the question of "what if" there is a problem began to develop. At her yearly Pap smear visit Donna asked her gynecologist, who recommended they begin an evaluation. "Better find out now and begin," the physician advised. "Infertility evaluations can be a long, arduous process." *Infertility,* that word. Donna and Jim had moved out of a natural developmental process into a state of alarm and worry. For the first time, Donna felt out of control. She and Jim, like many American couples, had valued the control they had over their lives. They planned and saved for their first home. They enjoyed their long-range career plans. Having control over their lives gave them a sense of security and satisfaction. Now it seemed lost.

The expectation that once couples decide to have a child nature will take over has proven faulty for a number of couples in the United States today. During the last 10 years the trend toward delayed childbearing has spotlighted significant problems about fertility. About one half of all American couples who try to get pregnant have trouble doing so and as the couple age, the average time it takes to conceive increases. In addition to delayed childbearing there are other considerations that have affected couples. If a woman has ever had an intrauterine device she may have experienced pelvic inflammatory disease, which could damage her fallopian tubes. Any woman who has had three or more bouts of a sexually transmitted disease has increas ed odds of being infertile. And for men and women who have worked around h zardous chemicals there is evidence that infertility and sterility could occur. The e is no question that infertility is a problem now and it has been suggested that it v.ill only continue to increase (Aral & Cates, 1983). Estimates are that 15 to 20 percent of all couples in America have an infertility problem (U.S. Department of Health and Human Services, 1987). The impact of this crisis has been compounded with a decrease in available children for adoption. This is due not only to legalized elective abortion but to the phenomenon whereby more and more women are keeping their babies and not placing them for adoption.

Typically, the infertility evaluation process begins with a series of tests. These tests reinforce vulnerable feelings and, unfortunately for the individuals concerned, give couples very little opportunity to exercise any control or develop problem-solving techniques. The steps usually taken in this infertility process begin with a semen analysis collected by sample through masturbation and transported to the physician within two hours of ejaculation. This initial semen analysis establishes whether or not infertility could be traced to the male. Forty percent of infertility studies do find that it is with the male. If, however, the semen analysis is satisfactory, then the woman is subjected to a number of hormone tests which require repeated blood tests. The longer the infertility evaluation, the more invasive the tests become.

There are several procedures the physician may recommend. A hysterosalpingo-gram may be done, in which dye is injected into the pelvic region and X-rays are taken. An endometrial biopsy may be taken, in which a tiny piece of tissue is cut from the uterine lining. One test which couples find most uncomfortable is the postcoital test. The couple is asked to have intercourse on a number of scheduled mornings. The female then goes to her physician's office, where a swab of mucus is taken from her cervix to test both the mucus and the sperm's motilities in it. Finally, under general anesthetic a laparoscopy may be done, in which an instrument is passed into the abdomen through a tiny incision.

There is good news for about 90 percent of couples who go through an evaluation. For them the physical cause for infertility is found. Half of these 90 percent go through medical and surgical treatments, which also include such things as hormone shots, fertility drugs, surgery, and several forms of in vitro fertilization. However, procedures do take considerable time; money and treatments are not 100 percent effective.

A dilemma for many couples is that while they are proceeding through the infertility evaluation they are told not to apply for adoption. Many adoption agencies require that the couple no longer continue infertility treatment while they are in the process of adoption. Although some couples lie to agencies, the fear of being caught creates additional stress. The delay in applying for adoption prolongs any resolution of the problem. Thus the lack of resources, the expense, controversies about surrogate mothers, and other options can create extraordinary pressure.

Infertility as a Crisis Experience

E rikson (1969) noted that throughout the life cycle there are specific developmental tasks. Failure in these tasks inhibits growth. According to Erikson, one phase, *generativity*, is "primarily concerned in establishing and guiding the next generation." Parenting one's own children is not the only way to experience generativity, but is the most usual and accepted way. Erikson suggested it is more difficult but not impossible to achieve generativity without parenting. In this context, infertility is experienced as a crisis in the individual's psychosocial development. Thus the recognition that parenting may not occur may be a crisis event.

Not all patients experience infertility as a crisis, as defined by Parad (1965). Crisis is defined as "an upset in the steady state" (Parad, 1965). Golan (1978) names five components in a crisis situation: a hazardous event, a vulnerable state, a precipitating factor, an active crisis state, and the resolution of the crisis.

Hazardous Event

The impact of the diagnostic and treatment process for infertility is less likely to be heralded by one major event. This may make the crisis more difficult to recognize. While some couples may identify one event as threatening and emotionally difficult, it is usually a sequence of experiences that pushes patients or couples toward the active crisis state.

Infertility does shift the individual couple from the expected anticipation of parenting into a state of the unknown. The hazardous event may be laboratory test results, the first visit to the infertility specialist, the third failed in vitro fertilization, or the announcement that a close friend is pregnant. Whatever the experience, it is the *meaning attributed* to that experience that shifts couples' perceptions that their lives are "not conceiving according to their plan" (Mahlstedt, 1985).

Vulnerable State

As soon as the couple realize that they have an infertility problem, there are feelings of shock, disbelief, and helplessness. There is a sense of profound loss, which can be experienced in many ways. The loss of bodily function with threatened loss of a relationship, the loss of status, self-esteem, and other losses have a profound impact on the individual and couple, moving them into a state of vulnerability. A major problem experienced by many women is the lack of control over their own lives. For individuals engaged in an extensive infertility evaluation and treatment process, the focus and attention on bodily functions is a serious concern. Many couples find themselves reporting their sexual practices openly to a number of staff. Indeed, they are even expected to engage in sexual intercourse or masturbation in order to be ready for the next test or evaluation. The natural process of menstruation and ovulation is measured and often becomes an overriding concern. Sexual habits are noted systematically on a calendar, with a demand for sexual performance at particular times. As the couple begin to perceive and accept themselves as a couple with infertility problems, they become more disturbed by what should be, in their experience, a natural and happy anticipatory event.

Precipitating Factor

For most infertility patients who experience a crisis state, the event that triggers the crisis response is most apt to be related to the infertility medical process. Minor in a larger perspective, this "last straw" shifts the patient into an emotional state of fear, confusion, and anger. For example, the angry outburst at a friend or the receptionist may be the signal of that shift. Again it is not the event, which may have previously been routine; it is the change in the patient's response to the event that signals the crisis. For this reason, staff members who have consistent experience with the patient are in a good position to recognize this change as it appears atypical, extreme, prolonged, or even minimized.

Active Crisis State

Infertility professionals may not always have the foresight to predict a crisis, since office visits, tests, and treatment are so routine. Yet when the couple begin to show changes in coping patterns, it is a signal. Since so much attention is focused on physical functioning, it is often difficult to discriminate between what is overreaction and just interest in body function. Emotional signs are sometimes difficult to distinguish, since many women are treated with hormonal medication, which stimulates ovulation and also stimulates and changes emotional response. It may be, in fact, the lack of expressed emotionality that signals a crisis state.

The crisis state in reproductive failure becomes acute when the patient or couple exhibit difficulties in day-to-day coping. Infertility appears, in their perception, overwhelming to the extent that it consumes their thoughts, feelings, and actions. They see no end to it.

Resolution

Emotional support, coupled with hope, is an important factor in crisis resolution. The importance of medical hope was identified in the study of 343 men who were each part of an infertile couple. The men who knew that there was no hope of correcting the infertility by medical intervention did not resolve their crisis by adopting. Those who were less clear about the cause of their infertility felt a stronger desire to resolve the infertility crisis. The authors concluded that these men, who still held out hope in becoming parents, experienced more personal control regarding their infertility, while those males who had accepted their infertility gave up the goal of becoming a parent (Snarey, Son, & Kuehne, 1986). Leiblum, Kemmann, Colburn, Paspuale, and Delisi (1987) followed 28 women who had unsuccessfully completed one or more trials of in vitro fertilization. Although 52 percent reported that they had "resolved" their infertility crisis, 93 percent indicated they would participate in any new reproductive option that would enhance their likelihood of biological pregnancy. Therefore the opportunity to have final and complete resolution of this infertility crisis is hampered by the hope that new technology will afford an opportunity for pregnancy.

Miscarriage and stillbirth also complicate the process and may trigger an extended period of grief. Menning (1982) observed that feelings concerning these incompleted pregnancies are full of surprise, denial, anger, isolation, guilt, and grief.

As more opportunities to become pregnant are developed, a resolution of the infertility crisis may be delayed. Medical procedures are costly. Insurance coverage is often limited to diagnostic procedures or therapeutic interventions that treat disease, and infertility may not be viewed as a disease by many insurance companies. Given current competition in the medical field for patients, there is some concern that infertility patients are vulnerable to exploitation by eager profited-oriented marketing strategies. Advertising and promise of pregnancy may seem manageable at the initial stages of the infertility evaluation. However, as treatment continues, costs escalate and the couples have more expense than they originally anticipated. Therefore the active crisis state may be prolonged by intervening factors such as new technology and financial need.

The Psychological Impact on the Female

The reasons an individual wants a child are complex. Pregnancy is a confirming experience for couples. For a woman, having a child is an important component to her achievements as a female. Pregnancy may hold symbolic meaning. For some women having a child may appear to be the only way to achieve full adult status. Angela Barron McBride (1973, p. 17) says, "for a woman to be considered fully grown up in much of American society, she has to have children. If she wants people to listen to her as a responsible person, she has to show her credentials, Tom and Billy, Wendy and so forth."

Men and women confronted with infertility suffer injuries at many levels in their personalities, particularly self-esteem. Unresolved psychological conflicts may be activated and the resolution of these problems often depends on precrisis psychological strength and vulnerability. One important reaction to the infertility problem is not only the loss of control over one's life but indeed over one's body. A perception that she is defective can be the basis of many symptoms for the infertile patient. It is not uncommon for an individual to experience loss of sexual desire or the capacity for sexual response. This is compounded by the necessity for sexual intercourse at specified times.

There may also be depression from a sense of loss. Each menstrual cycle brings hope and anticipation, often intensified by treatment strategies, such as drugs which may prolong certain phases within the menstrual cycle, thus extending hope. When menstruation occurs, the woman experiences acute and deep depression. Infertile partners often fear that the spouse will abandon them for a fertile partner. Many experience themselves as unattractive and abnormal. For them, a sense of self-worth is based on an ability to produce a baby. Indeed, some women may differentiate between the ability to become pregnant and the ability to have a child.

Feelings of defectiveness may be compounded by earlier reproductive circumstances, such as previous pregnancy or an elective abortion. If the infertility is associated with venereal disease, guilt can be substantial. DeBrovner and Shubin-Stein (1975) describe the great lengths patients will go to in bringing up some past event to describe or explain their infertility. Often guilt over masturbation, sexual fantasies, and sexual desires plays a part. Some patients view their infertility as a punishment for sins or unworthiness. This eventually can be internalized, and clinical depression results. At some point patients may not be able to bear self-recriminations and their anger becomes directed outward to husband, physicians, members of the family, and to other, fertile women. There may be rivalry feelings with siblings and best friends.

Male reactions to the infertility crisis may differ from their spouses'. Kraft et al. (1980) described psychological experiences of childless couples who apply to adoption agencies. It was noted that the men had difficulty discussing the emotional pain of infertility. This was in contrast to Mahlstedt's (1985) findings which suggested that women talk a great deal with their husbands and the husbands feel powerless to take away the pain. This sometimes leads to husbands who stop listening. Men also associate infertility with their masculinity or sexual identity.

One study found that guilt and depression were experienced among 30 women who had tubal damage (Lalos, Lalos, Jaccobson, & von Scholtz, 1986). Both partners were interviewed and many of the symptoms reported in the interviews could be termed depression, guilt, and isolation. While the women generally experienced more depressive symptoms than the men, the male subjects often denied emotional reactions. Feelings of guilt were common among the women. It was also noted that the patients perceived relatives and friends as not giving genuine support. Pregnant women and other people's children all served as stimuli to negative feelings. This study suggested that couples require supportive counseling as their investigations and medical treatment continue.

Some 10 to 20 percent of couples desiring pregnancy cannot conceive for unexplained reasons (Aral & Cates, 1983). A common myth is that these couples are infertile due to psychological conflict. One resolution of infertility, then, is adoption. This impression has not been confirmed in the literature. Nonetheless, one would be remiss not to consider the effect of the individual's emotional set on the ability to conceive. Do anxiety and other symptoms of stress relate to the capacity to become pregnant? Serious methodological problems in many studies give an unclear picture to this complex problem. Earlier writings were focused on women and assumed a psychoanalytic traditional male viewpoint. Does psychotherapy produce a more positive outcome? And can this method take credit for the resolution of the infertility problem? In a comprehensive literature review, Pantesco (1986) states that nonorganic infertility still remains to some degree a mystery.

Motivation for childbearing and motherhood may be a factor that contributes to unexplained infertility. Sarrel and DeCherney (1985) followed couples with a history of secondary infertility that had no detectable organic etiology. Couples in one group were seen by a psychotherapist for an interview to assess whether or not there were previously unrecognized psychosexual problems and conflicts. Couples in the second group were not seen by a psychotherapist. The interview included the presence of both members of the couple and the infertility specialist. It was found that the psychiatric interview did uncover psychological conflicts. The most problematic was that between the woman and her mother, in which there was some confusion with psychological boundaries. Sexual problems, marital discord, and fear of pregnancy were other issues warranting clarification and attention. After an 18-month follow-up, six of the ten women in the couples who were interviewed had become pregnant and one woman of the nine in the control group had become pregnant. It is still difficult to determine whether or not this had a cause-and-effect result, particularly with the impact of one single interview. The authors argue that the interview did have a therapeutic effect. Certainly there may be questions of whether just additional time or other factors could explain this data.

Impact of Infertility on the Marital Relationship

T he difficulty couples may have in handling their feelings about infertility certainly will be affected by the strength of their marital system prior to the infertility crisis. Since many encounter infertility fairly early in their married life, when there have been relatively few major issues or problems to resolve, it has been suggested that they may not have developed the skills necessary for coping with a complex problem (Mahlstedt, 1985). Infertile couples often are isolated from each other and may have their own unique or idiosyncratic ways of dealing with infertility. Men and women may respond differently. A man's silence, Mahlstedt notes, sometimes confuses and upsets the woman, since she interprets the silence as uninvolvement on the part of her partner.

Lalos et al. (1986) noted that women generally manifest more depressive symptoms than men, who suppress or deny emotional feelings. The negative impact on marriages is often reflected in the fear of abandonment by the infertile partner or fear that the fertile spouse will remain in the relationship but will be resentful. It is not uncommon for infertile spouses to make offers of divorce as a solution for the fertile partner. Certainly the sexual performance pressure placed on the male to ejaculate at particular times for the purpose of impregnation has created serious issues between partners. However, it has been noted that the marital bond can be strengthened as a result of infertility if the man and woman show empathy for each other and share feelings (Kraft et al., 1980).

Some specific problems develop and affect the marital system. In addition to sexual dysfunction the conflict over the allocation of financial resources for infertility treatment can be a major source of conflict. This depends on the level of commitment each partner has toward resolution of the infertility. The expense of private adoption and surrogate parenting is astronomical. Many procedures used in treatment may or may not be paid for through medical insurance. In addition to emotional energies, the infertility problem can deplete financial resources.

Some couples find that they have value conflicts concerning methods used to resolve infertility. For example, artificial insemination has been extensively used as a possible solution. The loss of the genetic contribution of the husband and the genetic continuity may be an important factor. Many physicians mix donor semen with the husband's own semen so that there may be a physical opportunity for the child to be actually from the husband's biology. After artificial insemination is successful, exaggerated fears about how the baby will look and whether there will be a resemblance may develop. For some women the choice of adoption is denied them by the husband, who is steadfast in maintaining genetic control. The infertile woman may be experiencing tremendous pressure from her husband's need to resolve the situation. Males are rewarded for being problem solvers in many aspects of their lives, and to feel that they are contributing toward a solution, some men may overextend their financial resources by using private adoption or surrogate parenting as their solution to the infertility crisis.

Intervention

The use of individual, couple, and group counseling should be an integral part of the infertility process (Mahlstedt, 1985). One well-known group intervention is the self-help group called Resolve (Menning, 1982). By connecting infertile couples with each other, it lessens social isolation and provides emotional support. These groups, which are available in many communities, vary as to the involvement of professional staff. Some professionals work routinely with Resolve chapters (Barkman, 1985).

Many infertility programs do have mental health professionals as a part of the infertility assessment and treatment process. Most references reflect a supportive psychotherapeutic role. Since sexual dysfunction is common, referrals to marital and sex therapy resources are frequently indicated. The use of cognitively oriented groups and individual counseling can, in my experience, provide intervention which specifically addresses several key issues for the infertility patient: lack of self-esteem, attributes of defectiveness or imperfection, loss of control, hopelessness, and sexual and marital dysfunction.

Cognitive Therapy*

T he opportunity for cognitive distortion throughout the infertility process seems obvious from the previous discussion. Unlike many crises, a major problem here is the issue that the problem-solving process is out of the control of the individuals involved. One important aspect of cognitive therapeutic strategies is that the use of cognitive therapy can provide the infertile patient with a sense of personal control, if not over his or her body and medical treatment, then at least over his or her responses to the situation. Certainly the threat to self-esteem and the meaning that may have provide ample opportunity for irrational beliefs. The patient's self-perception as a defective person who cannot complete developmental tasks may hook into a number of previous self-doubts. Women may be more likely to experience these self-doubts, since they are socialized to believe their sexual identity includes childbearing.

Burns' (1980) listings of cognitive distortions suggested how distortions can be used by the infertile patient. Following are some examples:

All-or-nothing thinking. Burns defines this thinking as the tendency to evaluate one's personal qualities in the extreme either/or context. Certainly the woman most vulnerable to a psychological crisis about her infertility is the one who places all her self-worth on her ability to be feminine as defined by having a baby. Although life is rarely in an either/or context, it is quite easy for the individual who becomes consumed in the infertility process to think in what Burns calls *dichotomous thinking.*

Overgeneralizing. This distorted cognition is used to interpret that one bad thing that happens to you will happen repeatedly over and over again. Some women begin to interpret their infertility as part of a life struggle, and because they have always had such bad luck they feel hopeless.

Mental filtering. Picking out one negative detail in any situation and dwelling on it is an example of using a mental filter. There are many messages and concerns that are given to the infertile patient, with very few answers. A problem patients

---

*For a detailed description of the cognitive approach to crisis resolution, see Chapter 1 (pp. 11–14).

have is wanting to know very definitely what is happening and what the outcome will be. Physicians cannot give an absolute response because they may not be able to. This creates an opportunity for gathering data to support a cognitive distortion. Women report preoccupation with their body responses. Any deviation from the way their bodies should respond is negative data to support the cognitive distortion that they are failing.

Further, this filtering process is often used to support cognitive interpretations of what the rest of the world perceives. When one sees oneself as being incapable of having a child, many self-evaluations are filtered through this distortion.

Jumping to conclusions. Troubled infertility patients often get caught in mind reading, particularly of those individuals around them. Husbands, as noted before, are less likely to express their feelings, and therefore a silent husband is subject to having his mind read. Add this to the troubled patient who has low self-esteem, and she is likely to think, for instance, that her husband is no longer interested in her, does not care about the infertility process, or sees her as defective.

Fortune telling. In this cognitive distortion, entire future efforts are placed on making and having a baby. When fertility fails, the individual is apt to see the future in negative extremes.

Personalizing. This is a significant cognitive distortion for the infertility patient. Guilt derived from some previous behavior allows her to assume responsibility for the infertility.

Catastrophizing. This occurs when the only attribute that gives one reason for daily living is focused on the success of the current major treatment. Consequently, any deviation becomes a major catastrophe. Women deeply emotionally involved in the infertility treatment process manage their day-to-day lives by the treatment regime.

Time-Limited Cognitive Strategies

In the course of ongoing contact with the infertile couple, there are many occasions when the clinician can identify and challenge the presence of distorted thinking. One approach is to directly involve the patient or couple in their recognition of distorted thinking.

Women's groups have been significantly helpful in this regard. Infertility patients find mutual support from such groups and also use them to take control of their own thoughts and responses. While no specific evaluative data are available, my clinical impression is that this group experience is quite beneficial. Women report that major decisions were made during the group experience.

A major goal of the women's group is to impart information and provide opportunity for self-assessment and self-development. This is in contrast to many self-help groups. Self-help groups modeled after the successful Alcoholics Anonymous operate on the assumption that catharsis in an understanding, nonjudgmental, supportive atmosphere reduces stress. This implies that such awareness and support will be sufficient and that the individual can then take the responsibility for self-development. In a cognitive therapy group the emphasis is on information, using this to aid the participant in a supportive way, to further direct and develop her life. In my opinion the catharsis model often reinforces emotional understanding but does not stimulate further development and action.

One dilemma for the professional is identifying when the patient is most amenable to intervention using cognitive strategies. Rather than identifying specific points in time during the evaluation and treatment process, statements and behaviors that communicate a sense of vulnerability and loss prove to be an opportunity to offer group therapy as one intervention.

Another signal is for the patient to indicate she is isolated as a woman. Anger that she cannot accomplish what she expected to do as a woman—marry and have children—is a strong signal.

Some patients deny their problem, although others may strongly believe that this patient is in a crisis state. Should she be encouraged to join a group? Yes. Most individuals who initially resist because of their denial are most likely to give up their resistance at about the fourth group meeting. These women often give the argument that they don't like women's groups or don't get along with other women. What they may actually be communicating is low self-esteem or their own conflict about themselves and their gender role. The conflict is exacerbated by the infertility crisis. I confess to "selling" these women on attending the group, trusting from proven previous group experience that these women will usually end up the most positive about the group experience.

The extremely angry patient who displaces most of her anger on medical staff is not a good candidate for group intervention. This is particularly the case for the woman who is highly verbal and can be intimidating. Her extreme anger can be disruptive to the group process. Most of these angry women have histories of relationship problems prior to infertility, and have had extreme anger over other life events.

Not all women's group members are current infertility patients. However, as content moves to reproductive experiences many women express their belief systems and share experiences. These group sessions are limited to eight weekly two-hour sessions. Subsequently many participants pursue other self-development programs, career counseling, and individual counseling. Each session has a topic. The schedule of topics is flexible, depending on the particular issues represented in the group. Generally topics include identification of "shoulds" related to the traditional female role, consciousness raising, self-identity search, body image, communication techniques and role playing, developing and imaging affirmations, sexuality education, goal setting, relationship issues, and intimacy.

I have used the following exercises many times, and they prove to be quite popular and effective.

Opening Exercises

T he bonding of women's group members is facilitated by two exercises used at the first two meetings. In the opening of the first group meeting, each member is asked to give her life history in five minutes. This gives each member an opportunity to share her problem and learn about the problems of other members. At the end of this session, themes about women are identified. Many women, in their life histories, talk more about others than themselves, identifying the "other-directedness" of women. Alcoholism, sexual abuse, divorce, and losses are also common and serve to help each group member recognize that she is not the "only one." At the end of this session, members are asked to remember these themes and are reminded that women have much in common with each other, despite obvious differences such as lifestyle and age.

The second session focuses on what is termed the *good-girl role*. Members are asked to identify the numerous roles they were taught to believe women should be. "Mother," "wife," "maid," "teacher," "cook," and many more are called out and written on a chalkboard. Then these roles are challenged. For example, the leader argues, "Where is it written that a cook needs ovaries and a uterus to be a good cook?" Other members recall absurd messages and rules they were given. The absurd assumptions within these roles are challenged. Members frequently return at the third session with other memories and a new awareness of the many assumptions they were given as young girls as they grew into their traditional female role.

This consciousness raising is particularly helpful to the infertility patient, as it shifts her thinking from the traditional female role and suggests other options.

Correcting Cognitive Distortions

A major concern for the woman is dealing with her imperfect body and what this means to her self-esteem. Often, in her developmental years, she has not been supported in exploring and developing skills that confirm a sense of self-worth. Gilligan (1982) notes that for most women, being married and having babies is the confirmation of femininity. Thus, the infertile woman is reminded throughout the evaluation and treatment process of her imperfections. It is all too easy to use all-or-nothing thinking such as "I am a failure as a woman" or "I have nothing else to offer my husband." Each group participant is asked to list thoughts about herself. These lists are then exchanged and each participant is asked to respond to other thoughts with realistic challenges. The following is an example:

PARTICIPANT 1

Cognitive Distortion

My husband won't love me if I don't get pregnant. (All-or-nothing thinking)

I'm getting too old to be a good parent. (Fortune telling)

All I ever wanted to do was get married and have babies. There is nothing else I can do. (Fatalistic distortion)

All my neighbors have children. I don't have anything in common with them. They won't want me as a friend. (Overgeneralization)

We had an okay vacation. It would have been better if I was pregnant or we had a baby. (Disqualifying the positive)

PARTICIPANT 2

Realistic Thought

My husband loved me for many things before we decided to get pregnant. There is no indication his love for me has changed.

What does age mean when it comes to parenting? Older parents are often more experienced and mature and have more resources, like patience.

Many women who are not married and/ or do not have babies lead satisfying lives. These women are models for you to use.

Women form friendships on many levels and for many reasons. Common interests and experiences can go beyond children.

Couples who have babies can have fun without them. In reality, the vacation had many good and fun moments.

By sharing their "automatic" thoughts, patients also find their responses are common. It is easy to spot a cognitive distortion in another person, at the same time creating self-awareness of one's own automatic thoughts.

Body Image Exercise

Many women who experience extensive medical attention have negative body images. Often their reproductive organs become objects. Also, societal standards about the perfect female body frequently encourage women to be self-critical. Most women are not satisfied with their bodies. This dissatisfaction is exaggerated in infertility evaluations. Not only does the infertile patient's body look bad, it doesn't work. One fun exercise I have used has proved extremely positive in helping women recognize the cognitive distortions they have about their bodies and in challenging their own and others' distortions.

In group session the leader announces, "We are going to do an exercise to learn more about ourselves. We are going to pretend that each of us individually is going to rob a liquor store. Each of us will do it separately and differently. We are going to rob it *nude*. Our task today is to describe our nude bodies for the all-points bulletin."

Amid giggles and jokes, the leader then begins and always includes breast size and pubic hair. As the exercise progresses it is common for participants to leave out these parts of their bodies, even though it has been modeled for them. Invariably the women are critical of their breasts and rarely does one own up to positive attributes. Following all the descriptions, the participants share observations of self-criticism, unrealistic standards, and inhibitions. Members challenge criticisms and are frequently impressed that there is focus on a single negative feature that is usually unnoticed by others—the small scar on the face, large hands, a droopy eye.

This exercise permits women to share irrational beliefs and secret fears about their bodies. They also share bad medical experiences or experiences with abortion, plastic surgery, or rape. Some of these experiences are part of the distorted thoughts used by the patient to explain her infertility. Realistic thought responses by the leader and other group members challenge such thinking.

Self-Talk and Affirmation

Once the infertile woman becomes aware of her negative cognitive thoughts, she searches for new ways to respond. "Now that I know what I'm doing," said Wilma, "I have a blank mind. Now what do I say to myself?" By suggesting that the mind is like a computer which can be reprogrammed, the leader asks her to write affirmations. Helmsteeter (1986) recommends that affirmations be self-statements that are written in the present *as if* they are accomplishments. The patient is given a behavior prescription. In a relaxed state (sometimes early in the morning), the patient is directed to review her affirmations. As part of this review process, she is encouraged to use imagery.

Affirmations, to be effective, are personal, positive, in the present tense, clearly defined, realistic (believable), and emotionally dynamic. For the infertile patient, usually some affirmations are related to the medical process, but the women are also encouraged to have affirmations that are related to other parts of their lives. The following list is an example:

> I like maintaining a healthy balance in my marital relationship, my work, and my medical treatment.

> I enjoy being an excellent cook, confidently creating meals that are applauded and enjoyed.

I enjoy sex with my partner. It is one way of expressing my love and feeling close.

My automatic thoughts are positive, increasing my self-esteem and supporting my lifestyle.

Although study results are not yet available, the very use of affirmations appears to give patients a sense of personal control. Initially some report a silly feeling, only to find that continual use redirects them to actual behavioral change.

Hopeless No More

As infertile women begin to resolve their problems, one option is to shift attention to self-development in order to search for other life roles. Many women report that they have focused so much of their energy and attention on meeting the needs of others that they do not know who they are. In individual or group sessions, patients are asked if they know who they are. They can easily list who they think they *should* be—a list which is usually defined by external family and societal messages. Sher (1979) recommended a series of exercises beginning with answering the question "Who do you think you are?" In my experience most women begin with demographics and relationship description. Sher noted this does not tell anything about the individual. Instead, she suggested that the women describe what they do with energy and joy. They should be urged to list what they have a passion and a love for. This is a clue in learning about one's self. It is part of identity. Later in the exercise the patient is directed to childhood memories: What games, fantasies, activities did they enjoy? How were these special unique talents nourished? Women often find that they were discouraged in pursuing certain interests because it didn't fit into the "should" list of a traditional female role. By reviewing early wishes and goals, women often renew these goals and find hope and redirection. Women frequently report that their employment was not truly a career choice but rather a career imposed on them by others. "I always wanted to be a truck driver," commented one group participant. "I guess the easiest thing is a van full of kids! That's a silly reason to want children!" This woman started volunteering as a driver for a Meals on Wheels program.

Another exercise recommended by Sher is to fantasize five different lives. What would the woman be, how would she live those other lives? As one patient remarked, "I know there are other ways to be besides a mother. I was too hung up on that to go forward." By generating five different lives, the recognition of other options became apparent. The woman realized, "It never occurred to me I would be anything but a wife and mother." And another said, "If I don't have children, I can do many things, like travel, as much as I want. In some ways, there may be advantages to being childless."

Marital Pleasuring Exercise

O ne major problem for the infertile couple is that the goal of conceiving becomes the goal of sexual intercourse and any other intimate interaction. Conversation becomes oriented to the problem so that the marriage relationship becomes consumed. Sometimes a "vacation" from the infertility process is recommended. This, with all good intentions, is difficult to do.

Don and Mary had been trying for two years. Nothing they did was much fun anymore. In one session they were asked to recall what pleasurable activities they did prior to the infertility problem. As each began to remember, they noticeably relaxed. Following this, their assignment was to list things they like to do and what they like to do together. The Pleasure Predicting Sheet as described by Burns (1980) was used. At this point they were asked to list the activities and predict the actual fun or pleasure they might have doing the activity. They were also asked to add individual activities.

As they developed their lists, Don and Mary became aware of how focused they had become on "making a baby." "I haven't played the piano in weeks," noted Mary. Their next assignment was that each do one self-pleasuring activity and one mutual activity. They contracted to do this by a certain date. In the next session they listed their perception of actual fun. Don found that baking bread was less fun than it used to be, but Mary renewed her interest in the piano. They had an 85 percent actual fun time at the art fair (Table 12.1).

By listing specific activities, Don and Mary had direction in reviewing the positive aspects of their married life. Infertility issues seemed less intrusive, even as they continued in the process.

Table 12.1 *Don and Mary's Activities/Fun Chart*

ACTIVITY DESIRED	TOGETHER	PREDICTED FUN	ACTUAL FUN
Gardening	Together	60%	
Jane Fonda Tape	Mary	40%	
Golf	Together	70%	
Baking Bread	Don	70%	50%
Movies	Together	60%	
Art Fair	Together	60%	85%
Reading Mystery	Don	70%	
Playing Piano	Mary	60%	

Evaluation

P regnancy or adoption as an outcome is one way to resolve an infertility crisis. But making a baby is only one aspect of the infertility experience. Patients report that many new insights occur, such as awareness of relationship issues in the marriage, with their parents, and with siblings. Psychological and social maturing can be enhanced by this struggle and challenge. The use of cognitive therapy as an intervention strategy will not help the couple get pregnant, but it can help the couple respond positively to the crisis.

At this point there are no evaluative studies of infertility patients concerning the impact of interventions like cognitive therapy on individuals' and couples' psychological and marital adjustment. This may be the time, as study continues in this problem area, to be more definitive as to the effect of various interventions. For example, does supportive psychotherapy help maintain the patient in the infertility evaluation and treatment process? Does cognitive therapy further the resolution of the infertility crisis? Do women and couples who use self-help groups such as Resolve find faster or improved resolution of their infertility crisis? What personality characteristics or pre-crisis life problems interfere with or enhance the crisis resolution?

As new technology is developed, the infertile patient's chances to become a parent are increased. The challenge to the mental health researcher and clinician is to develop and evaluate interventions that allow this crisis to have a positive outcome, whether or not there is a pregnancy.

Summary

I nfertility is a developmental crisis with many complexities that affect the individual's self-esteem and the marital system. Cognitive distortions may occur at any point in the infertility evaluation. Through cognitive therapy and specific exercises, individuals involved may gain positive self-esteem and have some feeling of control in their response to this long, arduous and often frustrating process.

References

Aral, S., and Cates, W., Jr. (1983). "The Increasing Concern With Infertility: Why Now?" *Journal of the American Medical Association, 250* (17), 2327–2331.

Barkman, R. (1985). "A Comprehensive Approach to Treating Infertility." *Health and Social Work*, 46–54.

Beck, A. T. (1967). *Depression: Clinical, Experimental and Theoretical Aspects*. New York: Harper & Row.

Beck, A. T. (1976). *Cognitive Therapy and the Emotional Disorders.* New York: International Universities Press.

Berk, A., & Shapiro, J. L. (1984). "Some Implications of Infertility on Marital Therapy." *Family Therapy, 11*(1), 37–47.

Burns, D. D. (1980). *Feeling Good: The New Mood Therapy.* New York: Signet.

DeBrovner, C., Shubin-Stein, R. (1975). "Sexual Problems in the Infertile Couple." *Medical Aspects of Human Sexuality, 9,* 140–150.

Erikson, E. (1969). "Adult Stage: Generativity Versus Stagnation." In R. Evans (Ed.), *Dialogue With Erik Erikson* (pp. 50–53). New York: Dutton.

Gilligan, C. (1982). *In a Different Voice.* Cambridge, MA: Harvard University Press.

Golan, N. (1978). *Treatment in Crisis Situations.* New York: Free Press.

Helmsteeter, S. (1986). *What to Say When You Talk to Yourself.* New York: Pocket Books, Simon & Schuster.

Kraft, A. D., Palumto, J., Mitchell, D., Dean, C., Meyer, S., Schmidt, A. W. (1980). "The Psychological Dimensions of Infertility." *American Journal of Orthopsychiatry, 50,* 618–628.

Lalos, A., Lalos, O., Jaccobson, L., & von Scholtz, B. (1985). "Psychological Reactions to the Medical Investigation and Surgical Treatment of Infertility." *Gynecological Obstetrics Investigation, 20,* 209–217.

Lalos, A., Lalos, O., Jaccobson, L., & von Scholtz, B. (1986). "Depression, Guilt and Isolation Among Infertile Women and Their Partners." *Journal of Psychosomatic Obstetrics and Gynecology, 5,* 197–206.

Leiblum, S. R., Kemmann, E., Colburn, D., Paspuale, S., & Delisi, A. M. (1987). "Unsuccessful In Vitro Fertilization: A Follow-up Study." *Journal of In Vitro Fertilization and Embryo Transfer, 4*(1), 46–50.

Lukse, M. (1985). "The Effect of Group Counseling on the Frequency of Grief Reported by Infertile Couples." *Journal of OB/GYN Nursing* (Supp. 6), *14,* 675–705.

Mahlstedt, P. (1985). "The Psychological Component of Infertility." *Fertility and Sterility, 43*(3), 335–346.

McBride, A. B. (1973). *The Growth and Development of Mothers.* New York: Harper & Row.

Menning, B. E. (1982). "The Psychosocial Impact of Infertility." *Nursing Clinics of North America, 17*(1), 155–163.

Pantesco, V. (1986). "Non-organic Infertility: Some Research and Treatment Problems." *Psychological Reports, 58,* 731–737.

Parad, H. J. (1965). "Crisis Intervention: Selected Reading, Family Service Association." In B. L. Bloom (Ed.), *Definitional Aspects of the Crisis Concept* (pp. 303–311). New York: Family Service Association of America.

Sarrel, P. M., & DeCherney, A. H. (1985). "Psychotherapeutic Intervention for Treatment of Couples With Secondary Infertility." *Fertility and Sterility, 43*(6), 897–900.

Sher, B., with Annie Gottlief (1979). *Wishcraft: How to Get What You Really Want.* New York: Ballantine.

Snarey, J., Son, L., & Kuehne, V. (1986). "How Husbands Cope When Pregnancy Fails: A Longitudinal Study of Infertility and Psychosocial Generativity." (Working Paper No. 167). Wellesley, MA: Wellesley College Center for Research on Women.

U.S. Department of Health and Human Services (1987). *Fecundity, Infertility and Reproductive Health in the United States, 1982* (pp. 27–28). Washington, DC: U.S. Government Printing Office (Publication No. 87-1990).

Chapter 13

Male Erectile Difficulty: Crisis Intervention and Short-Term Treatment

BARRY COURNOYER, D.S.W., A.C.S.W.

B ob S., a 37-year-old single male, came to the agency with concerns about a new relationship. He reported that he had had several previous relationships with women but that almost all of them had ended badly. He said he was afraid that the current relationship would conclude in a similar fashion.

As the discussion proceeded and Bob S. began to feel more comfortable with the clinician, he reported that he was extremely attracted to his friend Beth and thought that she would meet the expectations he had for a long-term partner and wife. He mentioned that he was getting on in years and believed that if he did not find someone fairly soon he would probably not find a marital partner ever. He wanted very badly to be married and to have a family. Based on his track record and his age, he thought this present relationship might very well be his last chance at marriage.

Bob S. revealed that the relationship with Beth had developed over a period of approximately five weeks. He felt very positive about the way things were going and believed that Beth viewed the relationship in a similarly favorable way. He was hopeful that a long-term relationship might develop. However, over the previous weekend he and Beth had attempted sexual intercourse for the first time. He had not attained an erection and they did not complete coitus. Bob S. felt terrible—shaken, fearful, ashamed, and embarrassed. Although he reported that Beth was supportive and understanding, he believed that the relationship was now in serious jeopardy because of his sexual "failure." He was terrified that he would be unable to perform sexually during the next occasion.

The failure by a man to have an erect penis when he expects himself to do so may be psychologically and socially devastating. Regardless of the causes, the experience may provoke a state of disequilibrium significant enough to be classified a crisis. Nearly every man, at some point in his life, is likely to experience some erectile difficulty. Although such events may be quite normal, men dread their occurrence. Many men live in intense fear of impotency. This chapter will apply a crisis theory model to the phenomenon of erectile difficulty and describe strategies for crisis intervention and short-term treatment of men experiencing erectile problems. Crisis intervention and short-term treatment are often extremely effective in ameliorating erectile difficulties that are of recent onset, episodic, or situational in nature. Such attention is not usually applicable, however, to erectile dysfunctions of long duration, those which are secondary to severe marital or relationship distress or to psychopathology, those which are the result of illness or injury, or those which are caused by the use of alcohol, drugs, or certain medications. This chapter is intended to be of greatest utility to crisis intervenors who are not familiar with problems of male erectile difficulty and require an introduction to this extremely common concern.

Erectile Difficulty

Terminology

There are several fairly distinct sexual disorders that affect men. For example, in attempting to classify sexual dysfunctions, the American Psychiatric Association's *DSM-III-R* (1987) refers to the phases of the sexual response cycle as: (a) appetitive feelings or desire, (b) excitement or arousal, (c) orgasm, and (d) resolution. The diagnoses are then organized, generally speaking, according to those phases. Those which may apply to males include hypoactive sexual desire disorder, sexual aversion disorder, male erectile disorder, inhibited male orgasm, premature ejaculation, and dyspareunia. This terminology represents an improvement from the time, not very long ago, when *impotency* was nearly the only applicable term. It was "used to describe any male sexual dysfunction, including low sexual interest, difficulty with erection, dysfunctions of orgasm, failure to satisfy one's partner, and even problems of fertility" (Friedman, Weiler, LoPiccolo, & Hogan, 1982, p. 660). Despite some progress, however, the assessment and diagnostic picture remains seriously complicated by considerable confusion in the use of the relevant terminology.

Masters and Johnson (1970) were among the earliest to attempt a formulation of more precise classifications. For example, they distinguished between *primary* and *secondary* impotence.

> Primary impotence arbitrarily has been defined as the inability to achieve and/or maintain an erection quality sufficient to accomplish coital connection. If erection is established and then lost from real or imagined distractions related to the coital

opportunity, the erection usually is dissipated without an accompanying ejaculatory response. If diagnosed as primarily impotent, a man not only evidences erective inadequacy during his initial coital encounter but the dysfunction also is present with every subsequent opportunity.

If a man is to be judged secondarily impotent, there must be the clinical landmark of at least one instance of successful intromission, either during the initial coital opportunity or in a later episode. The usual pattern of the secondarily impotent male is success with the initial coital opportunity and continual effective performance with the first fifty, hundred, or even thousand or more coital encounters. Finally, an episode of failure at effective coital connection is recorded. (p. 149)

Masters and Johnson went on to caution that a man who experiences one or several experiences of erectile difficulty should not automatically be diagnosed as secondarily impotent. "Many men have occasional episodes of erective failure, particularly when fatigued or distracted. . . . When an individual male's rate of failure at successful coital connection approaches 25 percent of his opportunities, the clinical diagnosis of secondary must be accepted" (p. 149).

Helen Singer Kaplan (1974, p. 256) also attempted to be more specific in the use of relevant terminology. She raised questions about the use of the term *impotence*. "The use of the term impotence is objectionable, not only because it is pejorative, but also because it is inappropriate. Inasmuch as impotence is simply an impairment of penile erection, a more accurate term for this condition would be 'erectile dysfunction.' " Interestingly, Kaplan continued to use the term *impotence* in her writings.

The word *impotence,* currently so pervasive throughout the culture, the popular press, *and* the professional journals (see Elliott, 1985), was initially useful in calling attention to the problem of erectile difficulty and leading affected men to seek professional help. However, the word itself may now represent a part of the problem.

By suggesting that a man's power is located in his penis, the word *impotence* reinforces a man's self-consciousness about his penis, thereby reinforcing a likely problem: self-consciousness. In my work with men's groups, I find approximately 90 percent of so-called 'impotence' to be catalyzed by some combination of *self-consciousness and fear of rejection* or, on the other hand, simple *distraction.* When the catalyst occurs at a moment when we are expecting a body organ to change its shape, *the body organ cannot concentrate.* (Farrell, 1986, pp. 264–265)

Farrell (1986) implied that there is something inherently sexist about the common use of the term *impotence.* A man whose penis is soft—a perfectly natural and, depending upon one's definition of sexuality, an entirely sexual state—is often referred to as an *impotent male,* as if the soft penis characterized his entire being and captured his essence. The term *frigid woman* has a similar pejorative connotation. However, the differences in social and sexual expectations associated with gender are significant and, unlike the term *impotence,* still widely used by professionals in reference to men, the term *frigidity* is virtually absent from the contemporary vocabulary used by helping professionals in reference to women (Elliott, 1985). Farrell (1986, p. 256) suggested that a man would typically not characterize as frigid a female partner who "actively kissed him, touched him, and opened up, but had difficulty receiving him because she was not lubricated enough." However, a man who was physically affectionate, actively kissed and touched his female partner, but did not insert his penis because it was soft might very well be considered by his partner, and also view himself, as *impotent.*

Although all of the sexual dysfunctions warrant discussion, this chapter focuses on the crisis experienced by men who accurately or inaccurately perceive that they have problems associated with erection. Specifically, we are interested in men who are concerned about their ability to attain penile erection of sufficient stiffness to enable them, if they so chose, to penetrate the vaginal or anal orifice of a wanted and willing partner and to sustain that erection until orgasm. The term *erectile difficulty* has been used to refer to severe conditions of organic and/or psychosocial genesis as well as those temporary, occasional, or situationally specific experiences which may also generate crisis states among the men affected.

Etiology

The causes for erectile difficulty are varied and complex. Often a single causative factor cannot be identified; rather, the origin of erectile difficulty in many cases is the result of a combination of interacting influences. Masters and Johnson (1970) were among the earliest sex researchers to identify "contributing etiological factors" associated with the onset of what they called secondary impotence. These included premature ejaculation, an acute alcoholic episode, maternal dominance, paternal dominance, religious orthodoxy, and homosexuality. Masters and Johnson (1970, p. 181) also recognized that some forms of erectile dysfunction were due, at least in part, to physiological causes and, intriguingly, discussed the effects of inadequate counseling by helping professionals. "Careless or incompetent professionals inadvertently may either initiate the symptoms of sexual dysfunction or, as is more frequently the case, amplify and perpetuate the clinical distress brought to professional attention."

Kaplan (1974) discussed the effects of illness, drugs, and age on sexuality, and conceptualized the psychological determinants of sexual dysfunctions into four general categories: immediate causes, intrapsychic causes, relationship causes, and learned causes. She identified the following as some of the immediate causes for sexual dysfunction (Kaplan, 1974, p. 122):

> 1. . . . failure to engage in sexual behavior which is exciting and effectively stimulating to both. 2. Fear of failure, which is often exacerbated by pressure to perform . . . [and] overconcern about pleasing one's partner which is rooted in a fear of rejection. . . . 3. The tendency to erect perceptual and intellectual defenses against erotic pleasure. 4. Failure of the couple to communicate openly and without guilt and defensiveness about their genuine feelings, wishes and responses.

Kaplan also noted the importance of the relationship between the partners in the causation and maintenance of sexual dysfunction. Partner rejection (earlier recognized by Masters and Johnson) and marital (relationship) discord were established as general categories. Included among various forms of marital discord were problems associated with (a) transferences, (b) lack of trust, (c) power struggles, (d) contractual disappointments, (e) sexual sabotage, and (f) failure of communication.

Inaccurate information, exaggerated expectations, and mythical beliefs are likely to play a part in the etiology of much erectile difficulty. Zilbergeld (1978) identified some of the sexual myths American men commonly hold. They include the following:

1. Men should not have, or at least not express, certain feelings.
2. In sex, as elsewhere, it's performance that counts.
3. The man must take charge of and orchestrate sex.
4. A man always wants and is always ready to have sex.
5. All physical contact must lead to sex.
6. Sex equals intercourse.
7. Sex requires an erection.
8. Good sex is a linear progression of increasing excitement terminated only by orgasm.
9. Sex should be natural and spontaneous.
10. In this enlightened age, the preceding myths no longer have any influence on us.

Morton and Hartman (1985) have identified six generic themes which are commonly reflected among the subjective meanings or *covert statements* of men who experience sexual dysfunction. In reference to sexual dysfunction, covert statements are those things "the individual says to himself about himself, his partner, and the sexual situations in which he finds himself" (p. 307). The six themes identified by Morton and Hartman include

1. The "I will not" cognitions which often accompany sexual situations involving anger, resentment, and retaliation
2. The "I may harm you" thoughts which are often connected with situations involving fear of causing injury or death
3. The "I cannot have sexual relations because I have misbehaved or am bad" meanings which are associated with guilt, masochism, and depression
4. The evaluative "I am not (competent enough or attractive enough or well-equipped enough)" statements which often accompany feelings of inadequacy and fear of rejection
5. The evaluative "You are the wrong gender/not my mother/not attractive enough" statements which are often associated with the rejection of one's partner
6. The "I may be injured or killed" meanings which accompany fear of personal injury or death

Wolfe and Walen (1986) and Walen (1980, 1985) have also addressed the cognitive aspects of sexuality and have suggested that one's perceptual and evaluative cognitions are important in the development of sexual difficulties. Walen (1985, p. 131) suggested that *perception* significantly affects arousal and "can be viewed as a combination of three subprocesses: (a) *detection*—noting the presence of a stimulus or discriminating it from other stimuli; (b) *labeling*—applying descriptors to classify or categorize a stimulus; and (c) *attribution*—finding an explanation for a stimulus event.

A typical sequence involving erectile difficulty might proceed as follows. After a pleasant dinner and enjoyable conversation, a "first date" and I go to my apartment for a drink. We sit close together on the sofa, embrace, and kiss. I notice pleasant sensations in my penis (detection) and think, "I'm getting hard" (labeling). Another thought follows: "She turns me on" (attribution). At some point in this process, the second major cognitive factor in sexual functioning comes into play. *"Evaluation . . . involves a rating process along a good–bad continuum.* Obviously, evaluating a sexual stimulus as positive may enhance sexual feelings, just as a negative evaluation may diminish them (Walen, 1985, p. 132). I might say to myself, "She's more beautiful than any woman I have ever been with before" (evaluation). If I go on to think "My body is too flabby" or "My penis is too small (or not hard enough)," then I am very likely to diminish my feelings of pleasure and the strength of my erection. At this point I am unaware that I have just adopted the erroneous assumptions contained in at least eight of Zilbergeld's (1978) ten myths. Nor do I realize that I have reflected the subjective meanings associated with the "feelings of inadequacy and fear of rejection" theme suggested by Morton and Hartman (1985).

Men who experience erectile difficulties often have adopted various sexual myths or have engaged in maladaptive cognitive processes. Suffering from performance anxiety, fear of sexual failure, or fear of rejection, these men often assume the role of spectator (Masters & Johnson, 1970), monitoring and grading their performance, their partner's reactions, and the sexual encounter as a whole. Such beliefs and cognitive processes carry with them the potential for enormous psychological pressure and contribute to male erectile difficulty.

Increasingly, experts in the field have recognized that organic factors often contribute to erectile difficulty. The list of associated diseases, illnesses, and injuries continues to expand. Alcoholism, of course, has long been associated with sexual dysfunction, as has diabetes. In fact, erectile difficulty may be an early sign of a diabetic condition. Heart and blood vessel (both artery and vein) disease may also negatively affect sexual functioning. Kidney disease, hormone imbalances or deficiencies, testicular problems (including Klinefelter's syndrome) due to injury or disease, certain nerve diseases such as multiple sclerosis, and spinal cord injuries may contribute to erectile difficulty. Diseases of the penis, such as Peyronie's disease, or penis injury may influence erectile responsiveness. Some surgical procedures may also have an effect. These include prostate, bladder, rectal, penile, or testicular surgery (Berger & Berger, 1987).

Also growing is the list of medications and drugs which nay affect sexual responsiveness. Alcohol, tobacco, marijuana, amphetamines, and narcotics have all been associated with erectile difficulty, but the list also includes several antihypertensive medicines and diuretics; certain antianxiety medications; many of the antidepressants and major tranquilizers; some of the drugs for bladder or bowel spasms, Parkinson's disease, allergies, and motion sickness; certain muscle relaxants; drugs for irregular heartbeats; a variety of miscellaneous drugs such as timolol maleate eye drops; some of the medications for treatment of ulcers or for heart problems; and certain hormones (American Urological Association, 1984, cited in Berger & Berger, 1987).

Prevalence

Although it is virtually impossible to obtain definitive information concerning the frequency of sexual difficulties among men, it is clear that a substantial proportion of the male population experiences a period of sexual difficulty at some time in life. "Studies in Europe and the United States indicate that in the young adult population, approximately 8% of the males have Male Erectile Disorder" (APA, 1987, p. 292). Nathan (1986) reviewed the studies and concluded that "the rates of erection difficulties of varying severity found by the surveys have been in the 10–20% range, with the exception of the much higher rates reported for men over 60, among whom, presumably, organic factors make a substantial contribution" (p. 278). In addition, a large number of men may incorrectly interpret temporary, occasional or situationally specific erectile difficulty as indicative of waning masculinity, serious sexual dysfunction, or approaching sexual impotency.

The Kinsey interviews included the question "Have you ever had trouble getting or keeping an erection?" Approximately 36 percent of the male college respondents indicated that they had experienced "incidental" trouble (defined as "(1) justifiable impotence due to drunkenness, fatigue, interruption, etc., and (2) impotence which occurs rarely or infrequently") and about 6 percent reported "more than incidental problems" (Gebhard & Johnson, 1979, p. 125).

Kaplan (1974, p. 255) estimated that "approximately half the male population has experienced occasional transient episodes of impotence." In her study of male sexuality, Hite (1981) asked each respondent, "Have you ever had difficulty having an erection at a time you desired one?" Hite found that 69 percent of the respondents reported difficulty "having an erection at some time (39 percent infrequently; 17 percent sometimes; and 13 percent frequently, regularly, or always)" (p. 340). In response to the question "When are you likely to be so 'turned off' that you can't complete a sex act?" Pietropinto & Simenauer (1977) found that only 16.2 percent of the respondents "never got turned off." They concluded that "about 84 percent of men today have experienced some sort of potency difficulties" (p. 215). In their study of homosexuality, Bell and Weinberg (1978, p. 332) found that 60 percent of the 575 white and 37 percent of the 111 black homosexual males questioned reported "difficulty in getting or maintaining an erection." Certainly questions may be raised concerning the research methodologies of such surveys. However, the fact that so many respondents indicated that they had experienced erectile difficulty indicates the degree of concern among men in general.

Masters and Johnson (1970) believed that most, perhaps 90 percent, of the cases of impotency were psychogenic in origin. More recent estimates suggest that a significantly greater proportion are at least partly the result of organic factors (Krauss, 1983). However, LoPiccolo (1985, p. 219) suggested that "while some studies have reported very high rates of physiologic pathology in cases of erectile failure, it seems to be the case that selective referral accounts for such extremely high rates."

It is now clear that some instances of erectile difficulty are primarily the result of organic or biochemical factors, others are primarily caused by psychosocial factors, and still others are best understood as the result of a combination of organic and psychosocial factors (LoPiccolo, 1985). However, regardless of its cause, erectile difficulty constitutes a potential crisis for any man so affected. Even after an occasional or transient experience of erectile difficulty, many men inaccurately conclude that they are seriously sexually dysfunctional and are or will soon become permanently impotent. They often proceed into a crisis mode, becoming less rational, highly anxious, and often depressed. Whether the major cause for the erectile difficulty is organic, psychogenic, or some combination of the two, a crisis state often precedes, accompanies, and/or follows its occurrence.

Crisis Theory and Erectile Difficulty

W ithin the literature, which is collectively called *crisis theory*, many theoretical models exist. Several of these are mentioned in other chapters of this handbook. Such models have been used in efforts to understand some of the experiences and effects on people exposed to an incredibly wide array of phenomena (e.g., violence, natural disasters, disease, life transitions). Interestingly, sexual dysfunction generally and male erectile difficulty particularly have not often been conceptualized as crisis situations. However, for many of the men who have erectile difficulty the experience represents a crisis of immense psychological and interpersonal significance. The criteria for a crisis state as proposed by Caplan (1961, p. 18) seem applicable to the experience of male erectile difficulty. A state of crisis is "provoked when a person faces an obstacle to important life goals that is for a time insurmountable through the utilization of customary methods of problem solving. A period of disorganization ensues, a period of upset during which many different abortive attempts at solution are made. Eventually some kind of adaptation is achieved which may or may not be in the best interest of that person or his fellows."

As is often the case when exploring crisis situations, it may be difficult to determine definitively which are the causes and which are the effects for men with erectile problems. Fortunately, in providing crisis interventive and short-term treatment services it is not always crucial that such distinctions be made. In conceptualizing the crisis of male erectile difficulty, the developmental model of crisis situations as used by Naomi Golan (1978, 1986) has been selected. Golan, congruent with the views of several other leading crisis theoreticians, suggested that there are several stages to a crisis situation. However, these phases are not truly distinct or independent. They overlap, occur in differing sequence, and experiences in one phase may reemerge in another. Golan identified the following five stages: (a) the hazardous event, (b) the vulnerable state, (c) the precipitating factor, (d) the active crisis state, and (e) reintegration.

The Hazardous Event

Golan (1978) conceptualized the first phase of a crisis situation as the hazardous event.

> (It) is a specific stressful occurrence, either an external blow or an internal change, which occurs to an individual in a state of relative stability with his biopsychosocial situation and which initiates a chain of reverberating actions and reactions. It is the starting point that marks a change in the ecological balance and can usually be found by probing the person's relatively recent past. Such events can be classified as anticipated and predictable, or unanticipated and accidental (pp. 64–65).

In the case of potential erectile difficulty, hazardous events may include such disparate phenomena as job loss or change, alcohol ingestion, fatigue, change in status of an intimate relationship, and diagnosed or undiagnosed illness. This stage may also include a single or several episodes of erectile difficulty. For many men, sexual experiences in which they or their partners perceive that they have "come too fast" may constitute hazardous events and serve as precursors to erectile difficulty (Masters & Johnson, 1970).

In the case of Bob S. cited at the beginning of this chapter, the hazardous condition is perhaps best viewed as a series rather than a single event. Over the course of several years, Bob S. experienced the dissolution of several romantic relationships. Because he strongly desired a long-term, intimate relationship he began to fear that he might never enjoy such an experience. When he recently met someone for whom he felt great attraction, this represented a genuinely hazardous event, containing both the possibility of achieving his goal as well as the danger of another disappointment.

The Vulnerable State

According to Golan (1978, p. 65), "The vulnerable or upset state is the subjective reaction of the individual to the initial blow, both at the time it occurs and later." She suggested that "each person tends to respond to the hazardous event in his own way, depending upon his perception of it." Some may experience it as a threat, others as a loss, still others as a challenge. Depending on the nature of the perception, the person experiencing the hazardous event may feel anxiety or fear, sadness or depression, hope or excitement.

> During the vulnerable state the individual usually goes through a series of predictable phases. First, he experiences an initial rise in tension and responds with one or more of his usual problem-solving measures. If these do not work, he feels an increase in tension and a sense of ineffectiveness; he then mobilizes his "reserve troops" of external and internal resources which he does not ordinarily employ or may never have used before. If this further activity does not succeed in solving, mitigating, or even redefining the problem in a more acceptable way (to the individual and those around him), tension will continue to rise to a peak with increasing disorganization in functioning. (Golan, 1978, pp. 65–66)

Bob S. experienced the vulnerable state concurrently with his recognition that he, but especially she, might soon desire sexual intimacy. He felt intense pressure, fear, and anxiety, along with hope that things might be different this time. He predicted that the sexual encounter might make or break the relationship. If it could be positive and pleasurable for his partner, the relationship might continue to develop. If not, she might begin to withdraw and perhaps reject him. He therefore attempted to present himself in just the right way. He attempted to be especially considerate and thoughtful. He was tolerant and patient. He tried to model "perfect partnering."

The Precipitating Factor

Golan (1978, p. 66) stated that "the precipitating factor is the link in the chain of stress-provoking events that converts the vulnerable state into the state of disequilibrium." The precipitant may be the hazardous event itself or, as often happens, it may be a relatively minor occurrence which triggers an active crisis state.

The precipitating factor for Bob S. was the initial sexual encounter with his friend Beth. They were kissing each other in the living room of her residence. She suggested that they retire to the bedroom. Bob S. agreed and they continued to embrace, kiss, and caress one another. He became aware that his penis, which had been partially erect earlier when they had been in the living room, was now flaccid. He became extremely tense and felt guilt, shame, and embarrassment. He was also terrified that his partner would find him laughable or pitiable.

The Active Crisis State

"The state of active or acute crisis describes the individual's subjective condition, once his homeostatic mechanisms have broken down, tension has topped, and disequilibrium has set in . . . the individual's customary defense mechanisms during this stage have become weakened or have even disintegrated, his usual coping patterns have proved inadequate, and emotional discomfort and psychic pain are great, he is usually highly motivated to accept and use help" (Golan, 1978, pp. 68–69).

Although his partner communicated understanding and support, Bob S. became distraught. Later that night, he found that he could not sleep. He was terrified that he would never again be sexually competent and predicted that the present relationship was all but over. It was at this point that Bob S. made contact with the clinician at the agency. Had Bob S. not sought professional help, it is likely that over time he would have proceeded on to the final stage of crisis, reintegration. However, the resolution of the problem may not have been as adaptive or the outcome as positive as was the case with professional help.

Reintegration

"The stage of reintegration or restoration of equilibrium is actually an extension of the state of active crisis, as the tension and anxiety gradually subside and some form of reorganization of the individual's ability to function takes place. Since the stage of imbalance cannot continue for long, some new form of adjustment, either adaptive and integrative or maladaptive and even destructive, has to be found" (Golan, 1978, pp. 69–70).

Through the services provided by the clinician, Bob S. reintegrated rapidly and adaptively. Within three weeks he engaged in satisfactory sexual relations with his partner and expressed excitement and optimism about the future.

Crisis Intervention and Short-Term Treatment of Erectile Difficulty

Relationship Establishment and Information Gathering

Upon meeting Bob S. or any other client in crisis concerning sexual matters, the first steps are, of course, to establish a positive relationship and to gather information concerning the precipitating factors (Golan, 1978). The nature of the interviewing atmosphere and the clinician's attitudes are particularly vital when dealing with such tender and often taboo subjects as sexuality and sexual difficulties. During this process, the clinician should approach the prospective client with warmth, respect, and particularly with competence and a sense of clear direction. In crisis, the client usually feels much greater security with a clinician who is obviously comfortable talking about sexually intimate matters and who conveys a coherent but not inflexible structure to the interview. Assessment of sexual difficulties begins with a thorough exploration of the problem, including a detailed review of the sequence of events leading to the occurrence of the precipitant.

Guidelines for Information Gathering

Several leaders in the sex therapy field have developed protocols for extensive assessment and sexual history taking. For example, Masters and Johnson (1970) developed a "history-taking outline " by which to organize relevant historical information in chronological order. Lopiccolo and Heiman (1978) later proposed a framework for conducting a sexual assessment and history interview.

In addition to interview protocols, several paper-and-pencil inventories have been incorporated by clinicians during the data collection phase. For example, the Derogatis Sexual Function Inventory (Derogatis, 1976) provides for a multidimensional assessment of an individual's sexual functioning, and the Sexual Interaction Inventory (SII) also yields an assessment of sexual dysfunction (LoPiccolo & Steger, 1978). These paper-and-pencil inventories provide the clinician with a great deal of information of potential relevance to the client's concern. Often such a detailed process is required, particularly if the presence of severe or chronic sexual dysfunction is apparent. However, during the early portion of the interview process, when the crisis state associated with erectile difficulty is high, the clinician's initial tasks are to provide a safe context for the client to describe his concerns and to express himself emotionally. Later, as the clinician attempts to formulate an assessment and intervention plan, a more comprehensive sexual history may be needed. Initially, the clinician attempts to elicit information specifically related to the identified problem, the problem's development, the client's attempts to resolve the problem and the outcomes of those efforts, the client's current sexual and social situation, and the reciprocal influences of the situation on the problem and the problem on the situation. In addition, the clinician should inquire about the client's pattern of alcohol or drug usage and the relationship, if any, between such use and the identified problem. It is important that the clinician also explore the client's medical history and use of prescribed medications. Finally, the clinician should seek from the client his views about the possible causes for the problem as well as his goals for treatment.

Description of the Identified Problem.   Exploring the topic of sexual difficulty is likely to prove uncomfortable for the client. The effects of socialization and common stereotypes of masculine roles often impede open and free expression. The clinician can expect the client to experience heightened anxiety and discomfort. However, in most cases, if the clinician maintains his or her calm, unflustered demeanor the client's discomfort will begin to moderate. In collecting data concerning the sexual difficulty, the clinician typically should request that the client describe in detail the nature of the problem and his subjective reaction. Specific questions might include: Do erections ever occur? If so, how fully erect does the penis become? If full or partial erections do occur sometimes, how long do they last and at what point in the sexual process does the erection begin to diminish? Specifically, what happens preceding, during, following a sexual encounter when the difficulty occurs? Regarding the interaction, the worker is particularly interested in (a) the setting; (b) sexual partner or partners involved and their behavior, reactions, and communications; (c) the client's view of the interpersonal relationship between the partners; (d) the timing, sequence, and duration of sexual activities; and (e) the thoughts and images as well as the feelings and sensations which occur at different points before, during, and after the sexual encounter.

The clinician should be especially interested in the client's cognitive processes and the nature of his cognitive reactions to the experience of erectile difficulty. The clinician should seek to identify the presence of sexual myths, inaccurate information, and exaggerated expectations as discussed earlier in this chapter. Sometimes the client's religious beliefs may be relevant and require exploration. In addition, the clinician should attempt to discern whether "spectatoring" occurs and, if so, what might be the fears which precipitate the assumption of the role.

The clinician should also be interested in learning if there are occasions when the problem does not occur. Are there times when having or maintaining an erection is not a problem—for instance, when masturbating, with certain partners, or in some situations? Are erections ever present upon awakening during the night or in the morning?

Development of the Problem.   The clinician should be interested in exploring with the client the origin and development of the identified erectile difficulty. Questions might include: Has it always been a problem? Were there indications of a problem during your earliest sexual encounters? Did the difficulty emerge suddenly or was the onset gradual? When, under what circumstances, and with whom did the first indications of a problem become apparent? What was occurring in other aspects of your life at the time the problem first occurred? What were your reactions and those of your partners when the difficulty occurred? Prior to the onset of erectile difficulty, was premature ejaculation ever a problem? Were there periods in the past when erectile responsiveness was not problematic or less (or more) of a problem? Were there certain people with whom or circumstances when the problem did not occur or was more likely to occur?

Previous and Present Problem-Solving Efforts.   Congruent with crisis intervention principles, the clinician should be interested in the client's past and present attempts to resolve the difficulty. The clinician might ask: Have you discussed the problem with your physician? Have you sought or received professional treatment before? If so, with whom? What was the nature of the treatment and its outcome? Have you engaged in self-help activities intended to address this difficulty? What was involved? For example, have you read any how-to books, used any mechanical devices, ingested any chemical substances, employed a prostitute, or viewed erotic materials? If so, what were the outcomes of these efforts? In addition to the visit to the agency, are you now engaged in other problem-solving activities? What are they and how are they progressing?

Current Social Situation.   Because sexuality is often affected by various factors in the social system within which one functions, it is important that the clinician collect information concerning this sphere of the man's life. The clinician should certainly attempt to determine the relevance of relationship factors in the origin and maintenance of erectile difficulty. Sometimes the sexual problem plays a large part in a relationship system. In such cases, the partner may be invited to share information and perhaps participate in the treatment process. In many cases the clinician should ask questions such as: At the present time, are you sexually or emotionally involved with anyone? If so, what is the nature of the relationship or relationships? Are your partners aware of the erectile difficulties? If so, how do your partners react to the sexual difficulty? Are your partners aware of the degree of your concern? Do you talk about it with them?

In addition, the clinician should seek information concerning the client's family system and the nature of his relationships with family members—parents, siblings, children. The clinician should also want to know about the client's school or employment situation as well as living and housing arrangements. The clinician might ask: Do you live alone or with others? Is there opportunity and time for privacy with a sexual partner?

Finally, the clinician should seek to identify sources of stress in the client's life. The clinician might ask: In your current situation, what causes you to feel stressed or pressured? Are there stresses at work or school? How are finances? Have there been life changes, losses, or gains which may have contributed to feelings of stress?

Medical/Physical Information.   In all cases involving erectile difficulty, it is essential that the clinician gather information concerning the client's medical/physical status and history. As indicated earlier, there are many illnesses, injuries, drugs and medications, and surgical treatments which may affect erectile responsiveness. Of particular importance would be the discovery of a timely relationship between the occurrence of an illness or injury or the initiation of a medical treatment and the subsequent onset of erectile difficulty. In the vast majority of cases a physical examination by a medical doctor, often a urologist knowledgeable about male sexual disorders, is indicated.

Historical Information.   The clinician should elicit historical information of various kinds. However, the nature and extent of the history taking varies according to the information gathered thus far and the relevance of that data to the erectile difficulty. Included among the information sought are the client's recollections of any traumatic experiences, such as rape, incest, or molestation, that may have relevance to the present difficulty. The sexual, social, and religious attitudes and practices of the client's family may be areas which require exploration.

Assessment/Diagnosis

In crisis situations, one of the clinician's primary responsibilities is to assess the client's current level of psychosocial functioning, mental status, and risk of harm to self or others. In cases of erectile difficulty, the danger of suicide and/or violence to others is relatively low. However, as in all crisis situations, the clinician should conduct at least an abbreviated mental status and lethality risk assessment. The clinician should attempt to determine the degree and extent of affective distress and whether intoxicants may be present in the client's system. How anxious, depressed, and/or intoxicated is the client? Does the degree of distress outweigh the severity of the concern about erectile difficulty? Should that distress be addressed first?

Assuming, as is nearly always the case, that emergency lifesaving measures are not warranted, the clinician next should attempt to formulate an assessment concerning the nature of the reported erectile difficulty. On the basis of the collected information, the clinician should decide whether or not an erectile disorder is actually present. Quite often, clients who are clearly and fully sexually functional have erroneously concluded that they are dysfunctional. For example, a man might believe that he is impotent because he loses his erection for several minutes after orgasm and it takes him 30 minutes before he can have another erection. Such misinformation may be quickly corrected and the crisis resolved.

As mentioned earlier, the current *DSM-III-R* (APA, 1987) includes the diagnosis of male erectile disorder (302.72) to refer to erectile dysfunction. In the *DSM-III* (APA, 1980) the diagnostic classification had been "inhibited sexual excitement." These classifications refer to conditions which have previously been associated with the term *impotence*. The specific diagnostic criteria for Male Erectile Disorder include (APA, 1987, p. 294):

A. Either (1) or (2):

(1) persistent or recurrent partial or complete failure in a male to attain or maintain erection until completion of the sexual activity

(2) persistent or recurrent lack of subjective sense of sexual excitement and pleasure in a male during sexual activity

B. Occurrence not exclusively during the course of another Axis I disorder (other than Sexual Dysfunction), such as Major Depression.

Additionally, the classifications as used by the American Psychiatric Association in the *DSM-III-R* may not accurately refer to sexual dysfunctions which are "attributed entirely to organic factors, such as a physical disorder or a medication" (APA, 1987, p. 290).

While the *DSM-III-R* diagnostic criteria are indeed useful, they are not usually sufficient for the clinician attempting to formulate an assessment on which to base an intervention plan. Therefore, in dealing with the crisis of erectile difficulty and based on the information gathered, the clinician should when possible address the following questions (see Annon, 1976; Kaplan, 1983; Lobitz & Lobitz, 1978) as he or she formulates an assessment:

Is erectile capacity full (erections do occur and are sometimes completely strong, stiff, and hard), partial (erections do occur and there is some stiffness but erection is always incomplete), or absent (erections never occur and there is no stiffness whatsoever)?

Is erectile difficulty evident (at least one episode in which the man was capable of erection and desired an erection but did not become erect) or absent (man incorrectly assumes erectile difficulty but has never had an experience when he was capable of and desired an erection but did not become erect)?

Is the erectile difficulty primary (lifelong) or secondary (acquired)?

Is the erectile difficulty generalized (all partners and contexts) or situational (specific to one partner or situation, or to those partners or contexts which share certain common characteristics)?

Is psychiatric disturbance present or absent?

If present, is the psychiatric disturbance of sufficient severity to supercede the erectile difficulty as a treatment goal?

If a sexual relationship with another partner exists, is it characterized by harmony or discord?

During sexual activities, is there sufficient or insufficient stimulation?

And, tentatively based on the available information, is the erectile difficulty more likely to be of organic or of psychosocial etiology (See Graber and Kline-Graber, 1981; Maxmen, 1986; Skinner & Becker, 1985.)

Addressing these elements may help the clinician to formulate an assessment which is likely to yield an effective intervention plan. For example, we learned from Bob S. that he had never previously had difficulty gaining or maintaining an erection and that he had received a complete physical examination from his physician, who informed him that there was no indication of physical problems of any kind and that his sexual systems were physically fine. We also learned that he did not and had not ever used alcohol to excess and had never used drugs. (He had drunk one glass of white wine on the occasion in question.) He did not and had not ever taken medications of any kind. He did not feel unduly stressed at work and said his living situation and family relationships were extremely positive. There was no evidence of psychiatric disturbance nor significant intrapsychic conflict. Bob S. said he found Beth attractive and desirable—in fact, he often experienced a full erection when fantasizing about her—and he believed that she valued and respected him and found him sexually attractive as well.

Therefore, based on the information provided, a tentative assessment of Bob's situation would be full erectile capacity; no psychiatric disturbance; erectile difficulty evident—secondary, situational, and of psychosocial etiology.

Intervention

Obviously, not all persons with erectile difficulty who arrive for treatment can be treated by crisis intervention and short-term treatment. Clients who meet the following criteria may be considered good candidates: (a) men who have firm erections during sleep, upon awakening, when masturbating, or with some partners; (b) men who have only recently experienced erectile difficulties or who experience such difficulties only in certain specific circumstances; and (c) men who do not have a significant psychiatric illness, psychosocial problem, or substance abuse problem, which should take precedence over the erectile difficulty.

Men who are not appropriate for short-term, crisis-oriented treatment include those who (a) have never experienced a firm erection; (b) have physical problems, medical conditions (e.g., diabetes), and/or take medications which affect the sexual system and must be addressed before or along with treatment of the erectile difficulty; (c) have psychiatric illness (e.g., clinical depression) which may predate the erectile difficulty and should be addressed prior to the sexual dysfunction; or (d) have severe marital/relationship conflicts which require treatment before or along with the treatment of the erectile difficulty.

Three of the operational objectives of crisis intervention suggested by Rapoport (cited in Golan, 1978, pp. 71–72) are (a) the relief of symptoms, (b) the restoration of the client to the precrisis level of functioning, and (c) the understanding by the client of the relevant factors which led to the crisis state. In responding to the crisis of male erectile difficulty, however, the objective of relieving the symptom must be addressed carefully. In order to reach the overall goal of improved erectile functioning, "the immediate causes or antecedents of the symptom must be modified" (Kaplan & Moodie, 1982, p. 366) The clinician must recognize the nonvoluntary nature of the erectile response in men. As Masters and Johnson (1970, p. 197) noted, "Sexual functioning is a naturally occurring phenomenon and cannot be controlled, directed, or even initiated unless it is in some manner related to the natural cycle of sexual response. *No man can will an erection,* but he can relax and enjoy it." In formulating treatment objectives, the clinician and client must avoid the temptation to establish a goal for the client of having a full, firm erection when wanted. Such an objective adds to the pressure of performance. Instead, the causal factors should be addressed directly and objectives intended to alter those should be created. For example, Masters and Johnson (1970) identified three primary goals in the treatment of erectile dysfunction. These were (a) reducing the man's performance anxiety, (b) altering his tendency to assume an evaluating, spectator role to one of becoming an active and involved participant in the sexual encounter, and (c) reducing his partner's fears and anxieties about his sexual performance. Kaplan and Moodie (1982, p. 367) suggested that treatment "typically involves the reduction of sexual anxiety, reduction of interpersonal anger and resentment, acquisition of sexual information and techniques, improvement in partner communication about sex, [and] reduction in nonerotic obsessive thoughts. . . . In general, more extensive goals like personality change, resolution of deep conflict, and improvement in the couple's relationship are not pursued unless they are essential to progress toward the specific goal."

Of course, the specific treatment goals and objectives should be based on the unique circumstances and characteristics of the person or persons involved. The man who does not currently have a sexual partner but wishes to experience full erections during masturbation is likely to have somewhat different treatment goals than the heterosexual man married for 18 years who experiences erectile difficulty with his wife but does not with extramarital partners. However, the general themes of the treatment goals often have considerable similarity.

One of the earliest questions which must be addressed is whether the treatment should include the client's sexual partner. In many situations, of course, the client does not have a sexual partner or his partner is incapable of participating or unwilling to participate in the treatment process. Such men may be treated individually or in group contexts (Dekker, Dronkers, & Staffeleu, 1985; Reynolds, Cohen, Schochet, Price, & Anderson, 1981; Zilbergeld, 1975). In cases where a stable, generally positive relationship exists and the partner is willing to participate in treatment, it is desirable to include him or her (Kaplan, 1974; Kaplan & Moodie, 1982; Masters & Johnson, 1970; Paff, 1985) in some or all of the treatment sessions. However, the overriding factors determining the direct involvement of the partner in the treatment process are the preferences of the man and the partner and the nature of the relationship. In providing crisis intervention and short-term treatment to men with erectile difficulty, the use of sexual surrogates is not advised or suggested.

Although each case requires a unique intervention plan, there are general strategies which are often applicable in the short-term treatment of erectile difficulty. Following is a discussion of commonly used strategies.

Information-sharing concerning sexuality is an important element in the treatment of erectile difficulty. Many men and their partners lack basic understanding of the human body and the sexual response cycle. For example, many men are unaware that the clitoris is a primary pleasure center for women or that there is a refractory period between male orgasms. Men are often ignorant of the adverse effects of fatigue, alcohol, and stress on their sexual responsiveness. Correct information is vital and is sometimes all that is required to alleviate the crisis. Single-session treatments are not uncommon. It is often helpful in the information-sharing process to show photographs, films, or videotapes to illustrate various aspects of sexual functioning. Relevant sexual "self-help" reading material may also be of great value.

Cognitive procedures designed to identify and refute irrational, mythical, or unrealistic beliefs and self-statements may be an important component in the treatment process. The use of positive self-talk or rational disputation (see Ellis, 1975; Morton & Hartman, 1985; Munjack et al., 1984; Walen, 1985; Wolfe & Walen, 1986) has become a mainstay in the treatment of male sexual dysfunctions generally and erectile difficulty particularly. Of course, such procedures overlap with the sexual information-sharing dimension. In general, the cognitive strategies involve identifying the thoughts or beliefs related to the erectile difficulty and examining their rationality or utility. For example, a man whose penis remains flaccid during a sexual activity may engage in a variety of thoughts which tend to increase emotional upset and perpetuate erectile difficulty. His thinking might proceed as follows: "My penis is soft. It may *always* be soft in sexual situations. It should *never* be soft in sexual situations. I'm impotent. I'm not a real man. My partner will laugh at me. I will be humiliated. This is the worst thing that could ever happen." The clinician, in helping such a client to explore these beliefs, would encourage him to identify the cognitive distortions (Burns, 1980) of all-or-nothing thinking, overgeneralization and mislabeling, mental filtering, jumping to conclusions, catastrophizing, "*should*ing," and personalizing inherent in such thinking. Once the beliefs have been identified and the distortions classified, the clinician can help the client develop less distorted and more useful thoughts which would likely lead to reduced emotional upset. The client in question might adopt thoughts such as "My penis is sometimes soft when I would prefer that it was hard. However, I know that sexuality involves much more than insertion of an erect penis. I am fully able to provide great pleasure to my partner and enjoy enormous pleasure myself with or without an erection. Manhood has nothing whatsoever to do with my penis. If I relax and involve myself in pleasuring my partner and experiencing pleasure myself, my body will respond naturally."

Relaxation training (Jacobson, 1971, 1978), often in conjunction with systematic desensitization and/or covert imagery, may also be of considerable use in the short-term treatment of male erectile dysfunction (see Auerbach & Kilmann, 1977; Flowers & Booraem, 1975; Obler, 1973; Wish, 1975). The primary objective in the use of relaxation exercises is to increase the client's capacity to moderate the level of anxiety associated with sexual expression.

Assertion training, communication and social skills training, and dating skills training may be applicable to some cases of erectile difficulty (see Reynolds et al., 1981) where interpersonal factors are associated with the onset of the problem.

Behavioral exercises represent perhaps the central component in most short-term treatment approaches to male erectile difficulty. Almost invariably, the exercises are adaptations of Masters and Johnson's (1970) protocol and proceed in step-by-step fashion. For example, Kaplan (1979) suggested that the "performance anxiety . . . can be diminished in many cases by structuring the sexual interactions so that they are nondemanding and reassuring. The patient is encouraged to substitute the non-pressuring goal of pleasure for the stress-producing goal of performance, and the sexual situation is arranged so that it is highly stimulating but has a low level of demand for performance or pressure" (p. 45). In crisis intervention and short-term treatment, the behavioral tasks are often suggested as homework assignments (McCarthy, 1985) and closely follow those suggested by Masters and Johnson.

The first task involves nondemanding, nongenital pleasuring of one's own body or, in the case of couples, taking turns in nondemand, nongenital pleasuring of one another. The clinician instructs the person or couple specifically not to proceed to orgasm or intercourse.

Task two involves nondemand, combined genital and nongenital pleasuring of one's own body or, in the case of couples, taking turns pleasuring one another. The combined pleasuring usually results in erection but again should not proceed to orgasm or intercourse. It may be both enjoyable and useful to engage in "teasing" activities in which an erection, when it occurs, is allowed to return to its flaccid state by discontinuing the pleasuring activities. Then, when an erection recurs as a result of the resumption of pleasuring activities, the man experientially learns that erections which subside can and do return. Such experiences generate an increased sense of confidence in a man's sexuality.

Task three involves, in the case of the man without a partner, self-pleasuring to orgasm during the full erection. Because some men have learned to climax with a nonerect penis (Lazarus, 1965), it is advisable to postpone orgasm until full erection occurs. Men who believe they have problems of premature ejaculation associated with the erectile difficulty may wish to use Semans' (1956) "interrupted stimulation" or "start-stop" technique, which involves engaging in pleasuring activities until he is just beneath the threshold of orgasm, stopping until he regains a sense of control, and proceeding with the pleasuring activities again. Masters and Johnson's (1970) "squeeze technique" may also be used. This procedure involves interrupting the pleasuring activities just prior to orgasm by placing the thumb on the inside portion of the head of the fully erect penis and the first and second fingers on the opposite side of the head of the penis, and then squeezing strongly for about four seconds. Then the penis is released until control is regained. In the case of couples, task three involves brief intromission of the erect penis into the vagina or anus of the client's partner. While the client remains fairly still, the partner thrusts a few times before the penis is withdrawn prior to orgasm. Subsequent to this, pleasuring activities resume until orgasm occurs.

Task four, not applicable for the man without a partner, involves a longer period of intromission involving the thrusting of both partners and orgasm during the period of insertion.

During the initial portion of the short-term treatment of Bob S., the clinician, in conjunction with the client, agreed on the following treatment goals: (a) reduction of the fear of losing the relationship with Beth, (b) reduction of the fear and anxiety associated with sexual involvement with Beth, and (c) increase in knowledge concerning sexuality among men and women. The clinician predicted that achievement of these goals would likely ameliorate the erectile difficulty. However, the worker was careful not to specify achievement of a firm erection during intercourse with Beth. Rather, the clinician said, as part of the sexual education component, that "erections occur spontaneously when a man is relaxed, desires his partner, and is stimulated sexually. They cannot be planned or forced. Erections spontaneously happen when the time and circumstances are right. Therefore, our work together will focus on reducing your fear and anxiety, increasing your relaxation, and ensuring that the circumstances are comfortable and that there is plenty of sexual stimulation." In discussions with Bob S., the clinician learned that Beth had expressed a willingness to help in whatever way she could. Her cooperation significantly improved the chances for success. The plan for achieving the identified goals included (a) identifying and refuting the cognitive myths and unrealistic expectations which lead to increased fear and anxiety, (b) teaching Bob S. about certain aspects of sexual functioning, (c) instructing Bob S. in systematic relaxation, (d) encouraging Bob S. in covert imagery of sexual pleasuring experiences with Beth, and (e) assigning graduated sexual homework to Bob and Beth.

Not surprisingly, Bob's high level of anxiety had already moderated substantially as a result of the problem exploration and the subsequent explanation by the clinician concerning the association between fear or tension and erectile difficulty. Thereafter, some of the strategies cited earlier were implemented. Perhaps most helpful to Bob S. were the discussions concerning female sexuality, the identification and challenge of his sexual misconceptions and the tendency to become a "spectator" during sexual activities, and the relaxation training. The behavioral homework exercises proceeded as planned with the cooperation and support of his partner, and full erections returned. At the time of last contact, Bob S. reported satisfaction with both his sexual life and his relationship with Beth.

Summary

T his chapter explored the topic of erectile difficulty. Relevant terminology, including the term *impotency,* was discussed. The chapter examined prevalence of erectile difficulties and the various factors associated with their etiology and presented the notion that erectile difficulty often represents a *crisis* of considerable significance to the men affected (and to their partners). Also, a well-known, five-phase model derived from crisis theory was applied to the phenomenon of erectile difficulty.

A crisis intervention and short-term approach can be appropriate for the treatment of many instances of erectile difficulty. However, a significant proportion of such problems have, at least in part, a physiological cause and require medical evaluation and perhaps treatment. Other cases of erectile difficulty may be related to severe relationship discord or may be secondary to more life-threatening problems and thus would be considered inappropriate for a crisis and short-term approach. Therefore, extremely careful and thorough assessment processes are required. This chapter presented guidelines for information gathering and diagnostic interviews and finally presented intervention strategies commonly used in the short-term treatment of erectile difficulties.

References

American Psychiatric Association. (1980). *Diagnostic and Statistical Manual of Mental Disorders* (3rd ed.). Washington, DC: Author.

American Psychiatric Association. (1987). *Diagnostic and Statistical Manual of Mental Disorders* (3rd rev. ed.). Washington, DC: Author.

Annon, J. S. (1976). *Behavioral Treatment of Sexual Problems: Brief Therapy*. New York: Harper & Row.

Auerbach, R., & Kilmann, P. R. (1977). "The Effects of Group Systematic Desensitization on Secondary Erectile Failure." *Behavior Therapy, 8,* 330–339.

Bell, A. P., & Weinberg, M. S. (1978). *Homosexualities: A Study of Diversity Among Men and Women*. New York: Simon & Schuster.

Berger, R. E., & Berger, D. (1987). *Biopotency: A Guide to Sexual Success*. Emmaus, PA: Rodale Press.

Burns, D. (1980). *Feeling Good: The New Mood Therapy*. New York: Morrow.

Caplan, G. (1961) *An Approach to Community Mental Health*. New York: Grune & Stratton.

Dekker, J., Dronkers, J., & Staffeleu, J. (1985). "Treatment of Sexual Dysfunction in Male-Only Groups: Predicting Outcomes." *Journal of Sex and Marital Therapy, 11,* 80–90.

Derogatis, L. R. (1976). "Psychological Assessment of Sexual Disorders." In J. K. Meyer (Ed.), *Clinical Management of Sexual Disorders*. Baltimore: Williams & Wilkins.

Elliott, M. L. (1985). "The Use of "Impotence" and "Frigidity": Why Has "Impotence" Survived?" *Journal of Sex and Marital Therapy, 11,* 51–56.

Ellis, A. (1975). "The Rational-Emotive Approach to Sex Therapy." *The Counseling Psychologist, 5,* 14–22.

Farrell, W. (1986). *Why Men Are the Way They Are*. New York: McGraw-Hill.

Flowers, J. V., & Booraem, C. D. (1975). Imagination Training in the Treatment of Sexual Dysfunction." *Counseling Psychologist, 5,* 50–51.

Friedman, J. M., Weiler, S. J., LoPiccolo, J., & Hogan, D. R. (1982). "Sexual Dysfunctions and Their Treatment: Current Status." In A. S. Bellack, M. Hersen, & A. E. Kazdin (Eds.), *International Handbook of Behavior Modification and Therapy* (pp. 653–682). New York: Plenum Press.

Gebhard, P. H., & Johnson, A. B. (1979). *The Kinsey Data: Marginal Tabulations of the 1938–1963 Interviews Conducted by the Institute of Sex Research*. Philadelphia: Saunders.

Golan, N. (1978). *Treatment in Crisis Situations*. New York: Free Press.

Golan, N. (1986). "Crisis Theory." In F. J. Turner (Ed.), *Social Work Treatment: Interlocking Theoretical Approaches* (3rd ed., pp. 296–340). New York: Free Press.

Graber, B., & Kline-Graber, G. (1981). "Research Criteria for Male Erectile Failure." *Journal of Sex and Marital Therapy, 7,* 37–48.

Jacobson, E. (1971). *Progressive Relaxation* (3rd ed.). Chicago: University of Chicago Press.

Jacobson, E. (1978). *You Must Relax* (5th rev. ed.). New York: McGraw-Hill.

Hite, S. (1981). *The Hite Report on Male Sexuality*. New York: Knopf.

Kaplan, H. (1974). *The New Sex Therapy*. New York: Brunner/Mazel.

Kaplan, H. (1979). *Disorders of Sexual Desire*. New York: Simon & Schuster.

Kaplan. H. (1983). *The Evaluation of Sexual Disorders*. New York: Brunner/Mazel.

Kaplan, H., & Moodie, J. L. (1982). "Psychosexual Dysfunctions." In J. H. Greist, J. W. Jefferson, & R. L. Spitzer (Eds.), *Treatment of Mental Disorders* (pp. 365–386). New York: Oxford University Press.

Krauss, D. (1983). "The Physiological Basis of Male Sexual Dysfunction. *Hospital Practice, 2,* 193–222.

Lazarus, A. A. (1965). "The Treatment of a Sexually Inadequate Man." In L. P. Ullmann & L. Krasner (Eds.), *Case Studies in Behavior Modification* (pp. 243–245). New York: Holt, Rinehart & Winston.

Lobitz, W. C., & Lobitz, G. K. (1978). "Clinical Assessment in the Treatment of Sexual Dysfunctions." In J. LoPiccolo & L. LoPiccolo (Eds.), *Handbook of Sex Therapy* (pp. 85–102). New York: Plenum.

LoPiccolo, J. (1985). "Diagnosis and Treatment of Male Sexual Dysfunction." *Journal of Sex and Marital Therapy, 11,* 215–229.

LoPiccolo, J., & Steger, J. C. (1978). "The Sexual Interaction Inventory: A New Instrument for Assessment of Sexual Dysfunction." In J. LoPiccolo & L. LoPiccolo (Eds.). *Handbook of Sex Therapy* (pp. 113–122). New York: Plenum.

LoPiccolo, J., Stewart, R., & Watkins, B. (1972). "Case Study: Treatment of Erectile Failure and Ejaculatory Incompetence in a Case with Homosexual Etiology." *Journal of Behavior Therapy and Experimental Psychiatry, 3,* 233–236.

LoPiccolo, L., & Heiman, J. R. (1978). "Sexual Assessment and History Interview." In J. LoPiccolo & L. LoPiccolo (Eds.), *Handbook of Sex Therapy.* New York: Plenum.

Masters, W., & Johnson, V. (1970). *Human Sexual Inadequacy.* New York: Bantam Books.

Maxmen, J. S. (1986). *Essential Psychopathology.* New York: Norton.

McCarthy, B. W. (1985). "Use and Misuse of Behavioral Homework Exercises in Sex Therapy." *Journal of Sex and Marital Therapy, 11,* 185–191.

Morton, R. A., & Hartman, L. M. (1985). "A Taxonomy of Subjective Meanings in Male Sexual Dysfunction." *The Journal of Sex Research, 21,* 305–321.

Munjack, D. J., Schlaks, A., Sanchez, V. C., Usigli, R., Zulueta, A., & Leonard, M. (1984). "Rational-Emotive Therapy in the Treatment of Erectile Failure: An Initial Study." *Journal of Sex and Marital Therapy, 10,* 170–175.

Nathan, S. G. (1986). "The Epidemiology of the DSM-III Psychosexual Dysfunctions." *Journal of Sex and Marital Therapy, 12,* 267–281.

Obler, M. (1973). "Systematic Desensitization in Sexual Disorders." *Journal of Behavior Therapy and Experimental Psychiatry, 4,* 93–101.

Paff, B. A. (1985). Sexual Dysfunction in Gay Men Requesting Treatment." *Journal of Sex and Marital Therapy, 11,* 3–18.

Pietropinto, A., & Simenauer, J. (1977). *Beyond the Male Myth.* New York: New American Library.

Reynolds, B. S., Cohen, B. D., Schochet, B. V., Price, S. C., & Anderson, A. J. (1981). "Dating Skills Training in the Group Treatment of Erectile Dysfunction for Men Without Partners." *Journal of Sex and Marital Therapy, 7,* 184–194.

Semans, J. H. (1956). "Premature Ejaculation: A New Approach." *Southern Medical Journal, 44,* 353–362.

Skinner, L. J., & Becker, J. V. (1985). "Sexual Dysfunctions and Deviations." In M. Hersen & S. M. Turner (Eds.), *Diagnostic Interviewing* (pp. 205–242). New York: Plenum Press.

Walen, S. R. (1980). "Cognitive Factors in Sexual Behavior." *Journal of Sex and Marital Therapy, 6,* 87–101.

Walen, S. R. (1985). "Rational Sexuality." In A. Ellis & M. E. Bernard (Eds.), *Clinical Applications of Rational-Emotive Therapy* (pp. 129–151). New York: Plenum Press.

Wish, P. A. (1975). "The Use of Imagery-based Techniques in the Treatment of Sexual Dysfunction." *Counseling Psychologist, 5,* 52–55.

Wolfe, J., & Walen, S. (1986). "Cognitive Factors in Sexual Behavior." In A. Ellis & R. Grieger (Eds.), *Handbook of Rational-Emotive Therapy* (Vol. 2, pp. 183–200). New York: Springer.

Zilbergeld, B. (1975). "Group Treatment of Sexual Dysfunctions in Men Without Partners." *Journal of Sex and Marital Therapy, 1,* 204–214.

Zilbergeld, B. (1978). *Male Sexuality.* Boston: Little, Brown.

Chapter 14

Post-Disaster Mobilization and Crisis Counseling: Guidelines and Techniques for Developing Crisis-Oriented Services for Disaster Victims

RAQUEL E. COHEN, M.D., M.P.H.

Introduction

Increasing attention is being paid to the plight of individuals caught in overwhelming, stressful, accidental events that produce serious reactions and sequelae affecting both physical and psychological health. These events, which appear to be increasing in numbers and magnitude worldwide, are exemplified by disasters, both man-made and accidental, acts of terrorism, kidnapping, and violence.

John, a 9-year-old boy, describes the experience of being a flood victim:

When the lights went down, my mother wondered if the wind had blown one of the electric poles down. Then the lights went out and the TV went off. It was pitch dark, and my mother found a candle and lit it. The wind was shaking the windows and doors. I had never heard that shrieky noise and became afraid. We heard a bullhorn announcement telling us to come out and get in the boats before the flood increased the danger. They took us to a church, but the water was coming near the church also. They said we had to get into some buses, and the people were pushing me away from my mother. They were afraid and so was I. I was crying.

John and his mother lost most of their possessions as the coastal storm destroyed their house. They were assisted by federal relief programs and the Red Cross in reestablishing their living quarters, and by the mental health crisis team in their psychosocial needs.

At the time an earthquake occurred, Henry, a maintenance worker, was driving to work and Mary was getting her daughter ready for school. Two younger children were still sleeping. The mother gathered all the children and started to run out of the house as the walls collapsed around them, threatening to trap them. The 4-year-old was screaming and started shaking, clinging to her mother. After reaching the street and noticing the destruction of their neighborhood, they huddled with a group of survivors until they were transported to a shelter. They waited anxiously for news about Henry. After Mary spent several days without news, wondering whether Henry was dead or alive, the authorities had the sad task of informing her that a cement block had killed her husband.

A woman living with a relative after the destruction of her house by the explosion of a tanker truck was referred to a crisis clinician. The family's house had been badly damaged, and the husband, wife, and two children 6 and 8 years old had to live with the wife's relatives for three weeks. During that time the husband was angry and depressed, expressing all his negative feeling for the irresponsibility of the public and private authorities who allowed "accidents like this" to happen to citizens. He also lashed out at his family, and the household was in constant turmoil. The wife, upset by her husband's behavior and feeling she had to remain strong, repressed her feeling of anxiety, irritation, and frustration. Antagonism grew between the couple, and the relationship with their children deteriorated to the point that the children's behavior regressed to infantile levels. It was at this point, three weeks after the event, that the relatives asked for help from the crisis team assigned to the families which had suffered during the explosion.

The clinician's initial function with this family was to explore the ways in which the event, the loss of the home, and the difficult living arrangements were influencing the interaction between them. The clinician interviewed the couple, the children, and the family as a whole in order to understand the effects of the disaster on their feelings and behavior. The clinician was able to help them see how their communication patterns had suffered, how it was interfering in the mourning process of having suddenly lost their world, and how they were evading confrontation of the reality of their situation and the painful efforts that lay ahead of them to reconstruct what they had lost. The clinician also helped them through the process of seeking and receiving assistance from the company that acknowledged responsibility for the accident.

These examples set the stage in which the post-disaster crisis clinician can enter the "front lines" in an outreach, advocacy posture where role and function will demand specialized skills and methods. Professionals are not only interested in understanding human responses in these situations, but also through experiential participation and research operations they are interested in developing intervention programs designed to assist the victims of these stressful events. Many models are being developed to design these programs of organized mental health intervention. This approach of incorporating mental health assistance within disaster relief operations must have a clear focus in order to participate in collaboration with many other agencies already integrated into the relief effort. Although suffering from the lack of clear guidelines, well-designed research methodology, and scientifically founded evidence of effective outcome, mental health intervention in disasters is moving forward, based on the empirical and clinical activities of many professionals in this new area of work. Their observations and documentation have been used to build a body of knowledge upon which guidelines leading to methodology and appropriate skills—still in a state of flux and needing further experimentation and validation—are being developed, used, and applied to help victims.

This chapter will address some specific areas needed to implement crisis intervention to assist victims of disasters. It will first focus on the issues of mobilization to develop the resources and methodologies for crisis intervention. It will then single out the techniques necessary to develop crisis-oriented services linked within a major multilevel mental health emergency relief program designed, planned, organized, and implemented within the context of the reality of the situation, the event, the population affected, and the resources available during the post-impact period.

It is important to point out that this chapter will not address the multiple components of mental health activities that are an integral part of the total program. Among such activities, consultation, training, and education are paramount. These methodologies implemented by mental health professionals can assist the non–mental health workers in discharging their responsibilities and increasing their capabilities for problem solving. The mental health assistance may also provide support to the public and private disaster emergency program staff to retard or alleviate burnout of the clinician in the front lines.

Review of Post-Disaster Mental Health Research Literature

Our mental health journals and books increasingly are presenting theoretical formulations of stress effects and crisis theory, the variety of approaches that have been applied in post-disaster situations, and research which attempts to measure successful outcome (Ahearn & Cohen, 1984). This emerging knowledge has helped professionals modify and reformulate traditional intervention treatment modalities to focus on the person–situation configuration as the unit of attention in psychosocial treatment (Sowdes, 1985). These formulations were documented by H. J. Parad and G. Caplan (1966), who outlined the mechanisms families characteristically use to solve the problems of a crisis situation. Another pioneer who applied these concepts to disasters was Lindemann (1944), who documented the bereavement reactions of individuals after the Coconut Grove fire in Boston. Tyhurst (1951) documented time sequences and phases of behavior across crisis resolution and began to point the way to crisis intervention during the specific phases. Cohen and Ahearn (1980) contributed the basic and applied knowledge useful in developing strategies and methods for crisis intervention. Another important contribution that incorporates the psychophysiology of crisis processes has been reported by researchers studying stress response syndromes and coping and adaptation processes, and their relation to support systems. Lazarus (1966) has enriched the knowledge of coping by identifying the important role of the cognitive system as it affects the psychological "interpretation" of the traumatizing stressor event. Eth and Pynoos (1985) in their studies have differentiated psychic trauma response phenomenology from grief and mourning processes.

In the area of applied knowledge of crisis intervention methodology, Cohen (1976, 1982, 1984, 1985) has reported her experiences during different post-disaster phases. In 1974, Congress enacted the Federal Disaster Relief Act, which stated that "the President is authorized through the National Institute of Mental Health to provide professional counseling service, including financial assistance to state and local agencies or private mental health organizations to provide such service or training of disaster workers to provide such service, to victims of major disasters in order to relieve mental health problems aggravated by such major disaster or its aftermath." Following the availability of funding for crisis intervention in a disaster declared as such by the president, many professionals have documented their experiences with crisis intervention services (Lystad, 1985).

Practice Framework:
Key Concepts

Post-disaster crisis counseling is defined as a mental health intervention technique useful in post-disaster events that seeks to restore the capacity of the individuals to cope with the stressful situation in which they find themselves. Crisis intervention is aimed at (a) restoring the *capacity* of victims to handle such stressful situations, (b) helping the victims *reorder and organize* their new world through the specialized techniques of psychosocial interactions, and (c) helping the victims deal with the formal, public bureaucratic relief assistance programs in order to obtain the available resources. The purpose of intervention is to bring about a change in the victims' post-disaster beliefs, feelings, and behavior so victims can reclaim their healthy adaptive defenses for problem solving and negotiating the reconstruction of their lives. It is fundamental to have a clear focus and sense of direction in post-disaster counseling and reconstruction of the healthy capacity for self-management that most victims have.

There is a relation between the approaches by which problems are defined and the interventions chosen and translated into action. Mental health problem definitions reflect influences and assumptions about the causes of the problem. In the case of a post-disaster crisis reaction, one useful conceptualization is based on a biopsychoso-ciocultural model of the individual's functions. In it the individual's reaction following the disaster's sudden and intense impact is related to the following:

1. The individual's personality structure
2. The individual's age, gender, ethnicity, and economic status
3. The individual's usual coping (defensive) styles
4. The intensity of stressors (primary and secondary)
5. The available and appropriate "fit" between the individual's needs and availability of support systems
6. The extent of personal loss suffered
7. The availability of relief emergency resources

Using these identifying data for each individual, the problems faced by the victims in their specific context or situation offer guidance to the crisis clinician.

During crisis all of an individual's biological, psychological, and behavioral systems are affected and tend to reorganize and reequilibrate for survival. Each individual has a backup set of available biopsychological mechanisms that are geared specifically to be mobilized at times of stress. The degree of success depends on many factors in the environment and within the individual. The recognition that there are sets of bio-psychological mechanisms that continually are available to correct and balance the physiological systems has been fully researched in somatic medicine (Canon, 1953). But this recognition is still in the process of being researched in psychological studies of man's adaptation in crisis (Lazarus, 1966; Horowitz, 1986). The conceptual formula developed by Cohen and Ahearn (1980) to organize the multiple variables that play a role in the process of crisis resolution deals with the dynamic interaction of multiple systems within the individual and the external conditions. It focuses on the complex, interactive integration of multiple levels of the individual, each level with its own rhythm, rate, laws, and characteristic changes, which shift and change as the individual proceeds through the phases of post-disaster crisis resolution.

Stages/Phases of Post-Disaster Behavior

T he disruption of lifestyles, property ownership, and personal relationships due to the secondary effects of the loss of neighborhood and permanent or transitory relocations produces a variety of emotions, cognition, and behavior. Paradoxical emotional reactions are likely to be evident during therapeutic intervention, especially in the acute phase of the trauma.

As the clinician encounters the clinical and behavioral manifestations of human reactions to traumatic events, it is helpful to keep in mind the developmental phases of crisis reaction across time (Cohen, 1986). Although we do not have a well-documented body of knowledge based on research, the changes in psychological, interpersonal, behavioral, and social interactions appear to follow a sequentially organized process. The adaptive defense mechanisms available to the individual are such human characteristics as health, age, lifestyle, and experience upon which to build a response; and behavior or social skills which act as a barrier, regulator system, or a filter to modify the impact of the crisis event.

Analyzing the reactions documented by Cohen (1986), the post-disaster sequence appears to show the following mainfestations:

Immediate Post-Disaster Stage: Psychological and Emotional Reactions

The range of emotions expressed immediately after individuals realize they have survived a traumatic event largely revolve around fear and anxiety. Other emotions begin appearing as it becomes necessary to find safe shelter and locate loved ones. People experience worry, shame, and guilt as they become aware of their own, self-centered survival efforts. Self-awareness of their own perhaps unusual reactions and behavior toward their novel situation adds to the difficulties victims have in adapting and coping. Fear, anxiety, apprehension, and demoralization need to be controlled and managed by victims, who are struggling to survive and cooperate in the efforts of the emergency assistance agencies.

The adaptive defenses observed during this phase can be grouped under the category of *denial*. Denial appears to act as a buffer to help individuals adapt and cope with the immediate, painful, and unbelievable changes in their lives. The phrase "It is true that we lost our home, but we are alive, thank God" is usually repeated by victims during the first hours after a disaster.

Relations between victims and helpers can vary from docile and passive obedience to orders or regulations issued by rescue personnel, to rebellious, antagonistic behavior toward such rules, apparently reflecting the victims' need to be in control of their individual "space." Rebellious individuals are difficult to manage in emergency shelters and strive to develop their own routines dealing with meals, lights, taking turns, or waiting to be attended to. This attitude of demanding, complaining, and expressing a sense of entitlement or trying to scapegoat the authorities for the consequences of the disaster seems to represent an effort to control situations to avoid being overwhelmed by feelings that are too painful and intense.

As times passes, behaviors reflect different ways of managing emotions produced by the losses and change of lifestyle. Variations of self-management include rigid, obsessive behavior in interactions with other individuals, vacillation, and ambivalent reactions to suggestions and advice. Some individuals congregate and form groups extending support toward victims or helpers. At times, the style of their support behavior is intrusive, inappropriate, or is resented by the recipient. Each individual's effort, either to relate with others or to become isolated, seems to help the individual deal with the sense of crisis, emergency, and threat in the unfamiliar world into which he or she has been uncontrollably plunged.

As weeks pass, the victims' reactions change. A new psychological–emotional state and behavior emerges as the individuals leave the shelters and return to their neighborhoods, where they become aware of the consequences of the disaster on their properties. As the victims begin to ascertain what it will take to begin reconstruction of their lives, the well-documented emotional expressions of grief, mourning, and despair take their toll. The victims' task of achieving resolution and accepting their fate parallels the developmental phases of crisis behavior. Due to the difficulty victims have dealing with personal emotions and interpersonal relations while at the same time having to fabricate a new world while attending to daily living tasks, crisis clinicians are apt to witness episodes of intense disorientation, confusion, and feelings of helplessness at not being able to control the environment. Feelings of vulnerability can strip individuals of their usual coping defenses for a limited time. Victims' usual psychological mechanisms fail at times, making it very difficult to deal concurrently with the multiple demands and decision making needed in reconstructing their lives.

Understanding the variations and sequences of emotions, with the accompanying defenses, is at the heart of crisis intervention. This requires knowledge, skills, and the correct attitude. The disaster situation changes some of the traditional understanding of crisis resolution processes that are part of our clinical practices in working with personal disasters. In the disaster setting, feelings of the victim are easily hurt. Conflicts arise from the victim's need to ask for help and the clinician's own brand of skills to deliver such assistance. The victim's sense of humiliation at having to depend on emergency supplies influences the victim–clinician assistance processes. The victim's awareness of having lost a familiar sense of security and independence, without the knowledge of whether he or she will ever regain it, adds to the bitter pain of the present. A percentage of the victims assume a so-called "victim's" role, with its accompanying expressions of entitlement, learned helplessness, expectations of assistance, and reactions of depression when frustration begins to accumulate (Krystal & Niederland, 1968). All these reactions begin to alter and distort relationships between the individual and his or her support system, since in order to obtain assistance the victim must negotiate and interact with a diversity of people who are just as frustrated and exhausted. For most individuals, these feelings of self-disparagement slowly disappear, replaced by a reemergence of more characteristic personality traits and social skills.

Around three months after the disaster the clinician may begin to identify pathological adjustments in some disaster victims. Chronic anxiety and clinical syndromes increase in the patient rosters.

However, the majority of the victims reconstruct their lives, physical community structures and homes recapture their old appearance, and the rhythm of normalcy returns to the neighborhoods. Assistance relief agencies finalize operations and leave the affected area. Levels of individuals' healthy adjustment vary according to an array of variables that interact according to random chance and produce varying outcomes of adaptation. Most individuals seem to achieve resolution of the crisis situation and continue reshaping their individual patterns of adaptation and resignation to the experiences and losses they have survived. What their scars look like and what sad fantasies return when they hear, for example, a rumble reminding them of the beginning of an earthquake or storm are individual secrets.

Victims show an increased and continuous use of their available support systems for a long time following a disaster. There is a need to share experiences, to have others participate in the traumatic events, and to validate acceptance of behavior that still feels alien to the individual many months after the event. These memories become a milestone that bonds individuals and allows them to share a sense of history unique to the survivors.

The Sociocultural Context of Community Changes

All these individual reactions—the emotions, thoughts, and behavior—are embedded in their sociocultural context. The community, in varying degrees of geographical and social cohesiveness, is also changed after the impact of a disaster. Its sociocultural manifestations (including religious patterns and characteristics) will continue to inter-sect with (a) the victims' reactions, (b) the emergency relief operations, (c) the reconstruction, and (d) the support and facilitation of crisis intervention programs. Groups emerge to revitalize the community social structures and affected agencies in the stricken areas. It is important to recognize the characteristic cultural values of a community, identifying the subgroups of family tradition, belief values, and norms when developing post-disaster crisis counseling.

An important area of such community-oriented post-disaster counseling deals with migrant or immigrant families recently arrived in the United States. The stress this population suffers is compounded by inexperience in dealing with relief assistance requirements. This situation can also be aggravated when the crisis clinician is insensitive to the families' cultural values or cannot communicate in their language. The conceptual models to work transculturally in crisis intervention require additional skills from the clinician. An example of this situation presented itself to a clinician who was asked to assist a Hispanic family that had recently emigrated from Central America to the Los Angeles area. After their small apartment was damaged by an earthquake, they had to live in a rented cellar, where they stored their household supplies. They were asked to document their losses and estimate the funds necessary to purchase some of their lost belongings. When the crisis clinician, who was a professional from their own country, visited them at home, they spread before her their attempts to comply with the official requests. They appeared depressed, fright-ened, confused, and unable to determine how to proceed any further. They had used all their emotional energy compiling the material, but were not clear as to who should be presented with their handwritten pages. Though this is a typical problem of many disaster victims, it was exacerbated for this family because public agencies are geared mainly to aid mainstream citizens. The clinician helped the family fill out forms and made them aware that she would help them deal with the emotional reactions to their situation and the bureaucratic network. The family gradually revitalized, learned about their community assistance plan, and were able to begin assuming responsibility for their lives again.

As time goes by for the disaster victim, a sense of competence is regained and victim assistance shifts from the relief operation staff, who begin to leave the community, to the community mental health agencies. Organized religious activity continues, at times with increased celebration of reactivated or reestablished rituals, including prayers for the dead and thanksgiving for the living.

Planning and Mobilizing Mental Health Intervention

T o design, organize, and implement crisis-oriented services for victims of disasters, an integrated, interactive, flexible linkage system must exist between mental health organizations and emergency management agencies. Emergency management staff have a long tradition of rapid response, clear operational guidelines for control of community disorganization, and effective methodology to help the victims with basic needs such as shelter, food, and clothing. In contrast, mental health professionals are newcomers to this trauma assistance field in attempting to find the best approaches to (a) collaborate with governmental emergency programs, (b) organize their own systems, and (c) develop models of mental health intervention using the techniques of consultation, collaboration, education, and direct crisis intervention. The next part of this chapter will address the specific steps of planning and mobilization for crisis intervention teams in order to meet the objective of post-disaster intervention in a phase-specific manner. There is a relationship between the time that has passed since the disaster and the appropriate intervention strategies. It is important to realize that while the mental health crisis team is helping the victims, multiple activities are taking place within their own mental health system and within the local, state, and occasionally federal relief operations.

Although many theoretical conceptualizations exist to help understand the behavior of victims in a crisis situation, the key point in planning for intervention is to choose a model that meets the consensus of the professionals who will be participating in these efforts. Unless there are clear notions of what the mental health team accepts as its mission, the possibility for confusion and failure will influence efforts to alleviate the victims' problems. The problems which need solutions and the options for modes of intervention are not only the result of the psychological state of the victims, but also result from the impact of the complex bureaucracy which participates in the victims' efforts to reconstruct their physical world. The role bureaucracy staff members play in the aggravation or resolution of the victim's crisis has to be considered an important influence when attempting to understand the victim's feelings.

The complexity of becoming acquainted with the multitude of relief agencies and learning how to access their disaster resources for the benefit of a victim is exemplified by the following report by a clinician. One ill elderly couple had contact with HUD and Red Cross before being referred to the crisis team. "In two months of intensive work with this couple, we worked with HUD and the Mennonites to repair the storm damage to their house, with the Salvation Army and Catholic Charities for temporary financial relief, and with Social Security to investigate Medicare and Supplemental Security Income (SSI) benefits; they were eligible for the former, but not for the latter. We worked with the Department of Public Welfare for food stamps and with the town tax assessors for a tax abatement. One of the victims was hospitalized in the second month span, which involved us with the hospital, home care, the visiting nurse program, and the Council on Aging. An attempted mortgage foreclosure caused us to contact the Legal Aid Society in the knowledge that the need for services might extend longer than the duration of our post-disaster crisis counseling project. The couple's health problems, fixed income, and need for rebuilding their life would keep them vulnerable and dependent for some time." The mobilization of resources after a disaster is an amalgam of traditional assistance and new techniques available to victims of disasters within certain conditions and for a specific duration. How the array of these resources is organized to assist victims of disasters must be a part of the repertoire of crisis clinician's skills.

Planning and Mobilizing

The following principles should be considered when planning a crisis team:

1. All team activities should be guided by tight, practical procedures which will result in economic, short-term, rapid assistance to victims.

2. Decision making and problem solving cannot be effectively carried out without involving some other agencies in the emergency program. Continuous linkages are part of the team's efforts.

3. Priority of resources controlled by mental health professionals will have to be apportioned according to careful assessment of the ratio between the very high needs of the victims and the very few available resources. Mental health assistance activities and interventions must be limited to immediate, practical applications and the most effective modalities.

4. The mental health professionals will have to apportion a percentage of their time to developing and sustaining current knowledge of all the assistance/entitlements for victims, all of which are continually changing.

5. The characteristics of the team's activities will shift daily as both the victims' problems and the organization of the governmental disaster aid network develop and change.

6. Effective institutionalized support systems for mental health workers should be implemented from the beginning to prevent and control symptoms of burnout. The "contagion" syndrome for clinicians who become exhausted, overidentified, and obsessed in the need to help victims has been amply documented (Lystad, 1985).

Implementing: Mobilization of Crisis Intervention Teams

In mobilizing the teams that will enter the field of action, the disaster site itself, the following areas of knowledge will be helpful:

1. The intervention philosophy for mental health professionals will be based on their theoretical schools of thought. The philosophical position of a mental health crisis team is related to the objectives of intervention as they are translated to (a) operation of assistance methods, (b) participation with human services in an emergency, and (c) relations with other agencies, such as the Red Cross or the local Civil Defense.

2. The development of mental health resource allocation is closely related to (a) the objectives of intervention, (b) the number of professionals participating, and (c) their mix of training and skills in emergency procedures.

3. The administrative procedures relating to team formation should be flexible and rapid in order to (a) identify the available professionals, (b) recruit and employ them, (c) organize them, and (d) train them both conceptually and clinically so that they may best acquire the expertise necessary to work in the front lines of the post-disaster site.

4. The framework for intervention implementation should be developed with the objective of a task-oriented, problem-solving approach. The functions of programs within this objective necessitate specific individualized program action guidelines for the assigned professionals in order to identify and respond to the victims' needs. The mental health professional identifies a victim's problem, sets the therapeutic intervention objectives within the context of the post-disaster situation, selects the services needed, delivers the services, and monitors the outcome.

During a blizzard, tidal flooding damaged a number of homes in a neighborhood. The victims of this tragedy were left with the task of rebuilding their homes and their community. Mrs. Brown, a 75-year-old widow living on Social Security, was visiting friends in another town at the time. Upon her return, she found the first floor of her home covered with water and the foundation, roof, and porch severely damaged. Most of her furniture, clothing, and personal possessions were destroyed. These losses were overwhelming to a woman living alone on a small fixed income. Mrs. Brown felt upset, depressed, and destitute. Although she had family living in another part of the state, they took no interest in her predicament and offered neither housing nor financial or emotional support. A friend offered her assistance and took her into her home. At first Mrs. Brown was grateful and put up with the lack of privacy, adapting to the family schedule and the discomfort of boisterous children in and out of the house. After several weeks of this, however, she was unable to tolerate her living conditions but felt helpless and did not know what to do.

It was at this point that she called the crisis team for help. The clinician made an appointment and went to the house to meet with Mrs. Brown. The clinician found her to be alert but sad and pessimistic. She seemed confused about what she could do to get herself back on her feet. She expressed anxiety about dealing with the bureaucratic red tape of the public relief assistance program and the length of time she anticipated before any response was received. She had crying spells when describing how the damage to her home and lifestyle had left her feeling lost and overwhelmed.

The clinician assessed the condition of her situation, her personality strength, and her level of crisis resolution. It was clear that she was in need of support and guidance, as her host family could not devote the time and attention to relive her experience and mourn her losses. Mrs. Brown also needed technical assistance in procuring government aid to fix her house and purchase new furniture and possessions. The clinician both instructed and guided her through the bureaucratic maze of agencies assisting the elderly victims. She also worked with Mrs. Brown to recover her self-caring skills. Three months later, the clinician had to conclude the crisis work, leaving Mrs. Brown on her way to recovering from the impact of the disaster.

5. The useful data that accumulates during a disaster comes from professionals collecting statistics, the news media reporting daily events, and the government agencies that are in charge of disaster assistance planning. The use of this increasing knowledge will aid in the prioritizing of resource allocation through choices of strategies and the deployment of personnel.

Roles and Skills in Post-Disaster Intervention

T he role of the post-disaster crisis clinician who is a member of the emergency program is still ambiguous. Both subjective and objective aspects of the role contribute to these unclear perceptions. The professional who participates in post-disaster work usually has developed clear guidelines to deal with individuals who are labeled "patients." When the clinician must assist an individual who is a victim of a disaster but is not "sick," or when a Red Cross worker observes the work of a mental health professional in the front lines, misperceptions on both sides cloud the understanding of the role functions.

The evolution of this role can be found in some counterpart of emergency trauma and hospital crisis units. Novel expectations of mental health professionals, both for themselves and others, produce role discomfort and confusion. Although clinicians are sincere in their interest to assist the victim, they convey a sense of being unsure of their own and others' expectations in mental health activities. They are hesitant and unclear as to the procedures of participatory activities. It is important to train the clinician to be prepared to adjust to the unfamiliar situations of emergency disaster work and to develop methods for dealing with the reality of difficult access and rapid use of only minimal data. Experience will help shift traditional attitudes to develop flexibility in collaborating with other disaster aid professionals. In working with colleagues such as the Red Cross, a federal management agency, or the local Civil Defense, problems such as trust, communication style, and lack of familiarity of mutual tasks emerge. There are long-standing traditions that guide the behavior of different emergency assistance agency workers. Their guidelines have produced problems with mental health professionals in their quest to collaborate.

The problems that have been documented in several disasters are related to professional differences in cultural and value systems and conflicting ideologies of how to help disaster victims. Problems also arise from different role expectations, within both the mental health teams and the relief agencies staff. Status and professional behavior norms are coupled with differing methods of working within the various mental health disciplines (e.g., social workers, nurses, physicians) that generally comprise a disaster assistance team. Professional boundaries, as they exist in a clinical setting, not only define the structure and capacity of the clinical services, but also the domain and responsibilities of the clinician. A wide range of services is mobilized, including counseling, advocacy, moving assistance, and transportation, in response to the enormous needs of the community. This array of needed assistance presents a dilemma to the crisis clinician on the front line who may be the only professional assessing the crisis situation. The clinician needs to set the limits and boundaries as well as prioritize, as it becomes painfully clear that the clinician cannot fulfill all the needs encountered. Within this setting, two themes have emerged as difficulties to clinicians trained in traditional procedures. One of these is the strategy of entering the victim's personal "space" and intimate life without having been asked for help, in the ritualistic manner of making an a priori assessment of the type of problem presented by the individual, and before appointments are given at most clinics. The outreach methodology is the primary means of making contact with victims in a crisis situation.

The second area of concern to clinicians is the substantially increased degree of dependency bonds in the midst of post-disaster events due to the level of trauma, suffering, pain, and the helpful and generally altruistic efforts of the clinicians in assisting in all types of capacities. Some of these feelings are expressed by a clinician with whom I worked in one post-disaster program: "Our goal as workers using an outreach model required that we adopt two seemingly conflicting roles of 'active-advocate-mobilizer' and 'passive-receptive-counselor/therapist.' We continually needed to shift between these roles as the victim's situation dictated. In a clinical situation, the worker's role is clearly defined as counselor/therapist; thus the issue of occupying different stances with the individual which we are aiming to help does not arise. The issues we faced in disaster crisis counseling were, one, our need to define our role and the nature of the relationship; two, to set limits on that relationship as it developed; and three, the power that we had to assume to deal with all the agencies, tending to be perceived by the victim as their 'hero.' We also needed to become aware of our projected sense of omnipotence and rescue fantasies."

When developing the role configuration, consideration must be given to the continuously shifting context in which the victims find themselves; there is a constant relocation of groups, different housing settings, and new directives from governmental authorities in charge. Standard behavioral guidelines should be developed and implemented to facilitate informed and efficient problem solving among all the organized disaster relief professionals, who continue to shift roles as time passes. Agreements on how to process resources as part of crisis intervention and techniques to diminish the intensity of conflicts must be achieved in order to function effectively.

Clinical Issues

Skills Needed to Develop Crisis Intervention Assessment

Assessing the current post-disaster situation surrounding the victim's life setting guides the first approach in evaluating the current crisis stage. The awareness of the post-disaster time frame impact-recoil will guide the procedures that should be instituted to help the victims cope by gaining a sense of control over their shifting, unfamiliar, and stressful environment. Following are some helpful guidelines for post-disaster crisis intervention techniques.

Generally, the clinician will make contact with the victim days or weeks after the disaster. In order to develop and establish a relationship with a victim who is showing distressed behavior, the clinicians should familiarize themselves with the expected individual post-disaster reactions as documented in the literature. Each phase of the post-disaster sequence will have a unique configuration of needs, crisis reactions, and available resources. These variables have major influences on the choice of techniques to implement crisis intervention. Throughout the phases, the clinician should combine an attitude of support within the utmost economy and efficiency of time usage, a difficult factor for many traditionally trained clinicians. A balance must be struck between expressing empathy and reinforcing and rewarding the so-called "victim's" role. The clinician should support the healthier parts of the victim's personality and mobilize them to enhance the ability to hang on for the immediate future. Short time-lapse intervention on a daily basis, serving to increase the psychologically painful awareness of the trauma, characterizes the initial techniques to be applied to the victims.

After promptly establishing a helping relationship with the victims, the clinician must initiate on the spot a rapid appraisal of key problem areas and immediate assistance in mobilizing all disaster relief resources, including establishing a relationship with the relief or Red Cross workers.

Techniques used to rapidly achieve these objectives are defined as any active interaction that tends to supplement, complement, reinforce, or promote the ego mechanisms of the victims. The range of procedures (behavior, action, speech, face-to-face interactions) through which this therapeutic process occurs will depend on the characteristics of the situation encountered by the clinician. The objectives of therapeutic crisis intervention encompass all types of activity by which the clinician seeks to relieve the distress and modify the behavior of the victim through psychological methods. It encompasses all helping activities based on communication that is primarily, although not necessarily, based on language. Many of these traumatized individuals display a sense of hopelessness and demoralization. All forms of therapy use certain approaches to combat and control this painful effect. The behavior of demoralized victims reflects the feeling of being unable to cope with the multiple problems they are expected to handle. This state of mind can vary widely in duration and severity, but the following manifestations are often found among the victims:

1. Diminished self-confidence
2. Confused feelings and thoughts in reaction to the new, uncomfortable, unfamiliar world
3. Belief that failure will be the outcome of all their actions and decisions
4. Feelings of alienation, depression, and isolation
5. Feelings of fluctuating resentment and anger resulting from the seeming inability or unwillingness of others, upon whom the victims depended, to help; the unconscious feelings of entitlement that are part of the so-called "victim's" role and the accompanying sense of frustration and disappointment create a vicious circle between the victims, families, and crisis workers
6. Increased negativistic reactions and diminished faith in the group

The variations, complexity, and severity of crisis reactions encountered by the clinician as the weeks elapse present a challenge in developing intervention approaches. The following example identifies the multilevel activities developed by a worker in her quest to assist a family.

Mr. Gordon, 49, his wife, 47, and their five children are a white, middle class family who were the victims of a disaster. Mrs. Gordon, while housed in rooming donated by a church near the disaster site, contacted the post-disaster relief team to ask for help and because she wanted to find out if she was crazy. She sat down in the clinician's office and reported that she had noticed her feelings and behavior changing. She had heard from neighbors that behavior changes were expected after the trauma of the tornado which had frightened the family and damaged their house. In spite of this knowledge, she thought that what she was experiencing was beyond the normal post-traumatic reaction. She described feelings of depression, crying spells, and the inability to carry out her usual household routines. Nothing interested her, and she had difficulty managing her children. Her social drinking patterns had increased and her friends were worried about it.

The family's home had been damaged, they had received assistance from government agencies, and workers were due to start repairs. Although this part of the upheaval appeared to be proceeding in a satisfactory manner, the family was experiencing serious difficulties. Most of Mrs. Gordon's complaints and expressions of her difficulties centered on a husband who was suffering from multiple sclerosis, resulting in restrictions on movement. Despite this disability, he wanted to control all the house repairs and assistance money received from the agencies. Mrs. Gordon felt this added to the complications caused by the house repairs and thought Mr. Gordon should be housed with relatives while the workers were in the house. Her marital situation, already shaky, had worsened and she felt trapped. In the past she had been able to function with strong, realistic defenses and support from her friends. At the time she came to the clinician, everything seemed to be falling apart.

The clinician interviewed the husband, the two as a couple, and the family as a whole in order to assess their psychological state and to hear their perception of the family's problems. The clinician was able to ascertain that Mrs. Gordon was exerting excessive control in order to deal with her feelings about the trauma, felt responsible for the family's problems, and was unable to relinquish responsibility for the complex array of activities needed to deal with the disaster assistance bureaucracy. Her ego capacity to handle the reality of her life and process her emotions had suffered as the result of the tornado and its effects on the family's living situation, was ineffective, and had precipitated a crisis. The clinician helped Mrs. Gordon reassess and reevaluate her current situation. By getting relief through verbal expression of her feelings, then by collaborating with her husband rather than trying to control his dealings with the repair workers, she gained better control of her emotions. She was also helped to recognize her own internal feelings and how they related to the unfinished work of resolving the trauma she had sustained. As she noticed an increase in her efficiency, she began feeling more positive about her family. The clinician supported her in her difficult situation and expressed appreciation of how well she had managed the bureaucratic conditions to get the house repaired.

Such an example highlights the types of crisis intervention techniques used with victims after the basic, concrete assistance has been rendered to repair their living conditions, which for many individuals is simply not by itself adequate. This family had many problems before the disaster took place. The tornado unleashed latent family relations problems, aggravated by the unresolved crisis of Mrs. Gordon. The intervention boundary between crisis resolution and family therapy remains a difficult issue for mental health clinicians who participate in this type of work.

Aspects of crisis components can be categorized within certain sequences: (a) impact of the stressful event (the disaster), (b) the perception by the victim of the event as a meaningful threat, (c) the victim's response to the stress, and (d) the adaptation outcome level of functioning at every sequential post-disaster level.

Based on the theoretical construct, the understanding of the stress response, resolution, and reorganization behavior will guide the intervention procedures step by step. This has important implications for the development of skills, the use of human resources, and the evaluation of the effectiveness of the intervention techniques.

Identification of temporal and phasic aspects of the affective and emotional expressions in the crisis counseling process include the following:

1. Cognitive confusion affected by anxiety:
   a. Assist in identifying the problem and clarify aspects of need.
   b. Guide evaluation of reality and help in reconstruction of event.
   c. Participate in formulating and evaluating priorities and make current knowledge of available resources for the victims.

2. Structure disorganized behavior toward realistic goals:
   a. Correct the victim's cognitive perception of the situation by acquiring and sharing knowledge about the impact of the disaster. What "hardships" has the disaster produced for the victim?
   b. Help in the management of affect by assisting in labeling and expressing the victim's emotions. By being told that irrational attitudes are to be expected in such a catastrophic experience, the victim is assisted in restructuring expectations, allowing internal sensations to change, and finding a more comfortable behavior.
   c. Indicate the methods available in seeking additional help from the emergency resources by listing tasks necessary for problem solving. This will reinforce the victim's cognitive grasp of reality and sense of capability, and will assist in restructuring the victim's new environment.

Intervention Techniques According to a Coping–Adaptation Model: Steps in the Crisis Intervention Model

Post-Disaster Crisis Intervention

The following steps highlight the sequences followed by mental health teams assigned to work in post-disaster situations. Before starting the assistance operations, the team will have obtained data available from the news media describing the type, extent, and impact of the disaster. The chance to mobilize a team to enter the disaster site a few days after public officials have organized relief operations offers the mental health clinicians a challenging opportunity. The mental health clinician will need to obtain sanction and legitimacy to enter the relief operations setting, which is generally organized and controlled by local officials and the Red Cross. The senior staff representative of the mental health crisis team can establish lines of communication with the head of the relief operations and receive permission to send in the mental health team. Once the team enters the site, the stage is set for the first phase of crisis intervention within the shelters where victims are transitionally housed in large numbers.

Three types of investigations are necessary to develop objectives and deploy the use of resources:

1. What are the characteristics and schedules concerning victim housing? Generally, victims are housed in buildings that have ample space, are safe, and provide necessities such as bathrooms and kitchens. If these are not available, makeshift spaces are provided by tents, mobile homes, or barracks. In these settings, the team needs to identify and link into the network of other assisting individuals, guided by the knowledge of sanctions for the mental health operation obtained beforehand from the presiding representative in the formal hierarchy of the relief command.

2. What are the characteristics of the victims (age, gender, ethnicity) that are gathered in the setting? A rapid needs assessment of the displaced, traumatized population will aid in planning the team's activities. For example, do the victims have few resources with which to rebuild their lives (as with elderly, handicapped, single mothers)? Are there many families that have lost one or more of their members through death or disappearance? Whether the needs are minimal, moderate, or severe, a mental health intervention will have to be prioritized due to lack of sufficient resources to aid everyone.

3. How are collaborative procedures, including referral and follow-through, with governmental and voluntary agency staff to be identified, designed, established, and implemented? One method is to have a representative of the mental health team introduce, describe, and explain the services offered by the team, as well as their schedule and location.

Procedures During the Acute Post-Impact Stage

A triage operation is instituted during this first phase of post-disaster assistance. The triage operation precedes crisis operations, setting the stage for initial assessment of victims who are showing signs of psychological decompensation and immediate need of assistance. The triage operation entails assessing the severity of the symptoms, some of which may include insomnia, inability to swallow, continuous crying, disorientation, or inability to follow the rules of the shelter. A rapid evaluation of the appropriateness of the victim's reaction at this stage after the crisis will help decide what psychological and medical procedures are needed. Through this method, a group of victims which will require crisis intervention for the first few weeks after the disaster is identified.

Recoil Post-Disaster Phase

The setting for crisis intervention is generally made when victims are moved to transitory housing or go back to their own, possibly still damaged homes. The teams are organized to develop the outreach–advocacy objectives and begin to identify individuals in need of services through referrals, door-to-door research, or word of mouth. Educational publicity in this respect can substantially increase the clinicians' effectiveness.

A Red Cross worker requested assistance with a 38-year-old single white woman who appeared to be anxious and angry. The woman was complaining of not receiving the services she was entitled to as a victim. The responding clinician found that the woman had lost her apartment because of severe damage from a tornado and had been shifted to three transitional settings. She was told to find a more permanent place by herself. She complained of feeling weak and helpless to find a place at a rent she could afford. She also felt entitled to government assistance but was not receiving it. Due to her psychological distress, this woman was unable to use her usual capacity to manage her life or articulate her needs in a socially acceptable manner. The mental health clinician helped her ventilate her anger and disappointment at her losses and, with the help of the Red Cross worker, guided her through the steps of locating a living place, obtaining rent assistance, and regaining her usual competence.

Phase-appropriate and stage-specific post-disaster work is related to the stages of crisis resolution in the majority of victims. Some individuals will not show the signs of discomfort until several months after the disaster, while others will recuperate from a crisis quickly but will again show signs of decompensation shortly afterward. The bulk of the work is implemented within a certain period of time for which the team has been paid or assigned. The outreach, selective approach of finding victims and working with them in association with the agencies deployed to assist in post-disaster programs has a time limit. After this period, mental health clinicians return to their offices, where victims may later appear. This gives the clinicians the opportunity to continue the crisis intervention techniques.

Throughout all the phases, the following underlying guidelines characterize the procedures:

1. Help the victim develop an awareness of the problems facing him or her, their extent, and the priority of solutions—"first things first." This challenges the clinician's skill in precisely identifying the problem on the spot and, on the basis of rapid and accurate diagnostic assessment, helping to reduce the victim's anxiety. Data at this phase are generally absent, faulty, or minimal.

2. Respect the use of denial as an initial reaction to stress and handle it slowly and gently, but firmly delineate the victim's situation.

3. Support active management on the part of the victim and discourage regression, passivity, and dependency. Do not take over the victim's life.

4. Immediately demonstrate helpfulness by meeting some of the reality-based needs of the victim; anticipate this possibility.

5. Express confidence in the victim's ability to manage the situation, while offering support for the steps necessary to achieve solutions. This hopeful, contagious feeling is important to impart to the victim, who is feeling helpless and hopeless, although it may be difficult for the clinician to sustain the feeling for long periods of time. The support system for crisis clinicians in disasters (including specific rest and recreation periods) should be implemented in all service programs.

Summary

P ost-disaster crisis intervention is emerging as a new type of intervention and participation of mental health teams in relief operations following a catastrophic disaster. Well-organized and operationally defined structures are in place to help victims with shelter, food, loans, and medical help. The incorporation of mental health services must be designed to match many of the organizational characteristics of the total relief system, including speed of operation, flexibility of format, and collaboration and integration with the efforts of other professionals. The total efforts generally operate under a schedule of intense activity, ending at a certain predefined date. The mental health crisis team activities may end with the official efforts or may continue after team members return to their office settings.

Crisis counseling to directly assist victims in the post-disaster stages of impact, recoil, and recovery may or may not parallel the stages of crisis resolution. Victims may show the typical signs of crisis stages, starting in the first weeks after the disaster and proceeding to resolution with the assistance of the mental health clinicians, or they may not display such signs immediately and may appear weeks later with acute crisis symptoms and asking for help. The techniques that will prove useful are based on traditional skills, but differ substantially in their application due to the following:

1. The intensity of the acute traumatic impact on the victims and their personal "space"
2. The complexity of interacting with professionals assigned officially by governmental relief operations having the power to dramatically affect the victims' lives
3. The high ratio of victims' needs to mental health resources
4. The rhythm and rate of change in the relief operations sites, from the acute stages to the transitional and final operations
5. The novel, untried, unfamiliar, and conflicting roles of the crisis clinician in the different settings (e.g., shelters, door-to-door inquiries, storefront offices)
6. The need to apply prompt crisis counseling assistance in situations where data are missing, where interview formats differ from the usual, and where privacy/confidentiality rules may not apply

The specialized context in which the intervention must be applied demands from the clinicians additional knowledge, skills, and attitudes not usually acquired in the day-to-day operation of mental health institutions. Preparation and planning for disaster events is increasingly being instituted by many mental health units in the United States.

References

Ahearn, F. L., & Cohen, R. E. (Eds.). (1984). *Disasters and Mental Health: An Annotated Bibliography* (DHHS Publication No. ADM 84–131). Washington, DC: U.S. Government Printing Office.

Canon, W. B. (1953). *Bodily Changes in Pain, Hunger, Fear and Rage* (2nd ed.). Boston: Brandford.

Cohen, R. E. (1976). "Post-Disaster Mobilization of a Crisis Intervention Team: The Managua Experience." In H. J. Parad, H. L. P. Resnick, & L. G. Parad (Eds.), *Emergency and Disaster Management: A Mental Health Sourcebook*. Bowie, MD: Brady.

Cohen, R. E. (1982). "Intervening With Disaster Victims." In H. C. Schulberg & M. Killilea (Eds.), *The Modern Practice of Community Mental Health* (pp. 397–418). San Francisco: Jossey-Bass.

Cohen, R. E. (1984). "Consultation in Disasters: Refugees." In N. R. Bernstein & J. N. Sussex (Eds.), *Psychiatric Consultation With Children and Youth*. Jamaica, NY: SP Medical and Scientific Books.

Cohen, R. E. (1985). *Crisis Counseling Principles and Services (Disaster Handbook)*. Washington, DC: National Institute of Mental Health.

Cohen, R. E. (1986). "Developmental Phases of Children's Reactions Following Natural Disasters." *Journal of Emergency and Disaster Medicine, 1* (4).

Cohen, R. E. (1988). "Mental Health Aspects." In Gueri (Ed.), PAHO publication.

Cohen, R. E., & Ahearn, F. L. (1980). *Handbook for Mental Health Care of Disaster Victims*. Baltimore, MD: Johns Hopkins University Press.

Eth, S., & Pynoos, R. S. (1985). "Developmental Perspective on Psychic Trauma in Childhood." In C. R. Figley (Ed.), *Trauma and Its Wake*. New York: Brunner/Mazel.

Horowitz, M. J. (1986). *Stress Response Syndromes* (2nd ed.). New York: Aronson.

Krystal, H., & Niederland, W. (1968). "Clinical Observations on the Survival Syndrome." In H. Krystal (Ed.), *Massive Psychic Trauma*. New York: International University Press.

Lazarus, R. S. (1966). *Psychological Stress and the Coping Process*. New York: McGraw-Hill.

Lindemann, E. (1944). "Symptomatology and Management of Acute Grief." *American Journal of Psychiatry, 101,* 104–148.

Lystad, M. (Ed.). (1985). *Innovations in Mental Health Services to Disaster Victims*. Washington, DC: U.S. Department of Health and Human Services.

Parad, H. J., & Caplan, G. (1966). "A Framework for Studying Families in Crisis." In H. J. Parad (Ed.), *Crisis Intervention: Selected Readings* (pp. 53–72). New York: Family Service Association of America.

Sowdes, B. J. (Ed.). (1985). *Disasters and Mental Health: Selected Temporary Perspectives*. Washington, DC: U.S. Department of Health and Human Services, Center for Mental Health Studies of Emergencies.

Tyhurst, J. S. (1951). "Individual Reactions to Community Disaster: Natural History of Psychiatric Phenomena." *American Journal of Psychiatry, 107,* 23–27.

Part V

RESEARCH

IN the previous sections this handbook examined the principles and use of crisis intervention with vulnerable target groups, including cocaine users, battered women, and rape survivors. Although the primary focus has been to describe crisis intervention strategies and techniques, many of the chapters have also mentioned the effectiveness of the crisis intervention model and the need for further research. In this final part of the book there is a comprehensive explication of the methods most applicable to critically evaluating and conducting research on the effectiveness of crisis programs. The concluding chapter will be of special interest to all clinicians and graduate students who are planning to evaluate the effectiveness of crisis intervention.

The time-limited nature of crisis situations poses some unique challenges to the practitioner interested in research and evaluation in crisis intervention settings. Chapter 15 explores a range of quantitative and qualitative methods available for use by the accountable professional. It considers a variety of intensive or ideographic models of research that can be woven selectively and unobtrusively into the fabric of the clinician's intervention routines. The strengths and limitations of the time-series design are discussed, together with a number of other useful, albeit less rigorous, alternative treatment evaluation strategies. Goal Attainment Scaling (GAS) is proposed as a flexible evaluation option which can be used to help bridge the methodological gap between clinical and organizational interests. The chapter concludes with a consideration of how standardized measurement instruments can be used in conjunction with various evaluation methods in an effort to operationally define the kinds of problems typically encountered by clients in crisis.

Chapter 15

Designs and Procedures for Evaluating Crisis Intervention

GERALD T. POWERS, PH.D.

Crafty men condemn studies and principles thereof.
Simple men admire them; and wise men use them.

Francis Bacon

Introduction

T he overall efficacy of brief therapeutic encounters, including crisis intervention approaches used with various types of clients, has been well documented (Koss & Butcher, 1986; Slaikeu, 1984; Auerbach & Kilmann, 1977). Despite methodological limitations inherent in some of the studies designed to compare short- and long-term intervention strategies, though there is little empirical evidence to suggest that there exists significant differences in the overall effectiveness of the two approaches. In fact, Bergin and Suinn (1975) suggested that clients are likely to change over time even without therapeutic intervention. The main effect of therapy is that it accelerates the pace of change and may also influence its direction. Most crisis theorists consider the time-limited disequilibrium associated with crises to be a powerful motivational force which heightens the client's susceptibility to intervention (Koss & Butcher, 1986).

Ever since Lindemann's (1944) initial formulation of crisis intervention in his now classic study of the Coconut Grove Nightclub disaster, crises have been characterized as time-limited phenomena that are inevitably resolved one way or another in a relatively brief period of time. As Slaikeu (1984, p. 14) explained:

> All humans can be expected at various times in their lives to experience crises characterized by great emotional disorganization, upset and a breakdown of previously adequate coping strategies. The crisis state is limited (equilibrium is regained in four to six weeks), is usually touched-off by some precipitating event, can be expected to follow sequential patterns of development through various stages, and has the potential for resolution toward higher or lower levels of functioning.

Because of this narrow window of vulnerability to change, it is considered essential that the crisis victim be provided immediate assistance in order to maximize the potential for constructive growth. According to Morley (1965, p. 77), "Enduring positive changes can be achieved following a crisis, and crises may have widespread results in the adjustment and coping capacity of the individual in future crises and in his overall adjustment to life."

The importance of early and brief intervention is supported by the consistent finding that most clients remain in treatment fewer than six sessions (Rubinstein & Lorr, 1965). In a study of 11,000 clients from 53 different clinics, Rogers (1960) found that less than half continued in treatment beyond eight sessions. Similarly, figures reported by the National Center for Health Statistics (1966) indicated that 979,000 patients receiving psychiatric treatment during 1964 averaged fewer than five contacts per person. In his review of research pertaining to continuation in psychotherapy, Garfield (1971, p. 275) concludes that "on the basis of the data . . . it is apparent that, contrary to the usual expectations concerning length of therapy, most clinic clients are done with it after only a few interviews." Koss and Butcher (1986) concluded that the majority of therapeutic contacts last fewer than eight sessions, regardless of the reasons for termination. In the absence of any compelling evidence in support of long-term therapy as a more effective practice, it can be anticipated that brief therapies are likely to be employed more extensively in the future. The resulting savings in clinical time would appear to make it possible to reach more people in need of treatment in a significantly more cost-efficient manner.

Evaluation in Clinical Practice

From a clinical perspective, however, there are some important limitations associated with many of the studies that compare short- and long-term intervention. For the most part, they tend to treat the independent variable in a homogeneous fashion. Thus, they operate on the assumption that there are no important individual differences among clinicians with respect to what goes on during the therapeutic encounter. The measures of outcome also tend to be treated as if they represented some sort of global and homogeneous index of client improvement.

These "uniformity myths," as Kiesler (1966) coined them, deflect attention from possible important individual differences both within and between groups of clients and the therapists who treat them. Existing research seems to provide ample evidence in support of the relative effectiveness of short-term intervention strategies, especially in crisis situations. What is less apparent, however, are any clear-cut answers to Paul's now famous dictim, "*What* treatment, by *whom*, is most effective for *this* individual with *that* specific problem, and under *which* set of circumstances?" (Paul, 1966, p. 111).

The purpose of this chapter is to discuss a range of clinically grounded research models that are sensitive to the three major variables of the therapeutic paradigm as proposed by Kiesler (1966): the *client*, the *therapist*, and the *outcome*. In doing so, we will consider only models which properly fall within the definition of what Chassan (1967) and others have referred to as "intensive" designs of research.

Intensive as distinguished from *extensive* models of research are primarily concerned with the study of single cases (i.e., $N = 1$). While such methods contribute very little to the confirmatory process which leads to scientific generalizations, they are nevertheless of enormous value to the scientifically oriented clinician interested in evaluating the effectiveness of his or her own practice interventions. In addition to providing the means by which clinicians can evaluate the idiosyncratic aspects of their practice, intensive research models can also generate practice-relevant hypotheses suitable for testing via the more traditional extensive research approaches.

The distinction between extensive and intensive models of research relates to the long-standing controversy regarding the relative merits of nomothetic versus idiographic research as differentiated by Allport (1962). Advocates of the nomothetic approaches emphasize the primacy of the confirmatory aspect of scientific activity, in which the ultimate goal is to discover laws which apply to individuals in general. The aggregate is inevitably of greater importance to the nomothetist than are the individuals who comprise it. As a result, nomothetists devote their time to the study of groups in an effort to confirm or disprove hypothetical statements and thus arrive at scientific generalizations concerning some aspect of the empirical world.

In contrast, advocates of the idiographic approach tend to be more interested in the study of individuals as individuals. Rather than focusing their attention on the discovery of general propositions, they prefer to investigate the rich and intricate details of specific cases, including the deviant cases which prove to be exceptions to the general rule.

Both approaches contribute to the cushion of knowledge which informs our practice. To pit one against the other creates a spurious issue. As Kiesler (1971, p. 66) points out, "The idiographic–nomothetic distinction misleads to the extent that it dichotomizes the approaches, rather than representing them as different emphases with some overlap and much fruitful complementarity."

The intensive or idiographic models of research are emphasized here simply because they lend themselves more directly to the primary purposes of the clinician—that is, the assessment of the clinician's own practice on a case-by-case basis. There is no intent to discount the importance of the extensive or nomothetic approaches. In fact, the probability of success in practice is likely to increase to the extent that clinicians explicitly base their interventions on scientific generalizations that are the product of controlled observation and systematic verification. In this sense, the two approaches are indeed complementary, one generating scientific generalizations under controlled circumstances and the other applying and evaluating their utility in the idiosyncratic crucible of practice.

Requisites of Effective Evaluation

E ach of the preceding chapters in this handbook discusses the application of crisis intervention strategies with a different population at risk. While sharing much in common with respect to many of the technical characteristics of the crisis intervention process, it is clear that there is wide variability regarding various dimensions of the therapeutic experience, including the problem, the client, the clinician, the surrounding circumstances, and the expected outcome. Such heterogeneous configurations of diverse and sometimes conflicting factors have led some researchers to conclude that any attempt to definitively test the effects of therapeutic intervention on the basis of classical pre/post-control group designs is "doomed to failure" (Bergin, 1971, p. 253). Similarly, Kazdin (1986, p. 37) noted that "investigations of groups and conclusions about average patient performance can misrepresent the effects of treatments on individuals." In discussing the need for specificity in conducting outcome research, Bergin (1971, p. 253) cautioned that "it is essential that the entire therapeutic enterprise be broken down into specific sets of measures and operations, or in other words, be dimensionalized."

From a research perspective, the various dimensions of the therapeutic experience may be thought of as involving a series of interactions among groups of independent and dependent variables somehow linked together in a complex network of functional relationships. *Independent variables* operate as presumed causes and *dependent variables* operate as presumed effects in any functional relationship. An important first step in the evaluation process, therefore, is to sort out what are believed to be the causal connections operating in any given crisis situation. This involves a series of interdependent problem-solving steps which logically flow from the identification of the presenting problem to its ultimate solution (Powers, Meenaghan, & Toomey, 1985). Embedded in the logic of this problem-solving process is an implied hypothesis, the calculus of which can be stated as follows:

> *If A-B-C is employed as an intervention strategy (i.e., independent variable), then it is expected that X-Y-Z will occur as a predicted outcome (i.e., dependent variable).*

Efforts to evaluate the effects and the effectiveness of practice inevitably involve, in one way or another, the testing of this implied hypothesis. It requires that the clinician—researcher specify clearly exactly what it is he or she intends to do with or on behalf of the client, as well as what the consequences of those actions are expected to be. In order to do this, both the intervention and the outcome must be defined in operational or measurable terms. To say that emotional support will result in enhanced client self-esteem or that ventilation will reduce depression simply are not adequate statements of testable hypotheses. We need to be clear, by stating in perceptually public terms exactly what is meant by *emotional support* and *ventilation*. Similarly, we need to ask ourselves what we will be prepared to accept as observable evidence of therapeutic change in a client's *self-esteem* or *mood*.

The task of operationally defining concepts is certainly not an easy one, but it is essential to effective evaluation. The value of our research efforts will prove to be only as good as the empirical observations upon which they are based.

Intensive Designs of Research

Ideally, the clinician—researcher would like to be able to identify with confidence a causal relationship between the independent variable (i.e., the intervention) and the dependent variable (i.e., the target behavior). Any extraneous variables that are not controlled during the therapeutic process, however, represent competing hypotheses as far as possible causes of change in the target behavior. To the extent that this occurs, it raises serious questions with respect to *internal validity*, thus reducing the level of confidence warranted by any causal inferences that might be drawn. Campbell and Stanley (1966) have described a number of possible design weaknesses that pose threats to internal validity. Those designs which effectively control contamination from outside variables are said to be internally valid. As Barlow and Hersen (1984) point out, single-case study designs vary widely with respect to their ability to accomplish this goal.

Time-Series Design

The prototype for the intensive/idiographic model of practice research is the *time-series design* (Fischer, 1978). The process involves the measurement of change in some target behavior (usually the identified problem) at given intervals over a more or less extended period of time. Successive observations made during the course of therapeutic intervention enable the clinician to systematically monitor the nature and extent of change in a target behavior. The actual observations, and/or the recording of those observa-

Figure 15.1 *Two-dimensional graph illustrating how successive observations of a target behavior are plotted in relation to a series of time intervals*

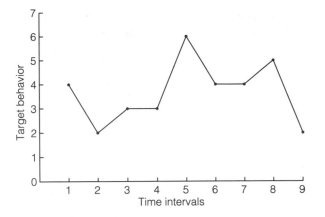

tions, may be done by the clinician, the client, or any other willing mediator with whom the client interacts on a regular basis, including, for instance, a family member, a friend, or a teacher.

Once a target behavior has been identified and an appropriate observational approach selected, it is a relatively simple matter to record any changes that occur during the course of intervention. The amount and direction of change are usually portrayed in the form of a two-dimensional graph, as illustrated in Figure 15.1.

The target behavior is plotted in relation to gradations (in frequency, duration, or intensity) arranged along the vertical axis. Successive observations are similarly recorded at regular time intervals, as indicated along the horizontal axis. The points are then joined in a continuous line which reveals the pattern of change over time.

If the identified problem involves an apparent absence, or an inadequate level of functioning in a given behavioral area (such as sexual assertiveness), then we would expect the target behavior (i.e., whatever it is we use as a measure of sexual assertiveness) to increase over time as a direct result of intervention. Conversely, if our intent is to reduce or eventually eliminate a dysfunctional behavior (such as domestic violence), then we would expect the observed pattern to go in the opposite direction in response to intervention.

While direct observations of this type can be very useful, caution needs to be exercised to avoid drawing unwarranted conclusions. As Barlow and Hersen (1984) point out, it is inappropriate to infer that any observed changes, which rely solely on the simple recording of repeated measures, are necessarily attributable to the clinician's intervention. Although positive (or negative) changes may occur concurrently with intervention, this approach does not permit us to rule out the possibility that other factors may be responsible for the observed change.

In order to address this limitation, a number of variations on the basic time-series design have been proposed (Barlow & Hersen, 1984), including the use of baseline measures. In such models the series of observations used to monitor change in the

Figure 15.2 *The shift from baseline to intervention*

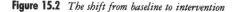
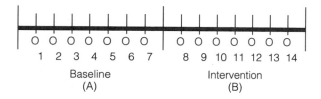

target behavior begin prior to the introduction of any formal treatment. This preintervention observation phase is referred to as the *baseline period.* The intent is to determine whether the pattern of behavior observed during baseline (i.e., Phase A) changes in the expected direction following the introduction of treatment (i.e., Phase B). If changes do occur during intervention, then the clinician has some basis upon which to infer that the treatment *may* have had something to do with it. The shift from baseline to intervention, which may be planned or in some instances the result of a natural interruption, can be illustrated in Figure 15.2, with "O" representing each successive observation.

Unfortunately, the practical realities of crisis intervention may not permit the luxury of collecting baseline data in advance of treatment. In most crisis situations delays in the initiation of treatment are not only likely to be viewed as theoretically questionable, but also may pose serious ethical implications (Kazdin & Wilson, 1978). Often the best one can expect with respect to the collection of baseline information may be a retrospective reconstruction of relevant data as reported by the client or some other available informant.

In some instances, as in the case of severe school phobia, reliable preintervention data concerning the target behavior (i.e., school attendance) may already exist in the form of available school attendance records. In other instances, such as those involving domestic violence, it may be possible for service delivery agencies to systematically reconstruct a reliable history of prior abuse.

For example, as an outgrowth of the Family Violence Project created by Boyd and Klingbeil in 1976, the Social Work Department of the Harborview Medical Center established protocol for the assessment of adult abuse. The purpose of such protocol is intended, in part, to document the incidences of abuse when they occur "using behavioral characteristics as opposed to traditional scales of measurement" (Klingbeil & Boyd, 1984). To the extent that such "hard data" are systematically gathered and recorded in relation to specific abuse victims, it may be possible to selectively exploit such information to create useful baseline measures. With some modifications, the strategy created at Harborview could be adopted by virtually any service delivery system which regularly interacts with clients who may subsequently be seen in a crisis situation.

It is apparent that the more rigorous the design, the more confidence one can have that threats to internal validity can be effectively ruled out. Unfortunately, the

Figure 15.3 *Two-dimensional graph illustrating the A-B-A-B reversal design*

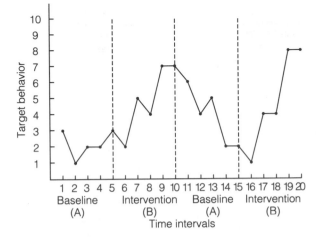

most rigorous designs require the use of baseline measures. Despite the limitations already noted, it is useful to understand some of the more sophisticated derivations of the time-series design. While they may not always prove to be of practical value in the evaluation of particular crisis situations, they do provide useful models against which to compare the rigor of alternative approaches.

Two of the most commonly encountered variants of the basic time-series design are the reversal design and the multiple baseline approach (Baer, Wolf, & Risley, 1968). In the *reversal design,* intervention is introduced for a prescribed period of time and then abruptly withdrawn, with the resulting circumstances essentially approximating preintervention or baseline conditions. In the absence of intervention, certain types of client behaviors might be expected to move in the direction of preintervention levels. When this occurs, it is generally considered to support a causal relationship between intervention and the target behavior. This is especially true if intervention is subsequently reinstated (A-B-A-B) with concomitant improvements in the client's functioning. Figure 15.3 depicts this type of reversal pattern.

Suppose, for example, a clinician was employing cognitive therapy as a means of reducing anxiety associated with inadequate sexual performance. The theory informing the use of intervention assumes that sexual encounters precipitate irrational thoughts, which in turn inhibit sexual performance and satisfaction. The clinician employs cognitive techniques and observes an improvement in the client's functioning during the intervention phase (B). The techniques are withdrawn. The client returns to his former state of irrational thinking during the second baseline period (A) with a concomitant increase in anxiety accompanied by prior levels of inadequate sexual functioning. The return to baseline conditions and ultimately to a second intervention phase provides the rationale for naming the process a reversal design.

The *multiple baseline approach,* like its A-B-A-B counterpart, is also used to minimize the possibility of behavior change due to chance. Unlike the reversal design, however, there is no withdrawal of intervention. Instead, baseline data are collected either (a) on more than one target behavior, (b) on the same target behavior but in more than one setting, or (c) on more than one but similar clients. Intervention techniques are applied in a sequential manner so that once a change in the initial target behavior is observed, the intervention is systematically introduced with the next target behavior or in an alternative setting (Fischer, 1978).

The sequential nature of the multiple baseline approach is especially useful in situations where there is more than one target behavior expected to be affected by the intervention. This is true in most crisis situations where the precipitating events typically affect various aspects of the client's overall social/psychological functioning. It is important to keep in mind, however, that the validity of any multiple baseline approach is based on the assumption that the selected target behaviors are themselves independent of one another. If changes in one behavior are somehow functionally related to changes in a second behavior, then those two behaviors can not be considered independent, and thus use of the multiple baseline approach would be inappropriate.

Both the A-B-A-B design and the multiple baseline approach begin to approximate the level of confidence achieved in what Campbell and Stanley (1966) refer to as *true experiments*. However, they are the most difficult to implement and, with respect to the evaluation of crisis intervention, have only limited utility for the practical, ethical, and methodological reasons cited earlier.

A final note is in order before we conclude our discussion of the time-series designs. In most instances, it is possible to determine whether meaningful change has occurred by means of simple visual inspection of the two-dimensional graph. Sometimes, however, it is impossible to determine from visual inspection alone whether the shift that occurs between the baseline and the intervention phases is dramatic enough to constitute a significant change. This is due to the fact that time-series data tend to be serially dependent (Gottman & Leiblum, 1974). *Serial dependency*—or *autocorrelation*, as it is sometimes called—means that future behavior can be predicted simply by observing performance from the past. In other words, the pattern of observations established during the baseline period appears to continue unabated throughout the intervention phase (see Figure 15.4).

When this occurs, the data are said to *drift*. In the presence of drift, it can not be inferred that change has occurred as a result of intervention. As Kazdin (1986, p. 41) points out, the plausibility that "changes are a result of treatment partially depends on the extent to which changes in the client depart from the expected and predicted pattern." Whenever the pattern of the data appears ambiguous with respect to the possibility of drift, reliance on simple observation alone may not be adequate.

Problems associated with serial dependency (i.e., drift) are not common. But when they occur, it is reassuring to know that there are available a number of fairly simple statistical procedures to assist us in analyzing and interpreting the data (Kazdin, 1984). When using statistics, however, we need to keep in mind that they should be employed only as a means to an end, and not as an end in themselves. In the final

Figure 15.4 *Two-dimensional graph illustrating the phenomenon of drift*

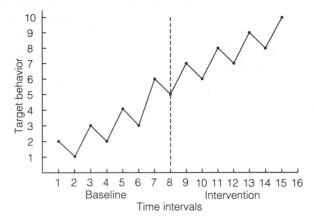

analysis, clinical judgment rather than statistical significance should serve as the ultimate litmus test of meaningful change.

Alternative Models

T hus far we have discussed a number of methodological variations derived from the basic time-series design as prototypes for the intensive or idiographic models of practice research. In light of the identified limitations, a number of recommendations have emerged recently involving adaptations of the single-system model. When viewed collectively, they provide added flexibility with respect to the evaluation process. When used alone, they are not as methodologically rigorous as some of the designs discussed in the previous section of this chapter. However, they do represent marked improvements over the methodologically soft or vague assessment techniques that typically characterize most efforts to evaluate clinical practice. Most of the research strategies discussed in the section that follows can be used in conjunction with various components of the more rigorous designs, thus providing a repertoire of techniques that can be used selectively in response to the idiosyncratic demands of a particular case. In addition, it is sometimes possible to employ several of the proposed evaluation strategies simultaneously within or across client systems. When this is done intentionally, it is referred to as *triangulation,* a process which enables the clinician to use each strategy as a means of cross-validating the findings generated by alternative strategies (Denzin, 1970).

Treatment Evaluation Strategies

Kazdin (1986) discusses a range of treatment evaluation strategies that can be especially useful to clinicians engaged in various forms of crisis intervention. Four of these strategies are relevant to our present concern because they address a variety of issues directly related to single-system evaluation:

treatment package strategy

dismantling treatment strategy

constructive treatment strategy

parametric treatment strategy

In the *treatment package strategy,* the impact of intervention is assessed as a total entity. It is understood that treatment is inevitably a multifaceted phenomenon. But no attempt is made to isolate the effects of the various components that comprise the treatment "package." In order to rule out potential threats to internal validity, such as changes attributable to motivation, spontaneous remission, or intervening historical events, some sort of control or comparison condition must be incorporated into the research design. This can take the form of direct comparisons between clients of a given type (e.g., a group of pregnant teenagers), some of whom are exposed to the treatment package, and some of whom are not. If waiting lists are not feasible for this purpose, it may be possible to split the target groups randomly into two or more subgroups and compare the relative effectiveness of alternative treatment packages.

Once it has been demonstrated that a treatment package, viewed as a totality, is capable of producing therapeutically desirable outcomes, we may want to analyze the relative contribution of the separate components that comprise the package. This involves the orderly removal of each component, accompanied by a careful recording of the apparent effects. This process of systematic elimination or isolation is what Kazdin (1986, p. 25) refers to as the *dismantling treatment strategy.* Its purpose is to enable the clinician to "determine the necessary and sufficient components for thera-peutic change." If we assume that $A + B + C$ represents a treatment package comprised of three distinct components, it is possible to illustrate the dismantling process as in Table 15.1.

From the available information in Table 15.1 it would appear that the inclusion of C in the intervention package is somehow related to the presence of Y as an observed outcome. When C is removed, Y is no longer observed. When B is also eliminated from the treatment package, outcome X disappears. This suggests that B may be

Table 15.1 *The effects of systematically dismantling a treatment package*

DISMANTLING PROCESS	TREATMENT PACKAGE	OBSERVED OUTCOME
Phase I	$A + B + C$	$X - Y - Z$
Phase II	$A + B$	$X - Z$
Phase III	A	Z

somehow functionally related to X. We are left with component A and outcome Z, which may or may not be related. We would, of course, need to eliminate A in order to confirm the possibility of an association between these two variables.

A brief example may help illustrate this otherwise rather abstract process. Let us assume that a client is referred to a substance abuse center experiencing a crisis precipitated by a recent history of excessive and uncontrolled alcohol consumption. The initial intake reveals that he is separated from his wife and family, was recently fired from his job, and was referred by the police department following an aborted attempt at suicide.

In conjunction with his admission to the detoxification unit, an assessment is performed which leads to a treatment plan comprised of three separate components. Component A involves participation in Alcoholics Anonymous. As a peer support group, it is expected that Alcoholics Anonymous will enable the client to share his experiences in an atmosphere of mutual support as well as help him develop strategies for overcoming his dysfunctional drinking patterns. Component B involves individual counseling, the purpose of which is to provide the client with an opportunity to engage in personal problem solving. Component C engages the client in an educational experience which utilizes various behavioral modification techniques designed to reduce stress.

Although the specific techniques employed in each component differ substantially, the primary goal of the overall treatment package is to control the dysfunctional drinking behavior and to reinstate a healthy personal adjustment. The clinician would, of course, need to operationally define *healthy personal adjustment* in terms of perceptually public target behaviors. Once this was accomplished and the treatment had been in effect for a long enough period to observe specific changes in the client's functioning, it would be a relatively simple matter to begin the dismantling process.

In an attempt to isolate the differential contribution of each component of the treatment package, the clinician would intentionally eliminate or temporarily withhold one of the three components (e.g., individual counseling) while closely monitoring the apparent consequences in relation to the identified target behaviors. Whether or not the component is later reinstated depends on the clinician's judgment concerning the component's apparent contribution to the goals of treatment. Components that prove effective may be reinstated; those that do not are likely to be rejected. Of course, at any given time the clinician may decide to intentionally dismantle, in any order, one or a combination of the components comprising the treatment package. Sometimes, however, unintentional disruptions occur, as would be the case were the client to unexpectedly stop attending Alcoholics Anonymous meetings. Whatever the case, the clinician should be prepared to systematically monitor the impact of such changes in relation to the identified outcome variables. Whenever an existing treatment component is either dismantled or subsequently reinstated, a new phase in the life of the treatment package is created.

It is possible to vary the order in which the various components comprising the treatment package are dismantled. This can be a useful strategy to employ with subsequent clients of the same type. It would certainly strengthen the level of confidence regarding possible causal links if outcomes could be accurately predicted on the basis of variations in the dismantling order. It is important to keep in mind, however, that it is up to the clinician to determine what aspects of the observed outcome represent the desired therapeutic effect and to retain only those treatment components that can be justified on the basis of the outcome.

Kazdin (1986, p. 26) points out that "dismantling research is greatly facilitated by having a tentative theoretical basis for explaining the techniques. The theory specifies the crucial interpretation of the mechanisms of treatment and directs the investigator to a particular set of components that warrant investigation." Thus, in our example, the more we know about the theoretical underpinnings of Alcoholics Anonymous, problem-solving focused counseling, and behavioral modification, the better informed we will be in our efforts to predict and explain the possible consequences of the dismantling process.

Clinicians may be reluctant to withdraw treatment components which they have reason to believe may be having an efficacious impact on the client. In such cases, it may be possible to employ a *constructive treatment strategy*. Constructive treatment is essentially the opposite of the dismantling strategy. It involves a process in which specific treatment components are added in an incremental fashion for purposes of monitoring their collective impact. The clinician employs a particular treatment technique, or constellation of techniques, as a point of departure. Then additional treatment components are systematically introduced in an attempt to enhance the overall effectiveness of the treatment package. As each new component is incorporated into the overall package, observable changes in the client's functioning are carefully recorded. Those components that appear to contribute to the therapeutically desired outcome are retained, and those that do not can be subsequently eliminated or dismantled.

Returning to the example cited earlier, the clinician might begin by involving the client in stress management training during the detoxification phase. Then, after the client is stabilized, a decision might be made to expand the treatment package incrementally to include referral to Alcoholics Anonymous, and subsequent involvement in individual counseling with a problem-solving focus. Additional components, such as family therapy or employment training, might also be added to the treatment package. As noted, the introduction of each new component represents a new phase in the evaluation of the treatment package. Each new phase in turn provides an additional opportunity to predict outcomes and observe changes.

Sometimes the question is not one of whether to add or subtract a particular component to an existing treatment package. Rather, it is to determine in what quantity and/or in what sequence the existing components are likely to have their most beneficial impact. By systematically manipulating one or more of the components comprising the treatment package, it is possible to monitor the differential effects. This type of evaluation, involving the fine tuning of an existing intervention plan, is referred to by Kazdin (1986) as the *parametric treatment strategy*. It involves the systematic manipulation of the established parameters—that is, the various components of the treatment package—together with a careful monitoring of the relative effectiveness of each modification. Unlike its dismantling and constructive counterparts, the parametric approach is used to evaluate the optimal configuration of a treatment package, the credibility of which has already been established.

When considered as a group, this cluster of four treatment evaluation strategies is similar to what Chassan (1967) described as "objectified case studies." In his discussion of this type of evaluation model, Fischer (1978, p. 103) stated that "objectified case studies basically are attempts to relate the process of intervention— what the worker does—to the outcome of that intervention—whether what the worker does reasonably can be concluded to be effective."

Goal Attainment Scaling

The time-limited nature of crisis intervention poses some fascinating challenges for the clinician interested in evaluating his or her own practice. Whatever evaluative efforts are employed, they must be initiated early and brought to closure fairly quickly. In addition, the methodology itself should not be experienced by the client as being in any way intrusive in the helping process. Consequently, the purposes of both the intervention and the evaluation should be compatible and mutually supportive. This suggests that no one methodological approach is likely to be appropriate for all types of crisis situations. The research challenge, as inevitably it is for practice as well, is to fit the method to the problem, and not vice versa. This requires a thoughtful selection of research strategies, the various threads of which can be creatively woven throughout the broader fabric of the overall intervention plan.

One evaluation model which would appear to be adaptable to a wide range of crisis intervention situations is the *Goal Attainment Scaling* approach introduced by Kiresuk and Sherman (1968). Goal Attainment Scaling (GAS) was originally proposed as a way of measuring programmatic outcomes for community mental health services. It is discussed here as an example of an evaluation model which combines a number of very useful idiographic as well as nomothetic methodological features.

GAS employs a client-specific technique designed to provide outcome information regarding the attainment of individualized clinical and social goals. Koss and Butcher (1986, p. 642) point out that "the time limitations of brief psychotherapy make many of the goals of traditional therapy such as extensive personality reconstruction or dynamic insight into psychogenetic origins of behavior impossible. Brief psychotherapy requires that 'therapeutic perfectionism' (Malan, 1963) and 'prejudices of depth' (Wolberg, 1965) be abandoned." This view is also shared by Bellak and Small (1978, p. 15), who argue that "the length of time that ordinary psychotherapy takes becomes one of the problems of its evaluation. Brief psychotherapy not only has the advantage of producing results sooner than more conventional psychotherapy, and therefore of providing a chance to follow-up its potential for therapeutic success, it is also—at least in our practice—a highly structured process with clear conceptualization and methodology." This structured quality, organized around the attainment of limited goals, articulates especially well with the methodological requisites of GAS.

GAS requires that a number of individually tailored treatment goals be specified in relation to a set of graded scale points ranging from the *least* to the *most* favorable outcomes considered likely. It is suggested that at least two of the five points comprising the Likert-type scale be defined with sufficient specificity to permit reliable judgments with respect to whether the client's behavior falls at, above, or below a given point. Numeric values are then assigned to each point, with the *least favorable* outcome scored -2, the *most favorable* outcome scored $+2$, and the outcome considered *most likely* assigned a value of 0. The net result of this scaling procedure is a transformation of each outcome into an approximate random variable, thus allowing the overall attainment of specific goals to be treated as standard scores, a feature that becomes important when GAS is used for program evaluation purposes.

This process is operationalized in the form of a Goal Attainment Guide. For example, the intervention goals for a particular suicidal client may include (a) the elimination of suicidal ideation, (b) the alleviation of depression, and (c) the enhancement of self-esteem. Table 15.2 illustrates how these goals might be defined in terms of expected outcomes that are relevant to a specific client. Although goals are tailored to each client's needs, a *Dictionary of Goal Attainment Scaling* is available to assist clinicians in their efforts to operationally define goals and construct Goal Attainment Guides (Garwick & Lampman, 1973).

The Goal Attainment Guide is constructed with a specific time frame in mind. The definitions for the expected level of success (i.e., the midpoint of the five-point scale) represent clinical predictions concerning client performance at some predetermined future date (e.g., four or six weeks following the formulations of the goals). The amount and direction of goal attainment can then be measured by comparing the client's level of functioning at the time the guide was constructed with the level of functioning on the target date. A check ($\checkmark$) is used to record the initial performance level and an asterisk (*) is used to record performance at the point of follow-up. The guide can be revised at follow-up to reflect new goals or anticipated changes in the performance levels of existing goals. Specific weights can also be assigned to each goal as a way of reflecting their relative importance in the overall intervention plan. Since weighting represents a relative rather than an absolute indicator of importance, however, the sum need not equal 100 or any other fixed total. The actual numerical value of the assigned weight is of significance only when GAS is used as a basis for comparing the relative effectiveness of alternative intervention approaches within or between programs.

The computing of GAS scores can be a simple or a complex matter, depending on the purposes for which the evaluation methodology is to be used. When employed as a program evaluation technique, which relies upon the availability of aggregate data, it is appropriate that composite standardized scores be derived. This is a fairly

Table 15.2 *Sample Goal Attainment Guide illustrating scaling procedure for hypothetical suicidal client*

LEVELS OF EXPECTED ATTAINMENT	GOALS		
	SUICIDE Weight: 40	DEPRESSION Weight: 20	SELF-ESTEEM Weight: 10
Least favorable outcome thought likely (−2)	Commits suicide or makes additional suicidal attempt(s).		
Less than expected success (−1)	√Preoccupied with thoughts of suicide as a possible solution to personal problems; says "life is not worth living."	√Complains of being very depressed all the time; eating and sleeping patterns irregular; cries daily; not working.	√Considers self a "bad person"; criticizes self; feels people would be better off without him or her.
Expected level of success (0)	*Occasionally thinks about suicide, but is able to consider alternative solutions to personal problems.	Complains of being depressed all the time; eat at least two meals a day; sleeps at least six hours a night; cries occasionally; misses work occasionally.	*Doesn't verbally criticize self, but says he or she is not very happy.
More than expected success (+1)		*Only occasional feelings of depression; eating and sleeping regularly; no longer crying; working regularly.	
Most favorable outcome thought likely (+2)	No longer considers suicide a viable solution to personal problems; talks of future plans.		Reports he or she likes self and way of living and/or reports being "reasonably happy."

complex process requiring some statistical sophistication (see Kiresuk & Sherman, 1968, p. 448). When used as a framework for the evaluation of a single case (e.g., individual, family, group), however, the process is much less complicated. In fact, the only meaningful determination is whether, or to what extent, the predicted goals have been attained. For those who prefer to quantify such judgments, it is possible to derive a composite score by determining the amount and direction of change occurring in relation to each goal and then summing their respective contributions. An average attainment score can be calculated by simply dividing the composite score by the total number of goals. This makes it possible to compare attainment levels across clients while controlling for the number of goals.

Any number of goals may be specified for a particular client and any subject area may be included as an appropriate goal. Even the same goal can be defined in more than one way. For example, the goal of alleviating depression could be scaled in relation to self-reports (as in Table 15.2) or in relation to specific cutoff points on a standardized instrument such as the *Beck Depression Inventory* (Beck, 1967). It is essential, however, that all goals be defined in terms of a graded series of verifiable expectations in ways that are relevant to the idiosyncrasies of the particular case.

Originally, Kiresuk and Sherman (1968) proposed that client goals be determined by a single goal selector or a goal selection committee. Subsequently, a number of variations in the goal selection process have emerged. In some instances, clients have been engaged in the process (Houts, Scott, & Leasor, 1973), while in others goals have been determined by clinicians and significant others as well as clients (Polak, 1970). From a research perspective there are some definite advantages with respect to objectivity in having a disinterested third party establish and monitor the goals. From a clinical perspective, however, it can be argued that clients are more likely to work toward goals that they have helped formulate than toward goals that have been formulated for them. In the final analysis, the clinician needs to weigh the relative merits of alternative goal selection approaches and use the one best suited to the clinical/research situation.

It should be emphasized that the use of GAS as a framework for the intensive study of a single case does not warrant inferences concerning causal relationships between intervention and outcome. In fact, by stressing the importance of outcome factors, it tends to deflect attention away from concern for issues directly involving interventions. While it can not be concluded that intervention is necessarily responsible for the attainment of goals, when expected goals are not realized it does raise serious questions concerning the efficacy of the intervention strategy. In addition, the construction of a Goal Attainment Guide can serve as a useful rallying point around which practitioners and clients can negotiate the particulars of an intervention contract, including the formulation of objectives, the establishment of priorities, and the assignment of responsibilities. In a study of the therapeutic effectiveness of goal setting, Hart (1978, p. 1242) concluded that "the goal attainment model with periodic monitoring may be useful in the therapeutic process to collect information, as an aid in organizing and recording the process of therapy, to design treatment for outpatients, as an outcome effectiveness measure, to evaluate therapeutic progress, and to provide new data for setting additional therapeutic goals." In sum, GAS provides a systematic yet flexible practice evaluation model which can help bridge the methodological gap between clinical and organizational interests.

Using Standardized Measurement Instruments

O ne of the most difficult aspects of evaluating clinical intervention is the task of operationally defining client problems. This is not surprising, in that many of those problems tend to be characterized in somewhat vague and nebulous language. Terms such as *stress, anxiety,* and *depression* are often used to describe important facets of a client's social/psychological functioning. Although commonplace in our professional jargon, such terms tend to carry rather subjective connotations, and as a result can be difficult to measure.

In recent years clinicians have begun to rely more heavily on the use of standardized instruments in an effort to achieve greater accuracy and objectivity in their attempts to measure some of the more commonly encountered clinical problems. The most notable development in this regard has been the emergence of numerous brief pencil-and-paper assessment devices known as Rapid Assessment Instruments (RAI). As standardized measures, RAIs share a number of characteristics in common (Levitt & Reid, 1981). They are brief, relatively easy to administer, score, and interpret, and they require very little knowledge of testing procedures on the part of the clinician. For the most part, they are self-report measures that can be completed by the client, usually within 15 minutes. They are independent of any particular theoretical orientation, and as such can be used with a variety of interventive methods. Since they provide a systematic overview of the client's problem, they often tend to stimulate discussion related to the information elicited by the instrument itself. The score that is generated provides an operational index of the frequency, duration, or intensity of the problem. Most RAIs can be used as repeated measures, and thus are adaptable to the methodological requirements of both time-series and GAS approaches. In addition to providing a standardized means by which change can be monitored over time with a single client, RAIs can also be used to make equivalent comparisons across clients. This feature is especially useful when working with couples or groups of clients experiencing a common problem (e.g., marital conflict).

One of the major advantages of RAIs is the availability of information concerning reliability and validity. *Reliability* refers to the stability of a measure. In other words, do the questions that comprise the instrument mean the same thing to an individual answering them at different times, and would those same questions be interpreted by different individuals in a similar manner? Unless an instrument yields consistent data, it is impossible for it to be valid. But even highly reliable instruments are of little value unless their validity can also be demonstrated. *Validity* speaks to the general question of whether an instrument does in fact measure what it purports to measure. There are several different approaches to establishing validity (Powers et al., 1985), each of which is designed to provide information regarding how much confidence we can have in the instrument as an accurate indicator of the problem under consideration. While levels of reliability and validity vary greatly among available instruments, it is very helpful to the clinician to know in advance the extent to which these issues have been addressed. Information concerning reliability and validity, as well as other factors related to the standardization process (e.g., the procedures for administering, scoring, and interpreting the instrument), can help the clinician make informed judgments concerning the appropriateness of any given instrument.

The key to selecting the best instrument for the job is knowing where and how to access the relevant information concerning potentially useful measures. Fortunately there are a number of excellent sources available to the clinician to help facilitate this process. The most comprehensive is a nine-volume series of *Mental Measurement Yearbooks* edited by Buros (1978) and Mitchell (1983a). This compendium of research instruments dates back to 1938. For inclusion in the *Mental Measurement Yearbook,* a test must be either new, revised, or have generated 20 or more references since its publication in an earlier volume of the yearbook. Each volume provides a wealth of information concerning literally thousands of published scales and indices, many of which have considerable potential as outcome measures. Each instrument is summarized in relation to a standard set of criteria, including data concerning reliability, validity, and utility. Many of the instruments are also critically evaluated by one or more independent reviewers, a feature which provides valuable information regarding a variety of methodological concerns.

A similar assessment of existing as well as more recently developed instruments can be found in *Tests in Print III* (Mitchell, 1983b), a periodically published volume which provides comparable information on any measurement devices that have appeared in print and are available for purchase or use. Both the *Mental Measurement Yearbook* and *Tests in Print* are extensively cross-referenced and can be found in the reference sections of most academic libraries.

A recently published sourcebook, *Measures for Clinical Practice* (Corcoran & Fischer, 1987), provides a valuable resource of more than 125 rapid-assessment instruments specifically selected for review because they measure the kinds of problems most commonly encountered in clinical practice. Corcoran and Fischer have done an excellent job, not only in identifying and evaluating a viable cross-section of useful clinically grounded instruments, but also in discussing a number of issues critical to their use. In addition to an introduction to the basic principles of measurement, they discuss various types of measurement tools, including the advantages and disadvantages of RAIs. They also provide some useful guidelines for locating, selecting, evaluating, and administering prospective measures. The instruments are classified alphabetically in relation to their appropriateness for use with one of three target populations: adults, children, or couples and families. They are also cross-indexed by problem area, which makes the selection process very easy. The availability of these, as well as numerous other similar references related to special interest areas, greatly enhances the clinician's options with respect to monitoring and evaluating practice.

In closing this discussion of measurement techniques, it should be noted that there are a variety of tools available to the clinician other than standardized measures (Corcoran & Fischer, 1987). Included among these are a number of direct behavioral observation techniques, self-anchored rating scales, client logs, projective tests, Q-Sort techniques, unobtrusive measures, and a variety of mechanical devices for monitoring physiological functioning. Together these methods provide a range of qualitative and quantitative measures for evaluating practice. Several of them are especially well suited for the assessment of practice based on the more phenomenologically and existentially grounded theories. Space limitations do not permit a discussion of these methods in this chapter. However, there are a number of excellent texts available which provide specific information regarding methodological considerations of each (see, for example, Lambert, Shapiro, & Bergin, 1986; Adams & Schvaneveldt, 1985; Goldstein & Hersen, 1978; Bloom & Fischer, 1982; Hersen & Bellak, 1981; Tripodi & Epstein, 1980; Stephenson, 1953).

Summary

T he empirical case establishing the efficacy of crisis intervention as a viable alternative to the more traditional long-term models of therapy has been well documented. The question is no longer whether crisis intervention or short-term therapeutic measures work, but rather what techniques work best with what kinds of clients and problems, and under what set of circumstances?

Throughout this chapter it has been argued that the best way to evaluate the relative effectiveness of alternative therapeutic strategies is through the creative use of various intensive designs of research. In recent years a range of quantitative and qualitative research methods have evolved. These ideographically grounded methods are of particular value to the clinician because they are specially designed for use in clinical practice situations where the primary unit of attention is a single client system (i.e., an individual, a family, a couple, or a group). For the most part, they are relatively simple, straightforward evaluation strategies which can be unobtrusively incorporated into the clinician's daily practice routines. When used appropriately they not only provide useful evaluative feedback, but also enhance the overall quality of the intervention itself.

Intensive designs of research make no pretense with respect to their contribution to scientific generalizations. They do, however, enable the clinician to test the utility of scientific generalizations within the crucible of practice.

We have noted some of the limitations of the classical time-series design as a prototype for the evaluation of crisis intervention. The time-limited nature of crises is such that both the intervention and the evaluation of them must be initiated quickly. In many instances it is necessary to proceed under less than optimal circumstances. The clinician is inescapably faced with the issue of somehow balancing the requirements of evaluation with those of practice, and of course, in any apparent conflict between the two, the interests of the latter must always be accorded primary consideration. It is not surprising, therefore, that methodological purists may at times be critical of our evaluative efforts. But the methodological rigor of any research endeavor is inevitably a relative rather than an absolute condition. Each evaluative effort represents an imperfect attempt to arrive at a closer approximation of the truth. As such, research provides no guarantee of certitude. It simply helps us reduce the probability of error in the face of uncertainty. If we can tolerate its limitations and exploit its possibilities, we can almost certainly improve the quality of services we provide our clients. In the words of the late John Cardinal Newman, "Nothing would ever be accomplished if a person waited so long as to do it so well that no other person could find fault with it" (Newman, 1902).

References

Adams, G. R., & Schvaneveldt, J. D. (1985). *Understanding Research Methods*. New York: Longman.

Allport, G. W. (1962). "The General and the Unique in Psychological Science." *Journal of Personality, 30,* 405–422.

Auerbach, S. M., & Kilmann, P. R. (1977). "Crisis Intervention: A Review of Outcome Research." *Psychological Bulletin, 84,* 1189–1217.

Baer, D. M., Wolf, M. M., & Risley, T. R. (1968). "Some Current Dimensions of Applied Behavior Analysis." *Journal of Applied Behavior Analysis, 1,* 91–97.

Barlow, D. H., & Hersen, M. (1984). *Single-Case Experimental Designs: Strategies for Studying Behavior Change* (2nd ed.). New York: Pergamon Press.

Beck, A. T. (1967). *Depression: Clinical, Experimental and Theoretical Aspects.* New York: Harper & Row.

Bellak, L., & Small, L. (1978). *Emergency Psychotherapy and Brief Psychotherapy.* New York: Grune & Stratton.

Bergin, A. E. (1971). "The Evaluation of Therapeutic Outcomes." in A. E. Bergin & S. L. Garfield (Eds.), *Handbook of Psychotherapy and Behavior Change* (pp. 217–270). New York: Wiley.

Bergin, A. E., & Suinn, R. M. (1975). "Individual Psychotherapy and Behavior Therapy." *Annual Review of Psychology, 26,* 509–555.

Bloom, M., & Fischer, J. (1982). *Evaluating Practice: Guidelines for the Accountable Professional.* Englewood Cliffs, NJ: Prentice-Hall.

Buros, O. K. (Ed.). (1978). *The Eighth Mental Measurement Yearbook* (Vols. 1-2). Highland Park, NJ: Gryphon Press.

Campbell, D. T., & Stanley, J. C. (1966). *Experimental and Quasi-Experimental Designs for Research and Teaching.* Chicago: Rand McNally.

Chassan, J. B. (1967). *Research Designs in Clinical Psychology and Psychiatry.* New York: Appleton-Century-Crofts.

Corcoran, K., & Fischer, J. (1987). *Measures for Clinical Practice: A Sourcebook.* New York: Free Press.

Denzin, N. (1970). *The Research Act.* Chicago: Aldine.

Fischer, J. (1978). *Effective Casework Practice: An Eclectic Approach.* New York: McGraw-Hill.

Garfield, S. L. (1971). "Research on Client Variables in Psychotherapy." In A. E. Bergin & S. L. Garfield (Eds.), *Handbook of Psychotherapy and Behavior Change* (pp. 271–298). New York: Wiley.

Garwick, G., & Lampman, S. (1973). *Dictionary of Goal Attainment Scaling.* Minneapolis: Program Evaluation Project.

Goldstein, G., & Hersen, M. (Eds.). (1978). *Handbook of Psychological Assessment.* New York: Gardner Press.

Gottman, J. M., & Leiblum, S. R. (1974). *How to Do Psychotherapy and How to Evaluate It.* New York: Holt, Rinehart and Winston.

Hart, R. R. (1978). "Therapeutic Effectiveness of Setting and Monitoring Goals." *Journal of Consulting and Clinical Psychology, 46,* 1242–1245.

Hersen, M., & Bellak, A. S. (Eds.). (1981). *Behavioral Assessment: A Practical Handbook* (2nd ed.). New York: Pergamon Press.

Houts, P., Scott, R. A., & Leasor, J. P. (1973). "Behavior Objectives and Mental Health: B. F. Skinner's Prophecy." *Ontario Psychologist, 5,* 14–18.

Kazdin, A. E. (1984). "Statistical Analyses for Single-Case Experimental Designs." In D. H. Barlow & M. Hersen (Eds.), *Single Case Experimental Designs* (2nd ed., pp. 285–324). New York: Pergamon Press.

Kazdin, A. E. (1986). "The Evaluation of Psychotherapy: Research Design and Methodology." In S. L. Garfield & A. E. Bergin (Eds.), *Handbook of Psychotherapy and Behavior Change* (pp. 23–68). New York: Wiley.

Kazdin, A. E., & Wilson, G. T. (1978). *Evaluation of Behavior Therapy: Issues, Evidence and Research Strategies.* Cambridge, MA: Ballinger.

Kiesler, D. J. (1966). "Some Myths of Psychotherapy Research and the Search for a Paradigm." *Psychological Bulletin, 65,* 110–136.

Kiesler, D. J. (1971). "Experimental Designs in Psychotherapy Research." In A. E. Bergin & S. L. Garfield (Eds.), *Handbook of Psychotherapy and Behavior Change* (pp. 36–74). New York: Wiley.

Kiresuk, T. J., & Sherman, R. E. (1968). "Goal Attainment Scaling: A General Method for Evaluating Comprehensive Community Mental Health Programs." *Community Mental Health Journal, 4,* 443–453.

Klingbeil, K. S., & Boyd, V. D. (1984). "Emergency Room Intervention: Detection, Assessment, and Treatment." In A. R. Roberts (Ed.), *Battered Women and Their Families* (Vol. 1, pp. 7–32). New York: Springer.

Koss, M. P., & Butcher, J. N. (1986). "Research on Brief Psychotherapy." In S. L. Garfield & A. E. Bergin (Eds.), *Handbook of Psychotherapy and Behavior Change* (pp. 627–670). New York: Wiley.

Lambert, M. J., Shapiro, D. A., & Bergin, A. E. (1986). "The Effectiveness of Psycho-therapy." In S. L. Garfield & A. E. Bergin (Eds.), *Handbook of Psychotherapy and Behavior Change* (3rd ed., pp. 157–211). New York: Wiley.

Levitt, J. L., & Reid, W. J. (1981). "Rapid-Assessment Instruments for Practice." *Social Work Research and Abstracts, 17,* 13–19.

Lindemann, E. (1944). "Symptomatology and Management of Acute Grief." *American Journal of Psychiatry, 101,* 141–148.

Malan, D. H. (1963). *A Study of Brief Psychotherapy.* London: Tavistock.

Mitchell, J. V. (Ed.). (1983a). *Ninth Mental Measurement Yearbook.* Lincoln: University of Nebraska Press.

Mitchell, J. V. (Ed.). (1983b). *Tests in Print III.* Lincoln: University of Nebraska Press.

Morley, W. E. (1965). "Treatment of the Patient in Crisis." *Western Medicine, 3,* 77.

National Center for Health Statistics. (1966). *Characteristics of Patients of Selected Types of Medical Specialists and Practitioners: United States July 1963–June 1964* (No. 1000, Series 10, #28). Washington, DC: Public Health Service Publication.

Newman, J. H. (1902). *The Idea of a University: Defined and Illustrated.* London: Longmans Green.

Paul, G. L. (1966). *Insight Versus Desensitization in Psychotherapy.* Stanford, CA: Stanford University Press.

Polak, P. (1970). "Patterns of Discord: Goals of Patients, Therapists, and Community Members." *Archives of General Psychiatry, 23,* 277–283.

Powers, G. T., Meenaghan, T. M., & Toomey, B. G. (1985). *Practice Focused Research: Integrating Human Service Practice and Research.* Englewood Cliffs, NJ: Prentice-Hall.

Rogers, L. S. (1960). "Drop-out Rates and Results of Psychotherapy in Government Aided Mental Hygiene Clinics." *Journal of Clinical Psychology, 16,* 89–92.

Rubinstein, E. A., & Lorr, M. (1965). "A Comparison of Terminators and Remainers in Outpatient Psychotherapy." *Journal of Clinical Psychology, 12,* 345–349.

Slaikeu, K. A. (1984). *Crisis Intervention: A Handbook for Practice and Research.* Boston: Allyn & Bacon.

Stephenson, W. (1953). *The Study of Behavior: Q-Technique and Its Methodology.* Chicago: University of Chicago Press.

Tripodi, T., & Epstein, I. (1980). *Research Techniques for Clinical Social Workers.* New York: Columbia University Press.

Wolberg, L. R. (1965). *Short-Term Psychotherapy.* New York: Grune & Stratton.

Glossary

A-B-C Model of crisis management
A three-stage sequential model for intervening with persons in crisis. The "A" refers to "Achieving Contact," the "B" to "Boiling Down the Problem," and the "C" to "Coping." See Chapter 6.

Adult abuse protocol A detailed assessment and intervention guide for the abused adult, based upon assessments made by multidisciplinary staff, such as a triage nurse, a physician, and a social worker. Using this protocol accomplishes two purposes: (1) it alerts the involved hospital staff to provide the appropriate clinical care, and (2) it documents the violent incident, so that if the victim decides to file a legal complaint, "reliable, court-admissible evidence" (including photographs) is available. One of the first adult abuse protocols was developed by Klingbeil and Boyd. See Chapter 6.

Alternative resource theory One theory offered to explain Hispanic underutilization of formal mental health services. Hispanics prefer to receive help for emotional problems from informal group structures such as family members, friends, acquaintances, godparents, and religious and spiritualist groups. See Chapter 11.

Ambivalence The behavior of a client expressed in apparently inconsistent thought and action. For example, an appointment with a clinician may be urgently requested, but the client does not attend. See Chapter 7.

Ataque Behavioral state often characterized by extreme hyperkinetic, convulsive actions. This hysterical conversion reaction is more common to Hispanic women and is a reaction to stress, often related to repressed anger or sexual tension. This behavioral state may be mistaken for a schizophrenic state by an inexperienced clinician. See Chapter 11.

Attachment theory This concept addresses the propensity that human beings have for forming strong, affectional bonds with each other. Attachment behavior is especially apt to be aroused in times of stress or fear. See Chapter 4.

Autocorrelation The phenomenon whereby there is a tendency for future behavior to be influenced by past behavior. In other words, the pattern of observations established during the baseline period appears to continue unabated throughout the intervention phase. See Chapter 15.

Autodiagnosing The process a counselor should go through before beginning work with sexual assault victims. In developing self-awareness, the clinician examines his or her own biases and prejudices with respect to the myths and stereotypes associated with sexual assault. See Chapter 7.

Barrier theory A theory used to explain Hispanic underutilization of formal mental health services. It proposes that the structure, policy, and program of many mental health centers do not accommodate the language, culture, and social class systems of Hispanic clients. See Chapter 11.

Baseline period The period of time during a preintervention phase when a series of observations are made to monitor subsequent changes in the client's target behavior. It provides a basis upon which to determine whether the behavior observed during baseline (ie., phase "A") changes in the expected direction following the introduction of treatment (ie., phase "B"). See Chapter 15.

Battered women's hotlines and shelters The primary focus of these services is to ensure the women's safety by crisis telephone counseling or provision of short-term housing at a safe residential shelter. Many shelters not only provide safe lodging but also peer counseling, support groups, information on women's legal rights, and referral to social service agencies. In some communities, emergency services for battered women have expanded further to include parenting education workshops, assistance in finding housing, employment counseling and job placement, and group

counseling for batterers. These crisis intervention services for battered women and their children exist in every state and major metropolitan area in the United States. See Chapters 1 and 6.

Brief therapy A type of intervention based on the premise that a system in crisis is more open to change, and that certain and often brief interventions into the unstable system can result in lasting changes in how the system functions. See Chapter 8.

Campus counseling centers interventions These efforts to help include crisis intervention, remediation, and development. *Level I interventions* focus primarily on the student and, under some circumstances, on those within the student's immediate environment. *Level II interventions* involve the staff, faculty, and student leaders who interact with students. *Level III interventions* include the ecological factors and social systems that affect student's functioning. See Chapter 5.

Compadragzo Family system in Hispanic culture in which godparents (*copadres*) become closely linked to the families of godchildren. Often *copadres* and natural parents rely on each other for mutual support and assistance. See Chapter 11.

Confianza Trust is considered an important cultural value for Hispanics and the most important aspect of interpersonal relationships. Hispanics may find it difficult to have *confianza* in a social worker who does not understand their language and culture. See Chapter 11.

Contagion syndrome A term describing burnout of workers that become exhausted, over-identified, and obsessed with the need to help victims. See Chapter 14.

Child abuse hotlines and referral networks These crisis intervention hotlines offer supportive reassurance, advice, and nonjudgmental listening from trained volunteers. They provide a stressed-out parent with information and referral to individual and group parenting treatment. Many communities have developed parental stress hotline services that provide immediate intervention for potentially abusive parents who are at risk of injuring their child. A number of states, cities, and counties have also developed child abuse hotlines for reporting suspected cases of child abuse and neglect. See Chapters 1 and 8.

Constructive treatment strategy A process in which specific treatment components are incrementally added to a treatment package in order to monitor their collective impact. As each new component is incorporated into the overall package, observable changes in the client's functioning are carefully recorded. This strategy is essentially the opposite of the *dismantling treatment strategy*.

Crisis The subjective reaction to a stressful life experience that compromises the individual's stability and ability to cope or function. The main cause of a crisis is a stressful or hazardous event, but two other conditions are also necessary: (1) the individual's perception of the stressful event as the cause of considerable upset and/or disruption; and (2) the individual's inability to resolve the disruption by previously used coping methods. Crisis also refers to "an upset in the steady state." It often has five components: a hazardous event, a vulnerable state, a precipitating factor, an active crisis state, and the resolution of the crisis. Crisis seems to be derived from the Greek word for "decision," or more broadly, "a turning point." In addition, a Chinese ideograph for crisis can be interpreted both as a "danger," in the sense that it threatens to overwhelm the individual and may result in serious consequences, and as an "opportunity," because during periods of crisis one tends to become amenable to outside influences. See Chapters 1, 6, 8, 10, and 12.

Crisis call to domestic violence hotline A telephone call to a hotline in which the caller is in imminent danger or has just been beaten. To determine whether the call is a crisis call, the worker should ask questions such as (1) Are you or your children in danger now? (2) Is the abuser there now? (3) Do you want me to call the police? (4) Do you want to leave and can you do it safely? and (5) Do you need medical attention? See Chapter 6.

Crisis intervention When a therapist enters into the life situation of an individual or a family to alleviate the impact of a crisis and to help mobilize the resources of those differentially affected. This clinical assistance may be given over the telephone or in person. See Chapter 1.

Crisis intervention service These services provide a person in crisis with the phone numbers of local hotlines, community crisis centers, crisis intervention units at the local community mental health center, rape crisis centers, battered women's shelters, and family crisis intervention programs, which then provide follow-up and home-based crisis services. Crisis intervention services are available 24 hours a day, seven days a week and are usually staffed by crisis clinicians, social workers, hospital emergency room staff, and trained volunteers. See Chapters 1, 6, 9, 10, 11, and 14.

Crisis-oriented treatments Treatment approaches that apply to all practice models and techniques that are focused on resolving immediate problems and emotional conflicts with a minimum number of contacts (usually one to twelve), and that are characterized as time-limited and goal-directed. See Chapter 1.

Crisis resolution The goal of interventions given by trained volunteers and professionals to persons in crisis. Resolution involves the restoration of equilibrium, cognitive mastery of the situation, and the development of new coping methods. An effective crisis resolution removes vulnerabilities from the individual's past and bolsters the individual with an increased repertoire of new coping skills that serve as a buffer against future similar situations. See Chapters 1, 7, 8, 9, 10, 12, and 13.

Dependent variables Variables that represent the presumed effect in any functional relationship.

Depressive syndrome This is frequently seen as a serious reaction to a stressful life experience. This syndrome is accompanied by feelings of depression and associated symptoms such as poor appetite, weight loss, and insomnia.

Dichotomous thinking Often called "all or nothing thinking," it is the tendency to evaluate one's personal qualities in an extreme either/or context. See Chapter 12.

Disequilibrium An emotional state that may be characterized by confusing emotions, somatic complaints, and erratic behavior. The severe emotional discomfort experienced by the person in crisis propels him or her toward action that will reduce the subjective discomfort. Crisis intervention usually alleviates the early symptoms of disequilibrium within the

first six weeks of treatment, and hopefully soon restores equilibrium. See Chapter 1.

Dismantling treatment strategy A strategy involving the orderly removal of one or more components of the treatment package accompanied by a careful recording of the apparent effects. This systematic elimination, or isolation, enables the clinician to "determine the necessary and sufficient components for therapeutic change." See Chapter 15.

Drift This is when the patterns observed during the *baseline period* appear to continue unabated throughout the intervention phase. In the presence of drift, the clinician cannot infer that change has occurred as a result of intervention. See Chapter 15.

DSM-III-R (1987) The latest revision of the *Diagnostic and Statistical Manual of Mental Disorders* of the American Psychiatric Association. See Chapter 2.

Educational intervention A worker's efforts to: (1) enhance the probability of recovery from the current crisis and prevent later crises through better self-care, and (2) counteract the patient's and family's sense of helplessness within a crisis situation. See Chapter 10.

Egocentrism A process of adolescent identity formation during which the adolescent retreats back into the self. See Chapter 1.

800-COCAINE This toll-free hotline provides callers with immediate assessment, crisis intervention, and referral. On May 6, 1983, New Jersey's Fair Oaks Hospital in Summit created the first nationwide hotline for cocaine and crack abusers and their families. As of 1988, the program was receiving an average of 1,200 calls per day, or 430,000 calls annually. See Chapters 1 and 9.

Erectile dysfunction The current *DSM-III-R* defines this state as either (1) "Male Erectile Disorder," or (2) "Inhibited Sexual Excitement." See Chapter 13.

Extensive designs of research Designs that emphasize the primacy of the confirmatory aspect of scientific activity. The goal of these designs is to discover laws that apply to aggregates of individuals rather than to the individuals who comprise the aggregate. In this approach, the ultimate goal is to discover scientific generalizations under controlled circumstances. See Chapter 15.

Fatalistic approach to life crisis Clients sometimes believe that whatever will happen will happen, and that they can do little to control their fate. This is antithetical to most theories of social work intervention, which stress the self- determination and efficacy of the individual. See Chapter 11.

Goal attainment scaling (GAS) This evaluation method measures intervention outcomes in which a number of individually tailored treatment goals are specified in relation to a set of graded scale points ranging from the least favorable to the most favorable outcomes considered likely. It is suggested that at least five points comprising a Likert-type scale be assigned with the "least favorable outcome" scored -2, the "most favorable outcome" scored $+2$, and the "most likely outcome" assigned a value of zero. See Chapters 8 and 15.

Idiographic research This approach focuses on the study of individuals as individuals, rather than on the discovery of general propositions. Idiographic research investigates the rich and intricate detail of specific cases, including deviant cases that prove to be exceptions to the general rule. See Chapter 15.

Impotence The inability to maintain an erection firm enough for sexual intercourse. See Chapters 1 and 13.

Impotence Anonymous (IA) A specialized support group for men with penile erectile difficulties. It has over 100 chapters. Every regular meeting of an IA chapter includes a group discussion with a consulting physician and a lay volunteer coordinator—a man who is now potent. Crisis intervention and time-limited brief treatment are very effective with impotence cases caused by psychological problems. See Chapters 1 and 13, which discuss erectile difficulties and disorders.

Incest Sexual contact between two people too closely related to marry legally. One of the individuals involved is typically under the age of majority. See Chapter 7.

Independent variables Variables that represent the presumed cause in any functional relationship. See Chapter 15.

Information and referral services (I and R) The goals of I and R services are to facilitate access to community human services and to overcome the many barriers that may obstruct a person's entry to needed community resources. These services, which number more than 4,900 in the United States, are operated under a variety of organizational auspices including traditional social services agencies, community mental health centers, public libraries, police departments, shopping malls, domestic violence shelters, women's centers, traveler's aid, youth crisis centers, and agencies on aging. I and R networks (funded by the United Way, Community Service Society, or the American Red Cross) provide crisis callers with phone numbers of local community agencies. See Chapter 1.

Intensive designs of research
Designs primarily concerned with the study of single cases. They provide the means by which clinicians can evaluate the idiosyncratic aspects of their practice. Intensive research models can serve to generate relevant hypotheses suitable for testing by the more traditional extensive research approaches. See Chapter 15.

Internal validity The level of confidence warranted by any causal inference. The designs that effectively control contamination from outside variables are said to be internally valid. See Chapter 15.

Intervention period The period of time, typically referred to as the "B" phase, in any time-series design during which treatment is purposefully administered. See Chapter 15.

Machismo Hispanic cultural value that esteems the power position and virility of men. Hispanic men, who are discouraged from expressing feelings, often do not seek help from mental health services. See Chapter 11.

Maladaptive reaction A codependent's tendency to continue investing time and energy to control a substance abuser's actions and behaviors despite repetitive adverse consequences. See Chapter 9.

Mental filtering Picking out one negative detail in any situation and continuing to dwell on it. See Chapter 12.

Multiple baseline approach A crisis intervention approach designed to minimize the possibility of behavior change due to chance. Baseline data are collected either (1) on more than one target behavior, (2) on the same target behavior but in more than one setting, or (3) on more than one but similar clients. Intervention tech-

niques are then applied in a sequential manner so that once a change in the initial target behavior is observed, the intervention is systematically introduced with the next target behavior or in an alternative setting. See Chapter 15.

Normal bereavement The reactions to loss of a significant person, which may not be immediate, but which rarely occur after the first two to three months after the loss. Normal bereavement involves feelings of depression that the person regards as "normal," although professional help may be sought for associated symptoms, such as insomnia or weight loss. Bereavement varies considerably among different cultural groups. See Chapter 2.

Objectified case studies Studies that attempt to relate the process of intervention (what the worker does) to the outcome of that intervention (whether what the worker does can be concluded to be effective). See Chapter 15.

Order maintenance activities Activities, normally undertaken by police officers, focused on service calls that involve assaults among family members, in neighbor disputes, in bar fights, in traffic accidents, and by individuals who are drunk and disorderly. The police may have the skills to intervene and resolve public disputes, but they are rarely qualified to provide crisis intervention and follow-up counseling with victims of domestic violence. See Chapter 6.

Parametric treatment strategies
Strategies that attempt to determine in what quantity and/or in what sequence the components of a treatment package are likely to have their most beneficial impact. By systematically manipulating one or more of the components of a treatment package,

it is possible to monitor the differential effects. See Chapter 15.

Parentification of the child The process in which a child may become overburdened with demands that he or she take care of underdeveloped parents and siblings and thus may never be given the chance to be a child in his or her own right. See Chapter 3.

Personalismo Hispanic cultural value that emphasizes the personal relationship over concepts and ideas. A clinician may find it is very important in working with Hispanics to relate on a personal level, rather than on a formal or theoretical level. See Chapter 11.

Post-disaster crisis counseling Intervention useful in post-disaster events, when the clinician seeks to restore the capacity of the individuals to cope with the stressful situation in which they find themselves. See Chapter 14.

Premorbid psychological history The history of a client that refers to previous psychiatric treatments, hospitalizations, medications, depressions, and suicide attempts. See Chapter 7.

Primary adolescent suicide prevention Programs offered in schools, churches, and recreational and social organizations, designed to serve as a deterrent to a suicidal crisis. These programs focus on education, peer counseling, and other prevention methods. Teaching about the prevention and identification of possible suicide attemptors may be part of these programs. See Chapter 3.

Primary impotence The inability to achieve and/or maintain an erection firm enough to accomplish coital connection. See Chapter 13.

Psychosocial crises Crises that are characterized primarily by psychosocial problems such as homelessness,

extreme social isolation, and unmet primary care needs, and that may contribute to physical and psychological trauma and illness. See Chapter 10.

Puerto Rican Syndrome See *Ataque*.

Rape crisis programs Programs that include specialized protocols for rape victims and that have been established by medical centers, community mental health centers, women's counseling centers, crisis clinics, and victim assistance centers. The protocol in these crisis intervention services generally begins with an initial visit from a social worker, victim advocate, or nurse while the victim is being examined in the hospital emergency room. Follow-up is often handled through telephone contact and in-person counseling sessions for one to ten weeks following the rape. See Chapters 1 and 7 (especially for a review of assessment and intervention strategies for rape and incest survivors).

Rape victim A person who reports having experienced sexual assault that meets the legal criteria for rape. The FBI's criterion for the major offense of forcible rape is "the carnal knowledge of a female forcibly and against her will." See Chapter 7.

Rapid Assessment Instruments (RAIs) Evaluation instruments that refer to any one of numerous assessment devices that are relatively easy to administer, score, and interpret and can be used to measure one or more dimensions of a client's target behavior. RAIs require very little knowledge of testing procedures on the part of the practitioner. The score that is generated provides an operational index of the frequency, duration, or intensity of the problem or target behavior. See Chapters 7 and 15.

Respecto Hispanic cultural value attributed to all interpersonal relationships, especially within the family. Respect is believed to be intrinsically owed to others based on age, role, and status within the family, regardless of external behavior. See Chapter 11.

Revictimization Victims may experience this process when the counselor, police officer, or prosecutor places himself or herself in the role of judging whether a reported rape or incest experience was "real," or whether the client was "provocative," "overreacting," "self-destructive," harbored "incestuous longings," or "enjoyed the experience" and is now expressing "guilt." See Chapter 7.

Reliability An evaluation term that refers to the stability of a measure. One aspect of reliability is whether the questions that comprise an instrument mean the same thing to one or more individuals answering them at different times. See Chapter 15.

Reversal designs Designs that involve a process in which an intervention is introduced for a period of time and then abruptly withdrawn, with the resulting circumstances essentially approximating preintervention or baseline conditions. In the absence of intervention, certain types of client behaviors might be expected to move in the direction of preintervention levels. See Chapter 15.

Secondary adolescent suicide prevention Process involving the identification of the at-risk adolescent and his or her family. The at-risk adolescent is often difficult to approach and may have withdrawn from friends, school, and family. See Chapter 3.

Serial dependency See *Autocorrelation*.

Single system designs Crisis intervention approaches that focus on the study of individuals as individuals. These designs investigate the rich and intricate details of specific cases, in-

cluding the deviant cases that prove to be exceptions to the general rule. See Chapter 15.

Somatic symptoms Physical concerns expressed by assault victims that can be classified as: disturbances in sleep (i.e., onset of insomnia, early morning awakenings, nightmares, disturbed sleep with muscle tension), disturbances in eating (i.e., marked decrease in appetite, nausea, stomach pains, gastric upset), and symptoms specific to the assault (i.e., headache, backache, rectal pain and bleeding, irritation to the mouth from oral sex, venereal disease, pregnancy, and so on). See Chapter 7.

Spiritism Belief system of many Hispanics in which the visible world is viewed as being surrounded by an invisible world inhabited by good and evil spirits that influence human behavior. Many hispanics are more likely to consult spiritualists (experts on spiritism) than mental health professionals. See Chapter 11.

Stress inoculation training (SIT) A useful treatment package for clients who have resolved many assault-related problems but continue to exhibit severe fear responses. A cognitively and behaviorally based anxiety management approach, SIT is designed to assist the client in actively coping with target-specific, assault-related anxiety. See Chapter 7.

Suicide prevention and crisis centers Centers that provide immediate assessment and crisis intervention to suicidal and depressed callers. The prototype for these centers began in London, England, in 1906 when the Salvation Army opened an anti-suicide bureau aimed at helping suicide attemptors. Today, there are over 1,400 suicide prevention and crisis centers in the United States and Canada. See Chapter 1.

Tertiary adolescent suicide prevention Prevention that requires the availability of a variety of sources to provide peer group support. Self-help groups, whether directly focused on suicide or not, allow the adolescent an opportunity to express and work out troublesome feelings before they become critical. Some of these groups are Alcoholics Anonymous, Al Anon, Narcotics Anonymous, Alateen, and Mental Health Anonymous. See Chapter 3.

Time-limited cognitive strategies Strategies that emphasize the treatment of cognitive distortions and irrational beliefs through cognitive restructuring, imagery, positive self-talk, and systematic desensitization. The client is encouraged to correct errors in thinking and maladaptive patterns with rational beliefs and adaptive cognitions. See Chapters 2, 8, 12, and 13.

Time-series designs Research designs that involve the measurement of change in some target behavior (usually the identified problem) at given intervals over a more or less extended period of time. Successive observations made during the course of therapeutic intervention enable the practitioner to systematically monitor the nature and extent of change in a target behavior. Typically, the phases of the time-series are referred to as baseline (A) and intervention (B). See Chapter 15.

Traumatic stress Type of crisis that refers to the highly intense level of psychological stress experienced as a direct result of some catastrophic event such as a devastating fire, serious illness, rape, or major operation. See Chapter 11.

Treatment package strategy A treatment evaluation strategy in which the impact of intervention is assessed as a total entity. In order to rule out potential threats to internal validity, such as changes attributable to motivation, spontaneous remission, intervening historical events, and the like, some sort of control or comparison condition must be incorporated into the research design. See Chapter 15.

Triangulation A process involving the use of several evaluation strategies simultaneously within or across client systems. When done intentionally, triangulation enables the clinician to use each strategy as a means of cross-validating the findings generated by alternative strategies. See Chapters 6 and 15.

24-hour hotlines Telephone services, often staffed by volunteers, that provide information, crisis assessments, crisis counseling, and referrals for callers with various problems, such as depression, suicide ideation, alcoholism, chemical dependency, impotence, domestic violence, and crime victimization. Because of their 24-hour availability, they can provide immediate, though temporary, intervention. See Chapter 1.

Uncomplicated bereavement Grief that continues to be characterized by guilt that is associated with things done or not done by the survivor at the time of death. See Chapter 2.

Validity An evaluation term that refers to the question of whether an instrument measures what it purports to measure. See Chapter 15.

Victim An innocent person, such as a victim of a violent crime or a victim of a disaster, who encounters physical injury, trauma, fear, acute anxiety and/or loss of belongings. See Chapter 1.

Index